The Enlightenment Qur'an

The Politics of Translation and the Construction of Islam

ZIAD ELMARSAFY

ONEWORLD

OXFORD

A Oneworld Book

Published by Oneworld Publications 2009

Copyright © Ziad Elmarsafy 2009

The right of Ziad Elmarsafy to be identified as
the Author of this work has been asserted by him
in accordance with the Copyright, Designs and Patents Act 1988

ISBN 978-1-85168-695-7 (Hbk)
ISBN 978-1-85168-652-0 (Pbk)

Typeset by Jayvee, Trivandrum, India
Cover design by Design Deluxe
Printed and bound in Great Britain
by TJ International, Padstow

Oneworld Publications
185 Banbury Road
Oxford OX2 7AR
England
www.oneworld-publications.com

Mixed Sources
Product group from well-managed
forests and other controlled sources
www.fsc.org Cert no. SGS-COC-2482
© 1996 Forest Stewardship Council

Learn more about Oneworld. Join our mailing list to
find out about our latest titles and special offers at:
www.oneworld-publications.com

*For the new family members and
those who brought them in*

CONTENTS

PREFACE

Translation is the most political art, all the more so when it involves re-presenting a text held sacred by those with whom relations are not always friendly. The forms of information and varieties of scholarship necessary for the translation of the Qur'ān into Western languages – a text not only sacred but considered by believing Muslims to be so powerful as to reduce its opponents to impotence – are driven by the complex ties that bind the Muslim and non-Muslim worlds. They are also shaped by politics of the sacred within the West itself. The following pages will trace the ways in which the trans-lation, the carrying over, of the language of the Qur'ān is negotiated by translators and readers across cultural differences, both between the Middle East and Europe and within Europe.

This study's focus on the long eighteenth century is deliberate, not only because past studies on the translation of the Qur'ān have dealt with other ages, but also because the Enlightenment holds a privileged position in the making of modernity writ large, seeing the consolidation of the values and institutions that run the contemporary world. This is when the vast projects of rationalization that started during the past two centuries finally come together. Between the Newtonian revolution in the sciences, the Lockean revolution in philosophy, the *Encyclopédie* project, Rousseau's revolution in both fiction and political science, and Voltaire's many revolutions in just about every area of human inquiry, the movement known as the Enlightenment made a decisive impact on the creation of the modern world. The consequences of all this activity, culminating in the American and French revolutions, Napoleon and the invasion of Egypt, are still with us today. In more than a banal, historical sense, the modern world is the product of the Enlightenment.

The eighteenth century saw the constitution of disciplines that organize the process of cultural exchange into the precursors of the modern social sciences – anthropology, sociology, psychology, and modern political philosophy. These discourses of observation and discovery center on the question of understanding the Other. All those cultural differences that threaten Europe – the "primitive" world, the violence of the "savages," the mores of non-European societies, the difference of physical characteristics, and systems of belief – are confronted and rationalized during the Enlightenment.

Among these other cultures, Islam is the one with which Europe was most familiar, though this familiarity did not necessarily lead to better understanding. It would be a mistake to claim that the rapport was defined by conflict alone: the many faces of Islam that appear in the literature of early modernity bear witness both to European fascination and bewilderment. This is perhaps nowhere more apparent than in the travel accounts of early modernity, where cultural differences often prompt emulation and altered self-definition rather than outright violence.[1] The literature of the period involves a constant re-evaluation of the boundaries between European and Muslim identity, with medieval opposition frequently giving way to identification between non-Muslims and Muslims.[2] This identification is increasingly focused on Muhammad himself, who starts to be seen as a great man and a wise legislator rather than the wicked voluptuary of medieval legend. Islam's manifestations speak simultaneously to one or another of the nascent forms of knowledge and the underlying mixture of curiosity and anxiety that coaxes the Western observer on. At the same time, many in Christian Europe were impressed by the example of inter-religious tolerance set by the Ottoman Empire. The awed and frequently puzzled gaze that the West brought to the Muslim world wrought serious changes in the gazers themselves, often to the point of defining their lives and careers: for better or worse, Montesquieu is still thought of as the author of the *Lettres persanes*, and Voltaire the student of religion is inseparable from the author of *Mahomet*. While these might be dismissed as accidents of reception, what is beyond doubt is the lasting mark left by the engagement with Islam and its central text, the Qur'ān. Furthermore, the turn to the Qur'ān comes at times and places that look, in retrospect, like turning points: Rousseau's construction of the legislator and the social contract, Voltaire's denunciations of fanaticism and nascent anti-clericalism, young Napoleon Bonaparte's invasion of Egypt, the young Goethe's oscillation between poetry and prophecy as literary paradigms, and the older Goethe's theorization of world literature. In all of these cases, the engagement with Islam enables a radical break with past traditions and the conception of something entirely new: a legislator who owes nothing to traditional contract theory (Rousseau), a view of universal history that goes well beyond the received idea of God's plan unfolding in human affairs, and in doing so inaugurates a new vision of modernity (Voltaire), a vision of a secular republic expanding outside Europe and into the Middle East and North Africa (Napoleon), a model of global literary production based on translation rather than creation (Goethe).

Of the developments that brought about these shifts of perspective, the new translations of the Qur'ān that were being produced in Europe after the mid-seventeenth century must take pride of place. André Du Ryer's pioneering effort in 1647 resulted in the first published translation from the Arabic into a vernacular language since the Middle Ages. Over the next 150 years, Ludovico Marracci, George Sale, and Claude Savary would translate the Qur'ān into Latin, English, and French respectively, adding a sizeable scholarly apparatus to the text: an introduction to Islam, cross-references to the available commentaries, and a very real effort to come to terms with Islam. This struggle gave rise to vastly different results – outright hostility in the case of Marracci (though the hostility was coupled with amazing erudition and excellent scholarship), something very much like genuine understanding in the case of Sale, and romantic mythology in the case of Savary. Perhaps because of its diffusion in whole and in part – the long "Preliminary Discourse" that served as an introduction to the Sale translation was quickly translated into French and added to the text of the Du Ryer translation – George Sale's translation was to exert the greatest influence on Europe's intellectual history, especially through the mediation of one of Sale's most intelligent readers, Voltaire. Savary's translation would prove influential in a far more dramatic manner: it seems to have been part of Napoleon Bonaparte's reading, along with a number of histories of the Orient. Were it not for Savary (among others), the invasion of Egypt might have followed a vastly different course. And were it not for all of the above (or at least Rousseau, Voltaire, and Napoleon), Goethe's – and consequently our – ideas about literature would have taken on a markedly different inflection.

In this study my aim is to look at these translations and their impact. I do not propose to write a detailed history of the production and dissemination of these texts – though these details certainly come into play – but rather to provide the reader with a series of snapshots of the dynamic interaction between Enlightenment Europe and the Muslim world. These snapshots take an in-depth view of the moments outlined above – the astonishing Sale translation, Rousseau's theory of the legislator, Voltaire's conception of the engaged intellectual, Napoleon's imperial gaze, and Goethe's hesitation between the poetic and the prophetic – in relation to the translation of the Qur'ān and the surrounding discourse on the Orient in which it is couched.

As will be seen, the politics of the translation of the Qur'ān reveal a great deal about the intellectual politics of the Enlightenment itself and the very long shadow that it casts over our own day and age. Whereas solid information about the Muslim world was available to Europe, its uneven penetration in various societies underlines the extent to which Westerners and Western intellectuals often choose to believe what they want to believe about Islam, rather than believing what the evidence suggests that they believe. Then as now, the Western world seems extremely reluctant to let go of the intellectual hooks by which its view of Islam is suspended. It is to be hoped that, by studying the period during which some of those cherished misconceptions were released, we can bring about a better understanding of the Muslim–Western dynamic today and save ourselves from the inexorable march toward a Huntingtonian "clash of civilizations."

ACKNOWLEDGMENTS

This book was written over several years, continents, and libraries. The entire process was made possible by funding from the Fulbright Foundation and the NEH, whose support is hereby gratefully acknowledged. Equally important were those who supported this project from the start and whose advice was critical in helping me to see it through: Anne Vila, Thomas Kavanagh, Elena Russo, and, as ever, Josué Harari. Critical to the fate of the project were the vision and encouragement of Adnan Husain, and the editorial and production teams at Oneworld. Jill Morris's scrutiny ensured the text's readability and the Leavis Fund generously supported the index.

At Kuwait University, the office of Dr. Ali Tarrah, Ms. Anfal Al-Awadhi, Dr. Ahmad Al-Baghdadi, and the office of Dr. Al-Sharif, Dean of the College of Shari'a and Islamic Sciences, were instrumental in enabling me to undertake basic research as a Fulbright Fellow. In Paris, the exemplary vision and dedication of the staff and faculty of the IISMM, especially Daniel Rivet, Hamit Bozarslan, and Gilles Ladkany, provided me with one of the most affable and stimulating research environments on the globe. Daniel Rivet's assistance in particular went well beyond the call of duty. At the BNF, Michel Fani helped set the course, while Philippe Chevrant found ways to make available material and resources that would otherwise have been impossible to obtain. At the Maison Suger, Jean-Luc Lory, Françoise Girou, and Nadia Cheniour and the rest of the staff ensured that my stay in Paris was as comfortable as it was productive. At York, Derek Attridge and Lisa Foggo went out of their way to bring me the texts I needed, often at very short notice. Steve Gran's expertise and Jane Elliott's reassurances saved this project – and much else – from an untimely death. To all of them, my deepest, warmest thanks.

The strongest influence on the content of this book is that of Alastair Hamilton, whose generosity with his time, counsel, and support, personal and institutional, were unsurpassed. I have also profited immensely from conversations and exchanges with Sayed

Abdallah, Asma Afsaruddin, Abdullahi Al-Naʿim, Mahmoud ʿAzab, Makram Abbas, Mustapha Bentaibi, Jacques Berchtold, Michael Bonner, Kenneth Brown, Christian Biet, John Bowen, Renée Champion, Eve de Dampierre, Matthew Dimmock, Assia Djebar, Walid El Khachab, Gérard Ferreyrolles, Bruce Fudge, Ferial Ghazoul, Henriette Goldwyn, Baber Johansen, Bernard Heyberger, Richard Jacquemond, Shereen Khairallah, Georges Khalil, Loubna Khayati, Gerald MacLean, Mona Mikhail, Pierre Larcher, Sylvette Larzul, Bénédicte Letellier, Pierre Lory, Samia Mehrez, Alain Messaoudi, Reinhardt Meyer-Kalkus, Natalia Muchnik, Sadek Neaimi, Angelika Neuwirth, Manar Omar, Andrea Polaschegg, Suzanne Pucci, John Renwick, Adel Rifaat, Mustafa Safouan, Recep Senturk, Tal Tamari, Abdulkader Tayob, Arnoud Vrolijk, and Gayle Zachmann. Jan Loop had a decisive impact on several aspects of the book, while Elizabeth Tyler and Gabriella Corona made sure that my Latin translations did not deviate as much as they might have. Audiences at the University of Massachusetts, Amherst, the University of Guelph, University College Dublin, the IISMM, and the University of York helped sharpen my thinking through their patient, considered responses to parts of this project.

Over the past few years, my friends and now expanded family have been the *sine qua non* that kept me going under sometimes difficult conditions. To all of them – my parents, my siblings, my new relatives, my new friends at York, Gerry, Frédérique, Vic, Sylvie, Kovie, Marc, Sheree, Jean, Lori, Riad, Laura, Stephen, Daniel, Michael, Alice, Michèle, Eva, Tim, Ora, Kathryn, Malina, Jachi, Iman, Wakako, Colette, Ariel, Jennifer, Françoise, Amal, Jihan, Nabil, Tareq, and Walid – I want to convey the sort of gratitude to which words cannot do justice.

1

TRANSLATORS AND TRANSLATIONS
OF THE QUR'ĀN

At first glance the most striking aspect of the translation of the Qur'ān into Western languages is that it exists at all. At second glance, the extant translations amaze by their quantity and the tendency many of them exhibit toward polemic and mythmaking. They bear witness simultaneously to a history of conflict – not only with Islam but within Christendom – as well as a secret attraction across the boundary between cultures and religions.

Perhaps inevitably, the earliest serious attempt at translating the Qur'ān was conceived at a key geographic and cultural interface between the Muslim and non-Muslim worlds; namely the Iberian peninsula. In 1142 Peter the Venerable, the hyperactive Abbot of Cluny, was invited to Spain by Emperor Alfonso VII in order to discuss certain financial and diplomatic matters.[1] Like the rest of Christendom, Peter's view of Islam was marked by the recent memory of the First Crusade, though he was exceptional in not being happy with the direction of the movement that increasingly saw war as an end in itself. Peter wanted to convert Muslims rather than exterminate them, and one means of doing so would be to study Islam the better to be able to refute it. Along with the trope of substituting words for weapons, this was to become a standard part of Christian anti-Muslim polemical and apologetic literature. While in Spain, he commissioned a translation of the Qur'ān and a number of auxiliary texts aimed at providing the reader with a solid source of information about Islamic history and Muslim doctrine. The Toledan Collection, as the result came to be known, was a group effort: Robert of Ketton translated both the Qur'ān and a compilation of Muslim traditions entitled *Fabulae saracenorum* (*Fables of the Saracens*); Herman of Dalmatia translated Saʿīd b. ʿUmar's *Kitāb nasab Rasūl Allāh* (*Book of the Genealogy of the Messenger of God*) as the *Liber generationis Mahumet et nutritura eius* and ʿAbdallāh b. Salām's *Masāʾil* (*Questions*) as *Doctrina Mahumet*, while Peter of Toledo and Peter of Poitiers co-translated an early Arabic Christian apology, the *Risālat ʾAbdallāh b. Ismāʿīl al-Hāshimī ilā ʾAbd al-Masīḥ b. Isḥāq al-Kindī wa risālat al-Kindī ilā-l-Hāshimī* (*ʾAbdallāh b. Ismāʿīl al-Hāshimī's Letter to ʾAbd al-Masīḥ b. Isḥāq al-Kindī and al-Kindī's Reply*).[2] The whole was accompanied by Peter the Venerable's summary, the *Summa totius haeresis saracenorum* (*Sum of All the Heresies of the Saracens*).

Robert of Ketton called his translation the *Lex saracenorum*, thereby setting another lasting trend that would be imitated by future translators. The idea of the Qur'ān as a source text of Muslim law, rather than the text that fulfills both doctrinal and liturgical functions, would hamper Western translators for centuries (though certainly not in the eyes of the translators), as would the sacred status of the language of the Qur'ān. Robert tried to produce a Latin translation marked by the elevated style associated with sacred rather than profane texts, frequently inserting material taken from exegetical commentaries on the Qur'ān into the text itself, with the result that his translation comes across as a well-informed paraphrase rather than an accurate rendition of the original.[3] One place where this is especially evident is in Robert of Ketton's "arrangement" of the Qur'ānic text, whereby the divisions between the various chapters ("Azoaras") correspond only occasionally to the divisions between sūras (mainly after Q10), and at other times follow the divisions between the *aḥzāb* (sixtieths), leading to a translation of the Qur'ān that contains 124 "chapters" instead of the canonical 114.[4] The titles of the "chapters" usually followed the Arabic name of the sūra in question accompanied in some copies by hostile rubrics emphasizing the falsity and incoherence of what was to follow. Later marginal annotations added to the polemical tone, thereby making it impossible to read Robert's translation (which, as Thomas Burman points out, is itself fairly restrained) without being as shocked as a Christian should be by the ostensibly heretical character of the Qur'ān. The coexistence on the same page of philological interest in the Arabic language and the obsessive concern with the safety of the Christian reader is probably one reason why, despite the liberties that Robert of Ketton took with the text, it was a lasting success, finding a place in numerous European libraries and serving as the basis for numerous future Western translations of the Qur'ān. Around 1210, Mark of Toledo started work on a more literal translation for the Archbishop of Toledo, Rodrigo Jiménez de Rada, giving his finished manuscript the title *Liber Alchorani* and adding a preface to make clear his hostile and polemical credentials. Despite the greater accuracy of Mark's version, or at least its greater similarity with the syntax of the original, the Toledan Collection's user-friendliness, aided and abetted by the Cluniac network, ensured its wider distribution and longevity. Its arrangement – framing the Qur'ān with abundant material and numerous polemical annotations while paying careful attention to the exegetical and philological dimension of the work – established a paradigm that would be followed for centuries.[5]

One key shift in the practice of the translation of the Qur'ān came about with the introduction of bilingual translations in the fifteenth century. In 1480–1481 Flavius Mithridates, a Jewish convert to Christianity who would later teach the Kabbalah to Pico della Mirandola, translated Q21 and Q22 into Latin with the Arabic on facing pages. His translation left much to be desired, but it was not without consequence. Soon thereafter Egidio da Viterbo followed the example of Peter the Venerable: having been named cardinal in 1517, he was sent to Spain as a papal legate and there commissioned a translation by a Spaniard, Iohannes Gabriel Terrolensis. The result is a translation that, like the Complutensian Polyglot Bible, seems designed for the student of the language of the Qur'ān and the culture of Islam rather than one interested mainly in anti-Muslim polemics. The translation was designed to occupy four columns: the Arabic text, its transliteration into Latin, the Latin translation, and notes on the translation, thereby allowing the reader quick and easy access to each part of the text. Unlike Robert of Ketton's translation, there is a deliberate and visible separation of text from commentary in Egidio's edition, a practice that would become increasingly evident in future translations. Remarkably, the notes attach far less weight to polemic than they do to philology – something that Marracci's bilingual translation would fail to do. Despite its quality, however, Egidio's edition did not circulate as widely as the Toledan Collection.

The Toledan Collection was printed in 1543 with numerous revisions by Theodor Bibliander (né Buchmann), a successor of Zwingli's at Basel, as part of a multi-volume reference work under the title *Machumetis Sarracenorum principis vita ac doctrina omnis ...*

(*The Life and Teachings of Machumet, Prince of the Saracens*).[6] The publication itself proved controversial: Bibliander's printer, Johann Oporinus (né Herbst), followed the usual practice of failing to inform the municipal authorities that he was about to publish the Qur'ān in order to speed up the process. He was denounced while the printing was well underway, and ordered to stop during the ensuing debate among the authorities on the suitability of his enterprise. Oporinus ignored the order again and was imprisoned for several days while his proofs were confiscated. Finally, he was then released on condition that he not contact anyone until a final decision was made, but by this point word had reached Bibliander and, through him, Protestant authorities elsewhere, leading to the interventions of Luther and Melanchthon. The fact that multiple parties intervened and numerous (sometimes contradictory) opinions were voiced bears witness to the degree of public interest in the Qur'ān.

The case against printing the Qur'ān relied on arguments forged during the long medieval tradition of anti-Muslim polemic. Under the leadership of Sebastian Münster, a former teacher of Bibliander who held the chair of Hebrew at Basel, the argument centered on the claim that there was nothing in the Qur'ān worth reading. Scholars and specialists may need access to the Qur'ān, but certainly not the general public. The Qur'ān was blasphemous and the public had to be protected. The opposite case was argued under the leadership of Oswald Myconius, another former teacher of Bibliander who had by then become the preacher of Basel and professor of New Testament exegesis. The Qur'ān did indeed contain much that was dangerous, but it was precisely in order to alert the public to its dangers that it had to be printed. In view of the continuing threat of Ottoman military incursions into central Europe and subsequent conversions to Islam, it was a matter of great importance that the Qur'ān be disseminated in order to inform the public about the true character of Islam. Finally, publishing this text in Basel would contribute to its prestige as a progressive center of liberal and tolerant thinking. Although the risk of anyone being converted by a mere reading of a book as difficult as the Qur'ān was small, the proponents of the printing advised adding some material to the publication to guide the reader through it theologically.

It was, in fact, after the addition of large quantities of such theological "guidance" (read: anti-Muslim polemic) that the Toledan Collection was finally published. Not only were there apologies by

Bibliander and Melanchthon, but a prefatory letter by Luther as well (though this was not added to all editions). Far from being prompted by any inclination toward Islam on Luther's part, this letter marks the culmination of a long series of works in which Luther tried to learn as much as he could about Islam as a way of fighting the Turks, the Pope, and heterodoxy within the church.[7] "Know your enemy" might stand as a useful summary of Luther's perspective on the necessity of translating the Qur'ān.[8] Bibliander's apology is equally forthright in its denunciation not only of Islam, but also of his own Christian enemies, not least among them being the Catholics and Anabaptists. Indeed, Bibliander argues, the latter are a case in point of what happens to a Christian society that is ignorant of its own traditions and consequently falls victim to pseudoprophecy. Bibliander's aim, in other words, was to show where true heresy was located.

Bibliander's edition contains a light re-working of Robert of Ketton's translation – his modest command of Arabic did not allow him to do much more than that. Bibliander's annotations, however, were copious, some bearing on the variants between the manuscripts that he used, some commenting on linguistic aspects of Robert of Ketton's translation – some even giving the Arabic original of a given word in Hebrew transcription, thereby attesting to the widespread importance of Semitic philology as a point of access to the study of Arabic and the Qur'ān at this point in time – and marginal comments, usually expressing dismay or contempt at what he takes to be the Qur'ān's contradictions and lies. Bibliander does not fail to add a significant number of notes on parallels between the Qur'ān and the Bible, usually ones bearing on a topic or story common to both. This particular use of textual points of contact as an exercise in comparative religious studies would become a regular feature of translations of the Qur'ān during the following two centuries. Although he consulted Arabic manuscripts of the Qur'ān, Bibliander did not consult any exegetical material at first hand. The three volumes of Bibliander's *magnum opus* are divided by function: first the sources, then the refutations, and, finally, history. The Toledan Collection takes up the first volume. The second contains polemical material, much of which was written after the twelfth century, including works by Riccoldo da Monte Croce, Juan Luis Vives, Savonarola, and Nicholas of Cusa. The inclusion of the latter's *Cribratio Alcorani* is a significant addition that demonstrates Bibliander's (and the reader's) interest in approaches to Islam that attempted to harmonize it with Christianity, albeit through a mystical lens, as well as the heuristic importance for Renaissance readers of parallels between the Qur'ān and the gospels.[9] The third volume contains several works on the history and political order of the Ottoman Empire by Luther, Giovio, and Pope Pius II, among others.[10] Thus the reader, according to his or her patience and attention span, is led from the origins of Islam to the politically strained relations between Islam and Christendom at the time.

Despite its questionable quality, the significance of this publication lies in the fact that it is the first published translation of the Qur'ān, as well as the fact that the Qur'ān has now become an integral part of polemics *within* Christianity as opposed to being used to address Christian–Muslim polemic. The pattern whereby a given theological opponent is accused of either being a Muslim or of being an ally of the Muslims acquires an additional dimension with the publication of the Qur'ān, so that Bibliander's "Protestant" project would soon be censored and banned by various Catholic authorities.[11] Arguments very similar to Bibliander's would be advanced during the second half of the seventeenth century in England, and again, Islam would prove "good to think with" in these polemics; a tool that would enable both traditionalists and radicals better to define their positions.

Two curious instances of this use of Islam within Christian polemic would come about in the same year.[12] Johann Albrecht von Widmanstetter published a summary of Robert of Ketton's translation joined with a polemical dialogue about Muhammad under the title *Mahometis Abdallae filii theologia dialogo explicata*. Widmanstetter imposed a polemical framework on summaries of the Toledan Collection that were circulating in manuscript by the late 1530s, with a view to providing the Catholic reader with a user-friendly tool to use in such instances.[13] Although the epitome of the translation of the Qur'ān is short (some thirty pages in print), Widmanstetter's annotations repeatedly refer to the Bible and Kabbalah. Thus there is more at stake in this project than anti-Muslim (and, since Widmanstetter was Catholic, anti-Protestant) polemic: part of the aim seems to have been the re-inscription of Islam within a larger corpus of comparative belief. Far less user-friendly was another work published in 1543 by Guillaume Postel (the most important Arabist of the sixteenth century, author of the first Arabic grammar in the West, a fervent Catholic, and occasional consultant to Bibliander), namely the *Alcorani seu legis Mahometi et Evangelistum concordiae liber*, in which he argued that the Protestants (of whom Bibliander was one) had a great deal in common with the Muslims, not least in their capacity for sowing discord and schism. Despite its title, the book does not contain a translation of the Qur'ān. Postel did, however, insert large tracts of the Qur'ān in a book he published the following year, the *De orbis terrae concordia*, in which he made a case for reconciling all the Abrahamic monotheisms under one religion; namely an improved Catholicism. The translations, which take up about a sixth of the total, are clearly made directly from the Arabic. Postel's translations indicate far greater familiarity with Arabic than Robert of Ketton, though Postel's vocabulary and diction are often inexact and occasionally weird. Postel went through the entire Qur'ān from beginning to end and chose what he considered to be the most important passages for his project. Nevertheless, the partial translations and esoteric character of *De orbis terrae concordia* limited the impact of Postel's work on the Qur'ān. It also bears pointing out that there is here a key instance of a pattern whereby Islam is used as part of a comparative system that tries to resolve the differences between the monotheisms. A century later, similar techniques would be used in a radically different register to argue against organized religion altogether.

In 1547 Andrea Arrivabene re-translated a much shorter, single-volume version of Bibliander's text into Italian while claiming to have produced a new translation from the Arabic text. What he did produce was a translation of the Qur'ān into a vulgar tongue, albeit one that was not translated from the Arabic.[14] In 1616 Salomon Schweigger re-translated Arrivabene's re-translation from Italian into German under the title *Der Türken Alkoran*, thereby indicating the extent to which "Muslim" and "Turk" were now synonymous, due in part to the reality of the Ottoman military threat in central Europe. In 1641, an anonymous Dutch translator re-translated Schweigger's re-translation of Arrivabene's re-translation of Bibliander's version of Robert of Ketton's translation of the Qur'ān, producing a text five times removed from the Arabic original.

As of the middle of the seventeenth century, Western readers mainly had access to versions of the Qur'ān increasingly distant from the Arabic text, along with multiple partial translations of selected passages and chapters. Nevertheless, the authorities were concerned with adding to what was known about the Muslim world without necessarily increasing the public's exposure to the Qur'ān. Thus Archbishop Laud obtained a royal letter requiring each Levant

Company ship to bring back one Arabic or Persian manuscript, except for the Qur'ān, since there were already enough of these in England.[15] The royal and university collections had yet to be filled with Oriental manuscripts, but somehow a sufficient number of Qur'ān manuscripts were in circulation to deem this exception to Laud's collecting strategy necessary. It was as if the Qur'ān were considered simultaneously desired and dangerous: desired because it is the Arabic book par excellence, the book of the "law of the Saracens"; dangerous because its reading could somehow "convert" the reader.[16] Laud's complementary strategies – founding the Laudian Chair of Arabic at Oxford and planning a "learned press" at Oxford using Arabic type – would have a lasting effect on early Orientalism and the translation of the Qur'ān.[17]

The quality of the Western translations of the Qur'ān took a dramatic turn for the better with the publication of André Du Ryer's (?1599–1672) *Alcoran de Mahomet* in 1647. Du Ryer had a long and varied career as a diplomat in the Middle East, with appointments in Alexandria, Cairo, and Istanbul. Though far more attentive than his predecessors to the form and literary qualities of the Qur'ān, Du Ryer nevertheless rendered the Arabic text into the elegant French that would be deemed acceptable for a seventeenth-century public without being overly concerned with an accurate rendition of the content.[18] Although it contains several serious mistakes, Du Ryer's translation is a vast improvement on what had gone before, as witness his openly acknowledged reliance on well-established exegeses, despite the fact that he occasionally gets the attribution wrong.[19] Instead of providing the reader voluminous compendia aimed at refuting the Qur'ān, Du Ryer contents himself with a six-page summary of "la religion des Turcs," openly derogatory in tone but arguably included to camouflage Du Ryer's sympathy with the Muslims and wide circle of Muslim friends.[20] Du Ryer takes the reader away from the mode of translation born of conflict and crisis toward a more genuine, if still troubled, inter-cultural connection, boasting of having made Muhammad speak French ("J'ay fais parler Mahomet en François").

Two years later Du Ryer's French text was translated into English.[21] Although the translator's identity is unknown, the name of Alexander Ross has been associated with this version since it appeared in 1649. The translation was published with several paratexts, including Du Ryer's preface, various diplomatic documents, a life of Muhammad (again, by an unknown hand), and text by Alexander Ross that makes the case for reading the Qur'ān. Ross takes pains to display his anti-Muslim credentials (possibly, again, in an attempt to foil any censors' attempts at accusing him of holding too favorable a view of Islam): the reader is promised a text in which "the great Arabian Impostor now at last after a thousand years, is by the way of France arrived in England, and his Alcoran, or gallimaufry of errors (a Brat as deformed as the Parent, and as full of Heresies, as his scald head was full of scurf) hath learned to speak English," and a lengthy "needful caveat" detailing the reasons for which reading the Qur'ān cannot do the reader much harm.[22] None of this stopped the Commonwealth authorities from issuing warrants for the seizure of the press and the arrest of the printer and bookseller. Nevertheless, the translation was published, and despite its poor quality went on to become one of the more popular books of seventeenth-century England (and, coincidentally, the first translation of the Qur'ān to be published in the United States of America [Springfield, 1806]).[23] Its greatest merit, perhaps, seems to be in diffusing the hysterical charge that greeted the publication of dissident views in early modern England. Ross attracted a great deal of criticism for his heterodox views. The promulgation of a comparative perspective on the world's religions in his *Pansebeia: or, View of All the Religions in the World* (1653) prompted a paradigm shift according to which the validity of religions other than Christianity became increasingly acceptable in seventeenth-century England, thereby paving the way for the outlook of the Sale translation.[24]

By the end of the seventeenth century Arabic studies and library collections in the West reached a point that enabled more complete and better documented translations of the Qur'ān.[25] One of the key Arabists of the age, Edward Pococke Sr. (1604–1691), had done much by mid-century to lay the ground for what would become the key translations with which we will be concerned in this study.[26] Arabic studies were already enjoying a revival in Europe for a number of reasons, chief among which were the importance of the language for both the study of the Bible after the Reformation, diplomacy, and the improvement of relations with the Christian populations of the Arab world.[27] All of these constituted the responsibilities of Edward Pococke Sr., who served as chaplain to the Levant Company at Aleppo from 1630 to 1635, and was appointed Laudian Professor of Arabic at Oxford in 1636 in addition to his appointment as Regius Professor of Hebrew.[28]

Before Pococke, William Bedwell, a pioneer of Arabic studies in England, proved instrumental in shifting the emphasis in the justification of Arabic studies from missionary to diplomatic, economic, and scientific uses.[29] Pococke's concern with the development of Arabic studies in England is evinced not only by the large number of Oriental manuscripts that he bought for the Bodleian, but by the shape of his publications. He translated an excerpt from the Syrian historian Bar Hebraeus (aka Ibn al-'Ibrī, Abū-l-Faraj) under the title *Specimen historiae arabum* in 1650. What is striking about this edition is the ratio of text to commentary: some fifteen pages are printed in Arabic (one of the earliest, if not the earliest, uses of Arabic type in England) with Latin translation on facing pages, but the whole is accompanied by some three hundred pages of notes and annotations bearing on every single point made by Bar Hebraeus in minute and very learned detail. The commentary effectively sets the record straight, giving the reader a proper account of the early rise of Islam, the lay of the land during the pre-Islamic period, and the structure of Muslim belief, including details of various legal schools and sects. Pococke takes care to correct errors and false claims repeatedly made by his predecessors, not least among them being Hugo Grotius, whose *De veritate religionis christianae* he would translate into Arabic in 1670. The arrangement of the material and the spirit of the project – compendious rather than critical or analytical[30] – anticipates and informs the work of the two key translators of the Qur'ān of the following century, Marracci and Sale, both of whom repeatedly seek recourse to the *Specimen* and Pococke's two other major historical works, the *Contextio gemmarum* (his translation of Eutychius's [aka Sa'īd b. al-Biṭrīq, the Melkite Patriarch of Alexandria] *Naẓm al-jawhar*, 1658) and the *Compendiosa historia dynastiarum* (a complete translation of Bar Hebraeus's *Al-Mukhtaṣar fī-l-duwal*, 1663).

While Pococke was working on his compendious histories and correcting the inveterate mistakes of his forebears, Ludovico Marracci was making his way as a regular member of the Order of the Mother of God, a teacher of rhetoric and Arabic, and confessor to Pope Innocent XI.[31] Marracci's relationship to the Arabic language – in which he claims to have been entirely self-taught, with some assistance from such native speakers of Arabic as he managed to meet and employ – was intense to say the least, and his reputation for piety and learning made it difficult for the Vatican to let go of him, despite his repeated requests for peace and quiet. By virtue of the age and order to which he belonged, Marracci was very much a man of the Counter Reformation. The Order of the Mother of God of Lucca was founded as a congregation by Giovanni Leonardi in 1574 before being promoted to the status of order in 1621 with the aim of fighting heterodoxy (read: Protestantism) through the instruction of the masses and the education of young minds. Coupled with Marracci's linguistic and philological gifts, as well as the ongoing advance of the Ottoman Empire and the siege of Vienna in 1683, this factor helps explain the outlook of Marracci's major lifework, his translation-cum-refutation of the Qur'ān, published in Padua in 1698. (Ironically, Padua and the Venetian republic were by then privileged points of entry for the "new philosophies" of Descartes and Spinoza into Italy.)[32] Marracci's ability as an Arabist had already been exploited by the Vatican on several occasions, first in helping to expose the Granadan Leaden Books as forgeries, and then much more significantly in bringing to fruition the Vatican's Arabic translation of the Bible in 1668 after the project had suffered numerous setbacks. Here, again, is an indication of the strong concern in the West with the spiritual and political salvation of Arabic Christians and a point of contention not against Muslims but against other Western Christians, such as those of the Levant Company. Nevertheless, Marracci gives the reader a very good idea of his orientation in dedicating the work to the man who had beaten the Ottomans at Vienna and then vindicator of Christendom, the Holy Roman Emperor Leopold I, whose alliance with Pope Innocent XI was seen to have been "rewarded" with victory over the Turks. This was more than a translation, therefore: for Marracci it was part of a vast war effort with roots extending to the Renaissance, undertaken with the aim of restoring the intellectual and theological glory of the Church of Rome and the memory of the Vatican as Europe's foremost center of Oriental studies.[33] His dedication to his project and the cause behind it was accompanied by a number of feverish efforts in Protestant Europe – mainly Germany – to produce a properly Lutheran translation of the Qur'ān.[34] Leibniz in particular seems to have been spurred by news of Marracci's undertaking to a hyperactive search for a suitable Lutheran counterweight, a task for which the nominees included Abraham Hinckelmann, the Hamburg pastor and Orientalist who would publish one of the earliest printed Arabic editions of the Qur'ān in 1694. Still, it was almost impossible to compete with Marracci's learning and excellent collection of sources at the Vatican library. As will be seen in the next chapter, this competition between rival Christian sects would prove to be a key impetus to the process of the translation of the Qur'ān in the West.

Marracci is, as Norman Daniel puts it, remarkable: on the one hand, his feeling for the Arabic language and culture are unparalleled; on the other hand, he dedicates his life to refuting the book that defines that language.[35] Pierre Martino gave what is probably the wittiest description of Marracci's translation a century ago:

> Un religieux italien, Maracci [sic], passa quarante années de sa vie à étudier le Koran, minant par avance chaque verset du livre maudit pour qu'il s'effondrât de lui-même. D'abord il publia une réfutation, afin que le remède fût connu avant le mal; puis, quand il fit paraître le texte lui-même et sa traduction latine, il eut soin qu'ils fussent enserrés entre les interminables colonnes où s'allongeaient les objections victorieuses: on eût dit un criminel, fluet, encadré entre d'énormes geôliers qui ne lui permettent pas de respirer.

> [An Italian priest, Marracci spent forty years of his life studying the Koran, undermining every verse of the book in advance so that it might fall apart automatically. First he published a refutation, so that the cure might be known before the disease; and then, when he published the text itself with its Latin translation, he saw to it that they were surrounded by endless columns of victorious objections: rather like a feeble criminal flanked by enormous prison guards that did not allow him to breathe.][36]

Marracci proceeded in stages, first publishing a prolegomenon to his refutation of the Qur'ān (the *Prodromus ad refutationem Alcorani*, 1691) in which he takes on the basic tenets of Islam, before publishing the *Refutatio* in 1698, along with a re-publication of the *Prodromus*, as a two-volume set, the *Alcorani textus universus*. Marracci presents a great deal of Arabic material in the *Prodromus*, almost all of it in print for the first time. After a preface to the reader, Marracci gives a life of Muhammad based entirely on Muslim sources, though he does not always manage to separate fact from fiction. The critique of Muslim doctrine in the *Prodromus* falls into four parts: the first attacks the Muslim claim that Muhammad's mission is foretold by Christian scripture; the second argues that, unlike Christianity, Islam cannot be a true religion because Muhammad did not perform any miracles; the third, that Christian dogma is true while Muslim dogma is false, and adduces the multiplicity of Muslim sects as evidence of the error inherent in their belief (adding a confession of Christian faith in Latin and Arabic); while the last section (inevitably) pleads for the superiority of Christian ethics over the violence and moral laxity of Islam. The thoroughness with which Marracci pursues these points is matched by his apparent intention to produce a new refutation of Islam on par with the great medieval polemics. The actual translation contained in the *Refutatio* is striking on a number of levels: the reader is met with the fully vocalized Arabic text of the Qur'ān,[37] followed by a detailed translation, followed by an impressive set of scholarly notes adducing multiple Arabic sources, exegetical and historical, usually quoted in the original and then translated into Latin. Unfortunately, the volume of all this valuable information is dwarfed by the painstaking "refutation" that Marracci adds to every translated passage. The refutations in question often surprise the reader by the obtuse approach that Marracci takes, deliberately ignoring or overlooking an obvious explanation for what he considers to be egregious mistakes. Despite the open hostility of Marracci's tone, his frequent recourse to military language – he brags about having fought the Qur'ān with the Qur'ān and "killed Muhammad with his own sword"[38] – and the often too literal quality of the translation, the sheer wealth of information contained therein makes it a good candidate for the title of the first proper encyclopedia of the Qur'ān. By Marracci's own admission, however, this refutation was clearly aimed at a Christian audience: at one point he states openly that he would not like it to be read by Muslims.[39] Marracci died in 1700, possibly worn out by the effort involved in translating the Qur'ān.

The years around the publication of Marracci's *magnum opus* would prove decisive to the future of Arabic and Islamic studies. In 1697, three books were published, all aimed at disparate audiences: Bayle's *Dictionnaire historique et critique*, a founding text of the European Enlightenment; Humphrey Prideaux's *True Nature of Imposture, Fully Display'd in the Life of the Prophet Mahomet*, a scathing critique of Muhammad in which the author repeated many of the same false claims about Islam that characterized Western discourse since the Middle Ages, written with a view to refuting Socinian/Unitarian and deist positions;[40] and finally Barthélémy D'Herbelot's *Bibliothèque orientale*, an encyclopedic, alphabetically arranged compendium that has been called the first encyclopedia of Islam. George Sale, on whom these three texts would leave their mark, and who would rely on them (along with many others) for a radically innovative translation of the Qur'ān, was born around the time of their publication.

Unlike Marracci, Sale did not take holy orders, though he did share his interest in Orientalism, which seems to have taken up more of Sale's time and energy than his ostensible profession, law. George Sale combined Enlightenment values and Christian commitment. In addition to the year of his birth, Sale's youth coincided with some key advances in European studies about Islam, among them Adrian Reland's *De religione Mohammedica* in 1705 (second edition, 1717; English translation of the first edition, 1712), and Jean Gagnier's *De vita et rebus gestis Mohamedis* in 1723. Reland and Gagnier in particular introduced key moments in the demythologization of Islam that would mark future scholarship permanently. Reland is remarkable for bringing to the study of Islam a perspective inspired by the growing Cartesianism of early eighteenth-century Utrecht, making a case for reading received ideas about Islam with skepticism and turning to Muslim sources for information about Islam and Muslims.[41] If anyone was fated to produce a good translation of the Qur'ān by being born at the right time, it was George Sale.

Bayle's dictionary needs no introduction, but what I would like to emphasize here is its status as one of the key vectors of critical and Spinozist thought that Sale would encounter. Bayle's article on Muhammad, "Mahomet," which was updated with every subsequent edition of the *Dictionnaire*, set out to deconstruct the received idea of Muhammad as a violent and licentious impostor. Bayle's critique of the idea that Muslims monopolized violence was probably informed by his own bitter experience as a Protestant refugee from Louis XIV's *France toute catholique*, as his comparison between French and Muslim armies makes clear:

> Mais enfin, comment résister à des armées conquérantes qui exigent des signatures? Interrogez les dragons de France qui servirent à ce métier, l'an 1685: ils vous répondront qu'ils se font fort de faire signer l'Alcoran à toute la terre, pourvu qu'on leur donne le temps de faire valoir la maxime, *compelle intrare, contrains-les d'entrer* [i.e. Luke 14:23]. Il y a bien de l'apparence que si Mahomet eût prévu qu'il aurait de si bonnes troupes à sa dévotion, et si destinées à vaincre, il n'aurait pas pris tant de peine à forger des révélations, et à se donner des airs dévots dans ses écrits, et à rajuster ensemble plusieurs pièces détachées du judaïsme et du christianisme. Sans s'embarrasser de tout ce tracas, il eût été assuré d'établir sa religion partout où ses

armes auraient pu être victorieuses; et si quelque chose état capable de me faire croire qu'il y a eu bien du fanatisme dans son fait, ce serait de voir une infinité de choses dans l'Alcoran, qui ne peuvent sembler nécessaires qu'en cas qu'on ne veuille point user de contrainte. Or il y a beaucoup de choses dans cet ouvrage qui ont été faites depuis les premiers succès des armes de Mahomet ["Mahomet," rem. N] …

Il faut avouer la dette: les rois de France ont établi le christianisme dans les pays des Frisons, et dans celui des Saxons, par les voies mahométanes ["Mahomet," rem. O].[42]

In the English translation of Bayle's *Dictionnaire*, a project with which Sale would later be associated, though it is not clear that it was necessarily he who translated the article "Mahomet," these passages are translated as follows:

[In] short, how is it possible to stand out against conquering armies, which demand your subscription? Ask the French Dragoons who were employed in that trade in the year 1685; they will answer that they will undertake to make all the world subscribe the *Alcoran*, provided they have a sufficient time allowed them to push that maxim, *compelle entrare*, i.e. compel them to come in. It is very probable that if Mahomet had foreseen that he should have at his devotion such good troops, and an army so resolute to conquer, he would not have taken so much pains in forging revelations, in giving himself such devout airs in his writings, and in adjusting so many detached pieces of Judaism and Christianity to his scheme. Without embarrassing himself in all this business, he would have been confident of establishing his religion wherever his arms could prevail; and if anything could make me believe, that he was pretty much tainted with fanaticism, it would be the observing an infinite number of things in the *Alcoran* which appear quite unnecessary, except upon the supposition that Mahomet did not mean to make use of compulsion. But there were a great many things in that work, which were wrote after his first successes in war … We must acknowledge our debt: the Kings of France established Christianity in the country of the Frisons and Saxony, by the Mahometan methods.

Europe's Most Christian Kings, in other words, are no better than the mythical version of Muhammad. Worse yet, intolerance is a Christian specialty, consistently and systematically used by one sect against another. If Muslims have used violence to spread their religion, they are only doing what French Catholics did after the revocation of the Edict of Nantes.[43]

In a key Spinozist moment, Bayle's article reminds the reader that Muhammad never claimed to have performed any miracles, but rather it was his followers who imputed them to him, thereby alluding to the radical argument that miracles are designed for the masses by a corrupt, manipulative clergy.[44] Many of Bayle's other footnotes take direct aim at the many myths about Muhammad and the Muslims that have circulated in Christendom, a point on which Bayle cites Marracci's argument that, far from advancing their cause, such behavior just makes Christians look ridiculous. Still, as the ambivalent tone of the passages quoted above demonstrates, Bayle's article is more of a balance sheet, establishing Muhammad's positive and negative qualities, rather than an outright defense or attack.[45] The many quarrels and polemics at work in Bayle's life color his portrait of Muhammad, leaving the reader better informed about Bayle's differences of opinion with those who have written on Islam before him rather than his own views. This is only to be expected, given Bayle's intention of writing a dictionary of past mistakes.

Barthélemy D'Herbelot's *Bibliothèque orientale* aims elsewhere. Like Bayle's dictionary, the *Bibliothèque* is very much a product of Louis XIV's France, though its focus is exclusively Orientalist and its political orientation far from critical of the regime, as D'Herbelot was a fervent Catholic who followed the tradition of studying Oriental languages better to understand the Bible. Edward Said's analysis of the excessively rational alphabetical grid into which D'Herbelot allegedly forces myriad facts about the Orient is too well known to require further comment, but it bears emphasizing that, since the *Bibliothèque* is essentially a series of translations from Oriental sources, chief among them being the monumental *Kashf Al-Ẓunūn* of the seventeenth-century polymath Kātib Čelebi (an annotated bibliographical dictionary of some 14,500 works in Arabic Persian and Turkish), it could hardly have been otherwise.[46] It is worthy of note that D'Herbelot chose (or was fortunate enough to possess) a relatively recent bibliography by the most conspicuous and productive scholar of the seventeenth-century Ottoman Empire in the *Kashf*, the first volume of which was completed in 1653–1654. D'Herbelot was thus aiming at the cutting edge of Oriental scholarship being produced in the Orient. Furthermore Kātib Čelebi's massive output included translations from Latin works dealing with the Ottoman Empire, including Mercator and Hondius's *Atlas Minor* as well as a sixteenth-century compilation of Western historical writing about the Orient spanning Byzantine, German, and Italian sources, the *Historia rerum in Oriente gestarum* (1587).[47] In dealing with this particular source of the *Bibliothèque*, therefore, we are confronted with a scholar whose work performs a key sorting and organizational function at the interface between East and West, rather than an Oriental entity passively suffering imperialist knowledge and control. Moreover, the vast compilation of facts in the *Bibliothèque* fit rather poorly under D'Herbelot's Arabic headings (which seem designed to frustrate the Western reader), with the net result that it is not the iron-clad container of knowledge about the Orient that Edward Said makes it out to be. Henry Laurens explains the curiously disappointing character of the *Bibliothèque orientale* by the same token whereby it enchanted its contemporaries: despite its erudite and restrained tone, the concatenation of translations from some thirty Oriental sources in the *Bibliothèque* obliges the reader to integrate the content of the articles into what can at best be called a personal, rather than an informed, opinion:

> La *Bibliothèque orientale* n'est en fait qu'une série continue de traductions et les efforts d'interprétation sont naturellement consacrés au domaine religieux, formant un ensemble particulier au sein de l'ouvrage. Le problème de la traduction impose un nombre relativement restreint de sources vraiment utilisés: notre trentaine de sources [covered in pp. 49–61 of Laurens' study]. Et ce caractère de traduction va donner un style, un cachet particulier à la *Bibliothèque orientale*.

> [The *Bibliothèque orientale* is in fact only a series of translations; any attempt at interpretation is naturally devoted to the field of religion, which constitutes a specific unit in the middle of the work. The problem of translation imposes restrictions on the number of sources actually used: whence our collection of about thirty sources. And this attribute of translation gives the *Bibliothèque orientale* its style and character.][48]

We are not far, then, from the aesthetic that drove Du Ryer's translations: the aim is to make the Orient readable without overwhelming the reader with erudition. On this particular count, D'Herbelot seems to have failed: the *Bibliothèque* was found to be a very useful work of reference, but hardly a readable one. D'Herbelot's will to exoticize the material is strong, and the tone is not far removed from Galland's *Mille et une nuits* – hardly surprising in view of the fact that Galland completed and updated the project after D'Herbelot's death.[49] When it comes to the articles on Muhammad and the Qur'ān, D'Herbelot keeps to the conservative positions that were typical of his age, choosing those two topics as privileged moments for the exercise of a critical faculty that he refuses to use on his own material, and concluding that the Qur'ān is a random collection of texts drawn from multiple informers – not unlike the *Bibliothèque* itself.[50] Conservatism and exoticism aside, the *raison d'être* of the *Bibliothèque* is, as Nicholas Dew explains, to substitute comparability, standardization, and compatibility for particularity and material copiousness.[51] That this substitution, in the end, produced something that most readers, like Gibbon, found "indigestible" is testament enough to the fact that the mere collection of facts was no longer enough as an approach to the Orient or Muslim world, and that something more was needed.

Like Bayle, Adrian Reland was concerned with demythologizing and correcting Western views of Islam. His application to the task was sufficiently thorough to result in the aforementioned *De religione Mohammedica*, a work described as "the first scientific description of the institutions of Islam" by Goldziher, probably the most important Orientalist of the nineteenth and early twentieth centuries.[52] A gifted polymath who combined remarkable learning (adding command of East Asian languages to the Orientalist's standard arsenal of biblical and Near Eastern ones), Reland set out to separate fact from legend in the representation of Islam once and for all. His *De religione Mohammedica* went through two editions and was quickly translated, making its way to multiple libraries and changing minds across Europe. Reland's influence was not limited to an academic audience: John Toland owned a copy of his work.[53] Reland's motives are couched in the usual language of "defeating" Islam, but it is clear that he is sincerely interested in a better understanding of Islam for its own sake:

> Truth, wherever it is, should be search'd after; and it is, in my Opinion, a laudable Exercise, to put a stop to Lyes, and to give a view of a Religion, which hath spread so far, to every one that pleases; not as it is disguis'd and cover'd with the Clouds of Detraction and Error, but as it is taught in the Mahometan Temples and Schools, that so we may be able to attack it with sure Blows; and if we are not able to shew the Vanity of it to the Turks, we may at least be convinc'd of its Vanity our selves.[54]

Reland compares the false claims thrown at Islam with those that the various Christian sects use against each other, thereby demonstrating his lucidity as to where the real gist of the quarrel about Islam lay in the early eighteenth century. Catholics and Protestants, says Reland, accuse each other of resembling Muslims, but whether these polemics bring either side to a clearer comprehension of Islam is very much in doubt.[55] These polemics are further compounded by the fact that the Western reader is rarely, if ever, encouraged to find things out about Islam for him- or herself, but rather informed by institutions that are far from being unbiased and often wrong in their assessment of Islam. In fact the only thing the hapless student of Islam is encouraged to do by some of these authorities is to burn the Qur'ān.[56]

The logic of Reland's approach – letting Muslim sources speak for themselves – comes through in the first part of *De religione Mohammedica*, which opens with the phrase "In the Name of the most Merciful God" and continues "Praise and Glory be to God, who hath brought us to the Faith."[57] The reader, in other words, is clearly reading what a Muslim has to say. The rest of the first part, an annotated translation of a Muslim text detailing the Muslim creed, lays out in lucid detail the five pillars of Islam and provides accurate descriptions of the rituals of prayer, ablution, alms, fasts, and pilgrimage. The second part of his book lists and corrects numerous misconceptions about Islam, mostly of the sort that are attributed by Western writers to the Muslims. The full range of Reland's learning comes out in this section, wherein we learn that Bartholomew of Edessa accuses the Muslims of believing that Mary became pregnant by eating dates and that Euthymius Zigabenus claims that Muslims believe that man was created out of a leech, among other things.[58] These laughable samples of patristic and medieval polemics are dealt with alongside weightier matters such as the Muslim view of salvation and the nature of paradise. Overall, Reland synthesizes the projects of Bayle and D'Herbelot: in a marvel of brevity (the English translation of *De religione Mohammedica* fills just over 100 printed pages) he lists, and refutes, the errors of past commentators on Islam while at the same time providing the reader with an authoritative introduction to Muslim dogma based on Muslim sources.

Humphrey Prideaux's *True Nature of Imposture* has a self-explanatory title, inviting the reader to see in Islam the true nature of imposture (as opposed to the imposture falsely imputed to Christianity by the deists) and urging him or her to remain within the true faith.

Prideaux writes to protect the Christian reader from the dangers that are sweeping across the land, chief among which is the multiplicity of sects and schisms. This multiplicity is, according to Prideaux, what made the Eastern churches such easy prey for the Muslims. The fate of the Church of England will almost certainly be that of the Eastern churches if such dangerous trends as deism are tolerated:

> Have we not reason to fear, that God may in the same manner raise up some Mahomet against us for our utter confusion; and when we cannot be contented with that blessed Establishment of Divine Worship and Truth, which he hath in so great purity given unto us, permit the Wicked One by some other such instrument to overwhelm us instead thereof with his foulest Delusion? And by what the *Socinian*, the *Quaker* and the *Deist* begin to advance in this Land, we may have Reason to fear that Wrath hath some Time since gone forth from the Lord for the Punishment of these our Iniquities and Gainsayings, and that the Plague is already begun among us.[59]

In order to terrify the reader, Prideaux narrates the life of Muhammad, who embodies "the true nature of imposture." For Prideaux, Muhammad is a frustrated, ambitious man who used imposture to reach his ends: political power. Had his father lived, Prideaux notes (correctly) that he would have inherited the leadership of the Quraysh effortlessly. Having been orphaned, however, he had to seek other means, and spent the first forty years of his life laying a wicked plan for the seduction of his peers.

> His two predominant passions were *Ambition* and *Lust*. The course which he took to gain *Empire*, abundantly shows the former, and the multitude of women which he had to do with, proves the later. And indeed these two run through the whole frame of his *Religion*, there being scarce a Chapter in his *Alcoran* which does not lay down some Law of War and Bloodshed for the promoting of the one; or else give some liberty for the use of Women here, or some promise for the enjoyment of them hereafter to the gratifying of the other.[60]

Nor is this all. In his appendix, the "Letter to the Deists", Prideaux proceeds to establish a semiotics of imposture, the better to enable his reader to identify imposture in matters of religion. The impostor is and has a character, in La Bruyère's sense of the term, which allows him to be recognized. The last and most important of these signs of imposture is the use of violence to propagate the false religion, "That it can never be established, unless backed by force and violence."[61] Imposture, for Prideaux, is unconvincing; its claims do not stand up to close scrutiny, unlike the true faith, whose hold on hearts and minds is undeniable. Hence the need for force.

The debate around imposture and religion in the late seventeenth century was not limited to Islam, but was inscribed in the wider questions dealing with salvation, "natural" religion, and reason. Indeed, the two decades from 1660 to 1680 saw the publication and dissemination of the largest number of texts centered on the theme of imposture in religion all over Europe, reflecting both interest in and anxiety surrounding the issue.[62] The debate was naturally linked to the many sects that so frightened Prideaux, chief among them being the Socinians (aka the Unitarians) and the deists.[63] The Socinian movement in England grew steadily during the seventeenth century, despite repeated persecution. In 1690 Arthur Bury argued in his *Naked Gospel* that Muhammad "possessed all the articles of the Christian faith, and declared himself not an Apostate, but a Reformer; Pretending to purify it from the corruptions wherewith it had been defiled."[64] Taking advantage of the relative weakness of Eastern Christianity, Muhammad founded the true (Unitarian) gospel. Bury's argument anticipates both Prideaux's attempt at a rebuttal and the argument that would become increasingly common in deist circles; namely that the true enemy of faith is the incomprehensible discourse in which religious beliefs are shrouded by a corrupt clergy. In his *Brief History of the Unitarians* (1687), Stephen Nye had argued that the Unitarians were the true heirs of early Christianity, invoking the Nazarenes, an early Judeo-Christian sect, as the first example of this pristine belief and again anticipating arguments that would be presented in more provocative form by John Toland, who made much of the parallels between Nazarene belief and Islam. Common to both Bury and Nye was the assumption that the doctrine of the Trinity was a corruption introduced by later Christians at Nicea in order to continue an age-old pattern of oppressive and mendacious behavior. The Anglican counter-polemic also built on the parallels that the Unitarians proposed, charging them with making common cause with the Muslims to bring about the downfall of Christendom. Prideaux was largely capitalizing on this trend in the composition of his *True Nature of Imposture.*

In 1720 there appeared an anonymous text that has been attributed to George Sale, though recent research has called this into question.[65] "Mahomet No Impostor," which takes explicit aim at Humphrey

Prideaux, was published somewhat incongruously as part of a literary miscellany, the *Miscellanea aurea*, and brings a cool skepticism reminiscent of Spinoza to Prideaux's alarmist claims. (The rest of the miscellany consists of prose and verse epistles exemplifying the moral laxity at which Prideaux took aim in *The True Nature of Imposture*.) Over the course of some twenty pages, the hoary concept of Muhammad's "imposture" is carefully deconstructed: far from establishing a false religion, Muhammad took the unity of the Godhead as his first principle, proceeding therefrom to the establishment of His worship, the elimination of idolatry, and the enforcement of moral principles. If anything, he was a reformer who delivered his people from error. If Muhammad practiced polygamy, so had Jacob and David. Unlike the lands where Christianity holds sway, Muslims still adhere to the principles that Muhammad taught them. What is remarkable about Sale's text (assuming that he is the author) is the trouble he takes to speak as a Muslim and a defender of Muhammad and Islam. He does this some three years before Montesquieu adopts a similar strategy in his *Lettres persanes*. Unlike Montesquieu, however, the aim of the piece is less a critique of the West through Eastern eyes than the defense of Muhammad as a prophet and statesman.

In the 1720s Sale became involved with the Society for the Promotion of Christian Knowledge. Founded in 1699 in reaction to what its members considered the prevailing moral laxity of the age, the society's policies had missionary and educational goals: the building of charity schools and workhouses, the distribution of books to those who could not afford them, and a general re-invigoration of Anglicanism.[66] Unfortunately these were soon oriented along an anti-Catholic axis, eventually turning the SPCK into a spearhead among several other national societies opposed to "popery," with a watching brief on "the practices of the priests to pervert His Majesty's subjects" and tactics that included keeping track of English Catholics at home and English seminaries abroad, plans for the conversion of Irish Catholics, and the use of a *Protestant Catechism* in their schools aimed, in part, at teaching children the basics of Anglicanism and the "Principal Errors of the Church of Rome."[67] In 1720 the SPCK added to its activities the publication of an Arabic translation of the New Testament aimed at the Eastern Christian communities in the Levant. Two Syrian Christians living in England at the time, Salmon Negri and Carolus Dadichi, were involved – indeed, Negri's correspondence with the SPCK repeatedly stressed the need for such a translation in view of the inaccessibility of the Arabic Bible in the Middle East, cleverly suggesting that the Levant Company at Aleppo be charged with its distribution, and attracting the approval and encouragement of none other than Humphrey Prideaux.[68] It is probably from Negri and Dadichi that Sale learned, or at least perfected, his Arabic, and with Negri that he worked on the corrections to the Arabic New Testament, having become a corresponding member of the SPCK and accepted the assignment of corrector in 1726.[69] The result, العهد الجديد لربنا يسوع المسيح (*The New Testament of Our Lord Jesus Christ*), was published and shipped in 1727.

Apart from the Arabic New Testament Sale was involved with the English translation of Bayle's *Dictionnaire* – though he does not seem to have added much beyond the letter "A" and his name does not appear on the title page past the fourth volume – and an early historical encyclopedia and prototype of the French *Encyclopédie*, the *Universal History*, to the first volume of which (the *Cosmogony*) he made an important contribution.[70] He was supposed to act as general editor, but his erudition and breadth of mind were ironically held against him, resulting in the transfer of the editorial responsibility to George Psalmanazar.[71] Both projects attest to Sale's interest in the philosophy of systems of belief and a rare capacity for global perspectives. Both also bear witness to Sale's attraction to critical approaches to received ideas: among his sources for the *Cosmogony* were deist texts that called into question biblical accounts of creation. Sale's comfort with multiple perspectives on what were held to be sacred truths, which allowed him to propose multiple, but equally valid, chronologies for the story of the flood, displeased the *Universal History*'s readers, many of whom were middle-class professionals allergic to that sort of speculation.[72]

Sale's translation of the Qur'ān, where his learning and the intellectual skills honed by his work on the aforementioned projects served him very well, made him famous. Although he did not reproduce the Arabic text, Sale stopped at nothing to produce a balanced and informative rendition of the Qur'ān, so much so that the few anti-Muslim statements that one runs across in his paratexts come across as being perfunctory and insincere. (The anti-Catholic statements, however, seem to be heartfelt.) The translation, which is copiously annotated (there are footnotes and footnotes to the footnotes on every page), is preceded by a long "Preliminary Discourse" (the title is a riposte to Marracci's *Prodromus*) in which Sale presents the history and geography of seventh-century Arabia, the rise of Islam, the history of the revelation and collection of the Qur'ān, as well as a cursory map of the doctrines and schools of thought of Islamic theology. Sale clearly acknowledges his debt to the previous generation of Orientalists – Marracci and Pococke in particular – but the results of his research and skill as a translator are unparalleled.

Sale's method in the "Preliminary Discourse" draws on a number of contemporary trends to produce an authoritative introduction to Islam. The multiple footnotes and annotations imply that Islam is to be read against two axes: philosophy and history. The critical function is probably inherited by Sale's reading of Bayle and Spinoza (see below), while the historical dimension bears witness to the new sort of historiography that was spreading across Europe, citing sources while critically evaluating them, and making a point of backing up every claim.[73] What distinguishes Sale's "Preliminary Discourse" from the work of Pococke and D'Herbelot is precisely the fact that it is not a compendium or a series of translations: far from simply amassing or translating facts, Sale is interested in interpreting and re-presenting them. The predominant question in the "Preliminary Discourse" seems to be "Where does Islam come from?" Sale avoids the facile answers that satisfied his forebears (Islam is a heresy invented by an impostor) to locate Islam as a system of belief rooted in time, place, and, most significantly, the text of the Qur'ān.

Sale drew and added to a rapidly developing image of Muhammad as a statesman and legislator. Here again, he was writing against *The True Nature of Imposture*. Prideaux's loud denunciations of Muhammad as an impostor are underlined by the sense that the deception of the masses by a clever manipulator could take place in any period of moral laxity, be it seventh-century Arabia or eighteenth-century England. Unless the licentiousness that he associated with deism came to an end, a new "impostor" would almost certainly appear and threaten Christendom – a lesson that found widespread appeal both in Europe and the American colonies.[74] Over against this discourse, the image of Muhammad as a legislator that appears in the eighteenth century owes much to the revaluation of all values underway as part of the Enlightenment. Henry Laurens sums up the situation thus:

> Dans une société qui commence à s'interroger sur une possible refonte globale de ses structures, tout antécédent historique sert

d'exemple et de révélateur du problème. Mahomet devient, plus que
tout autre personnalité historique, l'exemple même du surhomme au-
dessus des lois et doté de tous les pouvoirs, ce qui constitue l'une des
solutions envisageables. Il occupe dans la conscience occidentale du
XVIIIe siècle une place qu'il ne pouvait avoir avant, et qu'il n'aura
plus après. Mais ce personnage a un champ d'action géographique
qui lui était propre. L'Orient est le lieu d'élection du grand homme,
qu'il soit conquérant, législateur ou fondateur de religion. Le propre
de Mahomet est de posséder ces trois aspects.

[In a society that is starting to ponder a fundamental transformation of its structures, every historical precedent acts as a revealing
example of its problems. More than any other historical character,
Muhammad exemplifies the *Übermensch* who stands above the law
and is endowed with superhuman powers, thereby constituting one
conceivable solution. In the eighteenth-century Western imagination, he holds a place that he did not before and will not be able to
afterwards. But he had his own field of geographic action. The Orient
is the preferred location of the great man, whether he be a conqueror,
legislator or founder of a religion. Muhammad's essential quality is
the possession of these three aspects.][75]

Much ink is spilled during this period on the opposition between
the impostor and the legislator, with the term "legislator" enjoying
a strong positive spin.[76] Accordingly, the attribute that Sale most
frequently attributes to Muhammad is that of "legislator." This distinction is accompanied by the development of an English tradition stretching from Henry Stubbe to John Toland that re-wrote the
history of the three monotheisms as one of reforming legislators.[77]
Henry Stubbe commended Islam for its rationality and prudence in
his *Account of the Rise and Progress of Mahometism*, which was
completed in 1671 but only circulated as a clandestine manuscript
for the next fifty years, only seeing publication in the early twentieth
century. After presenting Christianity as a Jewish heresy in his opening chapter, Stubbe narrates the rise of Islam from the "decay and
debauchery" of Eastern Christianity; essentially a purified version of
the "Doctrines of the Nazarene Christians and the Arrians."[78] Taking
one element of anti-Muslim polemic, Stubbe argues that Muhammad
was a Machiavellian operator who capitalized on the geopoliti-
cal lay of the land to found a new religion and empire, concluding
that he was "the Wisest Legislator that ever was."[79] Stubbe dwells
on Muhammad's political skill, adding sententious observations to

frame a particular incident ("It is one of the most difficult parts of a Prince to adjust Employments to their Ministers, and to make use of suitable instruments for carrying on each Affair")[80] all with a view to emphasizing the complexity of Muhammad's mission and his intelligence in dealing with it. His creed depends on simplicity and common sense:

> This is the sume of Mahometan Religion, on the one hand not clog-ging Men's Faith with the necessity of believing a number of abstruse Notions which they cannot comprehend, and which are often contrary to the dictates of Reason and common Sense; nor on the other hand loading them with the performance of many troublesome, expensive and superstitious Ceremonies, yet enjoyning a due observance of Religious Worship, as the surest Method to keep Men in the bounds of their Duty both to God and Man.[81]

Finally, Stubbe demonstrates that Muhammad's legislative pow-ers outdid those of his predecessors, and even if some of his moral precepts were legislated for political reasons, their rational charac-ter ensures their success. Muslim religious duties are "plainly laid down, which is the cause that they are duly observed, and are in themselves very rational, tho' perhaps some of them were retained or instituted partly upon a political Account, as has been don by the wis-est Legislators in all Ages."[82] Stubbe also comments at length on the many Christian legends that circulated about Muhammad, showing them to be mere fables, thereby anticipating the task that would be performed with greater precision by Reland. Although it is far from perfect, and contains more than a few errors, Stubbe's account is well informed nonetheless, with frequent references to Pococke, the cut-ting edge of Orientalist scholarship at the time. It emblematizes the uses of Islam in freethinking circles during the late seventeenth and early eighteenth centuries: by inscribing Islam in the history of Judeo-Christianity, and by describing Islam as a return to a set of beliefs that had been corrupted by the church, Stubbe makes a strong case for Trinitarian Christianity as a form of imposture and religion as a human activity with a worldly, historical, and political dimension.[83] Sale's Qur'ān is distinguished by its reliance on, and dialogue with, the freethinking tradition that stretches from Stubbe to Toland.

The process of translating the Qur'ān – indeed the very act of translation – might usefully be compared to what Clifford Geertz, following Gilbert Ryle, calls "thick description," a term that Geertz applies both to the construction of meaning in both ethnography and reading. From this perspective, readers, ethnographers, and, I would add, translators must work their way through and find a way to render a "multiplicity of complex conceptual structures, many of them superimposed upon or knotted into one another."[84] The task of the translator is to analyze these strata of meaning in the text and convey them to the reader in a suitably thick description. Thick description is what sets Sale and Marracci apart from their predecessors, especially Du Ryer, who "introduces" his translation of the Qur'ān with a six-page "Sommaire de la religion des Turcs" and then relies on the language of his translation to convey the complexity of the Qur'ān, with marginal notes being kept to the bare minimum. To a certain extent, Du Ryer is responding to the expectation of the French reading public of the first half of the seventeenth century, who see the translator as a *littérateur* and who expect any text, be it the Qur'ān or Tacitus, to be made to sound like the language that has the sanction of the *Académie*, regardless of the emendations or "improvements" that the translator might bring to the original. Indeed, there is no gainsaying the role played by unfaithful translations (the "belles infidels") in the formation of French classicism.[85] The paradigm at work here is the same one that would later see in Louis XIV's France the rival, indeed the superior, of Greece and Rome, and lead Perrault to declare "C'est nous qui sommes les anciens." ["It is we who are the ancients."] This view minimizes the distance between the cultures and ages in play, as evinced by the triumphant claim in Racine's preface to *Iphigénie* that common sense is the same always and everywhere, and that "le goût de Paris s'est trouvé conforme à celui d'Athènes."[86] ["The taste of Paris turned out to be in conformity with that of Athens."] The idea that the past is not necessarily a foreign country informs both the translators of the Qur'ān and its readers, many of whom would probably have agreed with Voltaire's opinion that "L'homme, en général, a toujours été ce qu'il est."[87] ["Man, in general, has always been what he is."] It is precisely this belief in the contemporaneity of the past and the relative youth of the universe that allows a perspective on the Orient radically at odds with our own: Muslims might be different, but not so different as to be incomprehensible. This sense of similarity informs both the belligerence of Marracci, for whom the Crusades and the wars of religion are of a piece (but his co-religionists have somehow picked on the wrong enemy), and the goodwill of Sale. What exoticism there is in early Orientalism – in Galland, D'Herbelot, or elsewhere – does not necessarily translate into an essential difference between Muslims and Christians as different species, but simply as peoples who have had different histories that may well have been interchangeable. As Henry Laurens put it, the register of early Orientalism is one where the Athens of Pericles, Baghdad of Al-Ma'mūn, and France of St Louis are identical.[88]

George Steiner relates this isochronic outlook, whereby Parisians, Athenians, and Persians are not seen as being altogether very different, to the link between linguistic and geometric translation; the isomorphic mapping of a set of points from one locus to another and making of culture "the translation and rewording of previous meaning."[89] It is this sort of trans-lation, of carrying over from one physical and cultural space to another, that helps locate the difference between Du Ryer, Marracci, and Sale. There is nothing – apart, perhaps, from a concern with current standards of taste – to prevent Du Ryer from "thickening" his description either with a longer, fairer introduction, or more meaningful footnotes. Marracci and Sale, on the other hand, provide thick descriptions, and in Sale's case this in no way contravenes the production of a readable, fluid translation. Both Marracci and Sale seem to project the strata of meaning that they work through on to the format that they present to the reader – long introductions about Islamic history, theology, and law (the *Prodromus* and the "Preliminary Discourse"), the vocalized Arabic text with verse numbers (Marracci), translations, footnotes, citations, and footnotes to the footnotes (Sale) – so that the visual layout of the text actually reproduces the layers of meaning it is trying to render. The difference between Sale and Marracci, however, is that the latter's obstinate use of multi-page "refutations" of the pericope he is translating operates as a thinning agent, rendering what would otherwise have been an excellent thick description somehow irrelevant. Why, the reader is tempted to ask, provide all of this information if it is just going to be dismissed as being false anyway?[90]

Thus the differences between the translations and the surrounding descriptive framework depend on the political and theological stance of the translator. The history of the translation of the Qur'ān is bound inextricably with conflicts within the West rather than between the Muslim world and the West. In this the history of the translations is moving in line with the major trend that made confessional rivalry the primary motor of cultural change in Europe by the mid-seventeenth century.[91] The early modern study of Islam – like the early modern study of comparative religion generally – owed much to confessional quarrels that defined the "enemy" not as a Muslim but a Christian of a different denomination (and for some, *ipso facto*, no longer a Christian).[92] This curious situation is summed up nicely by Peter Harrison:

> While much comparison of "religions" took place in the seventeenth and eighteenth centuries, most of it was motivated not by any deep interest in the religious faith of other peoples, but by the desire to score points from theological adversaries. For this reason, the so-called religions of the Orient were made in the image of their presumed Western counterparts. Unfortunately, the paradigms of these new "religions" were the undesirable religious forms of Christendom – be it papism, Calvinism, Socinianism, deism, Presbyterianism, or episcopacy.[93]

For better or worse, confessional conflict, with all of its political ramifications, became a key site in the production of knowledge about the Orient, and nowhere more so than in the opposition between the Catholic and Protestant study of the Qur'ān.

Given the prevalence of such conflicts during the late seventeenth century, one might wonder why it is that Sale's reading of Islam only became possible in 1734 when much of the intellectual groundwork was ready some fifty years earlier. Apart from the reasons outlined above, including the advances made by Reland and Gagnier, and the sheer mass of material made available through the Marracci translation, it is important to note the impact of Spinoza and Spinozism: no longer a name but an entire climate of opinion by the turn of the eighteenth century.[94] The doctrine of the single substance, the denial of miracles, and the equivalence of all revealed religions as products of imposture paved the way for certain discursive practices that would have been otherwise impossible. Works based on Spinoza enjoyed remarkable diffusion despite their sometimes questionable quality. Chief among these is the *Traité des trois imposteurs*, also known as *L'Esprit de Spinosa*, a key vector in the spread of Spinoza's ideas in Europe alongside Bayle's *Dictionnaire*, where the article "Spinoza" is by far the longest.[95] The appearance of the *Traité des trois imposteurs* is symptomatic of a profound change in the European attitude toward monotheism, one that goes well beyond the efforts of the Socinians and Richard Simon at subjugating Christianity and scripture to the demands of reason and Cartesian philosophy.[96] The *Traité* enables the same sort of translatability that was once ascribed to the polytheistic religions to be allowed to operate among the monotheistic ones, albeit in a register of denunciation.[97] There is more at stake than a plea for toleration that would become common later in the eighteenth century: the *Traité*, like a great deal of Spinozistic literature, presents a strong critique of religion, parts of which would be put to good use by Sale.[98] Following this model, intercultural translatability depends on the assumed validity of the religions in question. With the publication of the *Traité des trois imposteurs* comes the idea that such translatability also works across cultural distinctions if one assumes the falsity of all the religions in question. The only instance in which there is a failure of translation is in the confrontation of a false with a true religion. As Jan Assmann put it, "False gods cannot be translated."[99] It is only once such equivalence is envisaged, if not actually established, in the minds of some, that an accurate reading of Islam becomes possible. In the case of Ludovico Marracci, we are faced with the impossibility of translation: the god of Islam is false (even though everything seems to indicate that it is the God of Abraham), and therefore no reconciliation with the Qur'ān is possible. In the case of Sale, the cultural boundary between Islam and non-Islam becomes sufficiently porous to enable translation of the older, "polytheistic" sort. The irony is that Sale relied on Marracci to a very large extent, and that he was a very committed Protestant, far from the vehement anti-religious tone of the *Traité*. Two radically different translations of the Qur'ān are enabled by the same data.

Thus the very possibility of seeing Islam as a legitimate religion (or at least set of laws worthy of respect) grows out of the leveling perspective adopted by the radical Enlightenment. If the *Traité des trois imposteurs* passed off all revealed religions as the products of imposture and manipulation, George Sale turned the argument on its head and made the case that all religions are thereby worthy of serious study instead of polemical dismissal. Furthermore, Sale's repeated description of Muhammad as a legislator on par with Minos and Numa adds further emphasis to the idea that certain aspects of Muslim life and law might usefully be compared to their counterparts in Greece and Rome – and, finally, that the Muslim state is less a monstrous scourge on humanity than a republic that gains from being compared with Rome and Venice.

Spinoza's name occurs once in the Sale translation, in the section of the "Preliminary Discourse" dealing with the Sunni–Shī'a split, and its political embodiment in the form of the conflict between Persia and the Ottoman Empire. Sale is amazed at Spinoza's ignorance:

> It seems strange that Spinosa, had he known of no other schism among the Mohammedans, should yet never have heard of one so publicly notorious as this between the Turks and Persians; but it is plain he did not, or he would never have assigned it as the reason of his preferring the order of the Mohammedan church to that of the Roman, that there have arisen no schisms in the former since its birth.[100]

In the footnote, Sale quotes a line from Spinoza:

> Ordinem Romanæ ecclesiæ – politicum et plurimis lucrosum esse fateor; nec ad decipiendam plebem, et hominum animos coercendum commodiorem isto crederem, ni ordo Mahumedanæ ecclesiæ esset, qui longè eundem antecellit. Nam à quo tempore hæc superstitio incepit, nulla in eorum ecclesia schismata orta sunt. (*Opera Post.* P. 613)

> [I grant the political and financial advantages that accrue from the order of the Roman church, and would believe it better designed than any other for the deception of the common people and the domination of their souls, were it not for the Mohammedan church, which surpasses it by far. Indeed since the start of that superstition (i.e. Islam) there has never been any schism in their church.][101]

The statement is taken from a long letter that Spinoza wrote to Albert Burgh, a former disciple who travelled to Italy and converted to Catholicism, eventually becoming a Franciscan friar, in 1675. Spinoza's letter was written in response to a lengthy missive by Burgh in which the latter attacks his system and defends the doctrine of the church. Both letters were published as part of Spinoza's *Opera Posthuma*, which is where Sale would have seen them, immediately becoming twin foci for religious polemic and debate in the ensuing years.[102] That Sale would have been drawn to one of Spinoza's more vehement anti-Catholic moments is hardly surprising. What is striking about Sale's reference to Spinoza is not, or not only, his defense of Islam, but rather the fact that he was sufficiently familiar with it to have it on his mind as he composed his account of Muslim sects and schools of thought.[103] Moreover, Spinoza's view of Islam as the religion best organized to dupe the masses and coerce them into submission and hence suffer no schism whatsoever is prominent throughout the *Tractatus Theologico-Politicus*, so Sale's return to this point at this moment in the "Preliminary Discourse" indicates that he was conversant with the ideas current in Spinozism and heterodox literature.

Two other names associated with this trend recur repeatedly in Sale's translation, bearing witness to the intellectual risks he was willing to take: Toland, whose name has already been mentioned, and Boulainvilliers. The latter is especially interesting as a case study in the conversion of a French nobleman from a "moderate" Cartesian outlook to a more radical set of beliefs, culminating in his *Vie de Mahomed*, a biography that faced difficulties so substantial that subscribers were asked to pay for the publication.[104] Both Prideaux and Sale were among the subscribers. The fact that the list of subscribers contains names associated with such divergent views demonstrates the reach of radical thought in debates about religion and Islam during the early eighteenth century. Boulainvilliers' text is less history than polemic, arguing that Islam is the purest of the three monotheisms and adapting Spinoza's mistaken claim about the absence of splits in Islam to "prove" its superiority over Christianity. Under Boulainvilliers' pen, Muhammad becomes an early avatar of Spinoza, bringing forms of belief so far superior to his predecessors that he singlehandedly changed the face of history and destroyed the mightiest empires of his day.

Having lived through the "domestication" of the French nobility by Louis XIV and the upheavals that accompanied the turn of the eighteenth century, Boulainvilliers spent much of his life looking for certainty and well-defined origins.[105] So it is with the *Vie de Mahomet*. Boulainvilliers emphasizes the happy state of the Bedouins before Muhammad's arrival, projecting on to them his view of what he supposes early French nobility must have been like before absolutism, referring to the "exclusion de rois, ou de chefs absolus."[106] In this golden age, genealogies were respected and bloodlines remained pure (which is why the Bedouins were necessarily not numerous). The Arab genius was neither intolerant nor excessively violent. Islam, far from being a religion of the poor, as was Christianity, attracted Mecca's best and brightest, who were drawn to its utter reasonableness: "Il [Muhammad] est venu à bout, non pas d'amener les hommes grossiers à une doctrine mystérieuse ... mais les plus sublimes héros de leur siècle, en valeur, en générosité, en modération et en sagesse."[107] ["He [Muhammad] managed to attract to a mysterious doctrine, not savage men… but the most sublime heroes of the age in valour, generosity, moderation and wisdom."] In other words the proud freedom-loving Bedouin were the raw material that Muhammad turned into the greatest people that the world had ever seen. Muhammad was a true prophet who gave his people the best laws that it was possible to have short of being Christian: "sans la grâce de la révélation chrétienne … il n'y auroit système de doctrine si plausible que le sien, si conforme aux lumières de la raison, si consolant pour les justes, et si terrible aux pêcheurs."[108] ["Without the grace of the Christian revelation … there would be no doctrinal system as plausible as his [Muhammad's], in such conformity with the light of reason, so comforting to the righteous, and so terrible to sinners."] Indeed, Muhammad's example proved that a religion could be true independently of Christianity.[109] So controversial were Boulainvilliers' claims that they displeased conservative and liberal alike: Jean Gagnier refers to the *Vie de Mahomet* as being closer to a novel than a history, and strenuously denied claims that is was he who completed the work, which was unfinished at the time of its author's death. Nevertheless, Boulainvilliers' tone makes itself heard throughout the second part of Sale's "Preliminary Discourse," dealing with the life of Muhammad.

John Toland started out attempting to refute Spinoza and ended up not only becoming a radical Spinozist himself, but also the one who did most to popularize the term "pantheist."[110] Apart from priestcraft – the corrupt, all-powerful clergy who worked with a tyrannous authority to forge "mysteries" that keep the masses in check – Toland's *bête noire* was the Catholicism that he abandoned in his youth, calling it "the insupportable Yoke of the most Pompous and Tyrannical Policy that ever enslav'd Mankind under the name or Shew of Religion."[111] Toland seems to have made his mark on Sale through his *Nazarenus, or Jewish, Gentile and Mahometan Christianity, containing the history of the antient gospel of Barnabas and the modern Gospel of the Mahometans, attributed to the same apostle* (1718). As its title implies, Toland's text argues for the possibility that all of the Abrahamic monotheisms are but variations on a theme, and can thus all be considered forms of "Christianity." Toland's text relies in part on the so-called Gospel of Barnabas, a forgery (unbeknownst to Toland) written apparently to vindicate the Qur'ānic account of Jesus. The impact of the *Nazarenus* is such that Sale not only returns to it in his translation of the Qur'ān – both in the "Letter to the Reader," and in a passage on the name of Muhammad – despite his awareness of its forged status, but also in his seeming adoption of Toland's outlook, whereby information about religion should be disseminated to the greatest possible number and other religions should be seen through a framework of similarities and differences rather than rivalry and enmity.[112]

The second part of Sale's "Preliminary Discourse," dedicated to the state of Christianity on the eve of Muhammad's birth, is very much of a piece with Toland's critique of clerical corruption, attributing the rise of Islam to the hapless state of Christendom and the error of its ways. The passage is a marvelous record of the anxieties surrounding the question of Christianity versus Islam, especially with respect to the rapid spread of the latter. Furthermore, it combines many of the discourses that have been described above, showing how they feed into Sale's account of early Christianity, Islam, and the Qur'ān:

> If we look into the ecclesiastical historians even from the third century, we shall find the Christian world to have then had a very different aspect from what some authors have represented; and so far from being endued with active graces, zeal, and devotion, and established within itself with purity of doctrine, union, and firm profession of the faith, that on the contrary, what by the ambition of the clergy, and what by drawing the abstrusest niceties into controversy, and dividing and subdividing about them into endless schisms and contentions, they had so destroyed that peace, love, and charity from among them, which the Gospel was given to promote; and instead thereof continually provoked each other to that malice, rancour, and every evil work; that they had lost the whole substance of their religion, while they thus eagerly contended for their own imaginations concerning it; and in a manner quite drove Christianity out of the world by those very controversies in which they disputed with each other about it. In these dark ages it was that most of those superstitions and corruptions we now justly abhor in the church of Rome were not only broached, but established; which gave great advantages to the propagation of Mohammedism. The worship of saints and images, in particular, was then arrived at such a scandalous pitch that it even surpassed whatever is now practised among the Romanists …
>
> This corruption of doctrine and morals in the princes and clergy, was necessarily followed by a general depravity of the people; those of all conditions making it their sole business to get money by any means, and then to squander it away when they had got it in luxury and debauchery …

It has been observed by a great politician [i.e. Machiavelli], that it is impossible a person should make himself a prince and found a state without opportunities. If the distracted state of religion favoured the designs of Mohammed on that side, the weakness of the Roman and Persian monarchies might flatter him with no less hopes in any attempt on those once formidable empires, either of which, had they been in their full vigour, must have crushed Mohammedism in its birth; whereas nothing nourished it more than the success the Arabians met with in their enterprises against those powers, which success they failed not to attribute to their new religion and the divine assistance thereof.[113]

Although the critique of the Church of Rome had become standard by the early eighteenth century, and some of Sale's arguments re-iterate those found in Bayle's *Dictionnaire*, what sets Sale's critique apart is its general tone: *every* Christian sect is guilty of corruption, and is therefore responsible for Europe's losses before the Muslim armies. Furthermore, the reference to Machiavelli bears witness to Sale's ability as a *bricoleur*, drawing in multiple sources and tradi-tions to make the case that Muhammad is not necessarily justified by his victories, but his behavior, as well as that of the Muslims, makes sense from the perspective of realpolitik. This is a much more sat-isfying explanation of Islam than the endlessly repeated charges of imposture, violence, and lust.

The translation of the Qur'ān quickly became synonymous with Sale's name, despite the fact that he died only two years after it was published, leaving his family in difficult financial circumstances. Eventually, myths began to emerge and circulate among the readership: Voltaire claimed that Sale had spent twenty-five years living in the Arabian desert, a mistaken impression created in part by the authentic sound of the text. The English translation was re-edited four times in the eigh-teenth century, and some sixty times in the nineteenth.[114] Naturally, re-translations quickly followed the publication of the first edition in 1734, with versions appearing in German (Theodor Arnold, 1764), Russian (Alexei Kolmakov, 1792), and Hungarian (Istvan Szokoly, 1854). Eventually, the "Preliminary Discourse" was translated and published separately in Dutch (Amsterdam, 1742), French (Geneva, 1751; Algiers, 1846; Paris, 1850), and Swedish (Stockholm, 1814), and coupled with the Du Ryer translation in an edition published in 1775. Remarkably, the "Preliminary Discourse" was also translated into Arabic in 1891, ostensibly to "prove" that the Qur'ānic account of the death of Jesus was not only correct, but actually accepted by certain Christians.

Once again, Sale's broadmindedness was held against him. Some, like the antiquary Thomas Hearne, who was a staunch supporter of Jean Gagnier, took issue with the vast amounts of information that Sale added to frame his translation, while others, like James Porter, who had served as ambassador to the Ottoman Empire from 1746 to 1762, criticized his tendency to "apologize" for the Qur'ān.[115] Worse yet, the translation that made him famous seems to have aggravated his relationship with the organization that did so much to make it possible, with which his contact became very infrequent after 1734. But his reputation as the man who produced a translation of the Qur'ān in line with the values of the Enlightenment, and one that can be read with profit to this day, remains intact.

The Sale translation is distinguished as a locus that combines multiple perspectives, from early Orientalism to radical philosophy. It is to this translation and its reception – the intellectual genealogies and exchanges that occurred around Sale, as well as the impact of this book on the subsequent history of the eighteenth century – that we now turn. Of necessity, this study is far from exhaustive, but it will hopefully give the reader an idea of the near-ubiquity of the translated Qur'ān in the project of the Enlightenment and the making of the modern world.

2

SALE, MARRACCI, AND
THE REPRESENTATION OF ISLAM

Semper miratus sum, Christiane Lector, quòd, cum tot doctissimi, sanctissimique viri, adversus alias Orthodoxae Religioni oppositas sectas immense volumina conscripserint: contra Mahumetum, impiamque ejus legem tam pauci, ac tam parcè calamo decertaverint. Arianam haeresim in ipsis incunabulis in trecentis decem & octo Nicaeni Concilii Patribus praefocatam, per aliquot deinceps saecula, cùm vegetiores spiritus resumpsisset, omnes ferè totius Christiani Orbis Scriptores validissime oppugnaverunt. Contra Eutychetis, Dioscori, Nestorii, Macedonii, aliorumque antiquiorum Haeresiarchum errores, non minor Catholicorum Doctorum acies insurrexit; atque ad eos profligandos plura Œcumenica Concilia celebrata sunt. Lutherum, Calvinum, Zwinglium, Melanchthonem, Servetum, aliosque recentiorum temporum Novatores, quis orthodoxorum in Italia, Hispania, Gallia, Germania, caeterisque Europae Provinciis non confutavit? Contra Mahumetum, Mahumetanicamque superstitionem, quae per annos supra mille perseverat, qui scripserint, sive ex antiquioribus, sive ex recentioribus, pauci, ne dicam paucissimi, numerantur. Quod verò dissimulandum non est, licèt quidam doctè satis, solidèque scripserint: nonnulli tamen ex rerum Saracenicarum ignorantia, vera plerumque omittentes, ficta ac fabulosa in medium protulerunt, quae Mahumetanis risus excitarent, eosque in errore suo obstinatiores efficerent.

[Christian reader, I have always been amazed that, while so many learned and good men have written so voluminously against other sects of the true religion, so few have written so little against Muhammad and his impious law. The Arian heresy was strangled in its infancy by the Nicene Council Fathers in those same books in 318 AD, and as it was renewed with greater vigor over the

succeeding centuries, nearly all the writers of the Christian world
fought it most valiantly. The battle of the Catholic scholars has in the
same way raged against the mistakes of the Eutychians, Dioscorians,
Nestorians, Macedonians, and other most ancient heresiarchs, to
whose overthrow several Ecumenical councils were dedicated.
Who among the faithful in Italy, Spain, Germany, France, and the
rest of Europe has not refuted Luther, Calvin, Zwingli, Melanchthon,
Servetus, and the rest of the more recent reformers? Yet those among
the ancients and moderns who have written against Muhammad and
the Muhammedan superstition, which has persevered for over a thousand years, are few; very few indeed. While it cannot be denied that
some have written with firmness and learning on the subject, many,
however, have made the Mohammedans laugh and persist in their
errors by their ignorance of the affairs of the Saracens and by their
omissions of numerous true facts while they bring forth fables and
inventions.][1]

Thus opens Marracci's refutation of the Qur'ān. Marracci likens the
situation of Christendom to that of pre-*reconquista* Spain, with multiple Christian factions warring against each other and none paying
much attention to the Muslim threat. Heresies ancient and modern
(such as the newfangled "innovations" of Luther and Calvin) have
all been subject to their fair share of attack and refutation, while the
arch-enemy of Christendom, Islam, remains immune to the assault of
the learned. Marracci sees his task as one of verbal warfare: it is time
to attack the Muslims with their own arguments and using their own
sources. For Marracci, the reading and translation of the Qur'ān is
really a secondary enterprise, undertaken only to ensure the success of
the first. Marracci has no illusions about his project: this is a task for the
happy few. Remembering his predecessors, from John of Damascus
to Savonarola, he adds the comment: "Verùm hactenus *Apparent rari
nantes in gurgite vasto*: vel potius, rari pugnantes contra exercitum
immensum. Quid [*sic*] enim sunt hi, si vel cum hostibus, à quibus penè
obruimur, vel cum nostris, qui contrà alias sectas dimicavere, com-
parentur?" ["Indeed, so far, *a few swimmers appear scattered in a vast
abyss*, or rather, a few lone fighters appear against an immense army.
Who indeed are those who can be compared either to the enemies, by
whom we were nearly defeated, or with our troops, who were busy
fighting other sects?"][2] Marracci transforms the description of the victims of the wreck of the ship carrying Orontes scattered on the ocean
(*Aeneid* 1:118) into another image: a handful of warriors taking on an

immense army. Like the Christian world he imagines, Marracci is at war. His strategy for winning this war is to provide Christianity with the intellectual means to refute Islam using Muslim materials; this feat of intellectual skill will unite the clergy in their struggle against Islam instead of their endless theological conflicts with each other.

Marracci's strategy did not work. His attempted refutation failed to unite Christians writing about Islam at the turn of the eighteenth century. The central question at the heart of Western debates about Islam during this period was not "How do we defeat the Muslims?" but rather "Who owns the representation of Islam?" Who best represents the Muslim world? Catholics or Protestants? Travelers or scholars? Arabists or Ottomanists? While these questions are current today, they also haunt much early Orientalist writing and motivate polemics during the Enlightenment. Thus George Sale, an Anglican, attacks Ludovico Marracci, a Catholic working for the Vatican, for having so mean an opinion of the Christian faith that he spends too much time "refuting" the Qur'ān. Jean Gagnier, another Anglican and former Catholic priest, attacks Boulainvilliers for having too positive an opinion of Muhammad and taking a deist position in his *Vie de Mahomet*, and accuses Marracci of "mutilating" (i.e. quoting out of context) Abulfeda's biography, *Al-Mukhtaṣar fī akhbār al-bashar*. David Durand, the presumed translator of Adrien Reland's *De veritate religione Mohammedica*, attacks quite a few others (including Boulainvilliers and Marracci) for being too lax as moralists, too literal as readers, too erudite as scholars, and generally too un-informative as writers.[3] Even if we take Sale's preface to his translation to be a marketing pamphlet, it still gives us a solid idea of the early modern public's horizon of expectations when it came to books about the Middle East. The frequency with which the above charges were repeated created a tendency to claim the "best Arabic authorities" as evidence of a solid, reliable source of information about the Muslim world (each writer claims to be the best representative of those representatives). In every preface, we see a transposition of the religious politics of the Enlightenment – the Catholic Reformation, the English Reformation, the deist quarrels – on to the politics of the representation of the Muslim world. In all of these cases, it is not so much a question of what Islam or the Middle East is about, but what *being about* them is about; what it means to talk about Islam, properly and authoritatively, in the early 1700s.

Much depends, therefore, on the ethical and political position that informs every participant in these debates. For all his hostility toward the Muslim Other in the wake of the Ottoman advances in Europe and the siege of Vienna in 1683, Marracci is nonetheless aware of the attractive character of Islam, and alerts the reader to it from the opening pages of the preface to his *Prodromus*:

> Habet nimirùm haec supersititione quidquid plausibile, ac probabile in Christiana Religione reperitur, & quae naturae legi, ac lumini consentaea videntur. Mysteria illi fidei nostrae, quae primo aspecti incredibilia & impossibilia apparent; & praecipuè quae nimis ardua humanae consentur, penitus excludit. Hinc moderni Idolorum cultores, faciliùs ac promptiùs Saracenicam, quàm Evangelicam legem amplectuntur; et in postremum amplectentur, nisi à Missionariis nostris, his, quae ego in meo opere pono, argumentis praeveniantur, ac praemuniantur.

> [This superstition (Islam) contains everything that is possible or probable that might be found in the Christian religion, and everything that seems to conform to the law of nature and the light of reason. It excludes all of those mysteries of our faith that seem improbable and impossible, especially those that are too difficult for human consent. Hence today's pagans embrace the law of the Saracens with greater speed and ease than they do the law of the Gospels, and will continue to do so unless our missionaries are armed with the arguments that I present here.][4]

Faced with a choice between the gospels and the Qur'ān, Marracci argues, any reasonable person would choose the latter. It is only once the reader is initiated into the mysteries of the true faith (and made to understand the falsity of Islam) that Christianity becomes the preferred choice. In a lengthy passage that verges on parody, Marracci imagines the prima facie reactions to the two texts and their religions.[5] Islam offers a single, omnipotent, omniscient God, who commands prayer, alms, fasting, and pilgrimage, enjoins justice and kindness, forbids theft, adultery, and murder, promising eternal and desirable rewards in the hereafter to the good and endless torment to the evil. Christianity, on the other hand, seems to present a series of contradictions and ordeals: a God that is simultaneously one and three, that became a pauper and was subsequently tortured and crucified, a God that died and was buried, a religion that demands coming to terms with the Eucharist and the penitential sacraments, a life perpetually joined to the cross involving indissoluble matrimony and kindness to enemies, supreme happiness that consists in things invisible and inaudible; withal things that exceed human understanding or require belief in unreal, unnatural conditions.

From the outset, then, Marracci considers the Qur'ān seductive in a very negative sense. Marracci takes pains to add that the truths of the Qur'ān are bound inextricably with falsities, mistakes, and absurdities, and that these truths are in fact found in purer form in the gospels. Muhammad, he says, merely took the eternal truths put forward by Judeo-Christianity and added a thick layer of entertaining superstition to hoodwink and bully his helpless victims; a layer which, once removed, would expose Muhammad and his followers to the same sort of ridicule that they find in the Christians. In doing so, however, Marracci overlooks the distinction between faith and reason: just because a "heathen" sees the reasons behind the form of Islam and the Judeo-Christian origins of its creed (most of which would be rather obvious in view of the repeated claims in the Qur'ān that Muhammad's mission was built upon the other Abrahamic monotheisms) does not necessarily mean that the said heathen will immediately choose Christianity over Islam. Having set up Islam as the religion any rational person would choose, Marracci then subverts his argument by introducing rational reasons for the putative rejection of Islam, overlooking the fact that belief has less to do with reason than it does with faith.

Not unexpectedly, Sale's paratexts take aim at Marracci together with Humphrey Prideaux, whose polemic against Muhammad seems to have preoccupied Sale's mind. In his remarkable opening salvo in the dedication to Lord Carteret, Sale situates Muhammad on par with the founders of the world's great civilizations:

> Notwithstanding the great honour and respect generally and deservedly paid to the memories of those who have founded states, or obliged a people by the institution of laws which have made them prosperous and considerable in the world, yet the legislator of the Arabs has been treated in so very different a manner by all who acknowledge not his claim to a divine mission, and by Christians especially, that were not your lordship's just discernment sufficiently known, I should think myself under a necessity of making an apology for presenting the following translation.[6]

Now, Sale could have started out by simply stating that Muhammad was a great man, and is therefore worthy of serious study. How much more rhetorically effective, though, is this sentence that asserts that Muhammad is the *legislator* of the Arabs rather than a warrior king, the founder of an empire, and, perhaps most significantly, a man who has "obliged" (i.e. served) his people by instituting laws that have made them prosperous and considerable in the world rather than ruling in a tyrannical or oppressive manner. In this perspective, Muhammad is the man who civilized the Arabs, the institution of laws being the sign of civilization in 1734. As such he has not been paid the great honor and respect that other founders of other states have been paid; whence the need for a new translation of the Qur'ān.

According to Sale, Muhammad "has given a new system of religion, which has had greater success than the arms of his followers." The use of the term "his followers" is significant: it is the Muslims, not Muhammad himself, who are violent. This is a veiled attack on Prideaux, who argues that *the* mark par excellence whereby the imposture of Islam might be recognized is that it was spread "by the sword." This is a key opposition that will run through the course of the Sale translation: the word versus the sword, with Sale decidedly on the side of the former. For Sale, the sheer discursive eloquence and novelty of Islam are even more powerful than the putative violence of the early (or contemporary) Muslims.

We find these issues combined in the second paragraph of Sale's dedication in the sentence following the previous citation:

> But as Muhammad gave his Arabs the best religion he could, as well as the best laws, preferable at least, to those of the ancient pagan lawgivers, I confess I cannot see why he deserves not equal respect, though not with Moses or Jesus Christ, whose laws came really from heaven, yet with Minos or Numa, notwithstanding the distinction of a learned writer [i.e. Prideaux], who seems to think it a greater crime to make use of an imposture to set up a *new* religion, founded on the acknowledgement of one true God, and to destroy idolatry, than to use the same means to gain reception to rules and regulations for the more orderly practice of heathenism already established.[7]

Apart from the contradiction of praising heathens when they are named Minos or Numa while condemning them otherwise, Sale's defense of Muhammad is cogently argued: if Muhammad really were a self-serving impostor, as Prideaux claims, why would he have gone through the trouble of instituting monotheism among the pagans instead of merely arrogating all rites and devotions to himself? Clearly he was more interested in substituting laws for chaos and monotheism for idolatry.

Sale's dedicatory epistle lays out a *mise en scène* of the Western confrontation with Islam. The novelty of Islam is something that has been sustained over the centuries. The frontiers of what might loosely be called the Muslim empire were in more or less continuous expansion until the late seventeenth century, which is to say about one thousand years after Muhammad's death. Islam was as "happening" in Sale's time as it had been in the age of John of Damascus. Finding explanations for this extraordinary phenomenon was a task every bit as urgent in Enlightenment Europe as it had been in Byzantine Syria. The struggles of modernity and modernization in Europe meant coming to terms with this puzzling, sometimes hostile "neighbor," and finding out which aspects of his behavior were worth imitating. Indeed, what both Prideaux and Sale have in common is the use they make of the study of Islam: Prideaux finds that by studying this imposture he will make the reader a better Christian, while Sale aims at making the reader a better citizen of his age: "To be acquainted with the various laws and constitutions of civilised nations, especially those who flourish in our own time, is, perhaps, the most useful part of knowledge."[8] Islam certainly was flourishing in Sale's time, and the knowledge gained from reading his translation of the Qur'ān was not merely curious or interesting, it was *useful*. The emphasis on the use-value of knowledge is, of course, part and parcel of post-Lockean Britain, where there was a growing consensus that the aims of learning should be practical rather than idealistic or speculative.[9] As if the point were not made with enough vigor in the dedicatory epistle, Sale repeats them more explicitly in the epistle to the reader: "if the religious and civil institutions of foreign nations are worth our knowledge, those of Mohammed, the lawgiver of the Arabians, and founder of an empire which in less than a century spread itself over a greater part of the world than the Romans were ever masters of, must needs be so."[10] Sale's legal background emerges here, since any student of English law would have had to study Roman law, and by induction any empire greater than that of Rome merits even more particular attention in its own right. The religion Muhammad has founded is (relatively) new, spreading, and misunderstood. If better representations of that religion and its founder were available to the West, it might be possible to learn from them and put the learning to good use.

Just what this use might be is made clear very quickly. The charge of mis-representing Islam is once again leveled at a very particular group of Western writers: Catholics. The well-read reader will quickly understand that Marracci is Sale's target:

> The writers of the Romish communion, in particular, are so far from having done any service in their refutation of Mohammedanism, that by endeavouring to defend their idolatry and other superstitions, they have rather contributed to the increase of that aversion which the Mohammedans in general have to the Christian religion, and given them great advantages in the dispute. The Protestants alone are able to attack the Koran with success; and for them, I trust, Providence has reserved the glory of its overthrow.[11]

The use of the word "refutation" is a deliberate allusion to Marracci. The Catholic polemic against Islam is, however, a clear failure in Sale's eyes, the end result being that the Muslims emerge stronger from the quarrel. The claim that only the Protestants are able to attack the Qur'ān with success, while ambiguous – Sale after all does not say that *he* is the Protestant in question – does clarify what is at stake for Sale: the enemy is not Islam but the Catholic Church. And the quarrel with the Catholic Church revolves not only around matters of doctrine but also – perhaps especially – of numbers.[12] The insistence on producing an English translation of the Qur'ān reflected Sale's concern not only with making it available to a wide audience, but also, perhaps particularly, as a veiled attack on Marracci's choice of Latin for his translation and refutation. Sale's project should therefore be seen in light of the Protestant opposition to the use of Latin in church services, which was seen as part of a policy aimed at keeping the believers in ignorance and the clergy powerful. If the flock were armed with proper knowledge of the scripture, the argument went, they would see the differences between Catholicism and true Christianity and shun the latter.[13] Furthermore, Sale's involvement with the SPCK adds theological weight to the English language as well as his references to the glory of the Qur'ān's overthrow being reserved for the Protestant Church.

Sale's concern with the uses of his translation and learning from the Muslim world alerts us to a key aspect of his project, namely its modernity. The numerous definitions of and approaches to modernity, understood as both the history of the march toward "progress" and the way in which that history is told, might usefully be placed under two opposing rubrics. The first inscribes modernity in the history of the descent of the transcendent into the immanent, be they understood as the coming of the kingdom of heaven (Augustine), the descent of God into human history, the operation of providence in human history (Bossuet), or the operation of reason in the history of humanity (Hegel). The other rubric looks askance at the word "modernity" and replaces it with the term "modernization." Modernization is what happens when two different cultures meet and learn from each other. It goes without saying that such meetings are not always pleasant or peaceful. However, this approach allows a better framework for understanding the Enlightenment.

In *Philosophie par gros temps*, Vincent Descombes re-orients philosophy's attitude toward modernity in terms of emulation and exemplarity. Like Louis Dumont, who casts a long shadow over his work, Descombes believes that modernization only happens via intercultural contact.[14] Both emphasize the importance of the process of modernization rather than the elusive state of modernity (an argument that might be compared with Kant's in *What is Enlightenment?*). With his usual wit, Descombes makes the case that modernization depends on imitation, or that you only modernize when you see a neighbor that you want to imitate:

> On ne modernise quoi que ce soit que parce qu'on a en face de soi un voisin plus moderne, qu'on imite. Loin que la modernisation soit l'expression historique d'une raison autonome qui viendrait de découvrir qu'elle doit se fonder sur elle-même, elle est ce que l'anthropologue appelle un procès d'*acculturation*. Lorsqu'une culture moderne et une culture traditionnelle sont confrontées, celle qui est moderne provoque l'autre à rétablir l'identité collective par l'invention de synthèses plus ou moins heureuses entre ce qui vient de l'autre et ce qui vient de soi.

> [We do not modernize anything unless we have before us a more modern neighbor to imitate. Far from being the historical expression of an autonomous reason that has just discovered that it should be based on itself, modernization is what anthropologists call a process of *acculturation*. When a modern and a traditional culture meet, the latter is stimulated into re-defining its constitutive collective identities through the invention of more or less happy combinations between what comes from the other and what comes from itself.][15]

This is precisely what happens during the Enlightenment: it is the openness toward the other that heralds the dawn of modernity. Dumont's and Descombes' arguments are all the more significant in view of the fact that they overturn the Hegelian paradigm of modernity arriving via the long march of reason from alienation to self-realization.[16]

This is the spirit of Sale's translation of the Qur'ān, where we see a very real desire not only to understand, but perhaps also imitate the other. Sale certainly was not the first to argue that there were Eastern locations that were more "reasonable" than the West; he was one of the few to do so in a spirit of humility rather than reformist zeal (as had been the case with Reland and especially his French translator, David Durand), or in the framework of a critical project (Bayle, Montesquieu). Marracci is stuck in the medieval perspective that sees in the Arabs and Muslims proof of God's judgment against unbelieving (or merely lax) Christians, which is to say a sort of descent of the transcendent into human affairs. Not so Sale, who sees in them an example to be followed.

Another definition of modernity operates within the more restricted preserve of Orientalism. Albert Hourani's analysis of the history of Orientalism as a discipline centers on the opposition between Islam as text and Islam as living thing: early Orientalists (roughly through the end of the eighteenth century) saw Islam as a text, something to be read, while later ones (after Goldziher) wrote about it as a living thing.[17] Early Islamists were readers and philologists – erudite scholars whose geographic distance from the lands of Islam put them on par with the distance between the classicist and ancient Greece – while later ones were readers and cultural anthropologists, whose task is to translate a foreign, but living, culture.[18] Sale's achievement inheres in his skilled description of Islam and Muslims as living entities rather than textual inscriptions. It is here, in fact, that the gap separating him from Marracci is at its widest: Marracci treats the Qur'ān as a text in relation to other texts; Sale treats the Qur'ān as a text in relation to other texts *and in relation to other people* within the scenario of acculturation and modernization described by Descombes. We have seen how Sale's paratexts foreground the novelty of Islam as something considerably more important than its putative violence, and read Islam as a religion in its own right rather than a set of lies or dangerous modifications to established doctrine.[19] Ethically, therefore, Sale is prepared to meet and learn from the Muslim other, while Marracci is intent on fighting this other by any means necessary.

In this respect, Sale anticipates Massignon's understanding of the other: "Pour comprendre l'autre, il ne faut pas se l'annexer, mais devenir son hôte." ["To understand the other, we must not annex him, but become his host/guest."] Marracci makes full sense of the word "hôte" as a host and as a guest of the Arabic of the Qur'ān; one to whom protection is due; a stranger, possibly an enemy.[20] Marracci would most probably have approved of annexation in the full military sense of the term. Massignon's sentence is part of a passage that pleads for the decentring of the reader, whereby his or her entire frame of reference is transposed, to allow for this hospitable understanding of the other, in a perspective meant to counter the violence of confessional conflict and colonial takeover.[21] The Western student of Arabic or Islam ought intellectually to put him or herself in the place of the Other, not by an "annexation" from without, but by substitution from within. It is this sort of substitution that, I believe, Sale accomplishes with a greater degree of success than either Marracci or Du Ryer.

The impact of this ethical stance on Sale's translation is pervasive. In his landmark study *After Babel* George Steiner represents translation as a sequence of four steps: trust, aggression, incorporation, and restitution.[22] Steiner seeks in this model a way out of the triadic structure that dominates theories of translation before his, composed of "literal" or word-for-word translation at one end, loose paraphrase at the other, and a *juste milieu* in between.[23] Good translation is defined as "that in which the dialectic of impenetrability and ingress, of intractable alienness and felt 'at homeness' remains unresolved, but expressive."[24] Following this model, Sale is more "faithful" to the Qur'ān, even if he is less literal, than Marracci. Marracci fails at the first step by failing to trust the text that he is translating,[25] except insofar as doing so will enable him to indulge his militaristic whims and "kill Muhammad with his own sword." Sale's faithfulness, on the other hand, inheres in accommodating the text's own claims to legitimacy, in trying to find, in English, an idiom and style smooth enough to contain the rich texture of the Qur'ān after it has undergone what George Steiner calls the aggression and incorporation that are involved in every act of translation.[26] Sale succeeds in restituting to the text something of the dignity and majesty of the Arabic original, thereby making it his own, while Marracci cannot keep himself from disowning the text through obsessive refutation despite his Herculean efforts at providing a proper Latin equivalent for every Arabic word. While it would be difficult to argue that the Arabic Qur'ān has "become" the target language, as did Gundolf in his study of Schlegel's Shakespeare,[27] there is no denying that a reader would have an easier time appreciating the force of the original without a translator constantly attempting to undermine its aesthetic beauty. The elegance of Sale's translation and his relative success in bringing the Qur'ān over into his idiom are the result of a constant giving and taking, of a graceful, sinewy moving to and fro, between the Arabic of the Qur'ān and his own English, as opposed to Marracci's imaginary war between the language that the Turks hold sacred and the language of the church. It is by seeing translation as a series of transactions between two individual idioms rather than the outright domination of one culture by the other that he manages to go farther than Marracci while seeming to do less.[28] It is in Sale's willingness to subsume his own voice to that of the text, like Borges's Pierre Menard, and in his knack for smoothing out the wrinkles where the strange and the familiar sit adjacent, that he succeeds in providing a better translation of the Qur'ān.[29]

Equally significant are the linguistic and stylistic differences between the two translations. One way of grasping these is through their differing approaches to the semantic polyvalence of the text before them. Like any text, the Qur'ān allows multiple readings and interpretations. What makes the Qur'ān unique as scripture is its open avowal of its polysemic potential. One of the verses where this is described in detail is Q3:7, a verse that introduces the fundamental opposition between the terms *muḥkam* (محكم ; roughly "fixed") and *mutashābih* (متشابه; roughly "polyvalent, allowing of multiple meanings"), and has given rise to a vast body of commentary and exegesis.[30]

هُوَ الَّذِي أَنْزَلَ عَلَيْكَ الْكِتَابَ مِنْهُ آيَاتٌ مُحْكَمَاتٌ هُنَّ أُمُّ الْكِتَابِ وَأُخَرُ
مُتَشَابِهَاتٌ فَأَمَّا الَّذِينَ فِي قُلُوبِهِمْ زَيْغٌ فَيَتَّبِعُونَ مَا تَشَابَهَ مِنْهُ ابْتِغَاءَ الْفِتْنَةِ وَابْتِغَاءَ
تَأْوِيلِهِ وَمَا يَعْلَمُ تَأْوِيلَهُ إِلَّا اللَّهُ وَالرَّاسِخُونَ فِي الْعِلْمِ يَقُولُونَ آمَنَّا بِهِ كُلٌّ مِنْ عِنْدِ رَبِّنَا
وَمَا يَذَّكَّرُ إِلَّا أُولُو الْأَلْبَابِ

Sale translates this in his typically straightforward manner, translating *muḥkamāt* as "clear to be understood" and *mutashābihāt* as "parabolical," both reasonable translations by contemporary standards:

> It is he who has sent down unto thee the book, wherein are some verses clear to be understood [آيَاتٌ مُحْكَمَاتٌ], they are the foundation of the book [أُمُّ الْكِتَابِ]; and others are parabolical [مُتَشَابِهَاتٌ] [footnote c]. But they whose hearts are perverse will follow that which is parabolical therein, out of love of schism, and a desire of the interpretation thereof; yet none knoweth the interpretation thereof, except GOD. But they who are well grounded in knowledge say, We believe therein, the whole is from our LORD; and none will consider except the prudent.[31]

Footnote c reads:

> This passage is translated according to the exposition of Al
> Zamakhshari and Al Beidâwi, which seems to be the truest. The con-
> tents of the Korân are here distinguished into such passages as are to
> be taken in the literal sense, and such as require a figurative accepta-
> tion. The former being plain and obvious to be understood, compose
> the fundamental part, or, as the original expresses it, *the mother* of
> the book, and contain the principal doctrines and precepts; agreeably
> to and consistently with which, those passages are wrapt up in meta-
> phors, and delivered in an enigmatical, allegorical style, are always
> to be interpreted.[32]

Sale ends the footnote with another footnote referring the reader to
Section 3 of his "Preliminary Discourse," where he discusses the textual character of the Qur'ān. Here we read:

> One of the most learned commentators [Al Zamakhshari] distin-
> guishes the contents of the Korân into allegorical and literal. The
> former comprehends the more obscure, parabolical and enigmatical
> passages, and such as are repealed or abrogated; the latter those which
> are plain, perspicuous, liable to no doubt, and in full force.
>
> To explain these severally in a right manner, it is necessary
> from tradition and study to know the time when each passage was
> revealed, its circumstances, state and history, and the reasons or par-
> ticular emergencies for the sake of which it was revealed [Ahmed
> Ebn Moh. Al Thalebi, *in Princip. Expos. Alc.*]. Or, more explicitly,
> whether the passage was revealed at Mecca, or at Medina; whether it
> be abrogated, or does itself abrogate any other passage; whether it be
> anticipated in order of time, or postponed; whether it be distinct from
> the context, or depends thereon; whether it be particular or general;
> and, lastly, whether it be implicit by intention, or explicit in words
> [Yahya Ebn al Salam al Basri, *in Princep. Expos. Alc.*][33]

What we have here is a brief exposition of the rules of *tafsīr* – exegesis
– according to categories that Al-Ṣuyūṭī would eventually codify in
his *Itqān*: Meccan versus Medinan verses, chronology, circumstances
of revelation, and so on. Sale is the first Western translator of the
Qur'ān since Mark of Toledo to maintain the distinction between and
accurately render the terms *muḥkam* and *mutashābih*.[34] This sensitivity to the literary aspect of the Qur'ān and the rhetoric of sacred
language is not to be underestimated. Sale translates the phrase *umm
al-kitāb* literally, before explaining in a footnote the relationship

between motherhood and fundament. Sale's use of commentaries in the translation of this verse is especially interesting, tactically coupling Zamakhsharī with a paraphrase of the texts and authorities that he found in Marracci's "De Alcorano" in the *Prodromus*.[35] *Ad* Q3:7, George Sale summarizes Zamakhsharī's lengthy and complex commentary on the verse. Zamakhsharī rehearses a number of arguments and explanations advanced by previous commentators, before adding a few of his own.[36] Among the more important questions raised by this verse is that of its scansion: what is the relationship between the adjacent words *Allāh* and *al-rāsikhūn fī-l-'ilm* ("those grounded in knowledge")?[37] The traditional readings separate the two, so that *Allāh* becomes the end of one sentence and those grounded in knowledge the start of another. Sale follows this practice. Zamakhsharī, however, had pointed out another possibility: that the letter *wāw* be read as the conjunctive *wāw al-'atf,* which would make that part of the verse scan as follows: "None knows their true meaning except God *and* those grounded in knowledge."[38] Sale's strategy in translating the verse as he does, without going into the many possible meanings afforded by the scansion of the verse, implies a degree of conservatism: he seems to be willing to concede the position that God is the ultimate guarantor of the meaning of the Qur'ānic verses. Moreover, by deciding not to reproduce Zamakhsharī's full argument, Sale's aim seems to be foregrounding the "reasonable" character of Islam and the comprehensible, familiar side of the Qur'ān: if there are multiple levels of meaning, there is also a knowing God who fixes them.

To a certain extent, Sale is also following Marracci's example. Marracci, too, separates *Allāh* from *al-rāsikhūn fī-l-'ilm*. Here is Marracci's translation:

> Ipse est, qui descendere fecit super te Librum, ex eo *sunt aliqui* versus sapienter dispositi; ipsi *sunt* mater Libri: alii verò assimilati *illis*. Porro illi, in quorum cordibus est declinatio (*à veritate*) sectabuntur, quod est assimilatum his ob desiderium schismatis, & ob cupiditatem interpretationis ejus: sed non novit interpretationem ejus nisi Deus. Stabiles autem in sapienta, dicent: Credimus in illud: totum est à Domino nostro. Et non recogitabunt *hoc*, nisi cordati.[39]

The literal character of Marracci's vocabulary is striking. The phrase "mater Libri" (as opposed to Sale's more palatable "foundation of the book") for *umm al-kitāb* shows this clearly enough. Whereas "sapienter dispositi" is a happy rendition of the phrase *āyāt muḥkamāt*,

the use of the word "assimilati" for *mutashābihāt* suggests a labo-
riousness born of Marracci's command of the Arabic language. Just
as the word *mutashābih* derives from the root شبه, which suggests
analogy, comparison, and similarity, so the term "assimilati," from
ad and *similum*, suggests proximity through similarity. Marracci's
strategy of translation therefore reduces the source language to its
root and seeks an equivalent root in the target language. Sale's, on
the other hand, looks for a contemporary equivalent in the target
language. Marracci's approach seems based on the assumption that,
between the languages of the sacred, the best translation is the one
that establishes diachronic, as opposed to functional, equivalence,
leading to the archaism of "assimilate" instead of "metaphorici" for
"mutashābih" as opposed to Sale's more sensible "parabolical."

In the Marracci translation there is, moreover, an echo of the related
verbs *adsimulo* (to reproduce, to fake), the noun *adsimulatio*, and the
adjective *adsimulatus* (invented, fictitious, counterfeit),[40] all of which
link (assimilate?) similarity and simulation, so that it becomes difficult
to avoid the feeling that, for Marracci, metaphor and falsity go hand
in hand, indeed, that the *mutashābih* is fundamentally *mashbūh*
(dubious, suspect). Marracci's failure to translate this verse adequately
is all the more puzzling in view of his reliance on commentaries that
make explicit the figurative connotation of the word *mutashābih*,
though it is not far fetched to suppose that he deliberately mis-repre-
sented the distinction between literal and figurative language in the
Qur'ān as a tactic to support better his "refutation." Although he knows
that "metaphorici" would have worked as a translation, he prefers
"assimilati," in a bid to emphasize the fact that whether or not certain
parts of the Qur'ān are metaphorical, and whether or not this brings it
closer to the Bible – there is, after all, figurative language in both texts
– the Qur'ān is still irremediably false, counterfeit, ad-simulatus.

Marracci's notes on this verse rehearse arguments from several
commentaries – the *Tafsīr al-Jalālayn*, Yahya b. Sallām (i.e. Ibn
Abī Zamanīn), and Zamakhsharī – covering the various possibilities
in play here (*muhkam* =clear, *mutashābih* = unclear, *muhkam* = legal
verse, *mutashābih* = everything else, *muhkam* = literal, *mutashābih*
= figurative, *muhkam* = retained, *mutashābih* = abrogated) and
indicating that the opposition between literal and figurative is one
among many alternatives. He also includes a passage from the *Jalālayn*
to explain that the phrase *umm al-kitāb* is itself a metaphor: they
are the "mother" of the book in the sense that they are its root and

foundation in matters of law ("radix et fundamentum ejus in senten-
tiis"; اصله المتعمد عليه في الاحكام). All of which leaves Marracci's reader
with the impression that he readily admits the existence of multiple
levels of meaning in the Qur'ānic text, despite his strategy of translating as literally as possible, seeking in Latin an equivalent based on an
Arabic root, and so on.

What comes in the refutation section two pages later is in stark
contrast to the possibilities suggested by all of this:

> Quod habet de duplici Alcoranicorum versuum differentia, (in qua
> tamen explicanda Mahumetani non conveniunt) non est dubium,
> quin per hoc subterfugium sese praemuniat ad quoslibet in Alcorano
> errores, vel excusandos, vel defendendos. Cum enim versus, quos
> *assimilatos* appellat, sint metaphorici, vel allegorici, & Deus solus
> illos intelligat: quoties in Alcorano absurdi aliquid, vel falsi, vel impii
> occurrerit, statim dicent Mahumetani, illas esse locutiones meta-
> phoricas, nec intelligi posse, nisi a Deo. At verò, quae utilitas in his
> versibus assimilatis, si eos nemo potest intelligere?

> [There can be no doubt that there is something duplicitous about
> the differences in the verses of the Alcoran (on the explication of
> which the Muhammedan commentators do not, however, agree),
> with which subterfuge it protects itself against whatever errors may
> be found there, either by excusing or prohibiting them. Since those
> verses that are called *assimilated* are metaphorical or allegorical, and
> only God understands them, then every time something absurd, false,
> or impious occurs in the Alcoran, the Muhammedans immediately
> say that it is metaphorical and can only be understood by God. Now,
> really, what use is there in these assimilated verses, if nobody can
> understand them?][41]

Marracci thus takes textual polysemy to indicate the total falsity of
the Qur'ān. Worse yet, the existence of obscure passages whose true
meaning is known only to God, the presumed source of the Qur'ān,
only proves its utter confusion and spuriousness. Marracci is further
horrified to observe that, in the absence of a Qur'ānic (as opposed
to exegetical) rule that constrains the reader to rely on the *muḥkam*
in order to understand the *mutashābih*, the Muslim reader is left to
interpret the Qur'ān as he or she sees fit, which is tantamount to reading all manner of nonsense – and license – into the text:

> Poterit igitur unusquisque Alcoranum ad libitum suum explicare,
> prout re ipsa Moslemi faciunt: & iis exceptis, quae vel naturae

lumine, vel ex sacrarum Scripturarum revelatione certa sunt (quorum nonnulla, licet plerumque depravata habet Alcoranus) caetera tricis & confusione plena erunt.

[Everyone shall therefore be able to explain the Alcoran as he wishes, which is precisely what Muslims do, and with the exception of those passages that are ascertained either through the light of nature or sacred Scripture, the greater part are full of nonsense and confusion.][42]

For Marracci, the very idea of such interpretive freedom is further proof of the fact that the Qur'ān is no sacred text. Even when he entertains the objection that the Bible is read both literally and figuratively, he says that such readings have the sanction of the church, which is more than can be said for the Muslim interpretive community, where the multiplicity of exegeses leaves Marracci with the impression that anything goes.

Another point of contention for Marracci concerns the phrase "*lā ya'lamu ta'wīlahā illa Allāh.*" If there are to be points in scripture so obscure that only God knows their meaning, he objects, then why should we bother with scripture at all, since it can never be a source of certain knowledge? The Bible might have its difficulties, but they are not such that they can only be understood by God: they can be explained by precedents and consequences in the text as well as by the learned and the faithful.[43] Not only does Marracci confuse agent and method of interpretation, but he completely overlooks the fact that the *doctiores* might belong to the same category as the *rāsikhūn fī-l-'ilm* – which would bring his position closer to Zamakhsharī's, with whose commentary he was familiar. Another point of convergence that Marracci seems deliberately to ignore is Zamakhsharī's argument *ad* Q3:7 that the *mutashābihāt* are a test of faith, constantly urging the reader to seek reconciliations between literal and figurative meaning and leading – hopefully – to divine inspiration in the interpretive process, with the attendant benefits of more solid belief and conviction [44].(ففتح الله عليه وتبين مطابقة المتشابه المحكم ، ازداد طمأنينة إلى معتقده وقوّة في إيقانه) Marracci seems to miss the point of all this: the fact that God is the only source of true knowledge of the sense of the Qur'ān does not mean that such knowledge is limited to God, nor does it rule out the possibility of God's bestowing some of this knowledge on a human being.

The rich complications surrounding this verse and its commentaries drove John Wansbrough to call it "the point of departure for all scriptural exegesis."[45] The relationship outlined above between hermeneutic activity and the bolstering of the reader's faith might be linked to a quality that Wansbrough identifies as being characteristic of scripture; namely, the need for exegesis or *Deutungsbedürftigkeit*. This term, which Wansbrough borrows from Erich Auerbach's study of the difference between Homeric and biblical narrative in *Mimesis*, becomes virtually synonymous with the activity of reading scripture:

> This is not merely to say that the content of scripture is enhanced by commentary, or that it may be made to bear any number of (complementary and/or contradictory) interpretations, but that the scriptural style is itself incomplete without commentary. Reasons for that condition were partly syntactic (*Abgerissenheit*, *Stilmischung*), partly rhetorical (*Vielschichtigkeit*, *Hintergründigkeit*).[46]

So important is *Deutungsbedürftigkeit* that Wansbrough makes it into a pillar of his taxonomy of the principles of Qur'ānic exegesis.[47] To read scripture, to read and interpret the Qur'ān, is to inhabit the space between the clear and the unclear, the known and the unknown, the *muḥkam* and the *mutashābih*, to heal the *zaygh* (waywardness, perversity) in the heart and become one of those believers "rooted in knowledge."[48] This is precisely the aspect of the Qur'ān that both Marracci and Sale fasten on to, though the former rejects and the latter accepts its claim to being scripture. For Du Ryer, it is still a merely literary work, a translation that if clearly executed does not require much in the way of further explication – whence the paucity of marginal notes involved.[49] Marracci and Sale both understand that the Qur'ān presents itself as scripture rather than as the "Book of Muhammad" and present their commentaries assiduously, not to say obsessively.

Auerbach links *Deutungsbedürftigkeit* to the totalitarian nature of scripture in relation to reality:

> If the text of the Biblical narrative, then, is so greatly in need of interpretation on the basis of its own content, its claim to absolute authority forces it still further in the same direction. Far from seeking, like Homer, merely to make us forget our own reality for a few hours, it seeks to overcome our reality: we are to fit our own life into its world, feel ourselves to be elements in its structure of universal history.[50]

Scripture says "This is the only Truth," tyrannically excluding all other truth claims, while Homer says "this is *a* truth." And so the reader's experience is necessarily different between the two: before Homer, we are as before a window on to the world of Greek gods and men, while before scripture we are drawn into that other world and are forced to start interpreting. The textual tyranny of the scripture is such that everything becomes part of its fabric, and the hermeneutic activity it inspires rapidly takes over other traditions and other domains: "As a result of this claim to absolute authority, the method of interpretation spread to traditions other than the Jewish."[51]

This point marks the difference between Marracci and Sale's position vis-à-vis their sources and the exegetical literature surrounding the Qur'ān. Both understand the "all-invasive" nature of scripture very well, but Marracci resists the Qur'ānic invasion by looking for (what he considers to be) lacunae and contradictions in text and commentary, so that the vast exegetic corpus to which he had access never fully completes the Qur'ānic text that he translates. Sale, on the other hand, uses his notes in much the same way as the exegetes themselves: as a way of *completing* his translation, and conveying to the reader the scriptural dignity of the Qur'ān. Hence, perhaps, the hostile reaction that met Sale's critical apparatus in some quarters, as made apparent by Thomas Hearne's comments:

> I think a bare translation had been sufficient. Nor can I see with what good design Mr. Sale hath published him with such glosses, unless it be to make people in love with this impostor. A bare translation would have sufficiently exposed the fictions and silly empty inventions of Mohamed, on purpose to delude the world … [52]

This re-invocation of medieval polemic against Muhammad departs from tradition in attacking Sale's notes rather than the substance of his translation or the content of his "Preliminary Discourse." In other words, the very thing that underlines the scriptural character of the Qur'ān in translation, independently of its own claims to being divine revelation, is what proves threatening.

This comparison between the two translations of Q3:7 and the surrounding scholarly apparatus brings out a pattern that we see repeatedly: even though they use the same data, Marracci and Sale emerge with vastly different results. Both see the multiple possibilities involved in translating a given text, both render some problematic verses in conservative fashion, and yet the end product of the translation process is vastly different in both cases. For Marracci, the fact that there are parts of the Qur'ān whose true interpretation is known to God only destabilizes the very possibility of the Qur'ān's being a religious text. For Sale, on the other hand, it *creates* that possibility.

The possibility of semantic polyvalence validating, rather than destroying, a claim to sacred status translates into two opposed outlooks regarding the literary quality of the Qur'ān and, consequently, with the literary quality of its translation. Both translators turn to other literary examples, and the allusions they make operate as tokens of belonging. Sale turns to Milton as a means of elucidating a given passage (Q6:31),[53] while Marracci repeatedly turns to the classics (mainly Homer and Horace) to deride Qur'ānic claims of *I'jāz* and drive home the point that the Catholic Church was only true heir to the cultural grandeur of Rome. The reference to Milton is all the more interesting insofar as it foregrounds Sale's attitude toward the Qur'ān: it is a work of literature, and as such its interpretation calls for an appeal to other works of literature. Marracci, admittedly, makes a similar case, but his hostility renders the exercise futile: it goes without saying that the Qur'ān will be found lacking when compared with the poets of the golden age. Sale's evocation of Milton belongs to another category of literary critical endeavor, namely reading one text against another in order to elucidate the imagery of both. The question under scrutiny in Q6:31 is: what does sin look like? How is hell to be represented? What language best renders the awfulness of evil?

In a footnote to his translation of Q6:31, Sale gives a graphic description of sin represented in the filthiest possible form on the day of judgment. The passage is remarkable not only by its explicit language, but also by its representation of sin as the mirror-image of the individual. Sale then alludes to *Paradise Lost* 2:737, a passage that starts a lengthy dialogue between Satan and two hideous monsters guarding the gates of hell: Sin, his erstwhile consort, and their son, Death. Satan is, to borrow a phrase, surprised by Sin, who is no longer the creature of light that he seduced, declaring, "I know thee not, nor ever saw till now / Sight more detestable than him [Death] and thee;" and prompting the retort, "Hast thou forgot me then, and do I seem / Now in thine eye so foul?" (*Paradise Lost*, 2:743–744, 746–747). Through his comparison between the shock of the sinner's encounter with his past in Q6:31 and Satan's horrified encounter with Sin and Death, Sale emphasizes the importance of the assumption of responsibility for individual behavior and, consequently, individual engagement with scripture. Sale makes it sound as if the *Tafsīr al-Jalālayn* actually cited Milton:

When an infidel comes forth from his grave, says Jallalo'ddin, his works shall be represented to him under the ugliest form that ever he beheld, having a most deformed countenance, a filthy smell, and a disagreeable voice; so that he shall cry out, GOD *defend me from thee, what art thou? I never saw anything more detestable!* To which the figure will answer, *Why dost thou wonder at my ugliness? I am thy evil works* [see Milton's *Paradise Lost*, bk ii v. 737 &c.]; *thou didst ride upon me while thou wast in the world; but now will I ride upon thee, and thou shalt carry me.* and immediately it shall get upon him; and whatever he shall meet shall terrify him, and say, *Hail, thou enemy of* God, *thou art he who was meant by* (these words of the Korân), *and they shall carry their burdens*, &c.[54]

The reference to Milton (the only one in Sale's translation) matters from the perspective of the history of reception of both epic and scripture. During the early eighteenth century, Milton had become the poet par excellence of the republican, anti-monarchist cause. Sale would, in all likelihood, have read Milton's prose in John Toland's edition of 1698, which capitalized on Milton's political and ecclesiastical writings to buttress the attack on priestcraft as well as royal and ecclesiastical authority.[55] In his biographical introduction to the 1698 edition, Toland underlines the moral and political function of epic poetry, concluding that Milton is the poet who can teach us the most about freedom:

An Epic Poem is not a bare History delightfully related in harmonious Numbers, and artfully dispos'd; but it always contains, besides a general representation of Passions and Affectations, Virtues and Vices, some peculiar Allegory or Moral. *Homer*, therefore, according to *Dionysus Hallicarnasseus*, expresses the strength of Body in his *Iliad* by the Wars of the *Greeks* and *Trojans*, but particularly by the valiant deeds of *Achilles*; and in his *Odysseus* he describes the generosity of Mind by the Adventures and Wanderings of *Ulysses* in his return from *Troy*. Thus *Torquato Tasso* has prefixt an Explication to his *Gerusalemme Liberata*: Nor was *Milton* behind anybody in the choice and dignity of his Instruction: for to display the different Effects of Liberty and Tyranny, is the chief design of his *Paradise Lost*.[56]

Toland proceeds to reproduce verbatim the closing paragraph of Milton's *Of Reformation in England* to underline the point:

But they contrary, that by the impairing and diminution of the true *Faith*, the Distresse and Servitude of their *Country*, aspire to high

> *Dignity, Rule* and *Promotion* here, after a shameful end in this *Life*, (which God grant them) shall be thrown down eternally into the *darkest* and *deepest Gulf* of HELL, where under the *despiteful Controul*, the Trample and Spurn of all the other *Damned*, that in the anguish of their *Torture*, shall have no other ease then to exercise a raving and bestial *Tyranny* over them as their *Slaves* and *Negroes*, they shall remain in that plight forever, the *basest*, the *lowermost*, the most *dejected*, the most *underfoot* and *down-trodden Vassals* of *Perdition*.[57]

The imagery of hell associated with the punishment of the unjust hints at George Sale's intentions in invoking Milton. There is more at stake here than an exegetical gloss on Q6:31: what Sale seems to be after is developing an eschatological perspective in which the unjust will be punished. The case might therefore be argued for the translation of the Qur'ān as a project with distinct freethinking and republican (read: anti-monarchical, democratic) sympathies. By invoking *Paradise Lost*, Sale is aligning himself with an intellectual genealogy that places the onus of scriptural interpretation and political engagement on the individual rather than the institution, urging the reader toward an internal voyage of spiritual self-discovery and independent strength.[58]

Nor is Milton Sale's only literary interlocutor. In the "Preliminary Discourse" Sale defends the traditional view of the miraculous eloquence (*I'jāz*) of the Qur'ān:

> And to this miracle did Mohammed chiefly appeal for the confirmation of his mission, publickly challenging the most eloquent men in Arabia, which was at that time stocked with thousands whose sole study and ambition it was to excel in elegance of style and composition …
>
> The style of the Korân is generally beautiful and fluent, especially where it imitates the prophetic manner and scripture phrases. It is concise and often obscure, adorned with bold figures after the eastern taste, enlivened with florid and sententious expressions, and in many places, especially where the majesty and attributes of GOD are described, sublime and magnificent; of which the reader cannot but observe several instances, though he must not imagine the translation comes up to the original, notwithstanding my endeavours to do it justice.[59]

Sale was among the earliest translators of the Qur'ān to accept fully the doctrine of its stylistic excellence.[60] Sale also inserts the following footnote to this section:

> A noble writer [i.e. Shaftesbury] therefore mistakes the question when he says these eastern religionists leave their sacred writ the sole standard of literate performance by extinguishing all true learning. For tho they were destitute of what we call learning, yet they were far from being ignorant, or unable to compose elegantly in their own tongue. See L. *Shaftesbury's* Characteristics, vol. iii p. 235.[61]

The allusion is to Lord Shaftesbury's *Characteristics*, an immensely popular complement to the *Spectator*, endlessly urging the reader to be a more virtuous person.[62] The passage that Sale has in mind is the following:

> The *Mahometan* Clergy seem to have a different Policy. They boldly rest the Foundation of their Religion on a *Book*: Such a one as (according to their Pretension) is not only perfect, but *inimitable*. Were a real Man of Letters, and a just Critick permitted to examine this *Scripture* by the known Rules of Art; he would soon perhaps refute this Plea. But so barbarous is the accompanying Policy of these Religionists, that they destroy all other Authors and Writings; and by this infallible Method, leave their SACRED WRIT *the sole standard of literate Performance*. For being *compar'd* to nothing besides it-self, it must undoubtedly be thought.[63]

Sale argues against Shaftesbury's claim, recalling the importance of the traditions of oral eloquence that were the cultural life of seventh-century Arabia, and narrating the story of the conversion of Labīd b. Rabīʿa. Given Sale's argument in the paratext that Islam was spread primarily by the word rather than the sword, his account of the style of the Qur'ān in this instance is a key complement to his earlier rebuttals to both Prideaux and Marracci. Disagreement aside, however, Sale's invocation of Shaftesbury re-locates the debate about the text of the Qur'ān to a sociable quarter within the republic of letters, one republican in outlook, critical of the powers of established religion and priestcraft – prominent themes in Shaftesbury's *Characteristics* – and firmly committed to a civil theology that promotes individual virtue against institutional entrenchment.[64] For Sale, Muslim culture has a valid claim to "politeness" and liberty as defined by Shaftesbury: it is a society ruled by a cultivated elite for whom ethics and aesthetics rather than birth and wealth are the joint determinants of power.

Marracci, on the other hand, is clearly translating for the entrenched institution rather than the virtuous individual. His view of the style of the Qur'ān leaves the reader in no doubt about his sentiments:

Est enim Alcoranus ita obscurus, concisus, perplexus, diffutus, atque elumbatus; ut, nisi illius Expositores suppetias ad ejus intelligentiam ferrent, Oedipo ipsi frustra explicandus traderetur. Verùm, Arabes etiam Interpretes plerumque divininant, sed falsò; & Prophetae sui ineptias in mysteria transformant ... Stylum Alcorani Arabes ad caelam efferent. Styli autem nomine elegantiam, & pulchram rerum, verborumque dispositionem intelligo. Est sanè in Alcorano fluxus quidam verborum ad aurium pruritium ac lenocinium accomodatus; praesertim ubi modum loquendi propheticam affectat, & Sacrarum Scripturam phrasin imitatur. Caeterùm ubi è proprio loquitur, nihil habet, nisi quisquilias, & meras ineptias, quas tamen Moslemi pro miraculo venerantur.

[The Alcoran is so obscure, choppy, intricate, diffuse and stylistically flimsy, that unless its commentators help with its interpretation, it would have been revealed to Oedipus himself in vain. Truly the Arabs make a number of false guesses, and transform their prophet's absurdities into mysteries ... The Arabs praise the style of the Alcoran to the skies. Now, I understand style to mean elegant and beautiful topics and verbal arrangement. And there is something attractive and alluring about the flow of the Alcoran, especially where it imitates Prophetic speech and the phrasing of the Sacred Scriptures. But elsewhere, when it speaks in its own voice, has nothing but rubbish and silliness, which however Muslims venerate as miracles.][65]

If there is any stylistic value to be found in the Qur'ān, Marracci claims, it is in those places where it comes closest to poetic and prophetic biblical loci. Those parts that cannot be matched against a biblical intertext are deemed worthless.

Later, in his translation of Q3, Marracci goes to great lengths to demonstrate why the battle of Badr, where some three hundred Muslims defeated an army three times their size, and which is often described as a miracle, was in fact no miracle, listing the prodigies of the Qur'ānic account before sarcastically dismissing the outcome: the angels descended from heaven and God involved His agency only to produce some seventy dead Qurayshis, adding "Parturient montes, nascetur ridiculus mus" (i.e. Horace, *Ars. P.* 139, "The mountains will part to give birth to a ridiculous mouse"), thereby following the usual pattern of turning to Horace every time he wants to deny the claim that anything about the Qur'ān is miraculous. In his *Prodromus* he cites *Carm.* 4:2. (which he calls 4:1)[66] in his refutation of Qur'ānic *I'jāz*.[67] Marracci cites the opening quatrain of the ode to imply that it would be stylistic suicide to try to match Pindar, and that all of the Qur'ān's claims to stylistic excellence are ridiculous. Apart from the irrelevance of the charge – it is far from clear that anyone in the Arabian peninsula had heard of, let alone sought to emulate, Pindar or Horace – Marracci's turn to what Gordon Williams calls "the poetry of institutions" is interesting insofar as it allows us better to understand the epistemological framework of the early Orientalists, for whom the classics of Greece and Rome constituted the primary aesthetic standard. Moreover, coming from the foremost Orientalist of the Vatican, the turn to, and identification with, a Horatian ode that was composed in anticipation of Augustus's triumphant return from a German campaign is not innocent, adding to the aforementioned association between the Catholic Church and imperial Rome the identification of Marracci's position with that of a military leader doing battle with the barbarians of his day.[68] By reading the Qur'ān through the classics, Marracci emphasizes his view that the book is a deliberately composed document rather than the result of poetic or divine inspiration. As makers of such texts, the seventh-century Arabs are inferior by far in Marracci's eyes to their Greek and Latin predecessors. According to Marracci, a far better choice of subject for the demonstration of a miraculous outcome of a military battle would have been the clash between Alexander and Darius (not a Homeric topic, which is what the subsequent section of the *Ars Poetica* might have led the reader to expect).[69] Here, the numbers are much more impressive:

Erant in eo praelio (ut vidimus) Coraisitarum mille, & aliquid minus, qui è Syria regressi, nihil de bello cogitabant. Mahumetus cum trecentis ac tredecim militibus eos inopinatò, & ex insidiis adorsus est. Ne verò Mahumetani ex hostium multitudine terrerentur; & ne hostes ex pauco Mahumetanorum numero audaciores fierent, divinitùs facum esse fingitur, ut Coraisitae Mahumetanis duplò minores; Mahumetani verò Coraisitis duplò, quàm ipsi, majores apparerent. En tibi unum miraculum. Audi alterum. Mahumetus arena, seu lapillis impletam volam conjecit in hostes, quorum oculis arena oppletis, omnes proni, ac penitùs caeci in terram corruerunt … Atqui ecce tibi intereà tertium miraculum: Deus è tertio Coelo, primò mille, deindè tria millia, postremò quinque millia Angelorum armatorum, duce Gabriele, in auxilium Mahumetanorum misit. Sed quid opus erat coelestibus armis ubi hostes prostrati, caecique jacebant? Ita se res habuit. Sed eventum belli audiamus: nimirùm: *Parturient montes, nascetur ridiculus mus*. Commisso certamine, septuaginta Coraisitae caesi sunt, & totidem capti. Ex Mahumetanis verò quatordecim periere. Hoccine est miraculum toties in Alcorano decantatum? Vix dignosci potest, posita tanta utriusque exercitus disparitate, ex cujus parte steterit victoria. Certe nullum hoc est miraculum: vel miraculum etiam & multò maius dicendum erit, quòd, cùm Darius Rex Persarum eum trecentis millibus, vel ut alii scribunt, sexcentis millibus militum Alexandrum Macedonum regem, cujus exercitus ad quadraginta millia militum non perveniebat, aggressus fuisset, initio proelio, centum ac decem millia ex Persis caesa sint: ex Alexandri verò militibus, centum octoginta tantum interierint.

[There were in that battle (as we have seen) somewhat less than a thousand Qurayshis coming back from Syria and not thinking about war at all. Muhammad, with some three hundred and thirteen soldiers, took them by surprise. In order that the Mohammedans not be frightened by the large number of their enemies, and that the latter not be encouraged by the small number of the Mohammedans, Providence made the Mohammedans appear twice as numerous as the Qurayshis. There's a miracle for you. Here's another. Muhammad threw some sand or pebbles at his enemies, whose eyes, being full of sand, fell, blind, on the ground ... Now here is the third of these miracles. God sent from the third heaven first a thousand, then three thousand, and then five thousand angels under the leadership of Gabriel to help the Mohammedans. But what need was there of heavenly reinforcements when the enemy lay blind and prostrate? Yet that is how the story is told. As for the outcome, to be sure: *Parturient montes, nascetur ridiculus mus*. In a decisive encounter, seventy Qurayshis were killed and as many captured. Of the Mohammedans fourteen perished. Is this not proclaimed as a miracle in the Alcoran? One can hardly tell, given the great disparity between both sides, which of the two can claim victory. Certainly there is no miracle here. Far more miraculous is what happened when King Darius, with three hundred thousand of his Persians, or as others write six hundred thousand, attacked Alexander the Macedonian, whose army did not reach forty thousand men: once the battle began one hundred and ten thousand of the Persians were killed, while a mere one hundred and eighty of Alexander's soldiers were killed.][70]

Unlike Sale, who uses classical sources to locate Islam within a panoply of religions, Marracci uses them to demonstrate the inferiority of the aesthetic and theological underpinnings of the Qur'ān. The charge that Marracci brings is, of course, preposterous, essentially accusing Muhammad, the presumed author of the Qur'ān, with ineptitude for neither following Horace nor imitating the authors of the Alexandrian histories. Ridiculous though it may be, it reveals an important element of the Western epistemology that reads the texts of Islam through the classics: originality counts for little as compared with the far greater literary value attached to revitalizing another Horatian *topos*; namely, tradition.

The differences between Sale's and Marracci's approach to the Qur'ān – emulating on the one hand, embattled on the other – demonstrate the complexity of the early modern attitude to the Muslim world. Sale's abandonment of the imposture thesis allows him to deal with Islam in ways that open up greater perspectives than those that he, as a translator, brought to the project of the translation, while Marracci's project, massive though it is, fails to go beyond itself, preferring to close questions and debates with foregone conclusions. Small wonder, then, that Sale's was by far the more popular translation, even among those who read Latin. Now, the attitude toward Islam is not the only criterion by which these two translations should be approached. The institutional backing of the two translations – Catholic in the case of Marracci, Anglican in the case of Sale – makes it equally important that they be examined with respect to the treatment of the Jesus story and Christianity in the Qur'ān. It is to this that we now turn.

3

TRANSLATING CHRIST AND CHRISTIANITY

Sale uses his translation of the Qur'ān to conduct an exercise in comparative religion. As is well known, the broad strokes of the Qur'ān's narration of the story of Jesus resembles that of the Bible and the Apocrypha, the most significant difference being the status of the cross and the doctrine of the Trinity. The virgin birth and miracles attributed to Jesus all have the status of signs (*āyāt*, آيات) sent by God to humanity that they might believe.[1] When Sale reaches those passages where Christianity in general, and the Jesus story in particular, are broached, he examines the points on which his (and, presumably, his Christian readers') beliefs coincide with the Qur'ān, and the points on which they differ. In this respect, his behavior is not unlike that of the adherent of a young religion, which seeks points of comparison before seeking points of contrast once confronted with another body of beliefs.[2] Where Sale differs from the adherent of a young religion in his confrontation with Islam is that he never quite reaches the point of sectarian distance and rejection. Indeed, as the following chapter makes clear, his translation and documentation of the Qur'ānic treatment of Christ and Christianity repeatedly returns to the scenario of interchangeability of the two creeds while minimizing the differences between them. In a manner not unlike, though certainly not identical with, the deists, the equivalence of religious belief across the Abrahamic monotheisms holds axiomatic status for Sale. From the Preface, where he argues, somewhat disingenuously, that Bishop Kidder's rules for the conversion of the Jews might also be applied in dealing with Muslims, Sale makes clear that confrontations between adherents of different religions have less to do with the construction of rigid boundaries than with exploring the possibility of the passage between them. Where others see the threat of conversion when Islam and Christianity meet, Sale, following Toland, sees the possibility of religious coexistence, a "union without uniformity."[3] In what follows, we will trace Sale's strategy of privileging inter-religious similarity over difference in his translation of the Qur'ān, with specific reference to the Jesus story.

The fourth section of Sale's "Preliminary Discourse" deals with matters of dogma and belief. It opens with the typical, unassuming manner:

> It has been already observed more than once, that the fundamental position on which Mohammed erected the superstructure of his religion was, that from the beginning to the end of the world there has been, and for ever will be, but one true orthodox belief; consisting, as to matter of faith, in the acknowledging of the only true GOD, and the believing in and obeying such messengers or prophets as he should from time to time send, with proper credential, to reveal his will to mankind; and as to matter of practice, in the observance of the immutable and eternal laws of right and wrong, together with such other precepts and ceremonies as GOD should think fit to order for the time being, according to the different dispensations in different ages of the world ... And to this religion he gives the name of Islâm, which word signifies resignation, or submission to the service and commands of GOD; and is used as the proper name of the Mohammedan religion, which they will also have to be the same at bottom with that of all the prophets from Adam ... That both Mohammed and those among his followers who are reckoned orthodox, had and continue to have just and true notions of GOD and his attributes (always excepting their obstinate and impious rejecting of the Trinity), appears so plain from the Korân itself and all the Mohammedan divines, that it would be loss of time to refute those who suppose the GOD of Mohammed to be different from the true GOD, and only a fictitious deity or idol of his own creation. [Marracci, p. 102.][4]

With this modest declaration, Sale places himself at the greatest possible distance from Marracci, who, as Sale rightly notes, sees all the similarities between Muslim and Christian dogma and yet concludes that Islam is mere idolatry. Sale, on the other hand, interprets the "one true orthodox belief" to be the same one that enables all the Abrahamic monotheisms, and acts on the corollary that the passage from one monotheism to another is more fluid than is commonly supposed. Sale's inclination – and Marracci's refusal – to acknowledge parallels between belief systems is in part the result of the intellectual atmosphere of the turn of the eighteenth century, wherein the idea of the equivalence of revealed religion was rapidly acquiring axiomatic status.

The propagation of this notion of similarity owed a great deal to John Toland, whose *Nazarenus* constitutes a turning point in the early modern understanding of comparative religion. This was the case for a number of reasons. Materially, the publication boom in patristic literature enabled the adduction of arguments from the history of the early church and their communication to a large lay audience. Institutionally, this boom was encouraged by both the Catholic and various reformed churches in order to buttress their positions as being the ones that continued the true faith of the ancients.[5] Needless to say, Toland's vehement anticlericalism and his opposition to the imposture of "priestcraft" were not at the service of any given church, though they certainly benefited from the marketplaces of books and ideas created by sectarian polemic.

As has been noted, the subtitle of *Nazarenus* proclaims the equivalence of the Abrahamic monotheisms. To this end, Toland relies on the Gospel of Barnabas to support the Muslim denial of the divinity of Jesus. The axioms that enable this argument are the ones of the fundamentally historical character of revelation and scripture, whose many different passages are aimed at different audiences, and that consequently, any attempt at a synoptic and simultaneous understanding of the gospels is ultimately futile. Toland argues against a view of religion that consists merely of "the most exact observation of externals … without one grain of religion," a phenomenon he blames on "bookcraft," whereas "true religion is inward life and spirit."[6] Minor theological details are of far lesser significance in the history of religion than potential union: *qua* monotheists, "the Jew and the Gentile, the Civiliz'd and the Barbarian, the Freeman and the Bondslave are all one in CHRIST, however different their circumstances."[7] Combining this with his reading of the Gospel of Barnabas, Toland claims that he has "given clearer account, than is commonly to be met, of Mahometan sentiments with relation to Jesus and the Gospel"; seeing in Muslims "a sort of Christians, and not the worst sort neither, tho farr from being the best."[8] In this reading, the sequence of revelations is cumulative rather than dialectical: "Jesus did not take away or cancel the

Jewish Law in any sense whatsoever."[9] Nor is this quality unique to Judeo-Christianity:

> Tis for the abovesaid reason, no doubt, of joining the *Pentateuch*, the *Psalms* and the *Gospel* to the *Alcoran* that I have heard some Arabians calls Mahometanism the religion of the four books, as the Christian Religion that of the two books … That the four books constitute the foundation of their Religion, is so much their general and constant belief, that one might as well be at the trouble of quoting authors to prove the Christians received the *Old* and *New Testament.*[10]

The final piece in Toland's arsenal of evidence proving that Muhammad came to complete, rather than abrogate, the mission of Jesus, centers on Toland's reading of the term "Paraclete":

> Every traveller almost will tell you, that where JESUS promises to send the *Paraclete* to complete or perfect all things, the Mahometans maintain that original reading was *Periclyte* [in footnote: Περίκλυτος, & non Παράκλητος], or the famous and illustrious, which in Arabic is *Mohammed*: so that their prophet was as much, in their account, foretold by name in the *Gospel*; as CYRUS is believ'd by the Jews and Christians, to have been foretold by name in the *Old Testament* [in margin: John 14.16.26 & 15.26 & 16.7 compar'd with Luke 24.49. Isaiah 44.28 & 45.1].[11]

Toland's reliance on progressive revelation rather than cancellation enables him to formulate a relationship of mutual interdependence between the religions: Christianity is meaningless without the Jewish law, but the latter requires confirmation by the former. A homologous relationship exists between Christianity and Islam: neither without either could or would obtain. Shorn of the corrupt accretions of "priestcraft," all three monotheisms promote the worship of the one true God, and might usefully be considered variations on the same theme. Whereas Marracci (whose translation served as an encyclopedic compendium for Toland as well as Sale) took the traditional view that every successive revelation abrogated or cancelled its predecessors even as it fulfilled their prophecy, Toland and Sale both understand that this fulfillment depends for its operation on the validation of precedent rather than its abrogation.

All of these factors come into play in Sale's treatment of the Jesus story. The structure of confirming precedent and validating future revelation is found in Q61:6:

وَإِذْ قَالَ عِيسَى ابْنُ مَرْيَمَ يَا بَنِي إِسْرَائِيلَ إِنِّي رَسُولُ اللَّهِ إِلَيْكُمْ مُصَدِّقًا لِمَا بَيْنَ
يَدَيَّ مِنَ التَّوْرَاةِ وَمُبَشِّرًا بِرَسُولٍ يَأْتِي مِنْ بَعْدِي اسْمُهُ أَحْمَدُ

which Sale translates as follows:

> And when Jesus the Son of Mary said, O children of Israel, verily I *am* the apostle of GOD *sent* unto you, confirming the law which *was delivered* before me, and bringing good tidings of an apostle who shall come after me, *and* whose name *shall be* Ahmed.[12]

Sale's footnote reads:

> For Mohammed also bore the name of Ahmed; both names being derived from the same root, and nearly of the same signification. The Persian paraphrast, to support what is here alleged, quotes the following words of Christ, *I go to my father, and the* Paraclete *shall come:* [see John xvi.7 &c: Nevertheless I tell you the truth; It is expedient for you that I go away: for if I go not away, the Comforter will not come unto you; but if I depart, I will send him unto you (KJV)] the Mohammedan doctors unanimously teaching that by the Paraclete (or, as they choose to read it, the *Periclyte*, or *Illustrious*) their prophet is intended, and no other.[13]

Let us note in passing that the text of John 16:7 makes the advent of the Paraclete dependent on the departure of Christ, adding further impetus to the dynamic of progressive revelations outlined above. Sale's footnote to Q61:6 also refers to his "Preliminary Discourse," where we read the following concerning this matter:

> The *Mohammedans* have also a *Gospel* in *Arabic*, attributed to St. *Barnabas*, wherein the history of *Jesus Christ* is related in a manner very different from what we find in the true Gospels, and correspondent to those traditions which *Mohammed* has followed in his *Korân* … This book [the Gospel of Barnabas] appears to be no original forgery of the *Mohammedans*,[14] though they have no doubt interpolated and altered it since, the better to serve their purpose; and in particular, instead of the *Paraclete* or *Comforter*, they have in this apocryphal gospel inserted the word *Periclyte*, that is, the *famous* or *illustrious*, by which they pretend their prophet was foretold by name, that being the signification of *Mohammed* in *Arabic*: and this

they say to justify that passage of the *Korán*, where *Jesus Christ* is formally asserted to have foretold his coming, under his other name of *Ahmed*; which is derived from the same root as *Mohammed*, and of the same import.[15]

In other words, far from being the idolatrous enemy, Muslims are represented as being monotheists who agree with Christians on most points, except for the Trinity and the authenticity of scripture.

Both Toland and Sale thus minimize the impact of abrogation *between* differing faiths. On the matter of abrogation *within* scripture, the differences between their position and that of Marracci are equally instructive. Toland makes the case for the historical basis of scripture and applies it to the three monotheisms.[16] Marracci's is the attitude of the obsessive grand inquisitor, who marshals the facts very carefully only to see falsity and evil everywhere. Finally, Sale's is the attitude of the rational translator, who finds in the doctrine of abrogation a method comparable to the hermeneutic framework that he and others use in reading the Bible. For Sale, texts are revealed in time, and the time of their revelation is of utmost importance in determining their meaning. As a concept, abrogation constitutes recognition of the fact that revelation occurs in real time, and that changes inevitably accompany the mutations of human history. Since human wisdom cannot possibly compete with the divine, it must needs content itself with incomplete information during its lifetime. These assumptions are part and parcel of the Qur'ānic science of *naskh*, whereby certain verses are abrogated by others. The time and context of a given revelation (*sabab al-nuzūl*) thereby acquires additional importance as a factor in Qur'ānic exegesis.

The status and history of *naskh* are employed for typically divergent aims by Sale and Marracci. For the latter the meaning of scripture must be synchronic in order for it to be legitimate: every word must make sense simultaneously. Since the Qur'ān openly admits the abrogation of certain verses, Marracci argues, it cannot possibly pretend to the status of scripture.[17] Marracci relies on a very respectable source, namely Ibn Salāma's *Kitāb al-nāsikh wa-l-mansūkh*,[18] much of which he summarizes in a section on abrogation in his "De Alcorano." Having transcribed and translated Ibn Salāma's typology of abrogation, according to which one verse abrogates either the letter or the meaning or both the language and meaning of another,[19] Marracci adds: "Quid enim magis risu dignum, quàm si Princeps ita per praeconem edicat: Sciant omnes, me nunc abrogare legem, quam deinde traditurus sum: itaque quando eam tradam, nullus eam observet, vel curet?" ["What could be more ridiculous than a prince announcing through a herald: 'Let all know that I hereby abrogate a law, that I will later command; thus when I command it, no-one will observe it, let alone care?'"][20] To support his claim regarding the incoherence of the theory of abrogation, Marracci gives the same examples and counter-examples mentioned by Ibn Salāma (namely that Q2:240 is abrogated by Q2:234 and Q50 which is abrogated by Q49, thereby contradicting the rule that the abrogated verse would precede the abrogating verse) to emphasize the point that there is nowhere given a good reason for the abrogations or the structure of Ibn Salāma's system. Marracci wonders what sense there is in an omniscient, omnipotent deity knowingly transmitting a law that will later be abrogated. Needless to say, Marracci finds it all preposterous, in the etymological sense of the term. Marracci thereby rejects two key aspects of the Qur'ān as scripture and historical event; as something that was orally revealed over twenty-three years and then underwent a long process of redaction before becoming the text that he translated. These aspects are not only central to a proper understanding of the Qur'ān, but prominent themes in Qur'ānic scholarship.[21] As usual, Marracci misses the Qur'ānic forest for the polemical trees.

Sale, on the other hand, is very comfortable with the historical and political condition of revealed scripture, a standpoint that easily accommodates abrogation. In a striking example of Sale's using the same data as Marracci but reaching radically different conclusions, Sale actually cites Marracci on abrogation in his "Preliminary Discourse," and even paraphrases Marracci's extract from Ibn Salāma's text, though he takes care to justify the doctrine with the phrase "for good reasons":

> There being some passages in the *Korân* which are contradictory, the
> *Mohammedan* doctors obviate any objection from thence by the doc
> trine of *abrogation*; for they say, that GOD in the *Korân* commanded
> several things which were for good reasons afterwards revoked and
> abrogated.[22]

After offering the reader several examples of abrogation, Sale refers, in a footnote, to Ibn Salāma via Marracci. The difference between Sale and his source inheres in the phrase "for good reasons": Sale relates the textual genesis of the Qur'ān without value judgments about the "laughable" process of transmitting a verse that will certainly be revoked later on. Once again, identical data (abrogation) give rise to two diametrically opposed readings.

The relationship between salvation history and abrogation in the Qur'ān is especially apparent in the literature surrounding Q2:62:

إنَّ الَّذِينَ آمَنُوا وَالَّذِينَ هَادُوا وَالنَّصَارَى وَالصَّابِئِينَ مَنْ آمَنَ بِاللَّهِ وَالْيَوْم

الآخِر وَعَمِلَ صَالِحًا فَلَهُمْ أَجْرُهُمْ عِنْدَ رَبِّهِمْ وَلَا خَوْفٌ عَلَيْهِمْ وَلَا هُمْ يَحْزَنُون

Sale translates this verse as follows:

> Surely those who believe, and those who Judaise, and Christians, and Sabians, [Sale footnote] whoever believeth in GOD, and the last day, and doth that which is right, they shall have their reward with their LORD; *there shall come* no fear on them, neither shall they be grieved.[23]

The standard exegetical literature on this verse tends to divide it into two parts, the first dealing with semantics and context, obsessing over the identification of the various sects and religions identified (much ink is spilled on the question of the Sabians [*Sābi'ūn*]), and the second focusing on their fate on the day of resurrection, with some arguing that this particular verse is abrogated by Q3:185 (following a tradition by Ibn 'Abbās), and that only Muslims shall be rewarded.[24] Sale's footnote covers all these points, though oddly enough he does not cite any of his three favorite exegetes directly:

> From these words, which are repeated in the fifth chapter, several writers (Selden, *de Jure Nat. et Gent.* sec. Hebr. l. 6, c. 12. Angel, a St. Joseph. Gazophylac. Persic. p. 365. Nic. Cusanus *in Cribratione Alcorani*, l. 3, c. 2, &c.) have wrongly concluded that the *Mohammedans* hold it to be the doctrine of their prophet that every man may be saved in his own religion, provided he be sincere and lead a good life. It is true, some of their doctors do agree this to be the purport of the words; (see Chardin's *Voyages*, vol. ii. p. 326, 331) but then they say the latitude hereby granted was soon revoked, for that this passage is abrogated by several others in the *Korân*, which expressly declare that none can be saved who is not of the *Mohammedan* faith, and particularly by those words of the third chapter, *Whoever followeth any other religion than* Islâm (*i.e.*, the

Mohammedan) *it shall not be accepted of him, and at the last day he shall be of those who perish* [i.e. Q3:185] (Abu'lkasem Hebatallah *de abrogante & abrogato*). However, others are of opinion that this passage is not abrogated, but interpret it differently, taking the meaning of it to be that no man, whether he be a *Jew*, a *Christian*, or a *Sabian*, shall be excluded from salvation, provided he quit his erroneous religion and become a *Moslem*, which they say is intended by the following words, *Whoever believeth in* GOD *and the last day, and doth that which is right*. And this interpretation is approved by Mr. Reland, who thinks the words here import no more than those of the apostle, *In every nation he that feareth* GOD, *and worketh righteousness, is accepted with him*: (Acts x. 35) from which it must not be inferred that the religion of nature, or any other, is sufficient to save, without faith in Christ. (Vide Reland. *de Rel. Moham*. p. 128 &c.)[25]

Sale's substitution of the vocabulary of salvation for the mercantile language of the Qur'ān (*lahum ajruhum 'inda rabbihim*) marks an important step toward his conclusion, namely that this verse does not provide grist to the mill of the deists. Sale represents the divisions of the *tafsīr* of this verse fairly and accurately, and correctly recapitulates the argument about its abrogation. What is especially worthy of note is Sale's ordering of these arguments: first, the apparent meaning of the verse, and the apparent latitudinarianism of orthodox Islam; second, the abrogation of the verse by another that limits salvation to Muslims only; and finally, presenting an alternative reading of the verse in question that allows of an interpretation that creates a parallel between Muslim and Christian belief. Relying on Reland, Sale claims that this verse serves the same function in the construction of the Muslim creed as Acts 10:35 in the Christian: in both cases we have the assertion of the necessity of faith for salvation.

Now, if Sale's aim were a negative representation of Islam, he could easily have presented the different exegetical positions in a different order, left out the alternative reading and the comparison with the Christian creed, or otherwise implied that the Muslim position is actually closer to the deist than the Christian position. The decision to stress the homologies between the structures of Christian and Muslim belief is the result of a deliberate effort aimed at demonstrating the ease with which one might pass from one set of beliefs to another. This is a far more radical position than "standard" deism, since no attempt is made at debunking the accepted structures of revealed religion. Instead, Sale seems to be saying that both Christianity and Islam are simultaneously "right," a claim based not on the content of their belief systems but on its structure. Sale will employ a similar strategy in his translation of the Jesus story in the Qur'ān.

By contrast, Marracci's approach to Q2:62 involves the condemnation not only of the Qur'ān and Muhammad, but of the exegetes as well, finding the extension of salvation to all of those who believe in God and his messengers in the *Tafsīr al-Jalālayn* on this verse "malicious." Marracci's allergic reaction to the meaning of the phrase "those who believe" goes so far as to condemn not only the Qur'ān and Muhammad, but the exegetes themselves:

> [*Qui crederunt*] Intelliguntur Mahumetani ipsi. Sed Gelal. [i.e. *Tafsīr al-Jalālayn*] malitiosè explicat من قبل آمنوا بالأنبياء , *qui crederunt in Prophetas anteà missos à Deo.* Sed in Alcorano آمنوا الذين , *qui crederunt*, perpetuò intelliguntur esse Mahumetani.

> [*Those who have believed*] The Mohammedans themselves are understood. But the *Tafsīr al-Jalālayn* maliciously glosses this to mean *those who have believed in previous prophets sent by God.* But in the Alcoran *those who have believed* is always understood to mean Mohammedans.][26]

The lengthy refutation of the verse and its commentaries multiplies the accusations of duplicity and malice, relying on the many other Qur'ānic verses that contradict or abrogate Q2:62. Having listed all of these verses, Marracci proceeds to reiterate the charges of hopeless incoherence in the Qur'ān based on the utter inconsistency of abrogation and revelation, concluding as he will so many times that Muhammad's revelation is too unstable to be valid or legitimate. For Marracci, this one point is the start of much anxious speculation, not only on the vexed problem of faith versus Islam, *īmān* versus *islām*, but also the order of the revelation and the possibility of making sense of the Qur'ān synoptically. The working hypothesis seems to be that if we assume falsity in one place, then it must be assumed to exist everywhere else. This is the stance of the inquisitor, not the translator. The net result is that the evolution of Muhammad's relationship with the Christians (and Jews) of Arabia is taken to be a sign of the falsity of Islam as a whole, rather than the result of changing political relationships. Unlike Sale, Marracci cannot conceive of a "good reason" for changing positions in matters of faith. Perhaps Marracci's weakest point is his failure to appreciate the different configuration of the eternal and the temporal in Islam: what is decreed in Q2:62 and elsewhere is not so much the relationship of Islam and Christianity as rival faiths, but rather the relationship between communities of Christians and Muslims at given points in time.

In addition to salvation history and textual abrogation, the narrative details of the Jesus story are foregrounded for polemical use in the Marracci and Sale translations, attracting the ire of the former and the understanding of the latter. At issue is the fact that the Qur'ān uses the same name, Maryam, to refer to both the mother of Jesus and the sister of Aaron. Since Maryam is the only woman referred to in the Qur'ān by name, a superficial reading might conclude that the text confuses the two Marys, thereby making Jesus the nephew of Moses and Aaron. This is precisely the interpretation of Marracci. Marracci's reading of Q3 returns obsessively to Islam's putatively false identification of Mary's genealogy.[27] The refutation starts:

> Ex ipso Surae hujus titulo, crassimus Mahumeti error ostenditur, dum Mariam Deiparam filiam Joachim confundit cum Maria filia Amran & sorore Moysis & Aaron. Id vero infra clariùs patet, ubi vocat Mariam Deiparam *Sororem Aaron*. Distorqueant quantum volent Mahumetani expositiores verba Alcorani, nunquam Prophetum suum ab hoc errore poterunt vindicare.

> [The most egregious Mohammedan error is demonstrated by the title of this Sūra, where the Virgin Mary, daughter of Joachim, is confused with Mary the daughter of Amran and sister of Moses and Aaron. This appears with greater clarity below, where the Virgin Mary is called *Sister of Aaron*. No matter how much the Mohammedan commentators distort the words of the Alcoran, they will never be able to clear their prophet from this mistake.][28]

Eight pages later we read:

> Iam superius indicavi, quam turpiter hallucinatus sit Mahumetus, existimando Beatissimam Mariam Deiparam eamdem fuisse cum Maria filia Amran & sorore Moysis & Aaron. Quidam Mahumetani …volunt Mariam illam filiam Amran usque ad haec tempora miraculose a Deo vivam conservatam fuisse. Sed in Libro Numer. Cap. 20 clare habemus, illam mortuam fuisse in Cades, & ibidem sepultam. Fortasse, ut Mahumetarum plerique tenent μετεμψύχωσιν, dicere poterunt animam unius Mariae in alterius corpus emigrasse. Verum Pythagorica deliramenta hae sunt.

[I have already indicated above how badly confused Muhammad is, imagining the Most Blessed Mary Mother of God to be the same Mary as the daughter of Amran and the sister of Moses and Aaron. Certain Mohammedans … imagine Mary the daughter of Amran to have miraculously lived long enough to last until that time [of the Virgin Mary]. But in Numbers 20 it says clearly that she died in Cades and was buried there. Perhaps, since many Mohammedans hold to *metempsychosis*, they can say that the soul of one Mary transmigrated into another body. Really, this is Pythagorean delirium.][29]

Marracci's acerbic tone seems all the more surprising when we observe that, *ad* Q19:28, where Mary is addressed as "the sister of Aaron," Marracci lists in his note a tradition clearly stating that this is *not* Aaron the brother of Moses, but another eponymous person, as well as Zamkhsharī's detailed refutation of the claim that Mary the mother of Jesus was the same person as Mary the sister of Moses.[30] Nevertheless, Marracci finds all of this unconvincing ("frustra, & rationibus prorsùs frivolis, ac ridiculis"), seeing in it evidence of the later commentators' desperation to cover up the confusion of Muhammad, whom he considers to be the author of the Qur'ān.[31] So attached is Marracci to this version of events (that Muhammad confused two Marys) that he repeats the argument briefly in the *Prodromus*.[32]

With which tortuous commentary and "refutation" compares Sale's more commonsensical explanation:

From the identity of names it has been generally imagined by *Christian* writers that the *Korân* here confounds *Mary* the mother of JESUS, with *Mary* or *Miriam* the sister of *Moses* and *Aaron*; which intolerable anachronism, if it were certain, is sufficient of itself to destroy the pretended authority of this book. But though *Mohammed* may be supposed to have been ignorant enough in ancient history and chronology to have committed so gross a blunder, yet I do not see how it can be made out from the words of the *Korân*. For it does not follow, because two persons have the same name, and have each a father and brother who bear the same names, that they must therefore necessarily be the same person: besides, such a mistake is inconsistent with a number of other places in the *Korân*, whereby it manifestly appears that *Mohammed* well knew and asserted that *Moses* preceded JESUS several ages. And the commentators accordingly fail not to tell us that there had passed about one thousand eight hundred years between *Amrân* the father of Moses, and *Amrân* the father of the Virgin *Mary*: they also make them the sons of different persons; the first, they say, was the son of *Yeshar*, or *Izhar* (though he was really his brother), the son of *Kâhath*, the son of *Levi*; and the other was the son of *Mathân*, whose genealogy they trace, but in a very corrupt and imperfect manner, up to *David*, and thence to *Adam*. It must be observed that though the Virgin Mary is called in the Korân the sister of Aaron, yet she is nowhere called the sister of Moses; however, some Mohammedan writers have imagined that the same individual Mary, the sister of Moses, was miraculously preserved alive from his time till that of Jesus Christ, purposely to become the mother of the latter.[33]

There are no assumptions of falsity or malice here, merely openness to the possibility that a given text might refer to two people who have the same name.[34] Not only did this possibility occur to Marracci, but he actually came across it in several commentaries, only to dismiss them out of hand as being silly and weakly argued.[35] The political implications of these two readings are clear: on the one hand, an obtuse insistence on the fact that Muslims get everything wrong, and on the other the will to solve an exegetical problem by widening the frame of reference.

Sale's treatment of the birth of Jesus builds on the strategy of expanding the frame of reference with a view to better understanding Islam, underlining the common denominators between Islam and Western religion writ large, as opposed to Christianity alone. *Ad* Q19:23, Sale notes the similarities between the Muslim version of the birth of Jesus and the birth of Apollo. Sale translates the verse thus:

> [A]nd the pains of child-birth came upon her near the trunk of a palm-tree. She said, Would to GOD I had died before this, and had become a *thing* forgotten, and lost in oblivion.[36]

before adding in a footnote that:

> It has been observed, that the *Mohammedan* account of the delivery of the Virgin *Mary* very much resembles that of *Latona*, as described by the poets, not only in this circumstance of their laying hold on a palm-tree (though some say *Latona* embraced an olive-tree, or an olive and a palm, or else two laurels), but also in that of their infants speaking; which *Apollo* is fabled to have done in the womb.[37]

Sale supports his comparison with footnotes referring to Homer and Callimachus, emphasizing the two motifs of childbirth in the shadow of a tree, variously described as a palm or olive-tree, and infant speech.[38] This leap, while not entirely unexpected coming from a man with the erudition of George Sale, underlines the perspective that enables translations such as this to take place. It could, of course, be argued that Sale is merely claiming that the Muslims got their sources wrong, and mixed up something that they might have inherited from the many Christian sects active in the Arabian peninsula with the "orthodox" Jesus story.[39]

For Sale, the Muslim account of Jesus cannot be accounted for only by measuring it against orthodox accounts; both must be inscribed within a comparative framework that assumes a culturally relativist perspective. For Marracci, the central question is "Is the Muslim account of Christianity accurate?" meaning "Is it compatible with our version of the story?" The answer, inevitably, is negative. Within this perspective, erudition becomes a weapon to be used against the Muslim adversary rather than a tool with which Islam might be understood. Marracci uses his vast repertoire of classical learning, invoking every author from Homer to Jerome, to counter claims of Islamic superiority and accomplishment. (Typically, he does not mention any classical parallels *ad* Q19:23.) Sale, on the other hand, transforms this question about the accuracy of the Muslim Jesus story into one that takes the nature of the material into account: "Where does the Muslim account of Jesus come from?" Once the question of theological correctness is thus displaced, a wholly different, radically new brand of inquiry becomes possible, one that familiarizes heterodox belief through a structural reading of its components.[40] By comparing structures across cultures, George Sale makes a strong case for the validity of Muslim belief and salvation history.

The third locus in the Qur'ānic Jesus story that attracts a great deal of attention is, inevitably, the death (or not) of Jesus. The first mention of the (non)-crucifixion of Jesus is found in Q3:54–55:

وَمَكَرُوا وَمَكَرَ اللَّهُ وَاللَّهُ خَيْرُ الْمَاكِرِينَ (54) إِذْ قَالَ اللَّهُ يَا عِيسَى إِنِّي مُتَوَفِّيكَ وَرَافِعُكَ إِلَيَّ وَمُطَهِّرُكَ مِنَ الَّذِينَ كَفَرُوا وَجَاعِلُ الَّذِينَ اتَّبَعُوكَ فَوْقَ الَّذِينَ كَفَرُوا إِلَى يَوْمِ الْقِيَامَةِ ثُمَّ إِلَيَّ مَرْجِعُكُمْ فَأَحْكُمُ بَيْنَكُمْ فِيمَا كُنْتُمْ فِيهِ تَخْتَلِفُونَ

Sale translates these verses as follows:

And *the Jews* devised a stratagem *against him;* but GOD devised a stratagem *against them;* and GOD is the best deviser of stratagems.

> When GOD said, O Jesus, verily I will cause thee to die, and I will take thee up unto me, and I will deliver thee from the unbelievers; and I will place those who follow thee above the unbelievers, until the day of resurrection: then unto me shall ye return, and I will judge between you of that concerning which ye disagree.[41]

These verses provide Sale with the occasion to re-iterate the Muslim rejection of the death of Jesus on the cross and its replacement by the belief that Jesus was raised to heaven by other means. In the lengthy footnote *ad* Q3:54, Sale explains that God's stratagem was "the taking of Jesus up into heaven, and stamping his likeness on another person, who was apprehended and crucified in his stead."[42] Sale also provides ample evidence from the apocrypha and patristic literature to support the Muslim position on this issue, tracing parallels with some ancient Christian sects, and naturally returning to the Gospel of Barnabas for added weight. Sale's reader would have been amply prepared for this by the fourth section of the "Preliminary Discourse," in which the differences of dogma and creed on this issue are laid out. Having treated the central difference between Islam and Christianity, and attempted to reduce the difference by referring to early Christian beliefs (albeit ones subsequently deemed heretical), Sale proceeds to cite Al-Baydāwī who, following Zamakhsharī, identifies Christians as Muslims.[43] The promise made in the second half of the verse – that Jesus's followers will be "above" the unbelievers until the day of resurrection – is also understood metaphorically. Sale cites Baydāwī's gloss that this superiority is to be understood in military rather than spatial terms:

> That is, they who believe in Jesus (among whom the Mohammedans reckon themselves) shall be for ever superior to the Jews, both in arguments and in arms. And accordingly, says al Beidâwi, to this very day the Jews have never prevailed either against the Christians or Moslems, nor have they any kingdom or established government of their own.[44]

This identification between Muslims and Jesus's followers can be traced to Zamakhsharī, who says that those who follow Jesus are "the Muslims, because they were his followers in the original sense of *islam* even if the laws were different [أصل الإسلام وإن اختلفت الشرائع هم المسلمون لأنهم متبعوه في], as opposed to those of the Jews and Christians who called him [Jesus] a liar and told lies about him."[45] In other words, Sale deliberately turns to those loci in the exegesis of the Qur'ān that reconcile the two faiths with respect to the mission of Jesus, notwithstanding the difference of their laws. The omission of any (or all) these details would have enabled Sale to represent the differences between Islam and Christianity as being larger than they are. A more literalist reading, such as Marracci's, would have had the same effect. Sale's decision to arrange the commentary in a certain sequence enables him, once again, to minimize those differences.

The most detailed description of the (non)-crucifixion of Jesus is found in Q4:157–159, which Sale translates as follows:

وَقَوْلِهِمْ إِنَّا قَتَلْنَا الْمَسِيحَ عِيسَى ابْنَ مَرْيَمَ رَسُولَ اللَّهِ وَمَا قَتَلُوهُ وَمَا صَلَبُوهُ وَلَكِنْ شُبِّهَ لَهُمْ وَإِنَّ الَّذِينَ اخْتَلَفُوا فِيهِ لَفِي شَكٍّ مِنْهُ مَا لَهُمْ بِهِ مِنْ عِلْمٍ إِلا اتِّبَاعَ الظَّنِّ وَمَا قَتَلُوهُ يَقِينًا (157) بَلْ رَفَعَهُ اللَّهُ إِلَيْهِ وَكَانَ اللَّهُ عَزِيزًا حَكِيمًا (158) وَإِنْ مِنْ أَهْلِ الْكِتَابِ إِلا لَيُؤْمِنَنَّ بِهِ قَبْلَ مَوْتِهِ وَيَوْمَ الْقِيَامَةِ يَكُونُ عَلَيْهِمْ شَهِيدًا

And [they, i.e. the people of the Book] have said, Verily we have slain CHRIST JESUS the son of MARY, the apostle of GOD; yet they slew him not, neither crucified him, but he was represented *by one* in his likeness; and verily they who disagreed concerning him were in a doubt as to this *matter*, and had no *sure* knowledge thereof, but followed only an *uncertain* opinion. They did not really kill him; but GOD took him up unto himself: and GOD is mighty *and* wise.

And *there shall not be one* of those who have received the scriptures, who shall not believe in him, before his death; and on the day of resurrection he shall be a witness against them.[46]

The passage spells out the Muslim version to the story of the crucifixion, asserting that Jesus was neither murdered nor crucified by his enemies, who were duped by a divine plan that placed the likeness of Jesus on the cross.[47] Sale's footnote *ad* Q4:157–158 reiterates what he has said before on the topic, again referring to Bayḍāwī's commentary. Relying on Zamakhsharī, Bayḍāwī and *Tafsīr al-Jalālayn*, Sale then explains the two possible readings of Q4:159: either that every individual Jew and Christian will believe in Jesus before he or she dies, or that all Jews and Christians will somehow be brought to right faith and belief when Jesus returns from heaven and lives out the rest of his earthly term. Sale's insistence on spelling out these details confirms his intention of finding ways to reconcile Muslim and Christian belief wherever possible by giving similarity the upper hand over difference.

Having made the case for the similarities between Islam and Christianity (or, in the case of Q4, Judeo-Christianity), Sale's rendition of the Christians of the Qur'ān leaves no doubt as to the parallels between the two faiths. By accurately translating the Qur'ān and its commentary, Sale represents the Christians of the Qur'ān as being Muslims in all but actual fact, true believers immune to the corruption of the sacred texts over the ages. In this respect, they closely resemble the Christians idealized by Toland and the Gospel of Barnabas, adherents of an Ur-monotheism where the relationship between God and humanity is not mediated by "priestcraft." Informed by the interchangeability of religious belief, Sale's translation of the Qur'ānic version of the Jesus story and Christianity comes arbitrarily close to the claim that (original) Christianity and Islam are two sides of the same coin.

4

VOLTAIRE: MUHAMMAD AND MOSES, OPPOSITION AND IDENTIFICATION

One of the more irritating stylistic habits of modern France is the widespread use of the phrase "la France de Voltaire" every time a crisis of religious difference – usually, though not exclusively, between Muslims and non-Muslims – threatens what some see as the sovereignty of the republic. Quarrels over headscarves and cartoons invariably see some journalist or other – usually, though not exclusively, in the right-wing press – invoke the sage of Ferney to trope secularism and an allergy to religion. In fact, Voltaire was a very serious and not entirely asympathetic student of religion, far removed from the versions of secularism that obtain nowadays. A further irony is Voltaire's engagement with Islam, which he used early in his life as a means of criticizing institutional Christianity, but which eventually became something that he used to trope tolerance, intellectual commitment, and war on the *infâme*. In what follows, I will attempt to trace the development of this relationship, mainly, though not exclusively, through Voltaire's reading of the Qur'ān and his steady identification with Muhammad.

Voltaire's tergiversations are well-known, perhaps none better than his frequent shifts of position with respect to Muhammad and Islam.[1] After using Muhammad as the embodiment of fanaticism and evil in his play *Mahomet*, Voltaire proceeds, slowly but surely, to rehabilitate him and recognize his ability as a statesman and "grand homme" whose existence changes history. Since Voltaire's fluctuations are well documented, the focus here will be less on whether he said good or bad things about Islam than the irrevocable fact that whatever theoretical phase Voltaire was going through – his preoccupation with fanaticism in the 1730s, his coming to grips with universal history in the 1740s and 1750s, his break with the *Encyclopédie* in the 1770s – his position is always defined with respect to Islam and Muhammad. Indeed, Islam becomes, for Voltaire, not only something that is good to think with, but something that defines him, something without which his witty, incisive *parti pris* would not be what they are.

In the 1730s, Voltaire was content to represent Muhammad as the epitome of evil and fanaticism. Although the image is offensive by contemporary standards, it is worth noting that the protagonist of *Mahomet* is part of a sequence of fanatics that Voltaire puts onstage. Before the premiere of *Mahomet*, *Brutus* was the play that presented Voltaire's sentiment against fanaticism to great acclaim, with the trademark scene of a family murder out of blind allegiance to a political cause – something we also see in *Oedipe* and *La Mort de César*. In any case, *Mahomet* was applauded in Lille and booed (and eventually banned) in Paris for the same reason: the audience saw very clearly that Voltaire was using his character Mahomet as a way of attacking the church.[2] By 1754, when pirated versions of what would later become *La Philosophie de l'histoire* and the *Essai sur les moeurs* were circulating in Europe, the situation had changed. Grimm reports the following in the January 1, 1754 issue of the *Correspondance littéraire*:

> On renouvellera sans doute le reproche qu'on a fait autrefois a M. de Voltaire a l'occasion de l'*Histoire des Croisades*, insérée dans le *Mercure de France*, c'est d'avoir un attachement secret pour la religion des Turcs; il les fait valoir tant qu'il peut, et presque toujours au dépens des chrétiens. Les mauvais plaisants disent que l'auteur ira se faire circoncire à Constantinople, et que ce sera là la fin de son roman.

> [The reproach that was leveled at Voltaire in the *Mercure de France* at the time of the *Histoire des Croisades* will probably be repeated; namely that he has a secret fondness for the religion of the Turks; he sides with them as much as he can, and almost always at the expense of the Christians. Wags say that he will go to get circumcized in Constantinople, and that that will be the end of this story.][3]

Things continue to change over the ensuing decades. By 1770, Voltaire has had his fill of anti-Muslim rhetoric. So much so that he chastises his compatriots thus:

Je vous le dis encore, ignorants imbéciles, à qui d'autres ignorants
ont fait accroire que la religion mahométane est voluptueuse et sensuelle, il n'en est rien; on vous a trompés sur ce point comme sur tant
d'autres.

Chanoines, moines, curés même, si on vous imposait la loi de ne
manger ni boire depuis quatre heures du matin jusqu'à dix du soir,
pendant le mois de juillet, lorsque le carême arriverait dans ce temps;
si on vous défendait de jouer à aucun jeu de hasard sous peine de damnation; si le vin vous était interdit sous la même peine; s'il vous fallait
faire un pèlerinage dans les déserts brûlants; s'il vous était enjoint de
donner au moins deux et demi pour cent de votre revenu aux pauvres;
si, accoutumés à jouir de dix-huit femmes, on vous en retranchait tout
d'un coup quatorze; en bonne foi, oseriez-vous appeler cette religion
sensuelle?

[I am telling you again, you ignorant imbeciles, whom other ignora-
muses have persuaded that the Mahometan religion is sensuous and
voluptuous, it is not true; you have been deceived on this matter as
you have been on so many others.

I ask you, you canons, monks, and prelates, if you had to obey the
rule of neither eating nor drinking from four in the morning until ten
at night when the fast falls in the month of July; if you were forbidden
from playing any game of chance under pain of damnation; if wine
were banned for the same reason; if you had to go on pilgrimages in
burning deserts; if you were enjoined to give at least two-and-a-half
percent of your income to the poor; if, having grown accustomed to
enjoying eighteen women at a time, fourteen of them were suddenly
removed; would you, in good faith, dare call this religion sensuous?][4]

Voltaire's method is telling. He uses the example of Islam as a foil to
Christian wrongdoing not by opposing actual examples of Muslim
behavior to other examples of Christian behavior, but by setting out
Islamic laws and prohibitions – the mandatory fast of Ramaḍān, the
ḥajj, compulsory alms-giving in the amount of two-and-a-half percent or more of income and asset value, no drinking, no gambling,
no more than four wives – to demolish once and for all the propagan-
distic claims about Islamic "sensuality." This argument would have
been very difficult to formulate without an accurate translation of
the Qur'ān. No quantity of travel narratives and accounts of palace
intrigue would have enabled Voltaire to make this argument, since
no quantity of empirical observation allows the absolute deduction
of legal codes: it comes straight from Voltaire's reading of Sale's
translation of the Qur'ān.

The Sale translation was first published in 1734, two years before the presumed composition of *Mahomet*. Although not unaware of Sale's work (he had certainly discovered it by August 1738), Voltaire proceeded with the composition and presentation of his play anyway, portraying Muhammad as a seventh-century Tartuffe who uses religion for personal ends and Séide as a haplessly fanatic servant, ripe only for manipulation. Notwithstanding the anti-Muslim appearance, the point of all this seems to be the indictment of fanaticism and the insanity of committing murder in the name of God. The character of Mahomet, while not historically accurate, serves as a foil to Voltaire's views on the relationship between faith, ethics, and political action. At this point, Muhammad is, in René Pomeau's memorable phrase, the "anti-Voltaire."[5] The historical Muhammad will continue this "foiling" role but Voltaire's views will frequently change.

Soon thereafter, Voltaire's tone in his private correspondence betrays a different image. On August 14, 1738, he writes to Thieriot that "Il y a un diable d'Anglais qui a fait une très belle traduction du saint Alcoran, précédé d'une préface beaucoup plus belle que tous les alcorans du monde" (D 1588). ["There is a devil of an Englishman who has made a very beautiful translation of the holy Alcoran, preceded by a preface far more beautiful than all the alcorans of the world."] Two years later, he writes to Frederick II that "M. Sale, qui nous a donné une excellente version de l'alcoran en anglais, veut faire regarder Mahomet comme un Numa, et comme un Thésée" (D 2386). ["M. Sale, who has given us an excellent translation of the Alcoran into English, wants us to regard Mahomet as a Numa and a Theseus."] These letters were written around the beginning of the Cirey period, the point at which Voltaire starts the composition of *La Philosophie dans l'histoire* and the *Essai sur les moeurs*. By 1748, Voltaire has added an appendix to a version of *Mahomet* that appeared in an edition of his collected works entitled "De l'Alcoran et de Mahomet," where at least some of the hostility has abated.[6] By the time he starts publishing parts of what would later become the *Essai sur les moeurs*, there is a marked shift in his attitude. This is connected not only with the subject – Islam – but with what Voltaire is doing with it: writing history rather than tragedy.

Voltaire's marginal notes on the Sale Qur'ān reveal some, though certainly not all, of the aspects that would preoccupy him in his future texts about Islam.[7] The themes that attract Voltaire's attention are those of internal and external differences between Islam and the other religions as well as within Islam itself. In the "Preliminary Discourse" Voltaire annotates, *inter alia*, passages on the religions of pre-Islamic Arabia, the Jews of Yemen, the sects of Islam, war on apostates, and Muhammad's skill as a legislator. Voltaire also marks passages from the Qur'ān dealing with numerous topics, listed here roughly in order of appearance:

1. Marriage, divorce, and inheritance (one of the few instances of detailed legislation in the Qur'ān: Q2:221, Q2:226–229, Q2:232–233, Q2:236–237, Q4:2–3, Q4:19–20, Q4:25, Q4:34–35).
2. The Muslim view of Jesus and Mary (Q2:253 [annotated "jesu fils de/marie chere a dieu"], Q3:41–47, Q4:154–157, Q4:172–173, Q19:16–27).
3. Verses defining virtue (Sale: "righteousness" البرّ [Q2:177]), punishment (Sale: "retaliation" القِصَاصُ [Q2:178–179]), tolerance (Sale: "let there be no violence in religion" لا إكْرَاهَ في الدِّين [Q2:256]), and charity (Q2:254).
4. The punishment of the Israelites (Q2:65, which he annotates "juifs changés en singes").
5. The prohibition of suicide (Q4:29).
6. Muhammad's fallibility and humanity (Q7:184–188).[8]
7. The unity of God according to Muslim doctrine (Q10:68, which Voltaire annotates, "god/hath no/children"), the Verse of the Throne (Q2:255).
8. The story of the *mi'rāj* and the children of Israel (most of Q17 is bookmarked).
9. The condemnation of poets (Q26:221–227) and proclamations of the divine origin of the Qur'ān (Q11:12–13).
10. The Moses story (Q28:13–32).
11. The description of paradise (Q55: 70–78, annotated "ouris").
12. Muhammad's quarrels with the Jews of Arabia (Q113, annotated "mahomet/freed from/the knots/of a jew/chapter/on/magick").

Voltaire works his reading of these passages into his universal history and later works dealing with Islam. Some of these passages are found in relatively unchanged form in Voltaire's texts. Voltaire's treatment of the dietary laws and the prohibition of alcohol in the *Essai sur les moeurs* in particular sound like translations from Sale's "Preliminary Discourse." Similarly, the description of the *houris* and paradise are clearly based on Q55:46–78. The overall spirit of Muhammad being the legislator who "gave the Arabians the best laws he could" comes through in Voltaire's description of Muhammad doing little more than "se conformer, pour le fond, aux usages reçus" ["conforming, for the most part, to custom"].[9] The most striking examples of this are marriage, the *ḥajj*, and the laws of war, each of which will now be covered in some detail.

Voltaire wastes no time in informing his reader that Muslim law is *not* designed to flatter men's voluptuous desires. In a passage that pre-figures his later denunciations of Western ignorance of Islam, he writes:

> C'est un préjugé répandu parmi nous que le mahométisme n'a fait de si grands progrès que parce qu'il favorise les inclinations voluptueuses. On ne fait pas réflexion que toutes les anciennes religions de l'Orient ont admis la pluralité des femmes. Mahomet en réduisit à quatre le nombre illimité jusqu'alors. Il est dit que David avait dix-huit femmes, et Salomon sept cents, avec trois cents concubines. Ces rois buvaient du vin avec leurs compagnes. C'était donc la religion juive qui était voluptueuse, et celle de Mahomet était sévère.
>
> C'est un grand problème parmi les politiques, si la polygamie est utile à la société et à la propagation. L'Orient a décidé cette question dans tous les siècles, et la nature est d'accord avec les peuples orientaux, dans presque toute espèce animale chez qui plusieurs femelles n'ont qu'un mâle. Le temps perdu par les grossesses, par les couches, par les incommodités naturelles aux femmes, semble exiger que ce temps soit réparé. Les femmes, dans les climats chauds, cessent de bonne heure d'être belles et fécondes. Un chef de famille, qui met sa gloire et sa prospérité dans un grand nombre d'enfants, a besoin d'une femme qui remplace une épouse inutile. Les lois de l'Occident semblent plus favorables aux femmes; celles de l'Orient, aux hommes et à l'État: il n'est point d'objet de législation qui ne puisse être un sujet de dispute. Ce n'est pas ici la place d'une dissertation; notre objet est de peindre les hommes plutôt que de les juger.
>
> On déclame tous les jours contre le paradis sensuel de Mahomet; mais l'antiquité n'en avait jamais connu d'autre. Hercule épousa Hébé dans le ciel, pour récompense des peines qu'il avait éprouvées sur la terre. Les héros buvaient le nectar avec les dieux; et, puisque l'homme était supposé ressusciter avec ses sens, il était naturel de supposer aussi qu'il goûterait, soit dans un jardin, soit dans quelque autre globe, les plaisirs propres aux sens, qui doivent jouir puisqu'ils subsistent. Cette créance fut celle des pères de l'Église du iie et du iiie siècle. C'est ce qu'atteste précisément saint Justin, dans la seconde

partie de ses *Dialogues*: "Jérusalem, dit-il, sera agrandie et embellie pour recevoir les saints, qui jouiront pendant mille ans de tous les plaisirs des sens." Enfin le mot de *paradis* ne désigne qu'un jardin planté d'arbres fruitiers.

[It is a widespread prejudice among us that Mohammedanism only made such great strides because it favored voluptuous inclinations. We do not think about the fact that all the ancient religions of the Orient allowed polygamy. Mahomet reduced to four wives a number that had been hitherto unlimited. It is said that David had eighteen wives, and Solomon eight hundred, along with three hundred concubines. These kings drank wine with their partners. It was therefore the Jewish religion that was lax, and the Mohammedan that was severe.

It is a great problem among politicians as to whether polygamy is useful for society and social growth. The Orient has settled this question for all time, and nature agrees with the Oriental peoples, for every animal species in which there are several females for every male. The time lost to pregnancy, childbirth and to women's native discomfort seems to demand reparation. In warmer climates, women stop being beautiful and fertile early. The head of a household who places his honor and glory in a large number of children needs a woman to replace a useless spouse. Western laws seem more favorable to women, and Oriental laws more favorable to men and the state: there is no subject of legislation that cannot also be a topic for discussion and dispute. This is not the place for a dissertation: our goal is to depict people, not to judge them.

The sensuous paradise of Mahomet is decried every day, but antiquity never knew any others. Hercules married Hebe in heaven as a reward for the trials that he suffered on earth. Heroes drank nectar with the gods, and since mortals were believed to be resurrected as their senses were excited, it is natural to suppose that they would enjoy the pleasures of the senses as they subsist, either in a garden on in some other world. This was the belief of the Fathers of the Church during the second and third centuries. It is what Saint Julian attests, in the second part of his *Dialogues*: "Jerusalem," he says, "will expand and grow more beautiful as it receives the saints, who will enjoy all the pleasures of the senses for a thousand years." Finally, the word *paradise* just means a garden planted with fruit trees.][10]

Voltaire's plan – the juxtaposition of Muslim and non-Muslim laws, the reliance on Montesquieu's theory of climate and classical sources – is a first step in explaining the historical development of Islam. The passage shows that, even if Muslim laws seem to favor men over women, they are still closer to the laws of nature, the customs described in the Bible, and classical ideals than is often claimed. It is interesting to note that the topics of marriage and paradise are the same ones that he bookmarks. Later in the same chapter he will declare that "toutes les religions ont emprunté leurs dogmes et tous leurs rites les unes des autres." ["All religions have borrowed their dogmas and rites from each other."][11]

Voltaire's reading of Q2 and Q4 shows him taking pains to present a positive version of Islam. Voltaire adds a list of the verses concerning marriage and divorce that he had marked in his copy of the Sale translation to the article "Alcoran, ou plutôt le Koran" that he wrote for the *Questions sur l'Encyclopédie*, with the aim of "réconcilier les femmes avec Mahomet, qui ne les a pas traitées si durement qu'on le dit" ["reconciling women with Mahomet, who has not treated them as cruelly as he is said to have"].[12] One of these passages – Q4:34–35 – contains the following verse defining male superiority and enjoining punishment if necessary:

الرِّجَالُ قَوَّامُونَ عَلَى النِّسَاءِ بِمَا فَضَّلَ اللَّهُ بَعْضَهُمْ عَلَى بَعْضٍ وَبِمَا أَنْفَقُوا مِنْ أَمْوَالِهِمْ فَالصَّالِحَاتُ قَانِتَاتٌ حَافِظَاتٌ لِلْغَيْبِ بِمَا حَفِظَ اللَّهُ وَاللَّاتِي تَخَافُونَ نُشُوزَهُنَّ فَعِظُوهُنَّ وَاهْجُرُوهُنَّ فِي الْمَضَاجِعِ وَاضْرِبُوهُنَّ فَإِنْ أَطَعْنَكُمْ فَلَا تَبْغُوا عَلَيْهِنَّ سَبِيلًا إِنَّ اللَّهَ كَانَ عَلِيًّا كَبِيرًا (34) وَإِنْ خِفْتُمْ شِقَاقَ بَيْنِهِمَا فَابْعَثُوا حَكَمًا مِنْ أَهْلِهِ وَحَكَمًا مِنْ أَهْلِهَا إِنْ يُرِيدَا إِصْلَاحًا يُوَفِّقِ اللَّهُ بَيْنَهُمَا إِنَّ اللَّهَ كَانَ عَلِيمًا خَبِيرًا (35)

Sale translates this passage thus:

Men shall have the preëminence above women, because of those *advantages* wherein GOD hath caused the one of them to excel the other, [Sale's footnote: Such as superior understanding and strength, and the other privileges of the male sex, which enjoys the dignities in church and state, goes to war in defence of GOD'S true religion, and claims a double share of their deceased ancestors' estates (Vide Al-Beidawi)] and for that which they expend of their substance *in maintaining their wives*. The honest women *are* obedient, careful in the absence *of their husbands*, [Sale's footnote: Both to preserve their husband's substance from loss or waste, and themselves from all degrees of immodesty (Idem [Al Baidawi], Jalaloddin)] for that GOD preserveth *them, by committing them to the care and protection of the men*. But those, whose perverseness ye shall be apprehensive of, rebuke; and remove them into separate apartments, [Sale's footnote: That is, banish them from your bed] and chastise them. [Sale's footnote: By this passage the Mohammedans are in plain terms allowed to beat their wives, in case of stubborn disobedience; but not in a violent or dangerous manner (Al Beidawi, Jallaloddin).] But if they shall be obedient unto you, seek not an occasion *of quarrel* against them: for GOD is high and great.

And if ye fear a breach between the *husband and wife*, send a judge [Sale's footnote: *i.e.*, Let the magistrate first send two arbitrators or mediators, one on each side, to compose the difference, and prevent, if possible, the ill consequences of an open rupture] out of his family, and a judge out of her family: if they shall desire a reconciliation, GOD will cause them to agree; for GOD is knowing and wise.[13]

In Voltaire's article, this becomes: "Les honnêtes femmes sont obéissantes et attentives, même pendant l'absence de leurs maris. Si elles sont sages, gardez-vous de leur faire la moindre querelle; s'il en arrive une, prenez un arbitre de votre famille et un de la sienne." ["Honest women are obedient and attentive, even during the absence of their husbands. If they are well behaved, beware of the slightest quarrel with them; if this should happen, take an arbiter from your family and one from hers."][14] Voltaire, in other words, avoids the issue of "chastisement" or the possibility of mis-reading the verse as an encouragement to domestic violence, all with a view to rehabilitating the image of Islam as a religion that legitimized and codified women's rights.[15] It is odd that Voltaire waited until the composition of this article to address the question, since as the above listing shows, the verses on marriage constitute the majority of those that attracted his interest. In view of the fact that the *Essai sur les moeurs* began as a set of notes intended for Mme du Châtelet, one might have expected him to present Muslim law under this positive light earlier. Nevertheless, it is quite significant that Voltaire details the Muslim law of marriage, divorce, and inheritance in French at a time when French law on such matters left much to be desired – marriage was a sacrament, divorce forbidden (though separations accepted *de facto*), lineage all important, and the power of the *paterfamilias* quasi-absolute.[16]

It seems that what prompted the composition of this text was, as Voltaire admits, the negative view of Islam prevalent at the time of writing, in the *Encyclopédie* and elsewhere:

Nos auteurs, qui sont en beaucoup plus grand nombre que les janissaires, n'eurent pas beaucoup de peine à mettre nos femmes dans leur parti: ils leur persuadèrent que Mahomet ne les regardait pas comme des animaux intelligents; qu'elles étaient toutes esclaves par les lois de l'*Alcoran*; qu'elles ne possédaient aucun bien dans ce monde, et que, dans l'autre, elles n'avaient aucune part au paradis. Tout cela est d'une fausseté évidente; et tout cela a été cru fermement.

[Our authors, who are far more numerous than the janissaries, did not have much trouble in attracting women to their cause: they persuaded them that Mahomet considered them merely intelligent animals, that they were all slaves according to the laws of the *Alcoran*; that they were to have no possessions in this world and would have no place in paradise in the next. All of this is obviously false, and all of this has been firmly believed.][17]

Voltaire's reliance on Muslim law is related to the ironic opening of this article:

Ce livre gouverne despotiquement toute l'Afrique septentrionale du mont Atlas au désert de Barca, toute l'Égypte, les côtes de l'océan Éthiopien dans l'espace de six cents lieues, la Syrie, l'Asie Mineure, tous les pays qui entourent la mer Noire et la mer Caspienne, excepté le royaume d'Astracan, tout l'empire de l'Indoustan, toute la Perse, une grande partie de la Tartarie, et dans notre Europe la Thrace, la Macédoine, la Bulgarie, la Servie, la Bosnie, toute la Grèce, l'Épire et presque toutes les îles jusqu'au petit détroit d'Otrante où finissent toutes ces immenses possessions.

[This book governs despotically all of North Africa from Mount Atlas to the Barca desert, all of Egypt, six hundred leagues of the Ethiopian Ocean coastline, Syria, Asia Minor, all of the countries that surround the Black and Caspian Seas with the exception of the kingdom of Astrakhan, the whole empire of Hindustan, all of Persia, large areas of Tatar land, and in Europe Thrace, Macedonia, Bulgaria, Serbia, Bosnia, all of Greece, Epirus and almost all of the islands up to the small strait of Otranto where these immense possessions end.][18]

If the reign of the Qur'ān is vast, the fact that it is a book of laws rather than a person who is governing "despotiquement" is significant. Voltaire thereby disqualifies the image of the "Orient" as a large area subject only to the whims of one man. The sovereigns of the Muslim world are subject to the "despotism" of Muslim law. Only those laws reign absolutely.[19]

The other area in which Muhammad's legislative skill emerges is the pilgrimage. The *ḥajj* has been cleverly described as a "sort of symbol of the permanent struggle of Islam against paganism."[20]

Here is Sale's account of Muhammad's struggle with this issue – one of the passages that Voltaire marked in his copy of the Sale translation:

> The pilgrimage to *Mecca*, and the ceremonies prescribed to those who perform it, are, perhaps, liable to greater exception than other of *Mohammed's* institutions; not only as silly and ridiculous in themselves, but as relics of idolatrous superstition. Yet whoever seriously considers how difficult it is to make people submit to the abolishing of ancient customs, how unreasonable soever, which they are fond of, especially where the interest of a considerable party is also concerned, and that a man may with less danger change many things than one great one, must excuse *Mohammed's* yielding some points of less moment, to gain the principal. The temple of *Mecca* was held in excessive veneration by all the *Arabs* in general … and especially by those of *Mecca*, who had a particular interest to support that veneration; and as the most silly and insignificant things are generally the objects of the greatest superstition, *Mohammed* found it much easier to abolish idolatry itself, than to eradicate the superstitious bigotry with which they were addicted to that temple, and the rites performed there; wherefore, after several fruitless trials to wean them therefrom, [footnote: See Kor. c. 2, p. 16. (i.e. Q2:77–87)] he thought it best to compromise the matter, and rather than to frustrate his whole design, to allow them to go on pilgrimage thither, and to direct their prayers thereto; contenting himself with transferring the devotions there paid from their idols to the true GOD, and changing such circumstances therein as he judged might give scandal. And herein he followed the example of the most famous legislators, who instituted not such laws as were absolutely the best in themselves, but the best their people were capable of receiving: and we find GOD himself had the same condescendence for the Jews, whose hardness of heart he humoured in many things, giving them therefore statutes that were not good, and judgments whereby they should not live.[21]

And here is Voltaire's typically succinct adaptation:

> Quant au pèlerinage de la Mecque, aux cérémonies pratiquées dans le *Kaaba* et sur la pierre noire, peu de personnes ignorent que cette dévotion était chère aux Arabes depuis un grand nombre de siècles. Le *Kaaba* passait pour le plus ancien temple du monde; et, quoiqu'on y vénérât alors trois cents idoles, il était principalement sanctifié par la pierre noire, qu'on disait être le tombeau d'Ismaël. Loin d'abolir ce

pèlerinage, Mahomet, pour se concilier les Arabes, en fit un précepte positif.

[As for the pilgrimage to Mecca, the ceremonies performed in the *Kaaba* and the black stone, few people are unaware that the Arabs cherished this rite for several centuries. The *Kaaba* was believed to be the oldest temple in the world, and even though three hundred idols were worshipped there at the time, it was sanctified mainly by the black stone, which was said to be the tomb of Ishmael. Far from abolishing this pilgrimage, Mahomet, in order to reconcile the Arabs (with his religion), made it a positive precept.][22]

As for the topic of war, which Sale places under the rubric of "civil laws" in another passage that Voltaire bookmarked (i.e. pp. 142–143 in the 1734 edition), Sale's argument is that Muslims do not have a monopoly on fighting the enemies of their religion, and that Muhammad's only fault, if it can be called a fault, lies in his ability to channel the "enthusiasm" of his followers. Commenting on the injunction of "warring against the infidels" and the rewards attached thereto, Sale writes:

Such a doctrine ... it must be allowed, was well calculated for his purpose, and stood him and his successors in great stead: for what dangers and difficulties may not be despised and overcome by the courage and constancy which these sentiments necessarily inspire? Nor have the Jews and Christians, how much soever they detest such principles in others, been ignorant of the force of enthusiastic heroism, or omitted to spirit up their respective partisans by the like arguments and promises.[23]

In Voltaire's adaptation, the word "enthousiasme" makes frequent appearances: "Après avoir bien connu le caractère de ses concitoyens, leur ignorance, leur crédulité, et leur disposition à l'enthousiasme, il vit qu'il pouvait s'ériger en prophète." ["Having studied the character of fellow citizens, their ignorance, their credulity, and their inclination toward enthusiasm, he saw that he could declare himself a prophet."][24] After the conquest of Mecca, "Il se trouvait à la tête de quarante mille hommes tous enivrés de son enthousiasme." ["He found himself at the head of forty thousand men, all intoxicated by his enthusiasm."][25] "Ces Ismaélites ressemblaient aux Juifs par l'enthousiasme." ["These Ishmaelites resembled the Jews by their enthusiasm."][26] "Les succès de ce peuple conquérant semblent dus

encore plus à l'enthousiasme qui l'anime qu'à ses conducteurs."
["The successes of this conquering people are due more to the
enthusiasm that motivates them rather then their leaders."][27] "Si
jamais puissance a menacé toute la terre, c'est celle de ces califes;
car ils avaient le droit du trône et de l'autel, du glaive et de
l'enthousiasme." ["If ever a power threatened the entire world,
it was that of the Caliphs; for they ruled over the throne and the
altar, with the sword and enthusiasm."][28] Finally, "Ce ne fut point
par les armes que *l'Islamisme* s'établit dans plus de la moitié de
notre hémisphère, ce fut par l'enthousiasme, par la persuasion,
et surtout par l'exemple des vainqueurs, qui a tant de force sur les
vaincus." ["It was not at all by arms that *Islamism* (sic) was established over half of our hemisphere; it was by enthusiasm, persuasion, and above all by the example set by the victors, which
has such great force over the vanquished."][29] This last sentence
demonstrates how far Voltaire has come since *Mahomet*. There
the grand enemy was *le fanatisme*.[30] By substituting the notion of
enthousiasme – a less extreme passion than *fanatisme* that can be
manipulated for political ends – Voltaire proclaims openly a version
of global history utterly at odds with the received idea of the conquering Muslim horde as a form of divine punishment. The key difference
in the context of the *Essai* seems to be that *fanatisme* is blind and
self-destructive, while *enthousiasme* looks outwards and builds
empires. Thus in India, "Les philosophes indiens se jetaient eux-
mêmes dans un bûcher, par un excès de fanatisme et de vaine gloire."
["The Indian philosophers threw themselves on the pyre, through an
excess of fanaticism and vainglory."][31] "Leur fanatisme [les bonzes]
se subdivise à l'infini." ["The fanaticism of the Bonzes is infinitely
divisible."][32] One of the few certainties in the history of the early
church is "qu'il n'y a que l'ignorance, le fanatisme, l'esclavage des
écrivains copistes d'un premier imposteur, qui aient pu compter
parmi les papes l'apôtre Pierre, Lin, Clet, et d'autres, dans le premier siècle." ["Only the ignorance, the fanaticism and the slavishness
of the copyists of a first impostor, who counted among the popes
the apostle Peter, Linus, Anacletus, and others during the first
century."][33] In his version of the early Muslim conquests, on the
other hand, Voltaire presents us with an army of believers whose
enthusiasm proves infectious and whose behavior invites imitation – the very dynamic of modernization through imitation that
we outlined above.

Such is the depth of Voltaire's conversion away from the fanaticism thesis that he takes his distance from Sale in his *Supplément à l'Essai sur les moeurs*:

> Le savant traducteur de l'Alcoran tombe un peu dans le faible que tout traducteur a pour son auteur; il ne s'éloigne pas de croire que Mahomet fut un fanatique de bonne foi. Il est aisé de convenir, dit-il, qu'il pût regarder comme une œuvre méritoire, d'arracher les hommes à l'idolâtrie et à la superstition et que par degrés, avec le concours d'une imagination allumée, qui est le partage des Arabes, il se crût en effet destiné à réformer le monde.
>
> Bien des gens ne croiront pas qu'il y ait eu beaucoup de bonne foi dans un homme qui dit avoir reçu les feuilles de son livre par l'ange Gabriel, et qui prétend avoir été de la Mecque à Jérusalem en une nuit sur le jument Borac; mais j'avoue qu'il est possible qu'un homme, rempli d'*enthousiasme* et de grands desseins, ait imaginé en songe qu;il était transporté de la Mecque à Jérusalem, et qu'il parlait aux anges: de telles fantaisies entrent dans la composition de la nature humaine …
>
> Il est vraisemblable que Mahomet fut d'abord fanatique, ainsi que Cromwell le fit dans le commencement de la guerre civile: tous deux employèrent leur esprit et leur courage à faire réussir leur fanatisme; mais Mahomet fit des choses infiniment plus grandes, parce qu'il vivait dans un temps ou chez un peuple où l'on pouvait les faire.

[The learned translator of the Alcoran is somewhat guilty of the weakness that every translator has for his author; he is not far from believing that Mahomet was a fanatic in good faith. It is easy to agree, he says, that he considered it a worthwhile task to tear people away from idolatry and superstition and that by degrees, with the help of an inflamed imagination, which is heritage of the Arabs, he believed himself actually destined to reform the world.

Many people will not believe that there was much good faith in a man who claimed to have received the leaves of his book from the angel Gabriel, and who claims to have been transported from Mecca to Jerusalem in one night on the winged horse Borac; but I admit that it is possible for a man full of enthusiasm and grand designs to have dreamed that he was transported from Mecca to Jerusalem, and that he spoke to the angels: such fantasies are part and parcel of human nature …

It is likely that Mahomet was a fanatic at first, just like Cromwell at the start of the Civil War; both men used their mind and their courage to make their fanaticism triumph, but Mahomet accomplished infinitely greater things, because he lived in an age or among a people where they could be accomplished.][34]

Voltaire's admiration for Muhammad's skill as a legislator – a great man who formed great men – is apparent in his detailed description of the similarities between Muslim law and other religions. The strategy of gradual compromise rather than outright contradiction is displayed in the adherence to established usage in such matters as circumcision, prayer, fasting, charity, and pilgrimage. Where differences do exist, they are decidedly to Muhammad's favor.

Voltaire's development of a new historiography, more concerned with being truly universal and less dependent on a literal reading of the Bible and the reader's edification, owes a great deal to his discovery of Islam. Voltaire's reading of Sale enables his passage through the difficult terrain of pyrrho-skepticism, which makes accepting anything as a fact rather than a fable well-nigh impossible, and the arrival at a point where divine is replaced by human agency. The demythification of biblical history, through which Voltaire attacks received ideas such as the chosenness of the people of Israel, the qualities of Moses as a leader and legislator, and most significantly, the miraculous as such, depends on a contrast with the history of Islam, where similar ideas operate but with the stress on believable events and ideas (men fighting rather than God, for instance).

In this context Bayle casts a predictably long shadow over Voltaire's historiography.[35] As a skeptic, Voltaire follows and differs from Bayle. On the one hand, he insists on adhering to strict standards of evidence. On the other hand, he wants to write histories that are instructive but go beyond the sort of pedagogy found in Bossuet's *Politique tirée des propres paroles de l'Ecriture sainte*.[36] Although the conflict between these two tendencies is never completely resolved, it will be seen that the turn to Islamic history enables a way out of the impasse. Voltaire's method can be summed up by his obsession with facts, following Fontenelle's admonition, "assurons-nous bien du fait avant de nous inquiéter de la cause." ["Let us be sure of the facts before worrying about causes."] Second, the total lack of respect for established authority, especially that of the Bible.[37] The credible and the likely, the *vraisemblable*, defeat the fabulous or the improbable. It will be Voltaire's task to separate the wheat from the chaff in an effort to come to grips with the reality of Islam. In this respect his project is reminiscent of the Abbé Banier, whose monumental *La Mythologie et les fables expliquées par l'histoire* (1738–1740) prescribes the systematic removal of any superstitious or unnatural claim made in a given myth as a means toward its proper understanding: "Il faut écarter d'une fable tout ce qui y paraît surnaturel."[38] Voltaire echoes Banier in his definition of history for the *Encyclopédie*: "C'est le récit des faits donnés pour vrais, au contraire de la fable, qui est le récit des faits donnés pour faux." ["It (history) is the narrative of facts presented as being true, as opposed to the fable, which is the narrative of facts presented as being false."] (*Encyclopédie* art: "Histoire.")[39] Overall, Voltaire completes the replacement of theology by modern historiography as the master discourse informing humanity of its place in the cosmos.[40]

As part of this process, one of Voltaire's tactics is to decentralize Jewish history. Bossuet, whose universal history was not universal enough to go outside the lands covered in the Bible, is again the target of choice:

> Cet éloquent écrivain, en disant un mot des Arabes, qui fondèrent un si puissant empire et une religion si florissante, n'en parle que comme d'un déluge de barbares. Il paraît avoir écrit uniquement pour insinuer que tout a été fait dans le monde pour la nation juive; que si Dieu donna l'empire de l'Asie aux Babyloniens, ce fut pour punir les Juifs; si Dieu fit régner Cyrus, ce fut pour les venger; si Dieu envoya les Romains, ce fut encore pour châtier les Juifs. Cela peut être; mais les grandeurs de Cyrus et des Romains ont encore d'autres causes; et Bossuet même ne les a pas omises en parlant de l'esprit des nations.
>
> Il eût été à souhaiter qu'il n'eût pas oublié entièrement les anciens peuples de l'Orient, comme les Indiens et les Chinois, qui ont été si considérables avant que les autres nations fussent formées.

> [This eloquent writer speaks briefly about the Arabs, who founded such a powerful empire and flourishing religion, as of a flood of barbarians. He seems to have written only to imply that everything in the world was done for the sake of the Jewish nation; that if God gave the empire of Asia to the Babylonians, it was to punish the Jews; if God made Cyrus reign, it was in order to avenge them; if God sent the Romans, it was once again to punish the Jews. It may be so, but the greatness of Cyrus and the Romans have other causes, too; and Bossuet himself has not omitted them in speaking of the spirit of nations.

> It would have been more desirable that he not completely forget the ancient peoples of the Orient, such as the Indians and the

Chinese, who were so considerable before the other nations were formed.][41]

Whence the plan of Voltaire's universal history, starting with what he took to be the oldest and most venerable civilization (China), though he does admit in this introduction that there may be older ones still.

By the time Voltaire has reached the history of Islam in the *Essai sur les moeurs*, his expansion of the world's origins, from biblical to Oriental, is well underway. His chapter on "De l'Arabie et de Mahomet" opens as follows:

> De tous les législateurs et de tous les conquérants, il n'en est aucun dont la vie ait été écrite avec plus d'authenticité et dans un plus grand détail par ses contemporains que celle de Mahomet. Ôtez de cette vie les prodiges dont cette partie du monde fut toujours infatuée, le reste est d'une vérité reconnue.

> [Of all the legislators and conquerors, there are none whose life was written with greater authenticity and in more detail by their contemporaries than was that of Mahomet. Remove from this life the prodigies with which this part of the world has always been infatuated, and the rest is recognizably true.][42]

This passage has a Salean ring to it. With this opening, Voltaire sets up the axes of his reading of Muhammad and the dawn of Islam. Muhammad is a legislator and a conqueror. Muhammad is not a myth, though many details of his life are shrouded in legend, much of it of Western provenance. By this point in the *Essai*, the reader knows the connotations: Muhammad belongs to the same select company as Alexander and Charlemagne. Indeed, Voltaire tells us that Muhammad had "l'intrépidité d'Alexandre, sa libéralité, et la sobriété dont Alexandre aurait eu besoin pour être un grand homme en tout." ["The intrepidity of Alexander, his generosity and the sobriety that Alexander would have needed to be a great man in everything."][43] After the victory of 'Umar b. Al-Khaṭṭāb at Madā'in, "Les Perses passent sous la domination d'Omar, plus facilement qu'ils n'avaient subi le joug d'Alexandre." ["The Persians passed under the domination of Omar, more easily than they suffered the yoke of Alexander."][44] (Even the defeated Parsis make the association between Alexander and Muhammad: "Les ignicoles maudissent depuis longtemps dans leurs prières Alexandre et Mahomet; il est à croire qu'ils y ont joint

Sha-Abbas." ["The fire-worshippers have for a long time cursed Alexander and Mahomet in their prayers; it is likely that they have added Shah Abbas."])[45] Muhammad is firmly situated at the center of world history, operating revolutions that change everything: "Le plus grand changement que l'opinion ait produit sur notre globe fut l'établissement de la religion de Mahomet. Ses musulmans, en moins d'un siècle, conquirent un empire plus vaste que l'empire romain." ["The greatest change that opinion has produced in our world was the establishment of the religion of Mahomet. In less than a century, his Muslims conquered an empire more vast than that of Rome."][46] This is a virtual translation of Sale's epistle to the reader, where Muhammad is described as "the founder of an empire which in less than a century spread itself over a greater part of the world than the Romans were ever masters of."[47] What sets Muhammad apart, and what makes him special for Voltaire the historian, is what can be known about him with some certainty. Indeed, the task of separating true from false in the accounts that have come down to us about Muhammad is, from Voltaire's perspective, made easier by the multiplicity of traditions and the ease of deciding what is *vraisemblable* and what is not: "Les Arabes contemporains écrivirent la vie de Mahomet dans le plus grand détail. Tout y ressent la simplicité barbare des temps qu'on nomme héroiques … On voit quels repas apprêtaient ses femmes: on apprend le nom de ses épées et de ses chevaux." ["The Arabs of the time wrote the life of Mahomet in the greatest detail. Everything about it smacks of the barbaric simplicity of the age that we call heroic … We see the meals that his wives prepared; we learn the names of his swords and his horses."][48] Here, then, is an important point of convergence between Voltaire and Muhammad: one solution to the dilemma of pyrrho-skepticism, at once verifiable *and* morally edifying, is the history of the life of Muhammad.

This oscillation between the true and the unlikely dominates Voltaire's reading of Muhammad. The relative absence of miracles in Muhammad's life (with the notable exception of the story of the *mi'rāj*, which poses no end of trouble for Voltaire) makes it somehow more palatable for Voltaire, at least more so than the histories of the other prophets as narrated in the Bible that involve the parting of the seas, the healing of the blind, and so on. For Voltaire, a miracle is a cosmic crime, a contravention of every known law. "C'est ce que la nature ne peut opérer; c'est ce qui est contraire à toutes nos lois." ["It is what nature cannot effect; it is what is contrary to all of our laws."][49]

Muhammad, for all his shortcomings, cannot be accused of having committed such a crime; it is only his followers who, in search of amazement, have imputed miracles to him.

The details of Muhammad's life parallel Voltaire's own. Like Muhammad, Voltaire took pride in having amassed a fortune, and saw this fortune as a means to an end: improving the world, mainly by changing the world's religious ideas, through his writing.[50] Needless to say, their experiences are far from peaceful and often combative. Like Voltaire, the activities that define Muhammad are writing and fighting: "Le fait est qu'il écrivait mal, et qu'il se battait bien." ["The fact is that he wrote badly and fought well."][51] Voltaire considered Muhammad to be the author of the Qur'ān and was openly skeptical of the thesis of Muhammad's status as an "unlettered" prophet. Despite Voltaire's opinion of Muhammad's "bad writing," he nonetheless advises his readers to "Lisez le commencement du *Koran*, il est sublime." ["Read the beginning of the *Koran*; it is sublime."][52] Voltaire foregrounds Muhammad's early experience with war – "Mahomet porta les armes des l'âge de 14 ans dans une guerre sur les confins de la Syrie" ["Mahomet bore arms at fourteen in a war on the Syrian border"] – and his skill as a businessman – "environ neuf cents francs de notre monnaie furent tout le patrimoine de celui qui devait changer la face de la plus grande et la plus belle partie du monde" ["about nine hundred of our Francs were the capital of the man who was to change the greater part of the world"].[53] Similarly, his rise to greatness from relative obscurity is expressed in terms with which Voltaire was familiar. In "De l'Alcoran et de Mahomet" Voltaire writes:

On l'admire pour s'être fait *de marchand de chameaux* pontife, législateur et monarque, pour avoir soumis l'Arabie qui ne l'avait jamais été avant lui, pour avoir donné les premières secousses à l'empire romain.

[He is admired for having turned himself from a *camel merchant* to a pontiff, a legislator and monarch, for having united Arabia, which had never been united before him, and for having made the Roman Empire tremble for the first time.][54]

Muhammad's exile confirms his similarity with Voltaire: "Cette fuite, qu'on nomme *hegira*, devint l'époque de sa gloire et de la fondation de son empire. S'il n'avait pas été persécuté, il n'aurait peut-être pas réussi." ["This flight, which is called *hegira*, became the epoch of his glory and the foundation of his empire. Had he not been persecuted, he would perhaps not have succeeded."] [55] This identification might explain the conditional clauses that abound in Voltaire's treatment of Muhammad. We have already seen one example ("S'il n'avait pas été persécuté [comme Voltaire], il n'aurait peut-être pas réussi"). Another instance is found in "De l'Alcoran et de Mahomet": "A quoi tiennent les révolutions? Un coup de pierre un peu plus fort que celui qu'il reçut dans son premier combat donnait une autre destinée au monde." ["What determines the outcome of a revolution? A stronger throw of a stone than the one that he received in his first battle would have given the world a different destiny."] [56] The uncharacteristically Pascalian tone (cf. Pascal's quip about Cleopatra's nose) struck in passages like these seems to imply that, were it not for a similar sequence of accidents, Voltaire might have ruled the world.

The first such accident is the victory at Badr: "Il battit d'abord, avec cent treize hommes, les Mecquois, qui étaient venus fondre sur lui au nombre de mille. Cette victoire, qui fut un miracle aux yeux de ses sectateurs, les persuada que Dieu combattait pour eux, comme eux pour lui." ["First of all, he beat the Meccans, one thousand of whom attacked him, with about one hundred and thirteen of his men. This victory seemed to his followers to be a miracle, persuading them that God was fighting for them as they fought for him."] [57] If Badr was a miracle, it was primarily one in the eyes of Muhammad's followers, but not necessarily in Muhammad's view. This distinction matters insofar as it confirms Muhammad's status – on the one hand he does not claim to have made any miracles and derives no authority therefrom, but his followers do. This distinction between great men and the agents of "priestcraft" is another constant in Voltaire's thinking and behavior. The more significant part of Badr, for Voltaire, is the belief that God was on the side of the Muslims: the active partnership between the early Muslims and God brings victory. Similarly, Voltaire's take on Muhammad's other conquests is worth close examination:

> De tous les législateurs qui ont fondé des religions, il est le seul qui ait étendu la sienne par les conquêtes. D'autres peuples ont porté leur culte avec le fer et le feu chez des nations étrangères; mais nul fondateur de secte n'avait été conquérant. Ce privilège unique est aux yeux des musulmans l'argument le plus fort que la Divinité prit soin elle-même de seconder leur prophète.

[Of all the legislators who founded religions, he is the only one who expanded his through conquest. Other people brought the fire and the sword to foreign nations, but no founder of a sect has also been a conqueror. In the eyes of the Muslims this unique privilege is the strongest proof that the Deity took personal care to support their prophet.][58]

In Voltaire's eyes, what makes Muhammad unique is the fact that he fights with his followers, rather than letting them take all the risks while he enjoys the benefits.

It is precisely on this point that Voltaire introduces the most important counter-example to Islam: Judaism. It is as if the increasing identification between Voltaire and Muhammad drove him to repeat emphasis of the great differences between the Jews and the Muslims. Voltaire's *Philosophie de l'histoire* takes direct aim at Bossuet's *Discours sur l'histoire universelle* as soon as he invokes the Arabs, adopting a remarkably hostile tone:

On ne les [les Arabes] avait jamais vus ni envahir le bien de leurs voisins comme des bêtes carnassières affamées, ni égorger les faibles, en prétextant les ordres de la divinité, ni faire leur cour aux puissants en les flattant par de faux oracles. Leurs superstitions ne furent ni absurdes ni barbares. On ne parle point d'eux dans nos histoires universelles fabriquées dans notre Occident. Je le crois bien; ils n'ont aucun rapport avec la petite nation juive qui est devenue l'objet et le fondement de nos histoires prétendues universelles, dans lesquelles un certain genre d'auteurs, se copiant les uns les autres, tous oublient les trois quarts de la terre.

[The Arabs were never seen invading their neighbors like ravished carnivorous beasts, nor were they seen slaughtering the weak, claiming divine orders as an excuse, nor were they seen flattering the powerful with false oracles. Their superstitions were neither absurd nor barbaric. They are never mentioned in the universal histories fabricated in our part of the world. I sincerely believe that they have no relationship to the small Jewish nation that has become the object and foundation of our so-called universal histories, in which a certain category of authors forget three-quarters of the world as they copy each other.][59]

The pattern continues in the *Essai sur les moeurs*. Here, both the early Jews and Muslims are described as being tough, warlike peoples. They share "la même ardeur à courir au combat, au nom de la Divinité; la même soif du butin, le même partage des dépouilles" ["the same arduous desire for battle in the name of the Deity; the same thirst for booty, the same division of the spoils"].[60] So much for the moral qualities of the two peoples (what Voltaire calls "les moeurs"). The national histories are, however, very different:

> Mais, en ne considérant ici que les choses humaines, et en faisant toujours abstraction des jugements de Dieu et de ses voies inconnues, pourquoi Mahomet et ses successeurs, qui commencèrent leurs conquêtes précisément comme les Juifs, firent-ils de si grandes choses, et les Juifs de si petites? Ne serait-ce point parce que les musulmans eurent le plus grand soin de soumettre les vaincus à leur religion, tantôt par la force, tantôt par la persuasion? Les Hébreux, au contraire, associèrent rarement les étrangers à leur culte. Les musulmans arabes incorporèrent à eux les autres nations; les Hébreux s'en tinrent toujours séparés. Il paraît enfin que les Arabes eurent un enthousiasme plus courageux, une politique plus généreuse et plus hardie. Le peuple hébreu avait en horreur les autres nations, et craignit toujours d'être asservi; le peuple arabe, au contraire, voulut attirer tout à lui, et se crut fait pour dominer.
>
> Si ces Ismaélites ressemblaient aux Juifs par l'enthousiasme et la soif du pillage, ils étaient prodigieusement supérieurs par le courage, par la grandeur d'âme, par la magnanimité: leur histoire, ou vraie, ou fabuleuse, avant Mahomet, est remplie d'exemples d'amitié tels que la Grèce en inventa dans les fables de Pylade et d'Oreste, de Thésée et de Pirithoüs. L'histoire des Barmécides n'est qu'une suite de générosités inouïes qui élèvent l'âme. Ces traits caractérisent une nation. On ne voit, au contraire, dans toutes les annales du peuple hébreu, aucune action généreuse. Ils ne connaissent ni l'hospitalité, ni la libéralité, ni la clémence. Leur souverain bonheur est d'exercer l'usure avec les étrangers; et cet esprit d'usure, principe de toute lâcheté, est tellement enraciné dans leurs coeurs, que c'est l'objet continuel des figures qu'ils emploient dans l'espèce d'éloquence qui leur est propre. Leur gloire est de mettre à feu et à sang les petits villages dont ils peuvent s'emparer. Ils égorgent les vieillards et les enfants; ils ne réservent que les filles nubiles; ils assassinent leurs maîtres quand ils sont esclaves; ils ne savent jamais pardonner quand ils sont vainqueurs; ils sont les ennemis du genre humain. Nulle politesse, nulle science, nul art perfectionné dans aucun temps chez cette nation atroce. Mais, dès le second siècle de l'hégire, les Arabes deviennent les précepteurs de l'Europe dans les sciences et dans les arts, malgré leur loi qui semble l'ennemie des arts.

[But considering only human affairs, and without regard for the judgments and unknown ways of God, why did Mahomet and his followers, who started their conquests in exactly the same way as the Jews, accomplish such great things, while the Jews accomplished such small ones? Might it not be because the Muslims took the greatest care to subject the vanquished to their religion, sometimes through force and sometimes through persuasion? The Hebrews, on the other hand, rarely allowed foreigners into their religion. The Arab Muslims incorporated the other nations; the Hebrews kept themselves separate. Finally it seems that the Arabs had a more courageous enthusiasm, a more noble and intrepid policy. The Hebrew people were horrified by other nations, and always feared being enslaved to them; the Arabs, on the other hand, wanted to attract everything to themselves, and believed themselves destined to conquer.

If these Ishmaelites had the enthusiasm and thirst for pillage of the Jews, they were far superior by their courage and magnanimity: their pre-Islamic history, whether it be true or false, is full of examples of friendship like those that Greece invented in the fables of Pylades and Orestes, of Theseus and Pirithoüs. The history of the Barmecides is simply a series of unheard-of acts of nobility that elevate the soul. These traits become the characteristics of an entire nation. In the annals of the Hebrew nation, on the other hand, we do not see any noble actions. They know neither hospitality, nor generosity, nor mercy. Their highest happiness is to practice usury with foreigners; and this sort of usury, which is the foundation of cowardice, is so deeply rooted in their hearts that it is continuously used in the rhetorical figures of their native eloquence. Their glory consists of bleeding and burning the little villages that they manage to conquer. They slaughter children and the elderly, sparing only fertile young women; they assassinate their masters when they are enslaved; they never forgive when they are masters; they are the enemies of the human race. No politeness, no science, no art have ever been perfected by this atrocious nation. But, ever since the second century after the *hijra*, the Arabs became the teachers of Europe in the sciences and the arts, despite their faith which seems to be the enemy of the arts.][61]

Voltaire's anti-Semitic gloss on the Bible drives home the point that only the Muslims can be compared to the greatness of ancient Greece and Rome, the true ancestors of the culture of Voltaire and his readers:

Il est évident que le génie du people arabe, mis en mouvement par Mahomet, fit tout de lui-même pendant près de trois siècles, et ressembla en cela au génie des anciens Romains ... Dès l'an 671, ils assiégèrent Constantinople, qui devrait un jour devenir mahométane; les divisions, presque inévitables parmi tant de chefs audacieux, n'arrêtèrent pas leurs conquêtes. Ils ressemblèrent en ce point aux anciens Romains, qui parmi leurs guerres civiles avaient subjugué l'Asie Mineure.

[It is evident that the spirit of the Arab people, once put in motion by Mahomet, worked by itself for almost three centuries, and in this respect resembled the ancient Romans ... Since the year 671, they lay siege to Constantinople, which would one day become Mahometan; the almost inevitable divisions among so many daring chieftains did not stop their conquests. In this respect they resembled the ancient Romans, who subjugated Asia Minor during their civil wars.][62]

Furthermore, the history of Arabia legitimizes the entire Western literary canon, from Homer and Herodotus to Ariosto and Tasso:

Il est évident que les combats des Amazones, dont parlent Homère et Hérodote, ne sont point fondés sur des fables. Les femmes de la tribu d'Imiar, de l'Arabie Heureuse, étaient guerrières, et combattaient dans les armées d'Abubéker et d'Omar. On ne doit pas croire qu'il y ait jamais eu un royaume des Amazones, où les femmes vécussent sans hommes; mais dans les temps et dans les pays où l'on menait une vie agreste et pastorale, il n'est pas surprenant que des femmes, aussi durement élevées que les hommes, aient quelquefois combattu comme eux. On voit surtout au siège de Damas une de ces femmes, de la tribu d'Imiar, venger la mort de son mari tué à ses côtés, et percer d'un coup de flèche le commandant de la ville. Rien ne justifie plus l'Arioste et le Tasse, qui dans leurs poèmes font combattre tant d'héroïnes.

[It is obvious that the Amazon battles that Homer and Herodotus mention are not founded on fables. The women of the tribe of Imiar, from Arabia Felix, were warriors who fought in the armies of Abubeker and Omar. We must never believe that there was a kingdom of Amazons, where women lived without men; but in the times and places where agrarian, pastoral lives were led, it would not have been surprising to see that women, who were raised in as tough a manner as the men, sometimes fought by their sides. In the siege of Damascus, we see one of these women from the tribe of Imiar avenging the death of her husband who fell by her side, and piercing the side of the commander of the city with an arrow. There is no greater justification for the poems of Ariosto and Tasso, who make so many heroines fight in their poems.][63]

Indeed, thanks to the Arabs and their extraordinary *moeurs*, history can become the rival of the epic:

> Les discours des héros arabes à la tête des armées, ou dans les combats singuliers, ou en jurant des trêves, tiennent tous de ce naturel qu'on trouve dans Homère; mais ils ont incomparablement plus d'enthousiasme et de sublime.

[The speeches of the Arab heroes at the heads of the armies, or in individual combat, or in swearing a truce, all have that natural quality that we find in Homer, but they are incomparably more enthusiastic and sublime.][64]

The implication seems to be that, by writing the history of the Arabs, Voltaire is reaching for epic status himself. It is difficult to avoid the feeling that Voltaire would gladly have written a tragedy on some topic taken from the history of the Arabs.[65] Indeed, so moved is Voltaire by the history of Harūn Al-Rashīd and the Barmecides that he breaks into song *and* seizes the occasion to boast of his writing ability:

> Mortel, faible mortel, à qui le sort prospère
> Fait goûter de ses dons les charmes dangereux,
> Connais quelle est des rois la faveur passagère;
> Contemple Barmécide, et tremble d'être heureux.
> Ce dernier vers surtout est traduit mot à mot. Rien ne me paraît plus beau que *tremble d'être heureux.*

[Mortal, feeble mortal, whom prosperous fate
Gives a taste of its dangerous charms,
Know the passing favour of kings,
Contemple Barmécide, and tremble in the face of happiness.
This last verse is translated word for word. Nothing seems to me more beautiful than *tremble in the face of happiness.*][66]

Of course, Voltaire does not tell his reader the "mot à mot" translation is based on a French text found in D'Herbelot's article "Barmekian" in the *Bibliothèque orientale.* The last paragraph of the article reads:

> Un Poëte Persien de ces tems-là voulant désabuser les gens de la Cour de la vanité des grandeurs du monde, & de la faveur des Princes par

l'exemple des Barmecides, fit un quatrain dont le sens étoit:
Nourrisson de la fortune qui succez pendant quelques jours le lait de
la prospérité qui coule de ses mamelles empoisonnées,
Ne te vante pas trop du bonheur de cet état, pendant que tu es dans le
berceau suspendu & branlant de la vie
Souviens-toi seulement du tems auquel tu as vu la grandeur des
Barmecides.

[A Persian poet of this period, wanting to disabuse the courtiers of the
vanity of this world and of the favour of princes using the Barmecides
as an example, composed a quatrain whose meaning was:
Fortune's infant, who suck for a few days the milk of prosperity that
flows from her poisoned breasts,
Do not boast of your happiness in this state, while you hang in life's
rocking cradle,
Only remember the time where you experienced the glory of the
Barmecides.][67]

Voltaire could not have failed to be moved, or at least identify with,
the rise and fall of Abbāsid court favorites and intellectuals.

In the *Essai,* the Qur'ān is introduced through a citation meant
to document Muhammad's status as an Abrahamic prophet (Q3).
Typically, Voltaire betrays a remarkable degree of understanding by
going straight to the heart of this long and complicated chapter which
is built around the leitmotif of Abrahamic genealogy. He also makes
Muhammad something of a deist like himself, dedicated to the worship of the one true God without the "disfigurations" of the other
religions:

Il prétendait rétablir le culte simple d'Abraham ou Ibrahim, dont il se
disait descendu, et rappeler les hommes à l'unité d'un dieu, dogme
qu'il s'imaginait être défiguré dans toutes les religions. C'est en effet
ce qu'il déclare expressément dans le troisième Sura ou chapitre de
son Koran. "Dieu connaît, et vous ne connaissez pas. Abraham n'était
ni juif ni chrétien, mais il était de la vraie religion. Son cœur était
résigné à Dieu; il n'était point du nombre des idolâtres." [i.e. Q3:66–
67: وَاللّٰهُ يَعْلَمُ وَأَنْتُمْ لَا تَعْلَمُونَ (66) مَا كَانَ إِبْرَاهِيمُ يَهُودِيًّا وَلَا نَصْرَانِيًّا وَلَكِنْ
كَانَ حَنِيفًا مُسْلِمًا وَمَا كَانَ مِنَ الْمُشْرِكِينَ]

[He claimed to restore the simple cult of Abraham or Ibrahim, from
whom he claimed to be descended, and to recall men to the dogma of
the unity of God, which he claimed had been distorted in all religions.
This is in effect what we read clearly in the third Sura or chapter of

his *Koran*: "God knows, and you do not know. Abraham was neither a Christian nor Jew, but he was of the true religion. His heart was resigned to God, and who was not at all among the idolators."][68]

Sale translates the verse in question, Q3:67, thus: "Abraham was neither a Jew nor a Christian; but he was of the true religion, one resigned *unto God*, and was not of the *number of the* idolaters."[69] It is significant that both Sale and, following him, Voltaire, translate the phrase that identifies Abraham's religion, *hanīf Muslim* [مسلما حنيفا], by "one resigned unto God" or, in Voltaire's more poetic rendition, "son coeur était résigné à Dieu," thereby accentuating the similarity between deism, as they saw it, and Islam. Voltaire's understanding of the Abrahamic genealogy of Islam and his comparison between Muslims and Jews may well have been influenced by Sale's notes to this and the other long sūras, where the revelation of numerous verses on the occasion of the disputes between Muhammad and the Jews of Arabia are spelled out in detail.[70]

Voltaire's skepticism about Muhammad's illiteracy is of a piece with his belief that poetry can change the world. The status of writing as a common element between the two is significant insofar as Voltaire considered Muhammad to be the author of the Qur'ān and questioned Muhammad's status as an "unlettered" prophet:

Ce n'était pas sans doute un ignorant, comme quelques-uns l'ont prétendu. Il fallait bien même qu'il fût très savant pour sa nation et pour son temps, puisqu'on a de lui quelques aphorismes de médecine, et qu'il réforma le calendrier des Arabes, comme César celui des Romains. Il se donne, à la vérité, le titre de prophète non lettré; mais on peut savoir écrire, et ne pas s'arroger le nom de savant. Il était poète; la plupart des derniers versets de ses chapitres sont rimés; le reste est en prose cadencée. La poésie ne servit pas peu à rendre son *Alcoran* respectable.

[He was probably not an ignorant man, as some have claimed. He must have been very learned by the standards of his nation and his age, since we have some medical aphorisms by him, and since he reformed the calendar of the Arabs, as Caesar did that of the Romans. It is true that he takes the title of the unlettered prophet, but one can know how to write without calling oneself learned. He was a poet; most of the verses of the last part of his chapters are in rhyme, the rest in cadenced prose. Poetry was quite useful in making his *Alcoran* respectable.][71]

Voltaire would probably have found it easy to identify with a learned man who used poetry to advance his ideas, and had been fascinated by the overwhelming importance of eloquence in seventh-century Arabia.

Les Arabes faisaient un très grand cas de la poésie; et lorsqu'il y avait un bon poète dans une tribu, les autres tribus envoyaient une ambassade de félicitations à celle qui avait produit un auteur, qu'on regardait comme inspiré et comme utile. On affichait les meilleures poésies dans le temple de la Mecque; et quand on y afficha le second chapitre de Mahomet, qui commence ainsi: "Il ne faut point douter; c'est ici la science des justes, de ceux qui croient aux mystères, qui prient quand il le faut, qui donnent avec générosité, etc" [i.e. Q2:2–3, very loosely translated][72] alors le premier poète de la Mecque, nommé Abid [i.e. Labīd b. Rabī'a], déchira ses propres vers affichés au temple, admira Mahomet, et se rangea sous sa loi.[73] Voilà des moeurs, des usages, des faits si différents de tout ce qui se passe parmi nous qu'ils doivent nous montrer combien le tableau de l'univers est varié, et combien nous devons être en garde contre notre habitude de juger de tout par nos usages.

[The Arabs took poetry very seriously; when a tribe had a good poet, the other tribes sent embassies of congratulation to the one that produced an author, who was considered inspired and useful. The best poems were hung in the temple of Mecca, and when they hung there the second chapter of Mahomet, which starts thus: "Let there be no doubt, this is the knowledge of the just, those who believe in the mysteries, who pray when they must, who give generously etc." [i.e. Q2:2–3 very loosely translated], the foremost Meccan poet named Abid [i.e. Labīd b. Rabī'a] tore his own verses that were hanging in the temple, admired Mahomet, and followed his law. Those mores, customs and facts differ so much from what happens among us that they demonstrate how varied is the scene of the universe, and how we must guard against our habit of judging everything by our customs.][74]

Far from being a mere warning against chauvinism, there is a hortatory note in this passage. Voltaire seems to imply that it would be a good thing if poets were as esteemed, and as influential, in the West as they were in Muhammad's day and age. Voltaire's historiography, open as it is to "other cultures," envisions possibilities undreamed of in the closed world of Bossuet.

Voltaire's treatment of the Qur'ān in the following chapter of the *Essai sur les moeurs* continues the pattern of sympathy and loose paraphrase. He finds that Muslim law conforms to nature (unlike the laws of other nations, which is completely un-natural): "L'Orient a décidé cette question [la polygamie] dans tous les siècles, et la nature est d'accord avec les peuples orientaux, dans presque tout espèce animale chez qui plusieurs femelles n'ont qu'un mâle."[75] ["The Orient has settled this question (polygamy) for all time, and nature agrees with the Oriental peoples, in almost every animal species where several females have only one male."] The Qur'ān is not the Bible, though both books preach a common morality:

Ce n'est point un livre historique dans lequel on ait voulu imiter les livres des Hébreux et nos Évangiles; ce n'est pas non plus un livre purement de lois, comme le *Lévitique* ou le *Deutéronome,* ni un recueil de psaumes et de cantiques, ni une vision prophétique et allégorique dans le goût de *l'Apocalypse;* c'est un mélange de tous ces divers genres, un assemblage de sermons dans lesquels on trouve quelques faits, quelques visions, des révélations, des lois religieuses et civiles.

Le *Koran* est devenu le code de la jurisprudence, ainsi que la loi canonique, chez toutes les nations mahométanes. Tous les interprètes de ce livre conviennent que sa morale est contenue dans ces paroles: "Recherchez qui vous chasse; donnez à qui vous ôte; pardonnez à qui vous offense; faites du bien à tous; ne contestez point avec les ignorants [i.e. Q7:199, loosely translated]."

[This is no historical book where the aim was to imitate the books of the Hebrews and our Gospels; nor is it a pure book of laws, like *Leviticus* and *Deuteronomy*, nor a collection of psalms and canticles, nor a prophetic apocalyptic vision in the manner of the *Apocalypse*; it is a mixture of all of these diverse genres, an assemblage of sermons in which we find some facts, some visions, some revelations, and civil and religious laws.

The *Koran* has become the code of jurisprudence, as well as canon law, in all Mahometan nations. All of the interpreters of this book agree that its moral message is contained in these words: "Seek those who persecute you; give to those who take from you; forgive those who offend you; do good to all and do not argue with the ignorant."][76]

Voltaire's source here is not Sale (or at least not only Sale), but D'Herbelot's article "Afu' & Afou" ["Forgiveness"] in the

Bibliothèque orientale. Voltaire's text echoes the third paragraph of the article, which reads:

> Au chapitre intitulé Aarâf [i.e. Q7] il y a un précepte de morale, que les Interprétes[77] disent être le plus excellent de tous ceux qui se trouvent dans l'Alcoran. Le voici: Regardez toujours ce qu'il y a de bon dans un chacun, & ne faites point d'attention a ce qu'il y a de mal: Pardonnez aisément aux autres, faites du bien à tous, & fuyez surtout la compagnie des ignorans, des opiniâtres & des querelleux [all three adjectives translate الجاهلين]. L'Auteur du Keschâf [i.e. Zamakhsharī] rapporte qu'après que Gabriel eut donné de la part de Dieu ce verset à Mahomet (car c'est ainsi que les bons Musulmans parlent) celui-ci lui demanda le sens, & l'explication de ce qui regarde le pardon. Alors l'Ange lui dit, Ces paroles signifient: Attachez-vous à ceux qui vous chassent:[78] donnez à ceux qui vous ôtent: pardonnez à ceux qui vous outragent; car Dieu veut que vous plantiez dans voz ames les racines de ses plus grandes perfections." L'imposture des Mahometans est visible en cet endroit, car il est très-certain que ce qu'il font dire dans l'entretien de Gabriel avec Mahomet, est tiré mot à mot des paroles de JESUS-CHRIST qui sont couchées dans l'Evangile.

> [In the chapter entitled *Aaràf* (i.e. Q7) there is a moral precept that the interpreters say is the most excellent of those found in the Alcoran. Here it is: *Consider the good that there is in everyone, & pay no attention to the bad: Forgive others easily, do good to all, & above all flee the company of the ignorant, the opinionated and the querulous* (all three adjectives translate الجاهلين). The Author of the Keschâf (i.e. Zamakhsharī) reports that after Gabriel had transmitted this verse from God to Muhammad (for it is thus that good Muslims speak) the latter asked him about their meaning and an explanation of pardon. The Angel then said to him, "These words mean: Attach yourself to those who persecute you; give to those who take from you; forgive those who outrage you; for God wants you to plant the roots of his highest perfections in your souls." The imposture of the Mahometans is visible in this place, for it is very certain that what they have Gabriel say in his conversation with Mahomet is taken word for word from the words of JESUS CHRIST as they are found in the Gospel.]

The fact that the Muslim understanding of forgiveness mattered to Voltaire is emphasized by the fact that this page is bookmarked in his edition of the *Bibliothèque orientale*.[79] Furthermore, Voltaire could not have failed to notice the prevalence of forgiveness and mercy as themes in the Qur'ān, whether as a form of divine grace or as an ethical imperative.[80] Although D'Herbelot adds the usual denunciation of imposture, refusing to believe that the Qur'ān could possibly command anything so close to Christian humility and forgiveness, Voltaire is happy to maintain the ethical parallel across the two faiths.

Voltaire finds the anti-Trinitarian Muslim confession of faith "sublime":

> Sa définition de Dieu est d'un genre plus véritablement sublime. On lui demandait quel était cet Allah qu'il annonçait: "C'est celui qui tient l'être de lui-même, et de qui les autres le tiennent; qui n'engendre point et qui ne s'est point engendre, et qui rien n'est semblable dans toute l'étendue des êtres." [i.e. Q112, لَمْ يَلِدْ وَلَمْ يُولَدْ (3) وَلَمْ يَكُنْ لَهُ كُفُوًا أَحَدٌ قُلْ هُوَ اللَّهُ أَحَدٌ (1) اللَّهُ الصَّمَدُ (2), loosely translated.] Cette fameuse réponse, consacrée dans tout l'Orient, se trouve presque mot à mot dans l'antépénultième chapitre du Coran.

> [His definition of God is of a more truly sublime sort. He was asked who was this Allah that he proclaimed: "He is the one who receives his being from himself, and from whom others receive theirs; who does not engender and who was not engendered, and whom nothing is equal in the entire extent of all that is" (i.e. Q112, loosely translated). This famous response, consecrated throughout the Orient, is found almost word for word in the ante-penultimate chapter of the Coran.][81]

So important is this issue to Voltaire that he inscribed a first version of his translation in the margins of his copy of the Sale translation, *ad loc.*: "dieu/est letre eternel/il n'a ny fils/ny pere, rien/n'est semblable a luy."[82] Sale's translation reads: "SAY, God is one GOD; the eternal GOD: he begetteth not, neither is he begotten: and there is not any one like unto him." Voltaire's paraphrase of Sale elides God's unity in favor of His status as absolute first cause and creator. Nor is this Voltaire's sole point of attachment on this issue. Elsewhere, he annotates Sale's translation of Q4:172 [لَنْ يَسْتَنْكِفَ الْمَسِيحُ أَنْ يَكُونَ عَبْدًا لِلَّهِ وَلَا الْمَلَائِكَةُ الْمُقَرَّبُونَ وَمَنْ يَسْتَنْكِفْ عَنْ عِبَادَتِهِ وَيَسْتَكْبِرْ فَسَيَحْشُرُهُمْ إِلَيْهِ جَمِيعًا]: "ne dites point/il y a trois/dieux,/jesu na/pas eu linso/lence de se/faire Dieu," thereby translating Sale's phrase "Christ doth not proudly disdain to be a servant unto God" [i.e. لَنْ يَسْتَنْكِفَ الْمَسِيحُ أَنْ يَكُونَ عَبْدًا لِلَّهِ] into much stronger terms – instead of "not disdaining to serve God," Voltaire's Christ has avoided the insolence of making himself a God.[83] This, too, helps explain the rapid spread of Islam: "Le dogme surtout de l'unité d'un Dieu, présenté sans mystère, et proportionné à l'intelligence humaine, rangea sous sa loi une foule de nations, et jusqu'à des nègres dans l'Afrique, et à des insulaires dans l'Océan indien."[84] ["Above all the dogma of the unity of God, presented without mysteries, and adequate to human intelligence, brought under his law a whole crowd of nations, including African negroes and Island-dwellers of the Indian Ocean."]

Overall, Voltaire's strategy in the second part of this chapter is, like Sale, to underline the familiar nature of Islam and the fundamental similarity of all religions: "Une chose qui peut surprendre bien des lecteurs, c'est qu'il n'y eut rien de nouveau dans la loi de Mahomet, sinon que Mahomet était prophète de Dieu."[85]["One thing that might surprise a number of readers is that there was nothing new about the law of Mahomet apart from the fact that Mahomet was the prophet of God."] And yet, in terms of historical development, Islam and Christianity are poles apart. The former starts from the stern law of Muhammad and the fanaticism of his followers to the flourish of Andalusia and the Abbāsid court. The latter starts with the sweetness of the savior, only to end in the spectacle of intolerance that is early modern Europe:

> Le législateur des musulmans, homme puissant et terrible, établit ses dogmes par son courage et par ses armes; cependant sa religion devint indulgente et tolérante. L'instituteur divin du christianisme, vivant dans l'humilité et dans la paix, prêcha le pardon des outrages; et sa sainte et douce religion est devenue, par nos fureurs, la plus intolérante de toutes, et la plus barbare.

> [The legislator of the Muslims, a powerful and terrible man, established his dogmas with his arms and courage; however his religion became indulgent and tolerant. The divine institutor of Christianity, living in peace and humility, preached pardon, and his holy, sweet religion became, through our fury, the most intolerant and barbaric of all.][86]

Apart from being written *contra* Bossuet, Voltaire's reading of world history owes much to Sale's translation of the Qur'ān. One further point of attachment for Voltaire comes in the narratives of the battle of Badr, which in the Qur'ān are modeled on the confrontation between Moses and the Egyptians.[87] Following his demythologization of Jewish history in his polemic with Bossuet, Voltaire proceeds to attack the latter's construction of Moses as *the* paradigmatic legislator. Voltaire writes about Moses repeatedly as a failed leader, both as a means of displacing the Bible and defining what it means to be a "grand homme." Voltaire's anti-Mosaic rhetoric is especially surprising in view of the numerous works in the eighteenth century – many of them by authors with which Voltaire was familiar (Spencer, Warburton, Toland, and Cudworth, among others) – that read Moses as a man initiated into all the mysteries of the universe, a natural philosopher, and prophet of deism *avant la lettre*.[88] The two qualities of Moses that are foregrounded in these contexts are his ability to legislate and his skill in decoding the secret language of the cosmos.[89] Voltaire's Moses, on the other hand, which is based on a very close reading of the Bible, comes across as being the hopelessly inept, inarticulate patriarch who led a most intolerant people on a quest for a supposedly promised land, and the latter as a bunch of cowards good only for conquest and oppression.[90]

Reading the Qur'ān probably gave Voltaire much food for thought in this regard. Moses is mentioned more frequently in the Qur'ān than any other prophet. Only Abraham seems to enjoy similar stature, though he runs a distant second.[91] A significant portion of Muslim identity and self-understanding, as gleaned from the Qur'ān, revolves around these two figures.[92] Like any nascent culture, Islam had to define itself against what was already there when it was formed. What was already there was, in very large part, Christianity and Judaism. Consequently, Islam behaved like young cultures do: first taking from those cultures what it needed to legitimize itself, before moving on to distinguish itself from its predecessors in its later stages.[93] This distinction is primarily mapped through normative inversion: reversing the laws of the predecessors.[94] The creedal and ceremonial history of Islam, therefore, proceeds from similarity to difference, starting out as a monotheism that resembles the others before becoming something opposed to them.

Voltaire re-traces this history through the oppositions between Arabs and Jews on the one hand and Muhammad and Moses on the other. Voltaire's contrast of the two prophets is not entirely original. Not only had Boulainvilliers done the same in his *Vie de Mahomet*, but the literature comparing the two figures goes back to the *Traité des trois imposteurs*.[95] But Voltaire's systematic attention to historical detail, his repeated returns to certain themes, and his impact on subsequent historiography are all reasons to examine his work in detail.

This strain runs through several of the historical and polemical works of the late Voltaire. Its import, as will be seen below, is instructive insofar as it operates not only as an attack on the institutional forms of Christianity, but also, and perhaps more significantly, as the moment that sets up the role of the modern intellectual. The sacerdotal class against which Voltaire takes aim repeatedly was itself charged with the interpretation of texts and laws. Through his writings Voltaire charges these readers and interpreters with a different task: to change the world.

The development of the Moses story in the Qur'ān and the early history of Islam involves the use of some key linguistic and thematic markers that establish their similarities and differences. Both Muhammad and Moses have "books": the former the Qur'ān, the latter the Pentateuch (which the Qur'ān calls the Torah). Furthermore, the existence of both books as divine texts is meant to divide the world history into pre- and post-revelation, and the audience into believers and unbelievers. Hence the other term that is used to describe these texts in the Qur'ān: *furqān* [فرقان], an almost untranslatable term, but whose root, *frq*, gives us the Arabic words for difference, distinction, division, and whose etymology has been linked to the Syriac *purqāna* (salvation).[96] The trajectory of the Qur'ānic account of Moses becomes a model for the evolution of Muhammad's message, from one based on breaking with Meccan norms to one aimed at founding a functional political community.[97] Variously defined as a criterion, as a marker and maker of differences, the *furqān* is the thing that makes the world intelligible after the advent of monotheism. Henceforth there will be an "us" and a "them," believers of the one true God and miscreants, Muslims and *kuffār*. Although Voltaire does not address *al-furqān* specifically, he seems to be one reader of the Sale Qur'ān who has fully grasped its operation and put it to good use in his own thinking.

For Voltaire, the history of the Jews is that of a beleaguered people who become cruel and bloodthirsty as they acquire kings and (meager) kingdoms. The Arabs, on the other hand, manage to conquer and civilize vast tracts of the globe under Muhammad's leadership. The reason as to why this should be so can be found in Voltaire's reading of the two religions. The difference between them is to be found in the contrast between the God of Islam and the God of Israel, between the prophets of the Old Testament and the Messenger of Islam.[98] One of the salient features of the God of Israel, in Voltaire's estimation, is his hyperactivity. He is a superagent, doing everything while his messengers and appointed representatives do nothing. In *La Bible enfin expliquée*, Voltaire writes:

> Si on demande pourquoi Josué fils de Nun ne ravagea pas, et ne conquit pas toute l'Égypte, toute la Syrie et le reste du monde pour y faire régner la vraie religion, et pourquoi il ne porta le fer et la flamme que dans cinq ou six lieues de pays tout au plus, et encore dans un très mauvais pays en comparaison des campagnes immenses arrosées du Nil et de l'Euphrate? Ce n'est pas à nous à sonder les décrets de Dieu. Il nous suffit de savoir que depuis Moise et Josué les juifs n'approchèrent jamais du Nil et de l'Euphrate que pour y être vendus comme esclaves; tant les jugements de Dieu sont impénétrables. Dieu ne cesse jamais de parler à Moïse et à Josué; Dieu conduit tout; Dieu fait tout; il dit plusieurs fois à Josué: sois robuste, ne crains rien, car ton dieu est avec toi. Josué ne fait rien que par l'ordre exprès de Dieu.

> [If the question were asked as to why Joshua, the son of Nun, did not lay waste to and conquer Egypt, Syria and the rest of the world to make the true religion reign there, and why he only brought the fire and the sword to five or six leagues of the countryside at most, and to very bad land at that compared with the immense landscapes irrigated by the Nile and Euphrates? It is not for us to examine the inscrutable decrees of God. It is enough for us to know that since the time of Moses and Joshua the Jews only approached the Nile and the Euphrates to be sold as slaves there; such are the impenetrable judgments of God. God never stops talking to Moses and Joshua; God manages everything, God does everything; he says several times to Joshua: be robust, fear nothing, for your God is with you. Joshua does nothing without God's express command.][99]

It bears pointing out that the "porter le fer et la flamme" phrase is Voltairean code for historical figures that he likes and respects: Charlemagne "porta le fer et la flame" all over Europe in the *Essai sur les moeurs*, as did Alexander the Great and Muhammad. The trouble with Joshua is that he did not take the same initiatives as these "great men"; he just restricted himself to a few leagues in the desert.

Voltaire's evaluation of Moses as a political leader follows a similar pattern:

> Il est peint décrépit et bègue. Il ne conduit ses suivants que dans des solitudes affreuses pendant quarante années: il veut leur donner un établissement, et il ne leur en donne aucun ... Il est à la tête de six cent

mille combattants, et il ne pourvoit ni au vêtement ni à la subsistance de ses troupes. Dieu fait tout, Dieu remédie à tout; il nourrit, il vêtit le peuple par des miracles. Moïse n'est donc rien par lui-même, et son impuissance montre qu'il ne peut être guidé que par le bras du Tout-Puissant.

[He is depicted as a decrepit stammerer. He just leads his followers into frightening solitudes for forty years; he wants to get them established somewhere, but he does not ... He is at the head of six hundred thousand fighters, and provides neither food nor clothing for his troops. God does everything, God remedies everything; he clothes the people through miracles. Moses is therefore nothing by himself, his impotence shows that he can only be guided by the arm of the Almighty.][100]

The God of Israel does everything; Joshua and Moses are merely passive instruments of his will with no ideas or plans of their own. Repetition from a mind as fertile as Voltaire's ("Dieu fait tout") implies importance: this is the defining trait of the relationship between the God of Israel and his prophets in Voltaire's opinion.

The image evoked by Voltaire at the start of the first passage quoted above – that of the prophet conquering the countries around him – is instructive, for that is precisely the defining characteristic of Muhammad. Unlike Joshua and Moses, Muhammad is an aggressive go-getter. Far from making him suspect in Voltaire's eyes as it had all other western commentators, Muhammad's engagement with the things of this world – war and peace, business, and conquest – endear him to the Enlightened philosopher's heart: "Il vanquit toujours, et toujours ses victoires furent remportées par le petit nombre sur le grand. Conquérant, législateur, monarque et pontife, il joua le plus grand rôle qu'on puisse jouer sur la terre aux yeux du commun des hommes ..."[101] Of course, he did not play the greatest role of all in Voltaire's estimation: "mais les sages lui préféreront toujours Confutzée, précisément parce qu'il ne fut rien de tout cela, et qu'il se contenta d'enseigner la morale la plus pure à une nation plus ancienne, plus nombreuse et plus policée que la nation arabe."[102]["He always won, and his victories were always carried off by a smaller number against a greater one. As a conqueror, legislator, monarch, and pontiff, he played the greatest role that can be played on earth in the eyes of the common people, but the wise will always prefer Confucius, precisely because he was none of these things, and because he was content to teach the purest morality to a more ancient, more populated, and more polite nation than the Arab nation."]

The moment that brings together the themes of distinction and conquest is the battle of Badr, which is described in Q8:41 as "the day of the *furqān*" [يَوْمَ الفُرْقان]. The day of the *furqān* might be rendered as "the moment of truth." *Furqān* is, as we have seen above, a criterion, an instance that sets up a fundamental distinction, a marker of difference that produces further differences. And the distinction, in this case, is between truth and falsity, orthodoxy and heresy, just and unjust, the communities of believers and unbelievers, consequently those against whom war was allowed and those against whom war would be illegitimate. After Badr, the Muslims know who they are and who the enemy is. Badr is a pivotal moment in a number of respects: after Badr both the Ramaḍān fast and *jihād* become an integral part of Muslim praxis, and once Voltaire reads the passage it seems to become part of his own. The traditional interpretation of this key event in the life of Muhammad is that his small army of believers won the battle (and, eventually, the war against Arabian polytheism [*kufr*]) because God reinforced their number with thousands of angels. Although Voltaire does not take the claim of a "miraculous" victory seriously, he does not contest it, contenting himself with the phrase "aux yeux de ses sectateurs" to underline the difference between sacerdotal and popular belief. In the Qur'ānic account of the battle of Badr, the heavenly reinforcements that God brought to Muhammad's army are repeatedly emphasized (Q8:9, 8:12, 8:65–66). Several writers have argued that Badr is to the narrative of Muhammad's prophecy what Exodus was to that of Moses: a moment of cleavage, of a radical break with a past and a place henceforth defined as the enemy.[103] Exodus marks the point in the Mosaic narrative where Voltaire loses respect for Moses. Not coincidentally, it is also the place where the Mosaic narrative expresses the distinction between true and false in religion – Egypt represents the polytheistic Other that has been rejected.[104] Richard Bell sums it up eloquently:

The occurrences of the word appear to come in revelations which may be dated shortly before and after the battle of Badr ... If the Furqān is a part of the Qur'ān, it is the aspect of it expressing the significance of the victory of Badr – the deliverance of the Muslims and their separation from the unbelievers, the assurance of divine approval, the establishment of the Muslims as a distinct community.[105]

It is therefore against the juncture of Exodus and Badr (Exodus being to Moses what Badr was to Muhammad) that we should read Voltaire's view of Islam. And this view decidedly favors Muhammad, who, unlike Moses, actually takes arms for his cause and emerges victorious.

This connection between Badr and Exodus was not lost on earlier commentators on the Qur'ān. George Sale inserts the following explanatory footnote *ad* Q8:5 ("As thy LORD brought thee forth from thy house with truth; and part of the believers were averse *to thy directions*" [كَمَا أَخْرَجَكَ رَبُّكَ مِنْ بَيْتِكَ بِالْحَقِّ وَإِنَّ فَرِيقًا مِنَ الْمُؤْمِنِينَ لَكَارِهُونَ] :)

"Mokdâd [Ebn Amru] in particular assured him that they were all ready to obey his orders, and would not say to him as the children of Israel did to Moses, *Go thou and thy LORD to fight, for we will sit here*; but, *Go thou and thy LORD to fight, and we will fight with you*."[106] Now, the first part of Mokdâd's statement is, as Sale notes, an allusion to another verse, Q5:24 [قَالُوا يَا مُوسَى إِنَّا لَنْ نَدْخُلَهَا أَبَدًا مَا دَامُوا فِيهَا فَاذْهَبْ أَنْتَ وَرَبُّكَ فَقَاتِلَا إِنَّا هَاهُنَا قَاعِدُونَ] : "They replied: O Moses, we will never enter *the land*, while they remain therein: go therefore thou, and thy LORD, and fight; for we will sit here."[107] The result of this diffident, impious attitude in the Qur'ānic version of Exodus is punishment: the Jews are condemned to wander the earth for forty years – "Moses said, O LORD, surely I am not master of any except myself and my brother; therefore make a distinction between us and the ungodly people. *God* answered, Verily the land shall be forbidden them forty years; *during which time* they shall wander *like men astonished* in the earth" [قَالَ رَبِّ إِنِّي لَا أَمْلِكُ إِلَّا نَفْسِي وَأَخِي فَافْرُقْ بَيْنَنَا وَبَيْنَ الْقَوْمِ الْفَاسِقِينَ (25) قَالَ فَإِنَّهَا مُحَرَّمَةٌ عَلَيْهِمْ أَرْبَعِينَ سَنَةً يَتِيهُونَ فِي الْأَرْضِ].[108] This is, of course, a punishment narrative: the Jews are condemned to wander the desert because they do not listen to Moses.[109]

Moses' words in this instance are especially important. When he asks God to "make a distinction" (افرق) his language recalls certain other instances in the Qur'ān where the just and the unjust are separated by divine will. Badr is one such moment; an overdetermined episode both in the text of the Qur'ān and in Islamic history. There are other moments where the word appears, noticeably in the title of Q25, which Sale translates simply as "Al-Furqān," but which is usually interpreted as another word for the Qur'ān. The Qur'ān is therefore the criterion that divides Muslims from other "people of the book" (other monotheists) and unbelievers.[110] The other notable instance in which this word appears is in reference to Moses in Q21:48 [وَلَقَدْ آتَيْنَا مُوسَى وَهَارُونَ الْفُرْقَانَ وَضِيَاءً وَذِكْرًا لِلْمُتَّقِينَ]: "We formerly gave unto Moses and Aaron the *Law* [al-furqān] being a distinction between good and evil, and a light and admonition unto the pious, who fear their LORD in secret, and who dread the hour of judgment."[111] This particular instance is especially important, because it re-emphasizes the relationship of *furqān* to the Mosaic narrative, and specifically to that part of the narrative that effects the distinction between the just and the unjust; namely Exodus. Although there is no verse in the Qur'ān explicitly saying something like "Badr is the Muslim Exodus," the use of the phrase "yawm al-furqān" in Q8:41 and the language of the narrative are revealing (no pun intended), constantly evoking the action of God *in conjunction with* (not instead of) human agency. Q8:17 reads: "And ye slew not *those who were slain at BEDR yourselves,* but God slew them. Neither didst thou, O Muhammad, cast *the gravel into their eyes,* when thou *didst seem to* cast *it,* but God cast *it,* that he might prove the true believers by a gracious trial from himself; for God heareth *and* knoweth [فَلَمْ تَقْتُلُوهُمْ وَلَكِنَّ اللَّهَ قَتَلَهُمْ وَمَا رَمَيْتَ إِذْ رَمَيْتَ وَلَكِنَّ اللَّهَ رَمَى وَلِيُبْلِيَ الْمُؤْمِنِينَ مِنْهُ بَلَاءً حَسَنًا إِنَّ اللَّهَ سَمِيعٌ عَلِيمٌ]."[112] Divine intervention is everywhere in evidence in the story of Badr, but only once the human initiative and will to fight have been asserted. The movement is therefore from an impossible situation – two armies of unequal size and strength – to divine intervention and to the conclusion that the world and its history is thereby permanently divided. This echoes the crossing of the Red Sea and the parting of the waters as narrated in Exodus ("Israel witnessed the great act that God had performed against the Egyptians, and the people venerated God; they put their faith in God and Moses his servant"). There is, however, an important difference: in the biblical narrative, the only human agent is Moses, and the only human action is his holding his hand over the water, while in the Qur'ānic narrative, the Muslims act and God acts with them. Badr, Exodus, and the Qur'ān are all instances of *furqān* – weighty criteria, distinctions that cleave the conceptual space they span and dictate subsequent law and behavior. And in a way, Voltaire's reading of Badr becomes the *furqān* that cleaves his own reading of Islam.[113]

For a reader as sympathetically cynical as Voltaire, the lesson is simple: God helps those who help themselves. The operative distinction, the Enlightenment *furqān*, that makes this lesson cohere is the binary opposition between those who change the world through their own initiative and those who wait for a higher power to do it for them. In this respect, the God of Islam might be compared to the "invisible hand," so prevalent in Enlightenment thought.[114] Whereas the God of the Old Testament did everything, the God of Islam helps his chosen army, but only after the latter had taken up arms against their enemies (and it should be pointed out that Badr was preceded by a few skirmishes and raids on the caravans of the Quraysh, but not proper wars). It is almost as if Voltaire chose the side of Islam out of sympathy with the prophet who fought for his own cause instead of relying on his God to do the fighting for him, just as Voltaire fought all of his own battles himself. Indeed, the evolution of Voltaire's relationship to Muhammad inheres in this: at the time of *Mahomet*, he considered Muhammad to be his anti-self due to his presumed fanaticism. After reading the Sale translation, Voltaire begins to see Muhammad as a second self, another prophet doing battle with *l'infâme* of seventh-century Arabia. In the Qur'ānic account of Badr, with its attendant Mosaic associations (formal and intertextual) and the subsequent emphasis on *jihād*, we find the germ of Voltaire's ethics: that as children of the Enlightenment, we all have a responsibility to do right actively rather than wait passively for a deity or an authority figure to do it for us.

Although the chapters on Islam come early in Voltaire's universal history, there is no gainsaying their crucial status. The story of Muhammad and the reading of the Qur'ān allow Voltaire to establish and advance models not only of demystified history, free of superstition, or of the man who single-handedly changed the entire course of world history, but also, and perhaps most significantly, of the unlimited potential of the power of the text, which can turn the Europe of *l'infâme* into "la France de Voltaire."

5

ROUSSEAU AND THE LANGUAGE OF
THE LEGISLATOR

There is no firm evidence that Rousseau actually read the Qur'ān.
However, the ideas contained therein, and especially in the
"Preliminary Discourse," were sufficiently widespread in the
eighteenth-century republic of letters that he would have almost
certainly come across them in his vast reading and constant
peregrinations.[1] The purpose of the following chapter is to trace
the impact of the altered climate of opinion in eighteenth-century
Europe, and in particular on the place of Islam within it, on two sets
of theories that would prove influential over the following centuries;
theories dealing with the legislator and the origin of language. As
will be seen, Rousseau's legislator is a prophet in all but name, and
as such the source of his power is linguistic and rhetorical. The
language that the legislator uses to establish his power and lead the
republic is therefore a question of some moment. Rousseau proposes
that this language be an Oriental one, most probably Arabic. In the
opening chapter we referred to the numerous texts in the seventeenth
and eighteenth centuries that set up Muhammad as a legislator and
lawmaker, among them works by Reland, Stubbe, Toland, and
Boulainvilliers, as well as their influence on Sale, who compared
Muhammad to Numa and Minos as a way of refuting Prideaux's
imposture thesis. These works attempt to theorize the legislator who
would lead the Republic, using Islam to enable political as well as
religious heterodoxy. Although there are some vestiges of the charge
of imposture (which writers used to protect themselves), Muhammad
now comes across as a man who learned from his experiences how
to govern well. Far from being the scourge of Christendom, Islam

becomes, once again, a tool that is "good to think with," especially where nascent political theories are concerned. The Enlightenment figure of the legislator – arguably its most enduring political legacy – would have been very different were it not for the increase and dissemination of knowledge about Islam.

Islam, for Sale, was not spread by the sword alone. It was, in fact, persuasive; it spoke to the hearer's heart and mind. In this respect Muhammad is not unlike the legislator of Rousseau, who succeeds precisely by making people want to obey the (his) law. There is, however, an important difference: Rousseau's theory of the legislator makes clear, however, that the distinction between a "true" legislator and an impostor is immaterial; the institution of laws has less to do with the legislator's private aims than the establishment of a functional body politic.[2] Rousseau's argument regarding the inconsequence of imposture is laid out in the letter to Christophe de Beaumont, which aims at buttressing the case for a civil religion as a basis for a functional republic. Rousseau imagines the wise men ("les hommes de sens," or the legislators) exhorting the masses to honor all the founders of all the religions, whether or not they believe in them:

Honorez en général tous les fondateurs de vos cultes respectifs. Que chacun rende au sien ce que qu'il croit lui devoir, mais qu'il ne méprise point ceux des autres. Ils ont eu de grands génies et de grandes vertus: cela est toujours estimable. Ils se sont dits les Envoyés de Dieu, cela peut être & n'être pas; c'est de quoi la pluralité ne sauroit juger d'une maniere uniforme, les preuves n'étant pas également à sa portée Mais quand cela ne seroit pas, il ne faut point les traiter si légérement d'imposteurs. Qui sait jusqu'où les méditations continuelles sur la divinité, jusqu'où l'enthousiasme de la vertu ont pu, dans leurs sublimes ames, troubler l'ordre didactique et rampant des idées vulgaires? Dans une trop grande élévation la tête tourne, et l'on ne voit plus les choses comme elles sont. Socrate a cru avoir un esprit familier, et l'on n'a point osé l'accuser pour cela d'être un fourbe. Traiterons-nous les fondateurs des Peuples, les bien-faiteurs des nations, avec moins d'égards qu'un particulier?

[Honor all the founders of your respective religions. Let everyone give to his own what is owed to him without holding the others in contempt. They had great genius and great virtues: this is always worthy of esteem. They claim to be God's Messengers: this may or may not be so; it is something that the multitude cannot judge since the evidence is beyond its reach. Even if it is not true, they should not be too quickly treated as impostors. Who knows where continuous meditations on divinity, where the enthusiasm of virtue, might have led the didactic order of crude ideas in their sublime souls? The head turns at high elevations, and things are no longer seen as they are. Socrates believed he had a familiar spirit, but he was not therefore accused of being a crook. Are we to treat the fathers of the people and the benefactors of nations with less consideration than an individual?][3]

The terms that Rousseau uses occur elsewhere: the legislator who founds a people but is open to the charge of "imposture" because the masses do not understand him is a character we also see in *Du contrat social*.

In *Du contrat social*, Rousseau's legislator is described as the miraculous, near-divine technician who designs the social universe and guarantees its smooth operation under the proper conditions:

S'il est vrai qu'un grand Prince est un homme rare, que sera-ce d'un grand Législateur? Le premier n'a qu'à suivre le modele que l'autre doit proposer. Celui-ci est le mécanicien qui invente la machine, celui-là n'est que l'ouvrier qui la monte et la fait marcher.

[If it is true that a great Prince is a rare man, what should we say of a great Legislator? The former only has to follow the model that someone must propose. The latter is the mechanic who invents the machine, the former simply the worker who mounts it and turns it on.][4]

This perspective is not entirely original to Rousseau – the literature of the eighteenth century is rife with references to the strong relationship between legislation and divinity.[5] God was routinely referred to as the supreme legislator during the seventeenth and eighteenth centuries. For Grotius and his French translator Barbeyrac, the legislator had to discover the law of nature whose author is God. James Harrington argued that every republic worthy of the name needed to be instituted by a great legislator. Consequently, the formation of the state by the legislator was equivalent to the creation of the universe by God. The value of the legislator, in whom resides the value of the social whole, and the divinity from whom he or she (usually he) derives his sovereignty, are of a piece.

Rousseau's legislator is thus like a prophet, an intermediary between God and humanity. In the domain of public affairs, the legislator's impossible task – "to command without violence and persuade without convincing" ("entraîner sans violence et persuader sans convaincre") – necessarily leads him to rely on the theatrical and ceremonial aspects of government. His skill, whereby citizens are persuaded actually to desire what he obliges them to do, is such that he might easily be mistaken for an impostor.[6] This ambiguity inevitably accompanies each and every legislator, whose claim to authority necessarily depends on the myth of his status as a divine emissary.[7] It is only the legislator's great soul and force of character – a miracle in Rousseau's eyes – that allows the appearances to gain the upper hand and persuades the people to believe and obey.[8] The legislator surpasses the prophet and patriarch alike: Rousseau has Moses say "J'ai fait un peuple, et n'ai pu faire des hommes" ("I have made a people, but I have not made men") while the legislator can actually "make men."[9]

As a mediator between the divine and the human, Rousseau's legislator is an outsider, since human beings can neither identify nor properly articulate the laws that they need. Because the Gods do not speak the same language as men, there is no way to check on the legislator's competence or authenticity. Worse yet, since law is the fundamental social bond in Rousseau's scheme, there is no way to exist socially without the legislator, which is to say that one can never be in a position to check as to whether or not the legislator thanks to whom one has a social and political existence is an impostor. The legislator claims to be heaven's messenger, and the citizens have no choice but to believe him, because dis-believing him is tantamount to social death. The legislator's claim, in turn, is necessarily false, being based on the fiction of a divine legation – the only possible means of persuading the masses:

Ainsi donc le législateur ne pouvant employer ni la force ni le raisonnement, c'est une nécessité qu'il recoure à une autorité d'un autre ordre, qui puisse entraîner sans violence et persuader sans convaincre.

Voilà ce qui força de tout temps les pères des nations à recourir à l'intervention du Ciel et d'honorer les dieux de leur propre sagesse, afin que les peuples, soumis aux lois de l'État comme à celles de la nature, et reconnaissant le même pouvoir dans la formation de l'homme et dans celle de la cité, obéissent avec liberté et portassent docilement le joug de la félicité publique.

Cette raison sublime qui s'élève au-dessus de la portée des hommes vulgaires est celle dont le législateur met les décisions dans la bouche des immortels, pour entraîner par l'autorité divine ceux que ne pourrait ébranler la prudence humaine. Mais il n'appartient pas à tout homme de faire parler les dieux, ni d'en être cru quand il s'annonce pour être leur interprète. La grande âme du législateur est le vrai miracle qui doit prouver sa mission. Tout homme peut graver des tables de pierre, ou acheter un oracle, ou feindre un secret commerce avec quelque divinité, ou dresser un oiseau pour lui parler à l'oreille, ou trouver d'autres moyens grossiers d'en imposer au peuple. Celui qui ne saura que cela pourra même assembler par hasard une troupe d'insensés, mais il ne fondera jamais un empire, et son extravagant ouvrage périra bientôt avec lui. De vains prestiges forment un lien passager, il n'y a que la sagesse qui le rende durable. La loi judaïque toujours subsistante, celle de l'enfant d'Ismaël qui depuis dix siècles régit la moitié du monde, annoncent encore aujourd'hui les grands hommes qui les ont dictées; et tandis que l'orgueilleuse philosophie ou l'aveugle esprit de parti ne voit en eux que d'heureux imposteurs, le vrai politique admire dans leurs institutions ce grand et puissant génie qui préside aux établissements durables.

[Since the legislator can use neither force nor argument, it is necessary that he seek recourse to an authority of another order, which can command without violence and persuade without convincing.

This is what has forced the fathers of nations from time immemorial to seek recourse to divine intervention and to honor the Gods with their own wisdom so that the people, who are subject to the laws of nature as well as the state, and acknowledging the same power in the formation of man and the formation of the city, obey freely and happily bear the yoke of public felicity.

This sublime reason which rises beyond the reach of the vulgar masses is the one that the legislator puts in the mouth of the immortals, in order to command through divine authority those who are not stirred by human prudence. But it is not for every man to make the Gods speak, or to be believed when he claims to be their interpreter. The great soul of the legislator is the miracle that must prove his mission. Any man can engrave stone tables, or buy an oracle, or feign some secret commerce with some deity, or train a bird to peck seeds out of his ear, or find other crude means to trick the people. And he who knows nothing but these tricks might even be able to gather a crowd of fools, but he will never found an empire, and his extravagant creation will perish with him. Vain charms create a temporary bond; only wisdom makes it last. The Jewish law which has survived to this very day, and that of Ishmael which has ruled over half of the world for ten centuries, still bear witness to the great men who founded them; and whereas proud philosophy or the sectarian spirit sees in them fortunate impostors, the real politician admires in their institutions that great and powerful genius that presides over lasting establishments.][10]

Rousseau's radical approach to the problem of the legislator's sincerity is nothing if not original. In the political space, even the most cynical impostor can create a respectable legal and political system. The only criterion for the evaluation of a legislator is not his intentions but the result: a good legislator is the one who creates a lasting political institution. Based on the necessity of resorting to the fiction of a divine mission, Rousseau does not see in the stance of Moses, Muhammad, or anyone else imposture so much as a necessary political device, in much the same way as microphones and television cameras today. The list of props attributed to the legislators of yore (stone tables, a bird trained to peck seeds from Muhammad's ear – a myth that Rousseau would have found in Grotius)[11] – far from confirming their imposture, actually proves the opposite: anyone can fool an audience with clever tricks like these, but few can write laws that stand the test of time. By this standard, Judaism and Islam bespeak the great men who founded them.

When Rousseau does criticize Muslims (specifically Arabs) it is in terms reminiscent of the first *Discourse*: namely that they became soft and weak as they became more civilized, thereby weakening the source of their strength, namely the link between religion and the state. Rousseau makes clear, however, that this is not Muhammad's fault:

Mahomet eut des vues très saines, il lia bien son système politique, et tant que la forme de son gouvernement subsista sous les califes ses successeurs, ce gouvernement fut exactement un, et bon en cela. Mais les Arabes devenus florissants, lettrés, polis, mous et lâches, furent subjugués par des barbares; alors la division entre les deux puissances [i.e. le culte et l'état] recommença; quoiqu'elle soit moins apparente chez les mahométans que chez les chrétiens, elle y est pourtant, surtout dans la secte d'Ali, et il y a des États, tels que la Perse, où elle ne cesse de se faire sentir.

[Mahomet had very sane views, he fastened his political system well, and as long as his form of government lasted under his successors, the Caliphs, this government was wholly unified and, to that extent, good. But once the Arabs flourished and became lettered, polite, soft and cowardly, they were subjugated by Barbarians. At this point the division between the two powers [i.e. religion and the state] started again, though it remains less conspicuous in Mahometan than in Christian states. It does exist nonetheless, especially in the sect of Ali, and there are states, such as Persia, where it makes itself felt everywhere.][12]

For Rousseau, a strong republic is founded on religious principles. The separation of religious and political power can only weaken the state. Islam provides Rousseau with an important case study with which to theorize the separation of church and state and the genesis of civil religion.

Rousseau's correspondence bears witness to his identification with or comparison to various legislators including Muhammad. Two themes predominate: Muhammad's status as a legislator and his exile from Mecca (an obvious point of comparison to the peripatetic Rousseau). One angry anonymous citizen of Geneva insists that Rousseau come clean and own up to being a crypto-Muslim in light of his *Confessions*, while Pierre de la Roche advises Rousseau to take his own advice on novels and burn his own books, like the mythical "Turk."[13] On June 16, 1763, Alexandre Deleyre wrote to Rousseau in terms that made this association both explicit and benevolent: "I have been looking for you since your flight into Switzerland, which I would willingly compare to the flight of Jesus into Egypt and Mahomet into Medina, though you are not the disciple of either of these two Legislators." ["Je vous ai cherché depuis votre fuite en Suisse que je comparois volontiers à celle de Jésus en Égypte et de Mahomet à Médine, quoique vous ne soiés le disciple d'aucun de ces deux Législateurs."][14]

The similarities between Rousseau and Muhammad drove Pastor Johann Heinrich Meister to refer to one of Rousseau's voyages as a "hégire."[15] Rousseau's erstwhile friend-turned-detractor Dusaulx, author of *De mes rapports avec Jean-Jacques Rousseau et de notre correspondance* (1798), describes the ageing

Rousseau's paranoiac megalomania in details worth quoting in full:

> La lecture des livres saints dont il s'étoit pénétré de bonne heure, n'avoit fait qu'attiser cette ame de feu, avoit tellement agi sur lui, qu'il s'étoit, pour ainsi dire, identifié avec les personnages de l'ancien et du nouveau testament; qu'il en avoit emprunté les passions, le langage et le brûlant enthousiasme; de sorte qu'avec le prophete-roi il n'a souvent, au milieu de ses triomphes, vu sur la terre que des ennemis conjurés contre lui; et qu'à l'exemple de l'homme-dieu, il s'est vu prédestiné a la régénération du genre humain.
>
> Un homme digne de foi, le citoyen Corancez, vient de nous apprendre que Rousseau se figuroit que le Tasse, dans son poëme, l'avoit, plusieurs siècles avant sa naissance, prédit aux nations. Mais voici un article entre plusieurs autres du même genre, qui semble autres du même genre, qui semble indiquer qu'il fut et l'imitateur et l'émule secret de Jésus-Christ: "Jésus, que ce siècle a méconnu parce qu'il est indigne de le connoître; Jésus, qui mourut pour avoir voulu faire un peuple illustre et vertueux de ses vils compatriotes; le sublime Jésus ne mourut pas tout entier sur la croix; et moi qui me sens un cœur dont aucun sentiment coupable n'approcha jamais, c'en est assez, mon cher Moulton [i.e. Moultou] pour qu'en sentant approcher la dissolution de mon corps, je sente en même temps la certitude de vivre etc."
>
> Plein de sa future apothéose, et ne vivant plus en quelque sorte que dans lui-même et dans la postérité dont il jouissoit d'avance, ils'étoit attaché des confidens, des dépositaires et des disciples éprouvés, à qui il avoit tracé la conduite qu'ils devoient tenir selon les occurrences, et surtout après sa mort. "Ceux qui m'aiment véritablement, écrivoit-il à son ami Moulton, se gardent bien dans les circonstances présentes, et lorsqu'il s'agit de moi, de se mettre en avant avec emphase: ils gémissent tout au bas au contraire, observent et se taisent, jusqu'à ce que le temps de parler soit venu, observent et se taisent, jusqu'à ce que le temps de parler soit venu, etc. Quand vous verrez la vérité, il ne sera pas pour cela temps de la dir ; il faut attendre *les révolutions qui lui seront favorables, et qui viendront tôt ou tard* ... C'est alors que le nom de mon ami, dont il faut maintenant se cacher, honorera ceux qui l'ont porté et qui rempliront les devoirs qu'il leur impose. Voilà ta tâche, o Moulton! elle est digne de toi, et depuis bien des années mon cœur t'a choisi pour la remplir etc." J'en demande pardon à Jean Jacques: en copiant cet article, je croyois entendre la voix de Mahomet.

[The reading of sacred books, with which he was preoccupied since his youth, only stoked his spirit's flames, and had such an influence on him that he identified, so to speak, with the characters of the Old and New Testaments; he borrowed their passions, their language and their burning enthusiasm, so that like the prophet-king he only saw enemies on this earth, and like Jesus Christ, he considered himself destined to regenerate the human race.

Citizen Corancez, a trustworthy man, has just informed us that Rousseau believed that Tasso had predicted his birth several centuries ahead of time in his poem. But here is one item among many of the same sort that seems to indicate that he was the secret imitator of Jesus Christ: "Jesus, who was misunderstood by an age unworthy of understanding him; Jesus, who died for wanting to make his vile compatriots into an illustrious and virtuous people; the sublime Jesus did not entirely die on the cross; and I who feel that I have a heart unblemished by blameworthy sentiment; this is enough, my dear Moultoun [i.e. Moultou], to make me feel the certainty of being alive as I feel the dissolution of my body etc."

Obsessed with his future apotheosis, and not living except in himself and in the posterity that he enjoyed in advance, he gathered around himself confidants, proven disciples and agents, to whom he prescribed how they should behave in any circumstance, especially after his death. "Those who truly love me," he wrote to his friend Moulton, "should be careful under current conditions, wherever I am concerned, not to speak up too forcefully: instead they groan silently, observe and stay quiet, until the time for speaking has come, etc. Even when you see the truth, that is not the time to declare it; *you must await the turns of events [les révolutions] that are favorable to it, and which are bound to come sooner or later* ... It is then that the title of my friend, which must now be hidden, will honor those who have had it and who will carry out the duties that it imposes on them. That is your task, my dear Moultou! It is worthy of you, and my heart chose you for it years ago etc." May Jean-Jacques forgive me; as I was copying this article I thought I heard the voice of Mahomet.][16]

Although Leigh denies any resemblance between Muhammad and Rousseau,[17] the announcement of Rousseau's mission by Tasso, the identification with Jesus, and the designation of Moultou as a caliph of sorts are all prophetic *topoi*. One might that Rousseau's fate of being chased from place to place is confirmation of the adage that "Nul n'est prophète en son pays." And, as John Wansbrough reminds us, exile is a key aspect of biblical and Qur'ānic theodicy.[18] Time and again, we see the figure of Muhammad being used to trope Rousseau's prophecy and/or imposture in the eighteenth century. To his followers, Rousseau was an unjustly persecuted prophet, on par with, if not greater than, Jesus and Muhammad. In their mind's eye, Rousseau did for his disciples what Moses did for the Jews and Muhammad did for the Muslims – he was the prophet/legislator who created their identity. Hence the following speculation in the *Voyage à Ermenonville*:

Les Romains ont deifie Numa, les Turcs ont fait de Mahomet un Prophête; les Juifs ont vénéré Moïse; les Chinois ne respectent rien tant que Confucius. Pourquoi sans être superstitieux ne serions nous pas aussi reconnaissans? Pourquoi Rousseau ne serait-il pas parmi nous l'objet de la vénération nationale? …

Le respect qu'on a pour le législateur tourne toujours au profit de la législation. On chérit l'ouvrage du mortel auquel on croit devoir des hommages: faire des loix est en quelque sorte une fonction de la divinité; il est de la prudence de tout état d'environner le mortel de qui il tient les siennes, de tout ce qui peut le rapprocher d'elle …

C'est en grande partie ce qui a fait des Juifs une nation qui fut toujours elle-même au milieu de tous les chocs qu'elle essuya … et si jamais fictions furent excusables, ce sont celles de ces grands hommes qui ont fixé l'esprit inquiet de ceux qu'ils gouvernaient, en faisant intervenir dans leur administration quelque chose de plus qu'humain, en imprimant à leurs ouvrages le sceau du respect.

Nous sommes trop éclairés pour être dupes du commerce de Numa avec la nymphe Egerie: nous ne sommes plus dans les tems où l'on prit des attaques d'épilepsie pour des extases, un pigeon pour l'ange Gabriel; les tonnerres du Mont Sinaï n'épouvanteraient pas des hommes qui ne croyent pas au miracles; mais l'éloge de l'orateur des mœurs ferait parmi nous couler bien des larmes: le temple érigé au mortel qui nous a montré la liberté ne serait pas sans adorateurs.

[The Romans deified Numa, the Turks made a Prophet out of Mahomet, the Jews venerated Moses; the Chinese respect nothing as much as they respect Confucius. Why, without being superstitious, should we not be as appreciative? Why should Rousseau not become an object of national veneration among us? …

The respect that is felt for the legislator always profits legislation. We always cherish the work of the mortal to whom we owe homage. Lawmaking is the task of the divinity in a way; it is a wise state that surrounds the mortal from whom it receives its laws with everything that could bring him closer to that divinity.

It is largely this that has made the Jews a nation that remained true to itself amidst all the shocks that they have suffered … If ever fictions were excusable, it is those that were invented by these great men to settle the anxious minds of the subjects, by introducing into their administration something super-human, by branding their works with the seal of respect.

We are too enlightened to be duped by the commerce of Numa with the Egeria: we no longer live in an age where epileptic seizures are taken for ecstatic states, or a pigeon for the angel Gabriel. Thunderstorms on Mount Sinai would not frighten people who do not believe in miracles, but the praise of the orator of morals would make many tears flow among us: a temple built for the moral who taught us freedom will not be without worshippers.][19]

The strengths of Rousseau's legislator have more to do with language than vision; he is more of a hearer and speaker than a seer.[20] What, then, does the divinely inspired legislator hear? What is the language of the gods that he re-transmits as law? In his study of the Qur'ānic *Weltanschauung*, Isutzu maps the non-verbal aspects of inspiration or *waḥy* between God and humanity, citing the many traditions wherein Muhammad described this state as one where he heard, *inter alia*, bells ringing, bees humming, and wings flapping.[21] These sounds, which we might usefully categorize as the sounds of the divine, are all the more interesting by their similarity with the description of soothsayers (*kahana*) and their inspiration by the *jinn*. Here, too, the inspired party hears non-verbal sounds variously described as those made by birds or bees. Whether or not one believes that Muhammad was the messenger of God, the link between non-verbal communication and the production of rhythmic or rhymed utterances is not to be overlooked. *Saj'* in particular was the sign of prophetic speech, an indication that the speaker was relaying information that had come from a super-human or divine source.[22] Thus one of the signs of the legislator–prophet is precisely his ability to speak musically, rhythmically.

Now, music also plays an important part in Rousseau's theory of the legislator. Indeed, music is the origin of all language for Rousseau, for whom every act of interpersonal communication carries with it an intensely spiritual, almost religious dimension.[23] As the *Essai sur l'origine des langues* argues, people sang before they spoke and used figurative before literal language. In bygone times, legislators had to use sophisticated rhetorical techniques to sway the free citizens of old, as opposed to the sorry subjects of Rousseau's day to whom the powers that be need say little more than "Tel est mon plaisir" and "Donnez de l'argent."[24] Christopher Kelly argues that the task of the legislator is as much aesthetic as it is political. In order to "persuade without convincing," the legislator must *move* the masses emotionally rather than rationally, for which process music is ideally suited. Indeed, in ancient societies, legislation and musical performance went hand in hand.[25] An early legislator would have sung as he spoke.[26] Among his many examples, Rousseau cites Athenaeus on the fact that the ancients sang their laws and exhortations to virtue, argues that the Israelites followed this pattern, and claims that Aristotle derived the etymology of the word *nomos* (meaning both law and song) from the fact that the ancients sang and wrote their laws. In the *Lettre à d'Alembert*, Rousseau remembers fondly, if perhaps fantasmatically, the virtuous mountain-dwellers of Nechâtel whose entire aesthetic and sole form of entertainment was to get together and sing the Psalms of David.[27]

Rousseau's predilection for the Cratylian implications of the words Numa and Romulus, even if it leads to fictitious linguistic claims, emphasizes his sensitivity to sound as a basis for the truth and the political impact of euphony. These issues come into play in Rousseau's description of the earliest languages in general, and Oriental languages in particular, all of which he finds more moving, and therefore more politically consequential, than the idioms of his day:

> Cette langue auroit beaucoup de synonimes pour exprimer le meme etre par ses differens raports [Rousseau's footnote: On dit que l'Arabe a plus de mille mots différens pour dire un *chameau*, plus de cent pour dire un *glaive* etc.] … Elle auroit beaucoup d'irrégularités et d'anomalies, elle négligeroit l'analogie grammaticale pour s'attacher à l'euphonie, au nombre, à l'harmonie, et à la beauté des sons; au lieu d'argumens elle auroit des sentences, elle persuaderoit sans convaincre et peindroit sans raisoner; elle ressembleroit à la langue chinoise à certains egards, à la grecque à d'autres, à l'arabe à d'autres. Etendez ces idees dans toutes leurs branches et vous trouverez que le *Cratyle* de Platon n'est pas si ridicule qu'il paroit être.

[This language would have many synonyms to indicate the same entity through its many relationships (Rousseau's footnote: They say that Arabic has more than a thousand different words meaning *camel*, more than a hundred for a *sword* etc.) ... it would have several irregularities and anomalies, it would neglect analogy through grammar in favor of euphony, number, harmony, and acoustic beauty; it would have laws instead of arguments, it would persuade without convincing and paint without reasoning; it would resemble Chinese in some respects, Greek in others, and Arabic in still others. Follow these ideas to their conclusions and you will see that Plato's *Cratylus* is not as ridiculous as it seems.][28]

This passage is striking on a number of counts. First, by the use of a phrase that the *Du contrat social* made famous: "elle persuaderoit sans convaincre." This, we might surmise, is the sort of language spoken by the legislator of the *Du contrat social*, who also has the mysterious ability to "entrainer sans violence et persuader sans convaincre." The language of the legislator abounds in synonyms and euphony. That cardinal rule of political rhetoric, namely the subjugation of reason to emotion, has its roots in the musical basis of language. Second, the sounds of this original legislative language: it would sound like Greek in certain respects, Chinese in others, and Arabic in still others. These, then, are the languages best suited to moving, persuasive legislation. Third, the natural relationship between sound and sense advanced in Plato's *Cratylus*, which in the current context could be taken to imply that the language of the legislator works because the words sound like what they signify: "L'onomatopée s'y feroit sentir continuellement." ["Onomatopoeia would be heard constantly."][29]

Most of Rousseau's ideas about these matters came from one of his favorite authors, Bernard Lamy, whose *Rhétorique* is echoed more than once in Rousseau's essay.[30] It is probably under Lamy's influence that Rousseau would have learned the importance of the legislator's verb, "persuader":

Rien de si important que de savoir persuader. C'est de quoi il s'agit dans le commerce du monde: aussi rien de plus utile que la rhétorique ... L'éloquence est dans les sciences ce que le soleil est dans le monde. Les sciences ne sont que tenebres, si ceux qui les traitent ne savent pas écrire.

[There is nothing as important as knowing how to persuade. This is what the way of the world is all about; there is therefore nothing as important as rhetoric … Eloquence is to the arts what the sun is to the world. Knowledge is nothing but shadows, if those who treat it do not know how to write.][31]

Like Rousseau, Lamy considers Greek, Chinese, and Arabic in his *Rhétorique*, though his aim is less the description of the first language of humanity, which, following Thomassin, he identifies as being Hebrew, than comparing the various characteristics of modern languages.[32] Unlike Thomassin, however, Lamy's framework pleads for the superiority of Greek and Arabic over Hebrew.[33] As against Thomassin, who wonders about the point of having one thousand nouns that mean "sword" and eighty that mean "lion," which is the case with Arabic, Lamy argues that this multiplicity of synonyms is a positive end in itself:

Il n'y a rien de si ennuyeux que d'entendre trop souvent les memes termes s'ils sont remarquables. La variete dans le discours fait qu'on ne s'aperçoit presque pas qu'on entend parler, on croit voir les choses memes. Quand cela arrive, un discours est parfait; comme la perfection de la peinture, c'est qu'on la prenne pour les choses mêmes qui sont peintes. Or la variete depend de la fecondité d'une langue.

[There is nothing as annoying as hearing the same remarkable terms over and over again. Variety in speech diminishes the perception that someone is speaking; we think we are seeing the very thing being said. When that happens, the discourse is perfect; like the perfection of a painting, where we think that we see the very thing painted. Now, variety depends on the fecundity of a language.][34]

By building on Lamy's theory of historical linguistics, Rousseau is essentially building a case for the genealogy of the divine language that is spoken by the legislator. His turn to Arabic in particular is also facilitated by the French translation of George Sale's "Preliminary Discourse" (1751), where the link between linguistic command and divine inspiration is made explicit:

The Arabians are full of the commendations of their language, and not altogether without reason; for it claims the preference of most others in many respects, as being very harmonious and expressive, and withal so copious, that they say no man without inspiration can be a perfect master of it in its utmost extent.[35]

It is accident, then, that properly used and uttered, the Arabic language, which is the language of Quraysh and the Qur'ān, can have some remarkable effects, both persuasive and legislative:

> It is probable that the harmony of expression which the Arabians find in the Korân might contribute not a little to make them relish the doctrine therein taught, and give an efficacy to arguments which, had they been nakedly proposed without this rhetorical dress, might not have so easily prevailed. Very extraordinary effects are related of the power of words well chosen and artfully placed, which are no less powerful either to ravish or amaze than music itself; wherefore as much has been ascribed by the best orators to this part of rhetoric as to any other. He must have a very bad ear who is not uncommonly moved with the very cadence of a well-turned sentence; and Mohammed seems not to have been ignorant of the enthusiastic operation of rhetoric on the minds of men; for which reason he has not only employed his utmost skill in these his pretended revelations, to preserve the dignity and sublimity of style, which might seem not unworthy of the majesty of that Being, whom he gave out to be the author of them; and to imitate the prophetic manner of the Old Testament; but he has not neglected even the other arts of oratory; wherein he succeeded so well, and so strangely captivated the minds of his audience, that several of his opponents thought it the effect of witchcraft and enchantment, as he sometimes complains.[36]

Armed with these ideas from Sale and Lamy, Rousseau argues that the legislator who speaks the wisdom of the ages can only do so in Persian or Arabic. Most Western languages would be unworthy of the sacred function of legislation:

> Le Francois, l'Anglois, l'Allemand sont le langage privé des hommes qui s'entre aident, qui raisonnent entre eux de sang-froid, ou de gens emportés qui se fachent; mais les ministres des Dieux annonçant les mistéres sacrés, les sages donnant des lois aux peuples, les chefs entraînant la multitude doivent parler Arabe ou Persan.

> [French, English, and German are the private languages of men who help each other, who reason calmly among themselves, or of angry people, but the ministers of God who announce sacred mysteries,

sages who give laws to peoples and chieftains leading the multitudes should speak Persian or Arabic.][37]

This text was composed roughly during the same period as the printing of the *Du contrat social*. The Arabic language and Rousseau's image of the legislator are therefore of a piece.[38]

The historical correlate to this process is found in Rousseau's account of how Muhammad's rhythmic recitation of the Qur'ān would have been persuasive enough to bring about instant conversions:[39]

> Tel pour savoir lire un peu d'Arabe sourit en feuilletant l'Alcoran, qui, s'il eut entendu Mahomet l'annoncer en personne dans cette langue éloquente et cadencée, avec cette voix sonore et persuasive qui séduisoit l'oreille avant le cœur, et sans cesse animant ses sentences de l'accent de l'enthousiasme, se fut prosterné contre terre en criant: grand Prophête, Envoyé de Dieu, menez-nous à la gloire, au martire; nous voulons vaincre ou mourir pour vous.

> [Those who can read a little Arabic smile as they leaf through the Alcoran, but if they heard Mahomet in person pronounce this eloquent and rhythmic language with that sonorous, persuasive voice that seduced the ear before the heart, constantly animating his laws with the accent of enthusiasm, they would have bowed on the ground before him crying out, "O great Prophet! God's Messenger! Lead us to glory and martyrdom! We want to vanquish or die for you!"][40]

This narrative is a minor variation on the story of the conversion of 'Umar b. al-Khaṭṭāb. This is a narrative that Rousseau would have come across in Gagnier's *Vie de Mahomed*, which he read to Madame Dupin while he worked as her secretary.[41] The narrative relates 'Umar's decision to kill Muhammad, his bursting into his sister Fatima's house, and his hearing al-Khabbāb b. al-Aratt reciting Q20:1–14 and being so struck by the beauty of the text that he decides to convert. Rousseau would have been especially sensitive to the opening verses of Q20, which Gagnier translates thus:

> Au nom de Dieu tres-misericordieux. Nous ne t'avons pas fait descendre l'Alcoran du Ciel, afin que tu fusses miserable; mais afin que ce soit un mémorial pour celui qui craint Dieu, &c. ... Certainement je suis Dieu. Il n'y a point de Dieu que moi. Sers-moi doc, & fais la priére en mémoire de moi seul (i.e. Q20:1–3,14).[42]

Sale translates this passage thus:

> We have not sent down the Koran unto thee, that thou shouldst be unhappy; but for an admonition unto him who feareth *God* … Verily I am GOD; there is no god besides me; wherefore worship me, and perform *thy* prayer in remembrance of me.[43]

The verses are addressed to Muhammad, but it is difficult not to imagine Rousseau identifying with someone who had been singled out for divine favor and the suffering that this caused him. Gagnier's account continues in terms not far removed from the compact version in Rousseau's *Essai sur l'origine des langues*:

> *Omar* vouloit d'abord se jeter à genoux; mais le Prophéte de Dieu l'en empecha. Il lui déclara ensuite le sujet de sa venüe: *Je viens*, lui dit-il, *pour croire en Dieu & en son Apôtre*; & incontinent il récita la formule de la double Profession de foi, en ces termes: *J'atteste, qu'il n'y a point d'autre Dieu que Dieu, qui n'a ni Compagnon ni Associé & que Mahomet est son serviteur & son Apôtre.* Toute l'Assemblée jetta alors un si grand cri de joye, que le bruit en fut entendu d'eux-mêmes qui étoient dans la Mosquée. Enfin *Omar* demanda instamment à l'Apôtre de Dieu, qu'ils allassent tous à la Mosquée, pour rendre à Dieu leurs actions de Graces. *Ô! Apôtre de Dieu* ajouta-t-il, *quelque chose nous arrive de la part des* Koraishites, *soit que nous vivions soit que nous mourions, ne sommes-nous pas dans la Vérité?*
>
> L'Apôtre de Dieu, admirant son zèle naissant, lui répondit: "Oui j'en jure par celui qui tient mon ame entre ses mains, vous êtes dans la Vérité, soit que vous viviez soit que vous mouriez." Sur cela, *Omar* lui dit: *Confirmez-nous dans ces grands mystéres.*

> [*Omar* wanted to kneel, but the Prophet of God prevented him. He then told him the purpose of his visit: *I come*, he said, *to believe in God and his Apostle*, and immediately recited the double Profession of faith, *I bear witness that there is no other God but God, who has neither companion nor associate, and that Mahomet is his servant and Apostle.* All assembled immediately rejoiced so loudly that the noise was heard by those who were in the Mosque. Finally *Omar* asked the Apostle of God that they all go to the Mosque immediately, to give thanks to God. *O Apostle of God*, he added, *something will befall us from the Qurayshis, but whether we live or die, are we not in the True Faith?*

> Admiring his nascent zeal, the Apostle of God answered, "Yes, by He who holds my soul in His hands, you are in the True Faith, whether you live or die." Whereupon Omar said to him, "Confirm us in these great mysteries."][44]

The scene that Rousseau sketches in the *Essai sur l'origine des langues* brings together the themes under discussion in this chapter: an eloquent legislator, a sacred text, and a sudden conversion. Rousseau turns to the Muslim world, and specifically to dramatic instances of spiritual discourse, in order to theorize the origins of language and law. Relying on Lamy, Sale, and Gagnier, Rousseau turns to the power of the Arabic language and examples of conversion narratives to think through the political impact of the legislator. Those aspects of Rousseau's political theory that began with the *Social Contract* are incomplete without the literary and linguistic dimension on the one hand, and the historical examples of Muhammad and 'Umar on the other. Given the uses to which Rousseau's name and philosophy would be put during the French Revolution, it would be no exaggeration to say that the metamorphosis of the French public depends in part on this passage through Islam. The transformation of the subject of the Most Christian King into the citizen of the republic relies on Rousseau's legislator, who is himself partially modeled on Muhammad. The shift from religious categories of political thought to secular ones is enabled by the dissemination of certain perspectives on Islam, aided and abetted by the translation of the Qur'ān.

As an epilogue to the past two chapters, we might consider the extent to which the trends exemplified by Rousseau and Voltaire – the idea of Muhammad as a legislator, and his association with other philosopher–legislators – had become standardized by the third quarter of the eighteenth century. Thus in 1775 François-Henri Turpin publishes his *Histoire de l'Alcoran*, where over the course of some eight hundred octavo pages the words "législateur" and "législation" are routinely used instead of "prophète" and "mission." Despite the first part of its title, Turpin's text is less a history than a detailed description of the Qur'ān, the life of Muhammad, and the laws of Islam, compiled from secondary sources that include Du Ryer, Marracci, D'Herbelot, Sale, Reland, Boulainvilliers, and Gagnier, undertaken with a view to showing Muhammad's sources.[45] Turpin's tone is decidedly ambivalent, routinely criticizing and denigrating Muhammad with some of the usual epithets inherited from the Middle Ages, while at the same time praising the rational, or at least expedient, character of his laws. This might have been the case due to the fact that the work is dedicated to Miromesnil, who held the post of Keeper of the Seals under Louis XVI. In his long and flattering dedicatory epistle, Turpin makes a point of underlining the natural fit between the legislator of seventh-century Arabia and the legislator of eighteenth-century France: "Une législation adoptée par les habitans de la moitié du Globe, ne pouvoit paroître que sous les auspices du Ministre de la loi." ["Legislation adopted by half the world's inhabitants could only appear under the auspices of the Minister of Law."][46] Especially worthy of note is Turpin's treatment of the Muslim laws of marriage and divorce; a subject on which he dwells at greater length than Voltaire, adding detailed ethnographic descriptions culled from travel accounts. Turpin devotes separate chapters in his second volume to marriage and polygamy in an attempt, like Voltaire, to overturn the image of Muhammad as a sensualist rake. Under Muslim law, marriage is a civil contract: "Sa Législation attentive à tous les moyens qui peuvent entretenir l'amour conjugal, défend tout ce qui peut l'affoiblir & commande tout ce qui peut lui donner des amorces."[47] ["His legislation is attentive to all the means that sustain conjugal love, prevents all that can weaken it and commands all that can strengthen it."]

The marquis de Pastoret's *Zoroastre, Confucius et Mahomet comparés comme sectaires, législateurs et moralistes* (1787) continues the comparisons of Voltaire's *Essai sur les mœurs*, situating Muhammad in a genealogy of legislators rather than prophets and/or classical figures – Minos, Numa, Moses, and Christ are all absent.[48] Pastoret inserts lengthy longitudinal comparisons between the three legislators of his title, finding in each one a certain superiority above the other two: as the founder of a religion, Muhammad takes first prize in Pastoret's scheme; as a legislator, Zoroaster beats Muhammad and Confucius, who in turn beats the other two as a moralist. Pastoret argues that Zoroaster's legislative superiority stems from his lengthy meditation on the effectiveness of his laws, while Muhammad's are the result of his inspired genius. Like Turpin, Pastoret makes all the familiar statements about Muhammad's "imposture," and, like Turpin, seems to have done so to placate the censors while praising Muhammad's ability as a legislator and rehearsing some familiar arguments in the process:

> Assurément l'erreur & l'absurdité déshonorent souvent la religion de Mahomet: mais serions nous assez injustes pour lui refuser les éloges dont elle n'est pas toujours indigne? Un systeme religieux qui asservit la moitié du monde, n'auroit-il donc rien que la raison pût avouer? Qu'on ouvre le livre sacré des Musulmans, & on y verra leur Apôtre annoncer par intervalle les vérites les plus sublimes du culte & de la morale. Maracci, dont certainement on ne suspectera pas le témoignage, ne craint pas de l'avouer. Ils ont conservé, dit-il, tout ce qu'on trouve de plus plausible & de plus probable dans la religion chrétienne avec tout ce qui nous paroît de plus conforme à la loi & à la lumière de la nature.

> [Assuredly error and absurdity often dishonor the religion of Mahomet, but will we be so unjust as to deny it the praise of which it is not always undeserving? Could a religious system that conquers half the world contain nothing that reason would admit? Let the sacred book of the Muslims be opened, and there their Prophet will be seen to announce at various intervals the most sublime truths of religion and morality. Marracci, whose testimony certainly cannot be suspect, does not fear to admit it. They have conserved, he says, all that is most plausible and most probable in the Christian religion with all that seems to us to conform to the law and light of nature.][49]

While Pastoret's account is not as lengthy as Turpin's, his reading of the Qur'ān is more careful, and his praise of Islam more generous (though it becomes attenuated once the comparison with Confucius gets underway). This is due in part to Pastoret's reliance on a new translation of the Qur'ān that was published three years earlier by Claude Savary, of which more will be said in the following chapter. Like Savary, Pastoret repeatedly refers to Muhammad as "le Législateur de l'Arabie."[50] Pastoret also relies heavily on Savary's imagery in his descriptions of Muslim dogma and the day of judgment showing a deep attraction to the unitary, transcendent God of Islam.[51] Methodologically, Pastoret's account synthesizes Reland and Voltaire (while relying on numerous other sources, including Prideaux, Gagnier, D'Herbelot, Chardin, and Marracci, as well as Savary), constantly attempting to save Islam from the false claims that have been made about it while critically evaluating it as a global legal system. Again, like Voltaire, the Muslim laws of marriage and divorce are read as a good example of legislation that protects women and establishes justice: with respect to the legislation on divorce in particular, and on the restrictions placed on husbands after divorce, Pastoret remarks: "On sent combien une precaution pareille, & en general toutes celles que Mahomet a prises, sont capables de mettre un frein aux caprices d'un mari bizarre & imperiuex." ["We see how such a precaution, and in general all of those that Mahomet took, are capable of restraining the caprices of bizarre and imperious husbands."][52] Pastoret does not hide his admiration for Muhammad's genius, emphasizing how well he knew his people and how well his ideas and beliefs worked as a basis for a global religion:

> Combien il est au-dessus de ses rivaux pour des ressources, l'étendue, la flexibilité du génie! Il fait servir à ses projets les obstacles même qu'il rencontre. Rien de ce qui peut flatter ou seduire n'échappe a ses regards perçants. On voit, a chaque pas, qu'il connoit parfaitement le peuple dont il change le culte & la législation.[53]
>
> Mahomet ne méanagea pas seulement les préjugés des Arabes, & les gouts, les sensations, les idées produites par l'influence du climat, il avoit un systeme trop vaste pour se borner a un peuple, a une opinion. Son projet, dont le succès seul a égalé la hardiesse, paroit avoir été de réunir toutes les nations sous une même croyance, & de cimenter ainsi une fraternité générale, par ce qu'il y a de plus sacré. Je ne crois pas me tromper en lui attribuant la grande pensée de soumettre les hommes a une religion universelle ... Ajoutons que ce faux apôtre se donne ordinairement pour un réformateur moins jaloux de renverser les principes reçus que de les concilier; & à ce dessein, il les réduit aux idées plus simples & les plus populaires.[54]

[How far ahead of his rivals he is when it comes to his resources and the extent and flexibility of his genius! He even makes the obstacles that he encounters serve his ends. Nothing flattering or seductive escapes his piercing gaze. At every step, we see that he knows the people whose beliefs and laws he is changing very well ...

Not only did Mahomet treat with consideration the prejudices of the Arabs, and the ideas, tastes and sensations produced by the climate; he had a system too vast to be limited to one people or one opinion. His project, whose daring is matched by its success, seems to have been to unite all nations under one set of beliefs, thereby cementing a global fraternity by that which is most sacred. I do not believe myself mistaken when I attribute to him the project of uniting all of humanity under one universal religion ... Let us add that this

> false prophet claims to be a reformer who cares less about reversing principles than reconciling them, and to this end reduces them to the simplest and most popular ideas.]

Despite the resemblance between Pastoret and Voltaire, his efforts had a decidedly different outcome, earning him an election to the Académie des Belles-Lettres et Inscriptions. This new trinity of Eastern religions and their founders would eventually be used to frame another translation of the Qur'ān into French by Kazimirski in 1840. The years between 1787 and 1840 were also full of other key developments in the Western history of the reception of the Qur'ān. They form the subject of the next two chapters.

6

SAVARY, NAPOLEON, AND EGYPT: VISIONS OF PROPHECY AND CONQUEST

There are few more momentous "applications" of European learning about Islam than Napoleon's invasion of Egypt. Although the Middle East was not invaded by texts, and few Orientalists could have been conscious of the use to which their work would be put, there is no gainsaying the impact of the improved understanding of the Orient on the success of Napoleon's campaign.[1] A learned man, Napoleon embodies the relationship between power and Orientalist knowledge. As Henry Laurens puts it, "Bonaparte n'invente rien mais, mieux que tout autre, il traduit en quelques principes simples la totalité du savoir orientaliste de son temps."[2] ["Bonaparte invented nothing, but he translated certain simple principles of the totality of Oriental learning of his age better than anyone else."] Napoleon saw the invasion of Egypt as part of the project of Enlightenment, a way of bringing truth and liberation to an underdeveloped people. This went hand in hand with the conception of the population of Egypt as a Middle Eastern "third estate" that was oppressed by a Mamlūk faction and which would benefit from the active intervention of an army bearing the ideals of the French revolution.[3] This idea would eventually work its way into the language of the first French proclamation in Egypt, dated 13 Messidor Year VI, a text in which Napoleon repeatedly emphasizes his credentials as a Muslim rather than a European invader and discredits those of the Mamlūks:

> Depuis trop long-temps ce ramassis d'esclaves achetés dans le Caucase et la Géorgie tyrannise la plus belle partie du monde; mais Dieu, de qui depend tout, a ordonné que leur empire finît.

Peuples de l'Égypte, on vous dira que je viens pour détruire votre religion; ne le croyez pas: répondez que je viens vous restituer vos droits, punir les usurpateurs, et que je respecte, plus que les Mamlouks, Dieu, son prophète, et la Qorân …

Qâdhys, cheykhs, Imâms, tchorbadjys, dites au peuple que nous sommes auss de vrais Musulmans. N'est-ce pas nous qui avons détruit le pape, qui disoit qu'il falloit faire la guerre aux Musulmans? N'est-ce pas nous qui avons détruit les chevaliers de Malte, parce que ces insensés croyoient que Dieu vouloit qu'ils fissent la guerre aux Musulmans? N'est-ce pas nous qui avons été dans tous les temps les amis du grand-seigneur (que Dieu accomplisse ses desseins), et l'ennemi de ses ennemis? Les Mamlouks au contraire ne sont-ils pas toujours révoltés contre l'autorité du grand seigeur qu'ils méconnoissent encore? Ils ne font que leurs caprices.[4]

[This bunch of slaves bought in the Caucasus and Georgia have tyrannized the most beautiful part of the world for far too long, but God, on whom everything depends, has ordained that their empire come to an end.

O people of Egypt, they will tell you that I have come to destroy your religion. Do not believe it. Answer them that I have come to restore your rights, to punish the usurpers, and that I respect God, his prophet and the Qorân even more than the Mamlūks.

Tell them that all men are equal before God, and that only wisdom, talent and virtue make differences among them …

O you judges, sheikhs, Imams and shorbadjis,[5] tell the people that we, too, are real Muslims. Are we not the ones who destroyed the Pope, who said that war must be made on the Muslims? Did we not destroy the Knights of Malta, those madmen who thought that God commanded them to wage war against the Muslims? Have we not always been the friends of the Grand Signior (may God accomplish his designs) and the enemies of his enemies? On the other hand, have the Mamlūks not always rebelled against the authority of the Grand Signior, that authority that they still do not recognize? They just do as they like.][6]

The synthesis of egalitarian rhetoric and praise for Islam in this proclamation grows out of the intellectual genealogy behind Napoleon's Egyptian campaign. The idea that the East was very much like Europe but took a wrong developmental turn somewhere was developed by a number of writers on the Orient during the late eighteenth century, notably Marigny, the Baron de Tott, Savary, and Volney, all of whom were subject at one point or another to Napoleon's studious attention. Several among them made the case that the course of Middle Eastern history might be changed for the better by the intervention of the West, going so far in some cases as to actively invite invasion of parts of the Ottoman Empire before other powers could profit from its inevitable demise.[7] The following chapter will map parts of the interplay between Orientalist text and Napoleonic military behavior.

Of the Orientalists who influenced Napoleon, Savary is the most literary. Although the writer with the greatest impact on Napoleon's views and policies toward the Orient is usually considered to be Volney, Savary's exoticizing tone was not without influence. Savary spent three years in Egypt (1776–1779), during which time he wrote a description of Egypt that propagated a certain mythology of the land of the pharaohs replete with the received ideas of Orientalist exotica: hot weather, palm trees, attractive women, despots, and so on. In 1784 he published his translation of the Qur'ān based on the Arabic he learned during those three years. Savary oscillates between translating from the Arabic text directly and offering a French translation of Marracci's text, though like Sale, Savary distances himself from the hard line of the Vatican. Savary's choice of Marracci's *Alcorani textus universus* as a source text is all the more significant insofar as it underlines the latter's *de facto* academic status – like Geiger in the mid-nineteenth century, Savary turns to Marracci for a complete encyclopedia of the Qur'ān, containing a fully vocalized text, annotations in the original languages, as well as a handy translation to help with the difficulties of Arabic. Like his predecessors, Savary provides a long introduction to his translation, along with occasional notes to the text, although these tend to be sporadic. Savary's accounts and translations are riddled with inaccuracies and dominated by hyperbolic imagery. There is here an important anticipation of what would later become the romantic imaginary. Overall, Savary is eager to convey to the reader a view of the Orient as a locus of monumental, exotic beauty inhabited by great men. Just the sort of place that would attract the military interest of someone like Napoleon.

The depiction of Muhammad in Savary's introduction combined the two poles of the opposition between legislator and demagogue, forced to resort to manipulation in order to lead.[8] The prophet of Islam is described in decidedly Promethean tones, beyond good and evil.

He did not so much change the world as "astonish" it: "La naissance de Mahomet, comme celle des hommes fameux qui ont étonné la terre, fut annoncé par des prodiges."[9] ["The birth of Mahomet, like that of famous men who have astonished the world, was announced by miracles."] His intellectual dominion over his peers is total: time and again, Savary refers to Muhammad's "empire" and "ascendant sur les esprits." Whereas most histories describe Muhammad's living conditions as being modest, Savary has him living in a "chateau" at Safa, going so far as to add a footnote informing the reader that the part about the castle of Safa is found in Abu'l Feda's biography of Muhammad.[10] There is a purpose behind Muhammad's every move. Muhammad produces miracles seemingly at will, but does so tactically. During the digging of the ditch around Medina, Muhammad manages to soften the rocky ground by spitting on it; a gesture that invites the following commentary:

Tel Annibal, se frayant une route à travers les Alpes, ranima le courage de ses soldats, en faisant répandre du vinaigre sur le rocher qu'il voulait percer. Partout le grand homme est le même, partout il aplanit les obstacles sous ses pas et fait céder la nature à ses efforts. Le charme invincible qu'il emploie pour produire des prodiges est l'assurance du succès dont il enivre les cœurs des mortels.

[Like Hannibal who, as he made his way across the Alps, revived his soldiers' courage by spitting vinegar on the rock that he wanted to break. The great man is everywhere the same: he flattens obstacles underfoot and makes nature yield to his efforts. The invincible charm that he uses to produce miracles assures the success with which he enchants mortal hearts.][11]

Muhammad considers his options wisely and acts decisively, which is what allows his followers eventually to conquer the remains of Byzantium: "Mahomet avait dessein de démembrer l'empire d'Héraclius; mais aussi sage dans ses mesures que prompt dans l'exécution, il sentit qu'avant de l'attaquer il fallait s'assurer des petits princes qui régnaient sur l'Arabie Petrée."[12] ["Mahomet had planned to dismember the empire of Heraclius, but being as wise in his actions as he was prompt in their execution, he felt that it was important to assure himself of the support of the petty princes of Arabia Petra before attacking him."] Overall, Muhammad is a prime example of an increasingly rare genius aided by circumstance:

Mahomet fut un de ces hommes extraordinaires qui, nés avec des talents supérieurs, paraissent de loin en loin sur la scène du monde pour en changer la face et pour enchaîner les mortels à leur char. Lorsqu'on considère le point d'où il est parti, le faîte de grandeur où il est parvenu, on est étonné de ce que peut le génie humain favorisé des circonstances.

[Mahomet was one of those extraordinary men who, born with superior gifts, show up infrequently on the face of the earth to change it and lead mortals behind their chariot. When we consider his point of departure and the summit of grandeur that he reached, we are astonished by what human genius can accomplish under favorable circumstances.][13]

Napoleon, who was an avid reader of Orientalist literature, would probably have identified with this rare genius who managed to conquer the world in a very short period of time.

Savary's translation of the Qur'ān follows the same stylistic lines. Consider the translation of Q83, where one verse is repeated (Q83:23 and 35) to emphasize the comfort and ease of those who are in paradise: عَلَى الْأَرَائِكِ يَنْظُرُونَ. This verse has prompted different tactical decisions on the part of its translators. Du Ryer only translates it once, separating verb from prepositional phrase and eliding the repetition at the end of the sūra through mere allusion: Q83:23 becomes "couchez sur des lits délicieux" (i.e. just *'alā-l arā'ik*) and Q83:35 becomes "ils verront les rigoureux tourmens des damnés" (i.e. just the verb *yanẓurūn* merged with Q83:34).[14] Marracci's literalism serves him well, as he repeats the same phrase verbatim, with an additional interpolation: Q83:23 becomes "Super lectulos sponsales aspicient" and Q83:35, "Super lectulos sponsales aspicient *infideles in Gehenna*."[15] The idea that the faithful will lie on comfortable couches and watch the damned being tortured in hell is based on Q83:34 ("At vero in die *illa*, qui crediderunt, de infidelibus risum captabunt") and the *Tafsīr Al-Jalālayn ad loc.*[16] Sale has interpolations for both verses, so that Q83:23 becomes "*seated* on couches they shall behold *objects of pleasure*," and Q83:35, "*lying* on couches they shall look down *upon them in hell*," both interpolations being found in the *Tafsīr Al-Jalālayn*. Here, now, is Savary's version: Q83:25: "Couchés sur le lit nuptial, ils porteront ça et là leurs regards;" Q83:35: "Ils les verront du sein des plaisirs."[17] Neither wholly accurate nor entirely inaccurate, Savary's translation adds details that leave the reader somewhere between bafflement and amusement: not only does he take the idea of "marital beds" from Marracci,[18] he emphasizes the state of pleasurable amazement that goes with being in paradise. The phrase "du sein des plaisirs" is entirely of Savary's invention, though based on the context, and adds to the image of a voluptuous paradise.

Napoleon, the demagogue and manipulator of people and ideas, displays more than a few parallels with Savary's portrait of Muhammad.[19] The ambiguous relationship between Napoleon and the idea of religion – religious when it was politically useful, agnostic otherwise – resembles Savary's image of Muhammad.[20] Napoleon's identification with Muhammad is a matter of record, both in the public proclamations to the Egyptians (see below) and in private communications. Napoleon thought he himself could have been Muhammad, whom he described as "un imposteur qui semble avoir été élevé à l'Ecole polytechnique, car il démontre ses moyens de puissance comme, moi, je pourrais le faire dans un siècle tel que celui-ci."[21] ["An impostor who seems to have studied at the École polytechnique; for he demonstrates his powers as I might do in a century like this one."] In other words, Napoleon would be to the eighteenth and nineteenth centuries what Muhammad had been to the seventh. After the Egyptian campaign he confided to one of his Dames du Palais, Madame de Rémusat, that on the way to Egypt, "Je créais une religion, je me voyais sur le chemin de l'Asie parti sur un éléphant, le turban sur ma tête et dans ma main un nouvel Alcoran que j'aurais composé à mon gré."[22] ["I was creating a religion, I saw myself leaving on an elephant on the way to Asia, with a turban on my head and in my hand a new Alcoran that I had composed to my liking."]

Napoleon's voracious reading and literary sensibility meant that his great actions had to be preceded by great literary examples. The fact that he saw in Corneille a born military strategist rather than a playwright meant that what mattered to Napoleon was the intuitive – inspired? – knowledge of military skill, and that once it took literary form it was only a matter of time before it was realized in real life. Literary texts like Corneille's battle scenes operated as sacred prophecies waiting to be fulfilled, most probably by someone like himself.[23]

Nor is this all. Napoleon's passionate involvement with the theatre drove him to put the playwright Arnault in charge of the artistic side of the invasion of Egypt, spending much time on board *L'Orient* in verbal jousts with him regarding the relative merits of the French classical playwrights.[24] On the eve of the battle of Austerlitz, Napoleon was busy discussing theories of tragedy and ways of reinvigorating French theatre with his generals.[25] Napoleon's behavior combines two registers: an actor on a stage and a prophet bringing a new religion to the East. Not coincidentally, this is the central theme of a short text that he wrote in 1787, "Le Masque prophète," essentially a two-page summary of the imposture and revolt of Al-Muqanna', the masked would-be prophet of Khurasān, in 160 AH/AD 177, with the usual heavy dose of Napoleonic identification.[26] Like Napoleon, Hakem is eloquent: "Hakem ... d'une éloquence mâle et emportée, se disait l'envoyé de Dieu." ["Hakem proclaimed himself the messenger of God with a passionate, masculine eloquence."] Like Napoleon, Hakem "prêchait une morale pure qui plaisait à la multitude; l'égalité des rangs, des fortunes, était le texte ordinaire de ses sermons. Le peuple se rangeait sous ses enseignes; Hakem eut une armée." ["Hakem preached a pure morality that pleased the masses; the equality of ranks and fortunes was the usual text of his sermons. The people assembled under his flags; Hakem had an army."] Napoleon's description is all the more interesting insofar as he translates the usual charge of excessive license that is leveled at Al-Muqanna''s ethics into the more respectable radical egalitarianism that would later be the hallmark of his army. Furthermore, Hakem's method anticipates opinions that Napoleon would later voice in his criticism of Voltaire's *Mahomet*, who is too elitist to succeed in Napoleon's opinion: "Les hommes qui ont changé l'univers ... n'y sont jamais parvenus en gagnant les chefs; mais toujours en remuant les masses."[27] ["The men who have changed the universe ... never did so by winning over the leaders, but always by moving the masses."] Hakem's career is short: in Napoleon's version he founds a sect, challenges the Caliph Al-Mahdī (Napoleon's "Mahadi"), and, seeing that his cause is lost, kills his followers and then himself. The moral of the story for the young Napoleon is rather ambiguous: "How far the fury of being illustrious can lead." ["Jusqu'où peut pousser la fureur de l'illustration!"] Of course, Napoleon, too, wants to be found illustrious, and, as will be seen below, finds himself preaching a radically egalitarian doctrine, leading armies against established powers, claiming to be the envoy of heaven when necessary, and even fighting wars against men named "Al-Mahdī" on occasion. For Napoleon, as for much of the nineteenth century, life imitates art.

Accordingly, Napoleon spent a great deal of time meditating

on the literary representations of Muhammad. Here is part of his commentary on Voltaire's *Mahomet*:

> Mahomet fut un grand homme, intrépide soldat; avec une poignée du monde il triompha au combat de Bender [sic]; grand capitaine, éloquent, grand homme d'état, il régénéra sa patrie, et créa au milieu des déserts de l'Arabie un nouveau peuple et une nouvelle puissance.

> [Mahomet was a great man, an intrepid soldier; with a handful of men he triumphed at the battle of Bender (sic); a great captain, eloquent, a great man of state, he revived his fatherland and created a new people and a new power in the middle of the Arabian deserts.][28]

Quite apart from the dramatic quality of these lines (and the literary historical irony whereby Napoleon uses the language of Voltaire's *Essai sur les moeurs* to criticize Voltaire's *Mahomet*) the misspelling of Badr – a mistake that Napoleon makes consistently – indicates another text that Napoleon probably had in mind here: Savary's "Abrégé de la vie de Mahomet," where the battle is called "Beder," one letter away from Napoleon's mistake.

Savary's account of Badr follows the usual breathless pace of his narration, eliding any mention of Muhammad's hesitation in attacking his tribe after the *hijra* or the Muslims' fear of the greater numbers of the Quraysh (both of which are points that recur frequently in traditional accounts of the battle and the glosses on the Qur'ānic verses where it is narrated):

> Il [Muhammad] n'avait avec lui que trois cent treize soldats ... tous déterminés à vaincre ou à périr ... Il partit sur-le-champ, et marcha avec tant de diligence, qu'il prévînt les ennemis, et campa sur leur passage ... Ils [les Coréïshites] ne tardèrent pas à paraître ... Les deux armées ne furent pas plutôt en présence, que, du côté des Coréïshites, *Otba*, *Shaïba* et *Waled* descendirent dans l'arène.

> [He (Muhammad) only had three hundred and thirteen soldiers with him ... all determined to vanquish or die ... He left immediately, and marched so diligently that he gained ground over the enemy and camped on their passage ... They (the Qurayshis) were not long in appearing ... The two armies were no sooner in each other's presence than *Otba*, *Shaïba* and *Waled* descended into the arena.][29]

The breakneck pace of the history of this battle also inflects Savary's translation of the Qur'ānic passages in which it is mentioned. Thus Q3:123, وَلَقَدْ نَصَرَكُمُ اللَّهُ بِبَدْرٍ وَأَنتُمْ أَذِلَّةٌ فَاتَّقُوا اللَّهَ لَعَلَّكُمْ تَشْكُرُونَ becomes "A la journée de Beder, où vous étiez inférieurs en nombre, le Tout-Puissant *se hâta* de vous secourir. Craignez-le donc, et soyez reconnaissants."[30] ["On the day of Beder, when you were inferior in number, the Almighty *hastened* to help you; so fear God, that you might be grateful." Sale: "And GOD had already given you the victory at BEDR, when ye were inferior *in number*; therefore fear God, that ye may be thankful."[31]] There is no mention of haste in the original. Similarly, Q3:124–125, إِنْ تَصْبِرُوا إِذْ تَقُولُ لِلْمُؤْمِنِينَ أَلَنْ يَكْفِيَكُمْ أَنْ يُمِدَّكُمْ رَبُّكُم بِثَلاثَةِ آلافٍ مِنَ الْمَلائِكَةِ مُنْزَلِينَ (124) بَلَى وَتَتَّقُوا وَيَأْتُوكُمْ مِنْ فَوْرِهِمْ هَذَا يُمْدِدْكُمْ رَبُّكُم بِخَمْسَةِ آلافٍ مِنَ الْمَلائِكَةِ مُسَوِّمِينَ becomes, "Tu disais aux fidèles: Ne suffit-il pas que Dieu vous envoie du ciel trois mille anges? Ce nombre suffit sans doute; mais si vous avez joint la persévérance à la piété, et que les ennemis viennent tout à coup fondre sur vous, il fera *voler* à votre aide cinq mille anges."[32] ["You (Muhammad) said to the faithful: is it not enough that God has sent you three thousand angels from heaven? This number is probably sufficient, but if you join piety to perseverance, and the enemy falls upon you suddenly, He will make five thousand angels *flee* to your aid." Sale: "When thou saidst unto the faithful, Is it not enough for you that your LORD should assist you with three thousand angels, sent down *from heaven*? Verily, if ye persevere, and fear *GOD*, and *your enemies* come upon you suddenly, your LORD will assist you with five thousand angels, distinguished *by their horses and their attire*."][33] The use of the verb "voler" is not implied by the original text or the commentaries, most of which work on the anthropomorphic assumption that the angels in question rode horses into battle. If anything, speed is one of the qualities of the angels that Savary imagines. Again, Savary's stylistic deviations (mistakes?) emphasize the dynamic quality of Muhammad's history. Since speed is nothing without dramatic rhetoric, Savary gives a similarly vivid, compressed translation of the first part of Q8:17, فَلَمْ تَقْتُلُوهُمْ وَلَكِنَّ اللَّهَ قَتَلَهُمْ وَمَا رَمَيْتَ إِذْ رَمَيْتَ وَلَكِنَّ اللَّهَ رَمَى as "Ce n'est pas vous qui les avez tués, ils sont tombés sous le glaive du Tout-Puissant. Ce n'est pas toi, Mahomet, qui les as assaillis, c'est Dieu."[34] ["It was not you who killed them; they fell under the sword of the Almighty. It was not you, Mahomet, who assaulted them; it was God." Sale: "And ye slew not those *who were slain at BEDR your selves*, but GOD slew them. Neither didst thou, O Mahomet, cast *the gravel into their eyes* when thou didst *seem* to cast *it*, but GOD cast *it.*"[35]] There is no mention of the sword of the Almighty in the original text. In all of these examples, Savary's imagination routinely supplies details that seem designed to appeal to a view of the Orient as a place where divine intervention is swift and overwhelming. This romantic perspective is further reinforced by the structure of Savary's account, which moves from battle to battle and victory to victory after the *hijra*. Badr, Uhud, the battle of the Ditch, and the reconquest of Mecca all take place in rapid succession. Again, this is not entirely original, but the compressed character and hurried tone of Savary's account lends further credence to the image of Muhammad as the Alexander of Arabia.

This romantic vision of the Orient reaches its apex in Savary's letters dealing with the revolt of Ali Bey, where Ottoman Egypt rivals Rycaut's Istanbul as the universal center of palace intrigue, treachery, and reversal of fortune.[36] Savary emphasizes the extent to which the Orient is simply an Occident whose history took a wrong turn. The Mamlūk armies are excellent but badly in need of European training.[37] Savary returns repeatedly to the themes of the impotence of the Ottoman Empire, and the extent to which any assistance from the Russians to Ali Bey would have ensured the former of a strong client in the Middle East and North Africa, an argument that stands as an effective invitation for military intervention in the region.[38] Any potential critique of imperial expansion is placed in the mouth of the treacherous arch-villain Abu Dahab, who addresses the Cairenes in the following terms in his last bid to turn the population of Cairo against Ali Bey:

> Braves chefs de la république, & vous Egyptiens, qui chérissez la loi de notre prophete, vous connoissez Ali. Il est chrétien dans le cœur, & a contracté des alliances avec les infidèles. Il veut soumettre ce pays pour abolir la religion de Mahomet, & vous forcer à embrasser le christianisme. Rappelez-vous ce que les Européens ont fait dans l'Inde; les Musulmans de ces riches contrées les ont accueillis avec bonté, les ont reçus dans leur ports, leur ont accordé des comptoirs, & ont formé avec eux des traités de commerce. Qu'en est-il arrivé? Les Chrétiens ont ravagé leur provinces, détruits leurs villes, conquis leurs royaumes, & après les avoir réduits en esclavage, ont établi l'idolâtrie sur les ruines de la vraie religion. Fideles Musulmans, un pareil sort vous attend. Ali, l'allié des Européens, va renverser la constitution de votre empire, ouvrir l'Égypte aux Infidèles, & vous forcer à devenir Chrétiens. Aidez-moi à repousser l'ennemi de

la république, de vos loix, de l'Islamisme; ou préparez-vous a tous les maux qu'ont soufferts vos freres du Bengale. Choisissez entre lui & moi.

[O brave leaders of the republic, and you Egyptians who cherish the law of our prophet, you know Ali: he is a Christian at heart and has forged alliances with the infidels. He wants to subjugate this country to abolish the religion of Mahomet and force you to embrace Christianity. Remember what these Europeans have done in India: the Muslims of those rich lands welcome them with kindness, received them in their ports, gave them trading rights, and signed commercial treaties with them. What was the result? The Christians ravaged their provinces, destroyed their towns, conquered their kingdoms, and after reducing them to slavery established idolatry on the ruins of the true faith. O faithful Muslims, a similar fate awaits you. Ali, the ally of the Europeans, will overturn the foundation of your empire, open Egypt up to the Infidels, and force you to become Christians. Help me to repel the enemy of the republic, the enemy of your laws, of Islam; or brace yourselves for all the harm done to your brothers in the Bengal. Choose between him and me.][39]

This critique resonates with modern attacks on imperialism. By placing them in the mouth of the villain of the piece, however, Savary is adding a layer of moral ambiguity that makes it seem an act of manipulation and demagoguery rather than a moment of liberation, effectively adding to what would become Napoleon's claim that he liberated Egypt to liberate it. Henry Laurens argues that the revolt of Ali Bey proves to Europe that a certain malleability has introduced itself into Middle Eastern politics, leaving some room for conquerors and conquest.[40]

The proclamations dictated by the French to the Egyptians make extensive use of Qur'ānic and apocalyptic language. The French texts sometimes lack the Qur'ānic allusion and are more succinct than the Arabic, but the implications of Napoleon's "Prophethood" are spelled out clearly. Consider the proclamation of 14 Jumādā I (2 Brumaire, year VII, which Al-Jabartī dates from Jumādā II 1213 AH). The verses of the Qur'ān are very much in evidence here, as befits a document signed by the twelve sheikhs of the first *dīwān*. In addition to pointing out that his is a project of liberation rather than occupation, Napoleon reminds the Egyptians that his victory is nothing less than the accomplishment of the will of God, and that opposing it would be suicidal, citing respectively Q2:247, Q5:1, and Q2:195 to this effect. The first two allusions occur in the sentence "rappelez-vous que Dieu donne l'empire à qui il veut, et ordonne ce qu'il lui plait."[41] Whereas Q5:1, إِنَّ اللَّهَ يَحْكُمُ مَا يُرِيدُ is accurately rendered by "Dieu ... ordonne ce qu'il lui plait," the use of the word "empire" in the first half of the sentence is unusual. The verse Q2:247 reads اللَّهُ يُؤْتِي مُلْكَهُ مَنْ يَشَاءُ, and refers to the story of another unlikely ruler, Saul (Ṭālūt), whose kingdom was the result of divine decree rather than popular consent – another parallel with Napoleon – and one of the few instances in the Qur'ān where the word *mulk* is used in connection with a human being rather than God.[42] The word *mulk* can be translated by a number of terms connoting power and property: "kingdom," "royalty," "sovereignty," or "dominion" are all valid possibilities.[43] Sale translates Q2:247 as "God giveth His kingdom unto whom he pleaseth," Du Ryer by "il donne la Roiauté à qui bon lui semble," Marracci by "Deus autem affert regnum suum cui vult," and Savary by the typically colorful "Le Tout-Puissant donne les diadèmes à son gré."[44] All of these translations revolve around the concept of kingship and crowns, reign and realm, as opposed to empire. Only Napoleon and the sheikhs of his *dīwān* go so far as to translate *mulk* by "empire." Similarly, the exhortation to the Cairenes not to do anything rash involves a tendency toward excess in the use of Qur'ānic language: "Nous vous conjurons donc de prendre garde de vous jeter dans le pécipice."[45] This is an allusion to Q2:195, وَلَا تُلْقُوا بِأَيْدِيكُمْ إِلَى التَّهْلُكَةِ. The jump from this formulation to throwing oneself into the precipice is, however, fairly large. Sale translates this verse thus: "throw not *your selves* with your own hands into perdition"; Du Ryer, "Ne vous jettez pas vous-même dans votre ruine"; Marracci, "ne projiciatis *vos ipsos* manibus vestris in ruinam"; and Savary, "N'opérez pas, de vos propres mains, votre ruine."[46] Again, the word "precipice" is entirely original to Napoleon and his translators. (Ironically, the gloss on this verse defines suicidal behavior by *refraining* from *jihād* rather than rushing into it as Napoleon and his collaborators would have it. Typically, only Marracci and Sale bother to point this out.)

The use of the Qur'ān and Sunna in the remaining proclamations serves to consolidate further the image of Napoleon as not only a follower of Muhammad, but a Mahdī destined to conquer the region. Consider the terms in which he addresses the population of Cairo some two months after the tax revolts that followed the invasion, in a proclamation announcing the formation of a new *Dīwān*:

Faites connoître au peuple que, depuis que le monde est monde, il étoit écrit qu'après avoir détruit les ennemis de l'islamisme, fait abattre les croix, je viendrois du fond de l'occident remplir la tâche qui m'a été imposée. Faites voir au peuple que, dans le saint livre du Qorân, dans plus de vingt passages, ce qui arrive a été prévu, et ce qui arrivera est également expliqué. Que ceux donc, que la crainte seule de nos armes empêche de maudire changent; car, en faisant au ciel des vœux contre nous, ils sollicitent leur condamnation; que les vrais croyants fassent des vœux pour la prospérité de nos armes.

Je pourrois demander compte à chacun de vous des sentiments les plus secrets du cœur; car je sais tout, même ce que vous n'avez dit a personne: mais un jour viendra que le monde verra avec évidence que je suis conduit par des ordres supérieurs, et que tous les efforts humains ne peuvent rien contre moi: heureux ceux qui, de bonne foi, sont les premiers a se mettre avec moi!⁴⁷

[Tell your people that since the beginning of time God has decreed the destruction of the enemies of Islam and the breaking of the crosses by my hand. Moreover He decreed from eternity that I shall come from the West to the Land of Egypt for the purpose of destroying those who have acted tyrannically in it and to carry out the tasks which He set upon me. And no sensible man will doubt that all this is by virtue of God's decree and will. Also tell your people that the many verses of the glorious Qur'ān announce the occurrence of events which have occurred and indicate others which are to occur in the future ... Indeed there are some of them who refrain from cursing me and showing me enmity out of fear of my weapons and great power and they do not know that God sees the secret thoughts, He "knoweth the deceitful of eye, and what men's breasts conceal" [Q40:19] [يَعْلَمُ خَائِنَةَ الأَعْيُنِ وَمَا تُخْفِي الصُّدُور]. And those who bear such secret thoughts oppose the decisions of God and they are hypocrites, and the curse and affliction of God shall surely befall them for God knoweth the secret things. Know ye also that it is in my power to expose what is in the heart of every one of you, for I know the nature of man and what is concealed in his heart at the very moment that I look upon him even though I do not state or utter what he is hiding. However, a time and a day will come in which you will see for yourselves that whatever I have executed and decreed is indeed a divine decree and irrefutable. For no human effort, no matter how devoted, will prevent me from carrying out God's will which He has decreed and fulfilled by my hand. Happy are they who hasten in unity and ardour to me with good intentions and purity of heart and that is all.⁴⁸]

Now, although the basic message is the same as that of the previous proclamations, the tone has been infused with an unprecedented degree of Qur'ānic allusion and auto-deification. No longer a mere exporter of the Enlightenment, Napoleon is now the arm of God; indeed, his omniscience makes him a God in his own right. Whence Al-Jabartī's allergic reaction to its "falsifications and weak-minded deceit and its audacious presumption in claiming Mahdīhood or Prophethood, and proving these claims by their antithesis"[لما فيه من التمويهات و الترييم على العقول الضعيفة و التسلق على دعوى]

النبوة والاستدلال على الدعوى بالنقيض].[49]

In a final instance of life imitating (rhetorical, dramatic, sacred) art, Napoleon the self-proclaimed prophet and successor to Muhammad (and Hakim Al-Muqanna') is met, and opposed, by a self-proclaimed Mahdī during the campaign in Syria.[50] Napoleon gave an account of the incident in a report to the Directory on the 1st of Messidor, Year VII.[51] Apart from the blatant imperialist tone of the report, where it is claimed that it would be more "reasonable" for the rebels to submit to than oppose Napoleon's "destiny," what is striking is the extent to which the events parallel those of Napoleon's novella "Le Masque prophète." Here, too, an impostor founds a sect, opposes the legitimate ruler, and ends up disappearing in a cloud of smoke. The theme of the masked prophet would therefore seem to be an overdetermined node for Napoleon: Muhammad, Hakem, Napoleon, and êl-Mahdy are all part of the same category; prophets who wear masks in order to legislate. However, only Napoleon and Muhammad succeed; Hakem and êl-Mahdy are done in by the "fureur de l'illustration." Still, Napoleon's hasty departure from Egypt is not unlike the imaginary flight to heaven of Al-Muqanna'.

As is well known, Napoleon's Egyptian campaign came to a sorry end.[52] Isolated and utterly demoralized, his soldiers and scientists left Egypt in 1801, having failed to export the republic. Four years later, Muhammad Ali would succeed where Napoleon failed, finally getting rid of the Mamlūks and inaugurating a programme of reform built, ironically, on the imitation and importation of French science and technology. Nor had the last round in the endless wars between Mahdīs and established powers been played: in 1881, another Mahdī came from the Sudan to oppose the occupying colonial powers. The romantic sensibility that fed the dream of conquest and the foundation of a lay post-revolutionary French republic in Egypt had not, in the end, counted on the hostility of the population or on the practical details of keeping a colony alive through a viable connection with the mother country. However, in the late eighteenth and early nineteenth centuries, another reader of the translated Qur'ān – one who met Napoleon – would start his own, more peaceful globalizing project in the register of culture rather than war. His endeavors form the subject of the next chapter.

7

GOETHE: POETRY AND PROPHECY, FROM *MAHOMET* TO WORLD LITERATURE

Goethe discovered the Qur'ān early, making of it an important tool with which he worked through his ideas about literature and writing. He had access to Theodor Arnold's German translation of Sale's translation by 1771, and reviewed David Megerlin's translation from the Arabic in 1772. He also had copies of Du Ryer's and Sale's translations in his library, and his notes include references to Marracci, which he would probably have known through Reineccius's abridgement of 1721. Goethe found the Megerlin translation a "wretched production," and sought occasional refuge in Arnold's re-translation of Sale for his *West-östlicher Divan* and its accompanying notes and essays. Katharina Mommsen's monumental study of Goethe and the Arab world shows conclusively that, in addition to all of the major translations of the Qur'ān extant in 1772, Goethe was also familiar with the major Enlightenment versions of Muhammad's life (Bayle, Reland, Gagnier, and Voltaire's *Mahomet*, as well as Thomas Arnold's translation of Simon Ockley's *History of the Saracens*).[1] Indeed, Goethe knew the translated text of the Qur'ān well enough to insert the occasional citation into his personal correspondence, as when he cites Q20:25 in his famous "Pindar letter" (in which he declares that he is living in Pindar: "Ich wohne jetzt in Pindar") to Herder (c. July 10, 1772): "Ich mögte beten wie Moise im Koran: Herr mache mir Raum in meiner engen Brust." ["I would like to pray like Moses in the Qur'ān: Lord open up my breast."][2] Mommsen points out that this is (one of) Goethe's ways of thinking through his anxieties about literary creation and his laborious relationship with Herder.[3] The fact that the breast-opening motif returns in his dramatic fragment "Mahomet" indicates that, for Goethe, that *inshirāḥ* (which he seems to associate with Moses as well as Muhammad) tropes creative activity, and that the prophet with the open(ed) breast is an archetype of the poetic genius that he attempts to become during his youth.[4] More generally, though, this letter sets a pattern in which Goethe's reflection on literary form is mediated by Islam and Muhammad. As will be seen, Goethe's reflections on creativity, literature, genius, and world literature see him return to Muhammad and the Qur'ān as ways of better defining his thoughts and self.[5]

Goethe transcribed other passages from various translations of the Qur'ān in his diaries and correspondence, some from Arnold's translation of Sale, some from the hapless Megerlin, and some translated by his own hand directly from Marracci, which is to say that Goethe did not bother with the polemical component of the translation.[6] Goethe reacted more to the literary quality of a given translation (especially Megerlin's and, to a lesser extent, Sale's) rather than its polemical bias. In his review of Megerlin's translation for the *Frankfurter Gelehrten Anzeigen* (December 22, 1772) he says that he would have wanted someone who could read and translate the Qur'ān with all of the poetic and prophetic feeling that he could muster:

> Wir wünschten, daß einmal eine andere [Übersetzung] unter morgenländischem Himmel von einem Deutschen verfertigt würde, der mit allem Dichter- une Prophetengefühl in seinem Zelte den Koran läse, und Ahndungsgeist genug hätte, das Ganze zu umfassen. Denn was ist jetzo *Sale* für uns?

> [We wish that, for once, another translation were produced under Eastern skies by a German, who would read the Qur'ān in his tent with all of his poetic and prophetic feeling, and who would be endowed with a sufficiently intuitive mind to contain the whole. After all, do we not already have (a prose translation in) *Sale* ?][7]

This wish would later be realized in a way on the title page of the *Divan*, which bears the curious Arabic title of الديوان الشرقي للمؤلف الغربي (i.e. *The Eastern Diwān by the Western Author*). We might note in passing the fact that, were it not for the dot above the final *ghayn*, the text would read "The Eastern Dīwān by the *Arabic* Author." In other words, we are a dot away from the wish expressed in the review penned during Goethe's youth, wherein Goethe, full of poetry and prophecy, becomes himself the author of the Qur'ān.[8] In Goethe's work, we find a mechanism similar to the one operative in the cases of Voltaire[9] and Napoleon: an identification with a great man (indeed, in 1806 Goethe described Napoleon as the "Mahomet der Welt").[10] For Goethe, however, it is Muhammad the man of words, the transmitter of the Qur'ān, rather than Muhammad the statesman, that matters.[11] Not for nothing does he locate the origins of poetry in scripture in his commentary on the *Divan*:

> Naive Dichtkunst ist bei jeder Nation die erste, sie liegt, allen folgenden zum Grunde; je frischer, je naturgemäßer sie hervortritt, desto glücklicher entwickeln sich die nachherigen Epochen.
> Da wir von orientalischer Poesie sprechen, so wird notwendig, der Bibel, als der ältesten Sammlung, zu gedenken. Ein großer Teil des Alten Testaments ist mit erhöhter Gesinnung, ist enthusiastisch geschrieben und gehört dem Felde der Dichtkunst an.

> [Naive poetry is each nation's first; it is the basis of all the poetry that follows; the fresher and more natural it is, the happier will be the development of all subsequent epochs.
> Since we are talking about Oriental poetry, we must mention the Bible as the most ancient collection thereof. A great part of the Old Testament is written in an exalted and enthusiastic style, and belongs to the field of poetry.][12]

Goethe's views are naturally inscribed within the trends prevalent in late eighteenth-century and early nineteenth-century Germany in the wake of Robert Lowth's *Lectures on the Sacred Poetry of the Hebrews*, whereby the Bible consolidated its position as a literary standard.[13] In Jonathan Sheehan's witty phrase, "The Bible was poetic because religion was poetic."[14] Goethe was probably also thinking of the extensive writings of Herder on Hebrew poetry as a text that founds a national culture and literature by making the sacred poetic.[15] In this respect, what makes the commentary on the *Divan* remarkable is its wide cultural range of reference: it is informed by the debates in Germany about the translation of the Bible, but also marks an opening up on to the Orient as an adjacent and similarly originary cultural space. Goethe will, in effect, use Islam to think through the age-old relationship between poetry and prophecy.

In the section on Muhammad, Goethe adds:

> Da wir bei unseren Betrachtungen vom Standpunkte der Poesie entweder ausgehen oder doch auf denselben zurückkehren, so wird es

von unsern Zwecken angemessen sein, von genanntem außerordentlichen Manne vorerst zu erzählen, wie er heftig behauptet und beteuert: er sei Prophet und nicht Poet und daher sein Koran als göttliches Gesetz und nicht etwa als menschliches Buch, zum Unterricht oder Vergnügen, anzusehen. Wollen wir nun den Unterschied zwischen Poeten und Propheten näher andeuten, so sagen wir: beide sind von *einem* Gott ergriffen und befeuert, der Poet aber vergeudet die ihm verliehene Gabe im Genuß, um Genuß hervorzubringen, Ehre durch das Hervorgebrachte zu erlangen, allenfalls ein bequemes Leben. Alle übrigen Zwecke versäumt er, sucht mannigfaltig zu sein, sich in Gesinnung und Darstellung gränzenlos zu zeigen. Der Prophet hingegen sieht nur auf einen einzigen bestimmten Zweck; solchen zu erlangen, bedient er sich der einfachsten Mittel. Irgendeine Lehre will er verkünden und, wie um eine Standarte, durch sie und um sie die Völker versammeln. Hierzu bedarf es nur, daß die Welt glaube, er muß also eintönig werden und bleiben, denn das Mannigfaltige glaubt man nicht, man erkennt es.

[Since, in these meditations, we use poetry as a point of departure and return, it would be suitable to relate first of all how this extraordinary man (Muhammad) vehemently claimed to be a prophet rather than a poet, so that his Koran should be considered a divine law and not a man-made book destined for study or entertainment.[16] Now, if we were to determine carefully the difference between the poet and the prophet, we would say that whereas both are possessed and enflamed by a God, the poet spends the gift that he has received on joy, and does so in order to produce joy, and to obtain glory or at least an enjoyable life through his production. He neglects all other aims, he aims for variety, showing an unbounded capacity for feeling and representation. The prophet, on the other hand, has a single precise aim, for the attainment of which he uses the simplest possible means. He wants to announce a doctrine, to assemble the masses through and for it, as if around a flag. In order for this to happen, it is enough that the world believe, and that the prophet keep playing the same tune; for we do not believe in the multifarious, we perceive it.][17]

In order to prove this point, Goethe proceeds to quote Q2:2–7 in Thomas Arnold's version, before proceeding to comment on the repetitious nature of the Qur'ān and its multifarious effects, alternately repelling and attracting, astonishing and impressing the reader. Two paragraphs later, Goethe describes the variation of the style of the Qur'ān according to the subject under treatment, by turns severe, elevated, threatening, and occasionally sublime, so much so that Goethe finds the doctrine of the uncreated Qur'ān perfectly natural.[18] In other words, Muhammad deconstructs the opposition that Goethe sets up between simple, straightforward prophecy and multifarious poetry: he fulfills the mission of the prophet with a text that bears more than a passing resemblance to poetry. Muhammad's capacity for founding laws and empires through the eloquence of the Qur'ān accomplishes what Goethe thought impossible: building a doctrine around the adoration (rather than the mere perception) of the multifarious through the One who created it.

If *Dichtung und Wahrheit* is to be believed, the similarities between Goethe and Muhammad, between poet and prophet, derive from his lifelong search for a religion with which he felt comfortable.[19] This had much to do with the Swiss poet and physiognomist Johann Kaspar Lavater, who had corresponded with Goethe while researching his *Physiognomie* and then spent some time with him during his tour of Germany, over the course of which several aspects of Christianity, and specifically the nature and physiognomy of the savior, were hotly debated.[20] Lavater's bizarre project – collecting as many possible faces as possible in order to reconstruct the physiognomy of Christ – did not alienate Goethe, though his obstinate insistence on "saving" his young proselyte seems to have done so. Before that stage, however, Goethe recounts how, during a conversation between Lavater and Susanna von Klettenberg, he came to the conclusion that people constructed their ideas of the deity after their own personalities, and that consequently men and women behave differently with their own ideas of Christ. Susanna von Klettenberg worshiped Christ as a lover in whom she placed her full confidence, while Lavater adored him as a friend and occasional rival whose example he tried to follow. Needless to say, Goethe agreed with neither, since he had his own *imago Christi* to contend with.[21] As he worked out his own theology and as he thought through his experiences with Lavater and other "men of action" such as the philosopher Johann Basedow – both of whom he seems to have considered prophets after a fashion – he began to compose his idea of Muhammad. Goethe links the conception of his project to his observation of Lavater's and Basedow's behavior, both of whom strained the relationship between the divine and the terrestrial by using spiritual means for earthly, this-worldly aims.[22] As these considerations ran through his mind, and as he sought other historical examples of people who combined the divine with the secular, he slowly conceived of the idea of writing a play about Muhammad, whom he had hitherto considered a mere impostor. Great men are driven to spread or ex-press the divine that is in them, but this expression is compromised by the realities of its contact with the outside world, which compromise eventually results in their being entirely deprived of that divine essence that they once wanted to share as they bring themselves down to the world's level.[23] Ex-pression becomes deprivation.

The superior (*vorzüglich*) individual's struggle between the spiritual and the earthly, between the other-worldly and the this-worldly, is of course Goethe's own. The dilemma he seemed to face in the early 1770s is precisely the one faced by a charismatic, wise, eloquent person like Muhammad, namely how to communicate the "Göttliche was in ihm ist" to the world. Worse yet, the young Goethe's voyage of self-discovery leads him to the appalling realization that the cultivation of one's virtues invariably leads to the cultivation of one's vices at the same time, thereby rendering such tragedies inevitable.[24] The more he cultivates his *vorzüglich* qualities, therefore, the likelier it is that the associated vices will come to the fore. By all accounts, Goethe had a great deal of *das Göttliche* in him: contemporary testimonies routinely compare him to kings, prophets, divinities, and pseudo-divinities.[25] Naturally, he faced the prophet's problem: on the one hand, he has his own theology and ideas about God; on the other hand, he feels no desire to defile them by bringing them into contact with the "raw" world for fear of losing them altogether. So it is with Goethe's Muhammad, whom he sees as the proper historical analogue for the tragic scenario of the great man's destiny.

Setting out to write a play about Muhammad allowed Goethe to work out the problem of his "destiny" while simultaneously undoing the opposition between the literary and theological registers. Goethe opts for poetry over prophecy not through an abandonment of the latter, but rather through the choice of an activity that can do the same thing as the liturgy without simultaneously solving the problem of worldly corruption:

Die wahre Poesie kündet sich dadurch an, daß sie, als ein weltliches Evangelium, durch innere Heiterkeit, durch äußeres Behagen, uns von den irdischen Lasten zu befreien weiß, die auf uns drücken. Wie ein Luftballon hebt sie uns mit dem Ballast der uns anhängt, in höhere Regionen, und läßt die verwirrten Irrgänge der Erde in Vogelperspektive vor uns entwickelt daliegen. Die muntersten

wie die ernstesten Werke haben den gleichen Zweck, durch
eine glückliche geistreiche Darstellung, so Lust als Schmerz zu
mäßigen.

[Real poetry reveals itself in this: like a worldly gospel, through inner
serenity and outer pleasantness, it delivers us from the earthly burdens that weigh us down. Like a hot-air balloon, it lifts us and the
ballast that we carry heavenward, giving us a bird's eye view of the
confused mazes of the earth stretched out beneath us. The lightest and
the most serious works have the same aim: to moderate joy and pain
through a fortunate spiritual representation.][26]

It is precisely to the production of such a worldly gospel ("weltliches
Evangelium") that Goethe dedicates himself.[27] Ironically, this
worldly gospel works by taking its readers outside the world and
giving them a world's eye view of their human condition. Its vector
of operation carries the reader from the realm of language to that of
the spirit, thereby conflating the literary and the spiritual.

This conflation can be connected to the idea of the genius, which
reached its peak during the *Sturm und Drang*. Navid Kermani
has made the case for the similarities between the Muslim idea
of the prophet and the concept of the genius: both produce work
of unparalleled aesthetic qualities whose origins are shrouded
in mystery – the divine, non-self-revealing God in Islam, and the
intuition of the genius that surpasses all understanding. Both Muslim
prophet and genius–artist mediate the absolute and infinite, neither
acts or speaks in his own name but rather ex-presses something that
is communicated through him, and both suffer a great deal as they
create. Kermani performs a remarkable experiment, substituting
rasūl for "artist" and *kitāb* for "art" in a passage from Schelling's
System of Transcendental Idealism to yield the following:

Just as the fatal man does not do what he wants to do, or what he
intends to do, but what he has to do, being under the influence
of an incomprehensible fate, just like him the *rasūl*, whatever he
might intend, seems to be under the influence of a power which
separates him from other human beings and which forces him to
express himself on matters or portray matters he himself cannot see
through and whose significance is tremendous. Since the absolute
coincidence of actions that flee each other is not explicable, but rather
an incident that cannot be denied – although it is uncomprehensive
– so the *kitāb* is the one and only and everlasting revelation existing,

and the miracle that would, even if it had existed just once, convince us of the absolute reality of the supreme.[28]

Goethe's exploration of Muhammad's life as a subject for a play is bound inextricably with the theory of genius and literary production, as well as his own identity as a productive genius.[29] Muhammad thus joins a panoply of other figures – Shakespeare, Pindar, Horace – all of whom stand for the towering sort of genius that Goethe would emulate.

What the foregoing seems to indicate is that Goethe's ideas about worldliness, and literature in the world, have much to do with religion in general and Islam in particular. Islam made sense in a way that Christianity did not: the former allowed Goethe to "rise above the world," especially in view of Christianity's violent history in Germany itself. Apart from Goethe's personal, pan-theistic attraction to Islam, the turn to Muhammad might also be read as an attempt at rising above the cultural memory of the Thirty Years' War, of which Goethe's mind was still full since he had just finished *Goetz von Berlichingen*. Writing about Muhammad not only permitted him to work out his plans for the future, but also (thankfully) to take his writing beyond the national historic passions in which he was so deeply invested at the writing of *Goetz* (he writes that Adelaide was so beautifully created that he fell in love with her).[30]

The plot that Goethe conceives of is of a prophet–poet of nature, who progresses through the same phases of adoration as Abraham in the Qur'ān: first he thinks the stars are God, then the moon, then the sun, before settling on the one eternal God of the monotheisms. Muhammad then converts his wife and Ali before trying to convert the Quraysh, whereupon he finds himself compelled to use trickery ("List") rather than force. Thus the earthly gains ground while the divine shrinks. ("Das Irdische wächst und breitet sich aus, das Göttliche tritt zurück und wird getrübt.")[31] At a certain point, having decided to conquer by any means necessary, Muhammad's methods turn against him: he is poisoned by the wife of a man whose execution he had ordered. As he feels the poisonous effects during the fifth act, Muhammad returns to himself and the higher calling that had set him on this course in the first place, thus provoking general admiration: "Seine große Fassung, die Wiederkehr zu sich selbst, zum höheren Sinne, machen ihn der Bewunderung würdig. Er reinigt seine Lehre, befestigt sein Reich und stirbt." ["His great composure, his return to himself and to higher things, make him worthy of admiration. He purifies his teaching, consolidates his kingdom and dies."][32] Overall, it is supposed to be a lesson in what genius can do to character and intellect, and about the resulting gains and losses.[33] The plot thus exposes the young Goethe's anxieties about art and action, about being a brilliant man of the word, and being a successful man of the world. If the very different trajectories of Werther and Goetz von Berlichingen were to be read biographically, we might see in them the two possible outcomes of a volcanic energy that is not sure how best to direct itself, and how best to avoid the seeming inevitabilities of self-destruction or the destruction of others.[34] Literature permits action through refinement ("List") without violence.

The initial result of Goethe's efforts was a dramatic fragment, "Mahomet," that remained incomplete until his death, although as will be seen it was only one of several decisive engagements over the course of Goethe's life. The fragment that remains consists of an opening hymn in which Muhammad, per Goethe's plan, re-enacts Abraham's "discovery" of monotheism. The starry setting of the play's opening and the cosmological language of the poem are based on the Abraham story as narrated in the Qur'ān, especially Q6:74–79. Not coincidentally this is one of the passages that Goethe felt strongly enough about to transcribe for future reference.[35] Instead of relying on Megerlin's translation, Goethe translates from Marracci's Latin to produce a version that approaches the conciseness and literary force of the Qur'ānic text:

> Abraham sprach zu seinem Vater Azar. Ehrst du Götzen für Götter? Wahrhaftig ich erkenne deinen, und deines Volks Offenbaren Irrtum. Da zeigten wir Abraham des Himmels und der Erde Reich daß er im wahren Glauben bestätiget würde. Und als die Nacht über ihm finster ward, sah er das Gestirn und sprach: Das ist mein Herrscher, da es aber niederging rief er: untergehende [sic] lieb ich nicht. Dann sah er den Mond aufgehen, sprach das ist mein Herrscher! Da er aber niederging sagt er: Wenn mich mein Herr nicht leitet geh ich in der Irre mit diesem Volk; Wie aber die Sonne heraufkam sprach er: Das ist mein Herrscher. Er ist größer. Aber da sie auch unterging sprach er: O mein Volk nun bin ich frei von deinem Irrtümern! Ich habe mein Angesicht gewendet zu dem der Himmel und Erde erschaffen hat.[36]

Abraham's progress is itself a sort of wish fulfillment, allowing Goethe to move from the adoration of nature to the adoration of its Creator.

In Goethe's literary idiom this narrative becomes a hymn of five stanzas, the middle three of which apostrophize various heavenly bodies – Jupiter ("Gad"), the moon, the sun – imploring them to become objects of adoration ("Sei mein Herr du, mein Gott") and each of which falls out of favor as soon as it sets. This leaves Goethe's Mahomet with the one all-creating God:

> Hebe liebendes Herz dem Erschaffenden dich!
> Sei mein Herr du! Mein Gott! Du allliebender du!
> Der die Sonne den Mond und die Stern
> Schuf Erde und Himmel und mich.

> [Raise yourself, my heart, to the Creator!
> You be my Lord! My God! You eternal one!
> You who created the sun, the moon and the star,
> Heaven and earth and me.][37]

The rest of the fragment contains a dialogue of the deaf between Mahomet and Halima in which Goethe's character bewails the ignorance of those, like Halima, who are still held by the shackles of idolatry and do not understand his message. Finally, the fragment contains the "Mahomets Gesang," a duo written for the characters Ali and Halima centered on the metaphor of a river. While there is no sure way of evaluating Goethe's strategy here – did he mean to compare Muhammad to a river? – the case has persuasively been made for tracing the language and imagery of the "Mahomets Gesang" to Goethe's reading of the classics.[38] Horace's comparison of Pindar's poetry to a boiling river swollen with rain (*Carm.* 4.2.5–8) was probably on Goethe's mind as he composed the "Mahomets Gesang," and Pindar was, as we have seen, very much part of Goethe's project of self-definition as a poet and writer in the early 1770s. The aforementioned Pindar letter of July 1772 sees citations from Pindar sitting near the Qur'ān (Q20:18) along with allusions to Horace and Quintilian.[39] Moreover, Pindar, who was regarded as a free verse poet at the time, became the impossible *exemplum* for Herder and Goethe, the former identifying his dithyrambs as being inimitable, while the latter did his best to imitate Pindar in the "Wandrers Sturmlied" (composed in 1771 but only published in 1815).[40] This literary genealogy leads to the curious composition of the "Mahomets Gesang," where the poet–genius (Muhammad? Goethe?) is described through the effects of his poetry, compared to a river flowing from the mountain springs and leading his brothers to the ocean, but nowhere explicitly named.[41] Muhammad and the Qur'ān are therefore key points of reference as Goethe defines his task as a poet and the *Sturm und Drang* aesthetics of his youth with the daring poetic experiments that they entail. Moreover, the juxtaposition of the Qur'ān, Pindar, and Horace is a none-too-subtle response to Marracci, who attempted to respond to the claim of *I'jāz* by citing, of all things, *Carm.* 4.2 (see above). From the outset Goethe had parochialism in his cross hairs and global culture in his purview: the trio of Pindar–Horace–Muhammad restitutes to the Qur'ān its literary and cultural value as a text on par with the texts that found his own (and eventually Europe's) literary historical being.

This collapse of Muhammad into Abraham is symptomatic of Goethe's view of the patriarch: someone who gazes at the world below from a joyous, lofty calm. At the opening of the *Divan*, Goethe invokes the happy life of the patriarch: "Flüchte du, im reinen Osten/ Patriarchenluft zu kosten" ("Hegire"). ["Flee to the pure East/To breathe the air of the patriarchs."] Breathing the pure air of the patriarchs probably also had much to do with Goethe's suffering in the stifling air of Napoleonic Europe's hyper-nationalisms.[42] Goethe was probably also thinking of the numerous debates in Germany regarding the "archaism" of the Old Testament and its translations; which archaism underwent an important shift from being negatively to being positively valued.[43] The poetry of the Old Testament, the patriarchal text par excellence, operates as a foundational text and literary example to whose force and influence the writer can only aspire. Elsewhere in the Goethe canon, the young Werther describes one of his few happy moments in his life as one lived in the "Züge patriarchalischen Lebens" (the "patriarchal way of life") as he reads Homer and cooks peas in Wahlheim.[44] In this setting, the patriarchs and Homer are of a piece; prophetic poets all. When Goethe "translates" Abraham into Muhammad, he is proposing cultural equivalence between Islam, Judeo-Christianity and the Greco-Roman heritage. Goethe inscribes his understanding of the relationship between poetry and prophecy within these three vertices: there can be no literature without divine inspiration, nor can there be inspiration unless one can literally inhale the air of the patriarchs (indeed, Werther says he chose Wahlheim because it is so close to heaven).[45] The turn to the East thus combines rejuvenation with spiritual and literary self-fulfillment.

One of the key intellectual historical developments that enabled Goethe's *Divan* and probably influenced his thinking about world literature was the publication of the *Fundgruben des Orients/Mines de l'orient* under the editorship of Joseph von Hammer. This encyclopedic collection of articles and annotated translations from Arabic, Persian, and Turkish into every major European language (French, German, Greek, Italian, Latin) stands, in effect, as the first instance of what could be called *Weltliteratur*. The contents fall under diverse headings – philology, poetry, history, geography, astronomy, bibliography, and so on – thereby communicating the full wealth of the treasures to be found in the "Oriental mine." This is announced from the title page, which is printed in three languages: Arabic, German, and French. Curiously, it is the Arabic title that is the longest and most detailed:

مخزن الكنوز المشرقيه
و معدن الرموز الاجنبية
تأليف
جماعة من الأدباء
بهمة زين الشرفاء
ونجسلاس قونت سياورشكي

قل لله المشرق و المغرب يهدي من يشاء الى صراط مستقيم

طبعت في مدينة وينا دار السلطنة الأيمبراطورية النمسوية
سنة تسع و ثمانمأية و الف بعد ميلاد المسيح اعني بها
سنة ثلث و عشرين و مأيتين و الف بعد الهجرة المحمدية [46]

The differences among the titles say a great deal about the project's conception. Quite apart from the fact the patron's name, Count Wenzeslaus von Rzewusky, appears only in Arabic,[47] the Arabic title makes clear that the book is a creative product of many hands: it is a *ta'līf jamā'a min-al-udabā'* rather than a mine "exploited" by an interested, if loving group ("Gesellschaft von Liebhabern"). Moreover, the wording of the Arabic title differs significantly from the German and French versions: calling the *Fundgruben* "The Warehouse of Eastern Treasures and the Mine of Foreign Symbols" in Arabic foregrounds the text's oscillation between Eastern and Western idioms. By invoking Q2:142, the editors (or probably just Hammer himself) reconcile the opposition between East and West under the ownership of the God of Islam and imply that the *Fundgruben* is one "straight path" (صراط مستقيم) through the Oriental cultural treasure.

Hammer's introduction to the *Fundgruben* bears this out. Having described the importance of Oriental studies to the West since the Dark Ages, and having rehearsed the difficulties of obtaining Oriental manuscripts and their impact on the intellectual development of the West, and the damage done to previous projects like his own by the speculation of publishers and editors, Hammer explains the reach of the project:

> Wir fühlen uns berufen, den wahren Pfad zur Vervollkommnung des orientalischen Studiums anzuzeigen, und somit auf unsere Unternehmung den Sinn unsers Titelspruchs anzuwenden:
>
> > *Sag: Gottes ist der Orient und Gottes ist der Occident;*
> > *Er leitet, wen er will, den wahren Pfad* [i.e. Q2:142].
>
> Also alles, was im Orient auf den Occident, und im Occident auf den Orient hinblickt, soll sich hier begegnen, und hülfreiche Hand bieten, aus den noch unbearbeiteten Fundgruben Schätze der Erkenntnis und des Wissens zu Tage zu fördern.
>
> [We feel that it is our task to show the true path for the improvement of Oriental studies, thereby applying the meaning behind our motto: "Say unto God *belongeth* the east and the west: He directeth whom He pleaseth into the right way." Thus all of those in the West who gaze at the East, and vice versa, will meet here, helping each other to extract from the raw mine treasures of knowledge and learning.][48]

Thus the *Fundgruben des Orients* is meant to go beyond D'Herbelot's *Bibliothèque orientale*. More than a series of translations, it is the point at which the Eastern and Western gazes intersect. The interdisciplinary, international, and multicultural character of the journal makes it a site of exchange moving in both directions, from the East to the West and vice versa, thereby anticipating the notion of international exchange and cooperation that inform Goethe's ideas about world literature; that plurality of cultures brought into one location, to which each researcher brings his or her wares.

The *Fundgruben* had an immediate impact on the *Divan*. One would not be far wrong in reading the *Divan* as a mise-en-vers of the *Fundgruben*.[49] Even the layout of the title pages bears more than a passing resemblance: as we have seen, Goethe's text also has an Arabic title that differs from its German one. Furthermore, the titles of the sections and poems of the *Divan* match many of the entries of the *Fundgruben*, among them: new translations of parts

of the Qur'ān by Hammer (undertaken as preparation for a translation in rhyme that would communicate the full literary impact of the
Arabic text), Silvestre de Sacy's translation of Attar's *Pend Nameh*,
Rosenzweig's translation of Jami's *Yusuf u Zulaikha*, as well as translations of Firdausi, Rumi, and Attar by various hands. The "motto" of
the *Fundgruben*, Q2:142, appears in the opening of Goethe's poem
"Talismane": "Gottes ist der Orient! Gottes ist der Occident!" The
original version had as its third and fourth verses, "Auch den Norden
wie den Süden/Hat sein Auge nie gemieden," thereby extending the
explication in the spirit of the title page of the *Fundgruben*.[50] Under
"Freisinn" we read an adaptation of Q6:97 into a quatrain: "Er hat
euch die Gestirne gesetzt/Als Leiter zu Land und See;/Damit ihr euch
daran ergötzt,/Stets blickend in die Höh." ["He has set the stars for
you/As guides on land and sea/So that you may be delighted/As you
look up above forever."][51] The eyes that are always gazing at heaven
are probably Goethe's own, whose interest in astronomy led him, as
we have seen, to use Q6:74–79 as a basis for the opening of *Mahomet*,
and would almost certainly have made him interested in the opening
piece of the *Fundgruben*, Hammer's article on Arab constellations,
and its epigram: "Er hat Euch die Gestirne gesetzt, als Leiter in der
Finsterniß zu Land und See."[52]

Hammer's ideas about translation, and especially his views
about the poetic qualities of Arabic and German, would certainly
have resonated with Goethe. In the introduction to the first set of
fragmentary translations for the *Fundgruben* we read the following:

> Das lebendige Wort, das die *sieben* göttlichen an der Kaaba
> ausgehangene Gedichte, weit hinter sich zurück ließ, konnte nicht
> die Frucht menschlicher Begeisterung, es musste im Himmel
> gesprochen und geschrieben sein von Ewigkeit her. Die treueste
> Übersetzung davon wird die sein, welche nicht nur den Geist,
> sondern auch die Form darzustellen ringt. Nachbildung der Rede
> durch Rythmus und Schall ist die unerläsliche Bedingung der
> Übersetzung eines Dichterwerks. Der höchste Zauber arabischer
> Poesie besteht nicht nur in Bild und Bewegung, sondern vorzüglich
> in des Reimes Gleichklang, der für arabisches Ohr wahrer Sirenton
> ist. Um also den poetischen Gehalt des Korans so getreu als
> möglich auszumünzen, muß die Übersetzung mit dem Originale
> nicht nur gleichen Schritt, sondern auch gleichen Ton halten; die
> Endreime der Verse müssen in Reimen übertragen werden, was
> bisher in keiner der uns bekannten Übersetzungen geschehen, und

in keiner europäischen Sprache getreuer geschehen konnte als in
der deutschen.

[The living word (i.e. the Qur'ān), which left the seven hanging
Odes far behind it, could not have been the fruit of human
inspiration: it must have been spoken and written in heaven from
eternity. The truest translation thereof would therefore be one that
struggles to represent not only its content, but also its form. The
reproduction of speech through rhythm and sound is the sine qua
non of the translation of a poet's work. The highest magic of Arabic
poetry consists not of imagery and movement, but in the superior
consonance of its rhyme, which to Arabic ears is a true sirensong.
In order to capture the poetic content of the Koran as authentically
as possible, the translation must not only follow the rhythm of the
original, but also its sound: the end-rhymes of the verses must also
be put into rhyme, which has not happened in any known translation,
and can happen in no European language more authentically than in
German.][53]

It is important to note here that we are dealing with a new generation of
Qur'ānic translation; one where sound and form matter as much as, if
not more than, content.[54] There is no exegetical apparatus attached to
any of Hammer's fragmentary translations in the *Fundgruben*. What
we see, with inconsistent results,[55] is a serious attempt at seducing
the Western reader with a functional translation of the magical sound
of the Qur'ān. We are not far, then, from the conflation of poetry
and prophecy that enthralled the young Goethe, now re-inscribed
into a global exchange of literature, ideas, and other disciplines that
bears a strong resemblance to the terms in which Goethe theorizes
Weltliteratur.

Among the many occasions that Goethe had to write about
world literature, there is one in particular that stands out: a review
of Carlyle's *German Romance*[56] where his reflection on the future of
global literary production reminds him of a passage from the Qur'ān
proclaiming God's mercy in sending to each people a prophet who
speaks their language:

Eine wahrhaft allgemeine Duldung wird am sichersten erreicht, wenn
man das Besondere der einzelnen Menschen und Völkerschaften
auf sich beruhen läßt, bei der Überzeugung jedoch festhält, daß
das wahrhaft Verdienstliche sich dadurch auszeichnet, daß es der
ganzen Menschheit angehört. Zu einer solchen Vermittelung und

wechselseitigen Anerkennung tragen die Deutschen seit langer Zeit schon bei. Wer die deutsche Sprache versteht und studiert, befindet sich auf dem Markte, wo alle Nationen ihre Waren anbieten; er spielt den Dolmetscher, indem er sich selbst bereichert.

Und so ist jeder Übersetzer anzusehen, daß er sich als Vermittler dieses allgemein-geistigen Handels bemüht und den Wechseltauch zu befördern sich Geschäft macht. Denn was man auch von der Unzulänglichkeit des Übersetzers sagen mag, so ist und bleibt es doch eines der wichtigsten und würdigsten Geschäfte in dem allgemeinen Weltverkehr.

Der Koran sagt: "Gott hat jedem Volke einen Propheten gegeben in seiner eigenen Sprache." So ist jeder Übersetzer ein Prophet in seinem Volke. Luthers Bibelübersetzung hat die größten Wirkungen hervorgebracht, wenn schon die Kritik daran bis auf den heutigen Tag immerfort bedingt und mäkelt. Und was ist denn das ganze ungeheure Geschäft der Bibelgesellschaft anders, als das Evangelium einem jeden Volke, in seine Sprache und Art gebracht, zu überliefern?

[A truly universal toleration would certainly be reached, if the special characteristic of distinct persons and peoples were laid to rest, and by the conviction that the most truly deserving quality that reveals itself thereby belongs to all humanity. The Germans have for a long time been contributing to this sort of mediation and many-sided acknowledgement. Whoever understands and studies the German language finds himself in the marketplace where all nations sell their wares: he plays the translator who enriches himself (through cultural exchange).

And so should every translator be seen as someone who tries to be at the centre of this universal culture business and manages its mutual exchanges. For no matter what one tries to say about the inadequacies of translation, it remains one of the most important and worthiest businesses in global commerce.

The Koran says: "God has sent to every people a prophet in their own tongue." So is every translator a prophet to his people. Luther's translation of the Bible has had the greatest possible impact, even if critics insist on finding fault with it to this day. What, after all, is the huge business project of the society of the Bible, if not to deliver the Gospel to every population in its language and after its manner?][57]

This passage synthesizes Goethe's entire career, from the question of tolerance that haunted his youth to the conception of world literature. The juxtaposition of *Weltliteratur*, the marketplace,[58] translation, the Qur'ān, and the Bible are indicative of Goethe's universalist frame of mind, which is broad enough to see in Luther's translation of the Bible the fulfillment of a Qur'ānic prophecy. The very existence of the global literary marketplace depends on the possibility of translations that bring the gospel to every population in their language and manner. The operation of literature is bound intimately with its role as an earthly gospel, and the task of the translator of literature is to bring this gospel to the many peoples and languages of the earth. The translator, therefore, operates between heavenly and earthly registers, like the Qur'ānic prophet (unlike the biblical model of prophecy, where no prophet is accepted in his own country [Luke 4:24]) who transmits God's message in a language that the people of a given community can understand. Goethe quotes Q14:4 (found, not coincidentally, in the sūra of Ibrahīm) in what would seem to be his own translation, as it stands somewhere between the Hammer and Megerlin versions, and which recalls part of Q13:8, which he had transcribed in Megerlin's translation in his youth.[59]

The convergence of the world's literatures, therefore, is not only a commercial enterprise, it is a religious one. Goethe's ideas on *Weltliteratur* have much more to do with religion than they do with buying and selling; that the commercial metaphor is just that: a *metaphor*, rather like the commercial metaphors that are used in religious texts. Thus when Goethe tells us that the interpreter is enriched by his business at the marketplace of world cultures, this has far less to do with the actual buying and selling of literary commodities and more with a figurative exchange. This matters because economic metaphors are a frequent recourse in religious texts, and especially in the Qur'ān and Bible, as a means of representing metaphysical gains and losses.

Goethe's speculations on world literature are conceived in relation to a specific set of translations (of his work into English). His opinions jump within a paragraph from those translations to the task of the translator to scripture. Although Goethe's views on world literature have gone through many interpretations and reappropriations, the religious component seems to have been overlooked, despite the fact that one of Goethe's working definitions seems to have been that which serves as a link among national literatures *and* transcends time and space.[60] It is clear, however, that in Goethe's mind, bringing the word of God to the masses and the genesis of world literature are part of one and the same process. Still, Goethe's commercial metaphors are not entirely clear: on the one hand, he speaks of markets and translators as middlemen constantly enriching themselves; on the other, he speaks of the arrival of world literature as part of a global transformation. Part of the eschatology of that world might be suggested by the Qur'ān, where commercial metaphors and eschatology go hand in hand.[61] The logic of this process is one of recognition: just as believers and unbelievers are brought together on the day of judgment and are recognized for their past actions, so are buyers and sellers brought together in the marketplace of literature and recognized for theirs. Since Goethe worked out his thinking about world literature in relation to translation, translation becomes the touchstone for the operation of world literature, now conceived of as a simultaneous interaction of global literatures in a process of ever-increasing speed and intensity.[62] Goethe speaks of an *age* of world literature as one would speak of a brave new world.[63] Historicizing world literature in this way enables him to formulate the concept as being dependent on the arrival of a sacred book, such as Luther's Bible or the Qur'ān in modern translation. Goethe's hesitation between promoting an international movement of translation from all to all (which is what is most frequently understood by *Weltliteratur*) and the promotion of German as being *the* privileged language of world literature, the understanding of which obviates the need to learn Greek, Latin, Italian, or Spanish, hinges on this very point: just as the Arabic Qur'ān exists in a privileged language but is, at the same time, intended for all humanity, so does German function as a linguistic space destined to serve as the meeting point for all humanity, so much so that in one conversation with Eckermann Goethe speculates that German speakers really have no need to understand other languages.[64] Nevertheless, Goethe always considered translation to be part of a given nation's literature: once when invited to contribute to an anthology of German resistance poetry in 1808, he advised the editors to include German translations of foreign poems, the better to understand the literary history that they were trying to construct. Moreover, Goethe considered translation to be a historical *process*, whereby the target text relates to the original first literally, then parodistically (Berman uses this term to describe transplanting the mentality of the source into the target culture), and then finally there arrives a phase where the translation works *from the place of* the source rather than acting in its stead.[65] Not coincidentally, this theory is developed in the notes that accompany the *West-östlicher Divan*.[66] It is precisely this last phase that allows source and target, or original and translation, to regard each other as specular

reflections or re-vivifications. The relationship of a text to its translation is therefore not one of pristine original to derivative copy, but one
of left- to right-handed images. Translation in the third phase is this
mapping of points across an axis of reflection that enables the inhabitants of a given space to see how a text works "in its place" ("an deiner
Stelle"). World literature is what happens when this mapping of texts
across reflective boundaries becomes the norm of literary production,
which henceforth has more to do with transmission than creation.
Hence the title *West-östlicher Divan*: it is not a mere translation of
Eastern literary topoi into a Western language, but the construction of
a series of specular relationships across the border between East and
West, whereby Hafiz is mapped on to Goethe, Timur on to Napoleon,
and so on, and whereby the idea that neither object nor specular image
– Eastern object and Western image or vice versa – could or would
obtain. Hence their inseparability: "Orient und Okzident sind nicht
mehr zu trennen." ["East and West can no longer be separated."][67]

The invocation of the Qur'ān and Luther's Bible in relation to
this question subverts the received idea of the author as creator, for
it would be difficult to speak of Luther as the author of the Bible
and downright heretical to speak of Muhammad as the author of the
Qur'ān. However, one would be correct in identifying both as trans-
mitters of a text considered to be the word of God across the axis that
separates the human from the divine, but which nevertheless allows
visual and oral communication (one cannot see, but one can hear,
God). The singularity of the prophet as messenger is replaced, in
Goethe's conception of world literature, by the multiplicity of translators as prophets. The advent of world literature becomes the event
that allows the author to become invisible without becoming dead: he
is always and everywhere revived through the transmission of his text
through prophets and translators. The life of the text and the invocation of the author inhere in its re-citation and exegesis rather than
its critical analysis. And it is here, perhaps, that we see the full
force of Goethe's work with the Qur'ān: by re-writing certain verses
in the *Divan*, Goethe makes it possible to recite the Qur'ān on the
other side of the mirror separating Arabic from German.[68] When we
hear a tenor sing Schumann's versions of "Talismane" or "Freisinn"
(both Op. 25), we are hearing the Qur'ān mapped on to a cultural
space different from, but not entirely foreign to, the one inhabited by
a given *qāri'* reciting Q14:4. This is enabled by the textual musical-
ity and oral character of the Qur'ān, insofar as a musical sequence

can be transposed into any key and remain identical, while a text must undergo some change to be translated.[69] Goethe seems to have aimed at doing to texts what happens in musical transposition, having well understood that a text lives through its recitation, and that the awesome power of the Qur'ān could only be rendered in translation through poetry and music. Moreover, the reach of his rendition bears witness to the extent to which the Qur'ān had worked its way into the fabric of Western culture by the nineteenth century.

Goethe's invocation of prophecy and scripture thus colors the universal vocation of world literature. The overarching force that regulates the operation of world literature is not the transcendent market but rather a universal humanity, of which the world's many particular literatures are seen as so many different manifestations – "das ewig Eine, das sich vielfach offenbart."[70] This concern with the Eternal becomes the fabric on to which the imaginary interaction of world literatures is projected.

Goethe's entire career seems to have been a struggle between theology and literature, between prophecy and poetry. His genius was such that he re-formulated the entire literary edifice of his day in order to allow it to perform the function of "worldly gospel." Furthermore, as one of the prophets who perfected the language of his people, and one who was concerned that it should play its "honorable part" in the international agora, Goethe modeled himself on the Qur'ānic prophets. In his outward-looking, forward-thinking manner, Goethe was in many ways the anti-Napoleon: whereas the latter thought of Muhammad as a warmonger on whom he could model himself, Goethe saw in Muhammad and in the Qur'ān a brilliant example of what words can do.

One immediate consequence of Goethe's reflections on world literature is found in Carlyle's description of Muhammad as a Great Man in *On Heroes and Hero Worship*.[71] Carlyle, whose relationship to Goethe provided important occasions for pronouncements on world literature, found in Goethe a source of spiritual relief from what he took to be the excessive materialism and "atheism" of English culture.[72] Carlyle's correspondence with Goethe describes the former's discovery of German literature in terms of a religious conversion, from unbelief "not in Religion only, but in all the Mercy and Beauty of which it is the Symbol; storm-tossed in my own imaginations; a man divided from men; exasperated, wretched, driven almost to despair, so that Faust's wild *curse* seemed the only fit greeting for human life" to "life spent in Literature, with such fortune and such strength as may be granted to me; hoping little and fearing little from the world." Toward those who, like Goethe, made this conversion possible, Carlyle is especially grateful, describing them in terms that recall Goethe's "Freisinn" and Q6:97:

> No wonder I should love the wise and worthy men by whose instructions so blessed a result has been brought about. For these men, too, there can be no reward like that consciousness that in distant countries and times, the hearts of their fellow-men will yearn towards them with gratitude and veneration, and those that are wandering in darkness turn towards them as to loadstars guiding into a secure home.[73]

After Goethe's death, Carlyle writes to his brother that, "Out of Goethe, who is my near neighbour, so to speak, there is no writing that *speaks* to me (*mich anspricht*) like the Hebrew Scriptures, though they lie far remote."[74] Whenever Carlyle thinks of Goethe, God and scripture are never far behind. This set of relationships molded Carlyle's belief that, despite the "wearisome" character of the Qur'ān (which Carlyle read in the Sale translation), Muhammad was a sincere prophet and a Great Man. Carlyle's sensitivity to the religious aspect of literature, as inflected by his reading of German literature and philosophy, allowed him to posit sincerity as the mark of Muhammad's greatness (as it is that of every hero), and, moreover, to valorize Muhammad's psychological struggles with his mission over their impact on world history. The net result is an account of Muhammad that overturns the routine accusations of imposture and ambition in favor of a man seeking, finding, and proclaiming answers regarding his place in the universe. According to Carlyle, via Goethe, those answers have universal reach:

> That God is great; and that there is nothing else great! He is the Reality. Wooden Idols are not real; He is real. He made us at first, sustains us yet; we and all things are but the shadow of Him; a transitory garment veiling the Eternal Splendor. "*Allah akbar*, God is great;" – and then also "*Islam*," That we must submit to God. That our whole strength lies in resigned submission to Him, whatsoever He do to us. For this world, and for the other! The thing He sends to us, were it death and worse than death, shall be good, shall be best; we resign ourselves to God. – "If this be *Islam*," says Goethe, "do we not all live in *Islam*?" Yes, all of us that have any moral life; we all live so.[75]

The universal message of Islam is made "receivable," comprehensible, by Goethe's reading of Islam and its translation – cultural as well as literary – by Carlyle. If, as Fritz Strich pointed out a half century ago, world literature is about the expression of relationships between nation and nation, those relationships are themselves transformed by the translation dynamic constitutive of *Weltliteratur*.[76] With Goethe the translated Qur'ān makes its way into the world literary system, as a text central to the understanding of what links nations and cultures to each other. Far from desecrating the Qur'ān, this development actually restitutes its scriptural status as a "worldly gospel." Although we are not done with the various defamations of Qur'ānic style and status, we are very far indeed from the warmongering polemics of Marracci. This is due, perhaps in part, to the reality of the Napoleonic wars: there is no sense in worrying about the Ottoman threat when faced with marauding armies coming from the other end of Europe. But it is also due to the very special engagement with the Qur'ān that was Goethe's, and the realization that the time had come to reach a new understanding of the link between poetry and prophecy; that literature would replace religion as the archive of humanity, and that the Qur'ān's place in the literary canon – not in opposition to, but together with, the concert of English, French, Italian, Spanish, Persian, Turkish, and other literary voices – was beyond dispute.

AFTERWORD

The uses to which the Qur'ān was put during the eighteenth century – describing the legislator, situating Europe in the context of global history, defining world literature – attest to its continuing importance and centrality even before the establishment of Orientalism as an academic discipline with all of the institutional trappings that accrue during the nineteenth century. The efflorescence of Oriental and Islamic studies during the nineteenth and twentieth centuries has been described (and condemned) elsewhere.[1] Much ink has been spilled on the course and impact of the fields and sub-fields of Arabic, Islamic, and/or Qur'ānic studies. In what follows I would like to pass a cursory glance at recent translations of the Qur'ān in order to establish what has and has not changed since the eighteenth century.

The most important of these changes is the history of Western imperialism and its painful aftermath. After Goethe, the translated Qur'ān is usually classified as a document belonging to a "world religion" and as the scripture of the Muslims. However, the encyclopedic translations of Marracci and Sale are a thing of the past (though Si Hamza Boubakeur's ambitious translation [1970] is an important exception in this respect). Curiously enough, this was happening while the entire Muslim world was being written out of world history as a static, unchanging entity, by specialists and non-specialists alike.[2] Albin de Biberstein Kazimirski's translation was first published as part of a three-volume set entitled *Les livres sacrés de l'Orient*, alongside translations of the *Shi King* and the laws of the *Manu*, under the editorship of the sinologist Pauthier.[3] Pauthier justifies his endeavor in world historical terms reminiscent of Voltaire, with the added impetus that comes from the need to understand religion better, as a way of countering the nefarious effects of Hegel's essentialist view of the Orient writ large as an unchanging entity. As Pauthier conceives it, the West's historical interaction with the Orient is not entirely innocent:

> C'est par la lecture de ce livre que nous pourrons apprendre à con-naître le caractère arabe et l'énergie fanatique de l'ennemi que nous avons à combattre dans l'Algérie, où la croyance dans le Koran est encore très-vive. C'est aussi par l'étude assidue du Koran que nous pourrons comprendre la politique des Arabes. Dans ce livre sacré la *déloyauté* en guerre est autorisée [Q8:58]; de même que la dépouille des ennemis [Q8:69]; la guerre doit se faire sans rémission [Q9:12–13, 24, 29, 36, 82]. On y trouve aussi prescrits *la guerre sainte* et les *mois sacrées* [Q9:5]. Les lâches, ou ceux qui ne veulent pas combattre les infidèles sont réprouvés et maudits [Q9:88, 91, 96].

> [It is by reading this book that we can get to know the Arabic character and the fanatic energy of the enemy that we have to fight in Algeria, where belief in the Koran is still very much alive. It is also by the assiduous study of the Koran that we can understand the politics of the Arabs. In this sacred book *disloyalty* in war is permitted (Q8:58), as well as despoiling the enemy (Q8:69); war must be waged relent-lessly (Q9:12–13, 24, 29, 36, 82). Similarly *holy war* and *sacred months* are prescribed (9:5). Cowards, or those who do not want to fight the infidels, are reproved and cursed (Q9:88, 91, 96).][4]

This passage stands strangely at odds with the body of Pauthier's introduction, most of which is very broad minded, and even includes a French translation of Sale's "Preliminary Discourse." Clearly, for Pauthier, reading the Qur'ān, understanding Islam, and ending the Algerian resistance to French occupation and its *mission civilisatrice* go hand in hand. The mixed bag that is Pauthier's introduction to the Kasimirski translation effectively underlines the extent to which Voltaire's reading of Muhammad overshadows his reception in the mid-nineteenth century: Muhammad was a man of the world, a leg-islator who founded an empire, but whose methods and example, all told, are still inferior to those set by Confucius. The inclusion of Islam alongside India and China as a constitutive culture of the Orient is coupled with a strong differential account that foregrounds the vio-lence inherent in the former and the pacific character of the latter. We are not too far removed here from Samuel Huntington's theses about the clash of civilizations.

The framework for this first edition of the Kazimirski translation marks the start of an important trend in the process of translating the Qur'ān into Western languages. The traditional polemics about the "validity" of Islam have now been replaced with the utility of the translation, not, as had been the case with Sale, in order to "emulate" the Muslims but rather in order to dominate them. (It bears pointing out that this was probably not Kazimirski's aim at all; it was simply the wrapping in which his work was brought to public attention.) It comes as no surprise, then, that as the process of decolonization gets underway, a similar process occurs in the opposite direction: Muslims translate the Qur'ān into Western languages in order to defend Islam against aggression by non-Muslims and, as an auxiliary aim, to persuade the reader of the beauty and rightness of the Muslim faith.

Consider the most prominent French translation by a Muslim after Algerian independence: the Si Hamza Boubakeur translation of 1972. In his preface Boubakeur says the following:

Nous nous sommes efforcés de traduire aussi fidèlement que possible le Coran et de faire connaître la vérité islamique à ceux qui l'ignorent encore, c'est-à-dire à la grande majorité du public européen et américain. Au cours de nos voyages dans le monde, nous avons été vraiment ahuris par une telle ignorance. Des esprits respectables ont encore sur l'Islâm des idées peu différentes de celles du monde chrétien du VIIe siècle. Pour des mobiles faciles à comprendre, aucune religion n'a été, en Europe, l'objet de tant de calomnies. Calomnies gratuites dont les effets subsistent encore dans les milieux les plus cultivés, par suite d'un manque d'information claire et objective. Puissent-ils se rendre compte à la lumière de ce travail, fruit d'un long et pénible labeur, que l'Islâm véritable est sans rapport avec l'image grossière que ses détracteurs se sont évertués à donner de lui, que son idéal spirituel ne correspond nullement à l'idée qu'ils continuent de s'en faire, à la suite d'une diffamation séculaire. Ils apprendront sans doute, grâce à ces pages, que l'Islâm proclame l'unicité divine absolue et exclut toute association à Dieu d'une autre divinité, tout panthéisme, toute incarnation, toute théorie d'un Dieu enfanté ou ayant enfanté, toute métempsycose, toute errance philosophique qui ne reconnaît pas à la foi, complément de la raison humaine limitée dans sa nature, la valeur de sa primauté et la réalité de son objet.

[We have done our best to communicate the Coran as faithfully as possible, and to bring the truth about Islam to those who still do not know it, that is, a large majority of the European and American public. Over the course of our voyages around the world, we have been truly astounded by this ignorance. Respectable minds still have opinions about Islam that differ only slightly from those of seventh-century Christendom. For reasons easily understood, no religion has been the object of so many calumnies in Europe. Gratuitous calumnies whose effects subsist in even the most cultivated circles as a result of a lack of clear and objective information. May they realize, in light of this work, which was the result of long and painful labor, that real Islam has nothing to do with the image that its detractors have tried so hard to create, and that its spiritual ideal in no way corresponds to what they continue to believe it to be, following long-term slander. In the following pages they will learn that Islam proclaims absolute divine unity and denies any association of another divinity with God, any pantheism, any incarnation, any theory of God having been born or having children, any metempsychosis, any philosophical specula-tion that does not grant faith, which is the complement of a naturally limited human reason, the value of its primacy and the reality of its object.][5]

For Boubakeur, summing up the tenets of Islam as the purest of the Abrahamic monotheisms is secondary to saving Islam from the "calumnies" that have assailed it "for reasons easily understood" (namely, the Algerian war and increasing hostility between Muslims and non-Muslims during the second half of the twentieth century). The Boubakeur translation comes with an impressive array of notes and annotations, effectively replacing previous encyclopedic single-volume translations like those of Sale and Marracci. Here, too, Boubakeur's will to save what he considers to be Muslim ortho-doxy from the assaults of the unbelievers is very much in evidence: in his introduction on the various schools and trends of exegesis he accuses khārijī exegetes of holding "shocking" opinions on such matters as divorce, prayer, and dog-eating, while his introduction to Q19 expresses horror at the fact that certain modern Christian readers doubt the immaculate conception and the virgin birth.[6] Furthermore, Boubakeur finds it necessary to make repeated claims regarding the primacy and originality of the Qur'ān in scientific matters. Eight out of the ten pages of Boubakeur's exegesis of Q1 are dedicated to an explanation of the term *'ālam* with a view to foregrounding the ways in which the Qur'ānic use of the term anticipates modern concep-tions of the universe, specifically the big bang and the big crunch.

Boubakeur adduces the absence of satisfying answers from cutting-edge cosmology to what preceded the big bang as further evidence of the solidity of the Qur'ān, proceeding to divide the history of science into Muslim and non-Muslim varieties in light of Q1:2:

> A la lumière de ce qui précède, on se rendra compte de la vertigineuse signification du vocable 'Alam et de la sublime majesté de son Auteur. Les astronomes musulmans auxquels, par parti-pris, on ne rendra jamais assez hommage, et leurs héritiers Copernic, Kepler, Newton ont ruiné la conception géocentrique de l'univers pour lui substituer celle plus réelle de l'héliocentrisme et une mécanique céleste toute nouvelle ...
>
> Le Coran enseigne une autre vérité qui plongeait dans l'ahurissement les savants non musulmans: c'est que tout ce qui est visible ou connu de la terre, tout le 'Alam est périssable, voué au néant. (S. LV, 26) Périssable, et soumis auparavant a des changements. (S. LXXXV, 13)
>
> Cette idée scientifique n'était pas courante avant le Coran. Dans le monde judéo-chrétien, comme chez les Hindous et chez les Chinois et même chez les Grecs, le ciel, les étoiles et leur mouvement sont toujours les mêmes. Le mot astronomie ne signifie pas autre chose que règles (nomos) qui régissent un univers d'une durée indéterminée.

> [In light of the foregoing, the vertiginous signification of the word 'Alam and the sublime majesty of its Author will be recognized. The Muslim astronomers, who will never be appreciated enough, and their inheritors Copernicus, Kepler, Newton have ruined the geocentric conception of the universe in order to replace it with the more real notion of heliocentrism and a brand new celestial mechanics ...
>
> The Coran teaches another truth that plunged non-Muslim scientists into amazement; namely that all that is visible or known about the earth, the entire 'Alam is perishable, condemned to nothingness. (S. LV, 26) Perishable, and mutable. (S. LXXXV, 13)
>
> This scientific idea was not current before the Coran. In the Judeo-Christian world, as in the cultures of the Hindus, the Chinese, and even the Greeks, the stars and their movements are fixed. The word astronomy signifies nothing other than the rules (nomos) that rule a universe of indeterminate duration.][7]

The tone of Boubakeur's comments on these issues (among others) combines defensiveness with a reformist outlook, repeatedly proclaiming the coherence, reasonability, and accuracy of the Qur'ān versus other scriptures, and adhering to the position that Islam is the only monotheism that fully respects all of God's messengers while simultaneously remaining fully compatible with the latest scientific discoveries.

A similar orientation informs prominent modern English translations of the Qur'ān by Muslims. In 1930 Muhammad Marmaduke Pickthall produced "the first translation by an Englishman who is a Muslim" under the title *The Meaning of the Glorious Koran*. In his introductory note to this very thinly annotated translation, Pickthall takes care to remind his reader that:

> The Koran cannot be translated. That is the belief of old-fashioned Sheykhs and the view of the present writer. The Book is here rendered almost literally and every effort has been made to choose befitting language. But the result is not the Glorious Koran, that inimitable symphony, the very sounds of which move men to tears and ecstasy. It is only an attempt to present the meaning of the Koran – and peradventure something of the charm – in English. It can never take the place of the Koran in Arabic, nor is it meant to do so.[8]

Among the "old-fashioned Sheykhs" to whom Pickthall refers is Rashīd Riḍā, whose opposition to the possibility and legality of translating the Qur'ān was linked not only to his conservative view of its inimitability, but also to a profound conviction that the translation of the Qur'ān and its dissemination would immediately bring about the disintegration of the community of believers. Riḍā's views were formulated against the backdrop of the abolition of the Ottoman Empire and the creation of the modern republic of Turkey. His perspective equated word with world: allowing translations of the Qur'ān would in effect be to continue the imperial dismemberment of the world of Islam. Fortunately, his was not the only legal opinion on the matter, and the views of those who, like Muhammad Al-Marāghī and Muhammad Shaltūt, realized that the translation of the Qur'ān would only strengthen an *umma* that was largely non-Arabophone, seem to have prevailed.[9]

The defensive tone that informs translators and "old-fashioned Sheykhs" recurs in the influential translation of Abdullah Yusuf Ali, whose 1934 translation entitled *The Holy Qur'ān* is something of a response to Pickthall. Yusuf Ali's preface divides previous translators into Muslims and non-Muslims, with the latter cast in a decidedly negative light and the former uniformly assumed to have produced positive contributions: "The amount of mischief done by these versions of non-Muslim and anti-Muslim writers [i.e. every major translator of the Qur'ān in the West since Robert of Ketton] has left Muslim writers to venture into the field of English translation."[10] Yusuf Ali's blanket condemnation of translations by non-Muslims is coupled with blanket approval of translations by Muslims, with the notable exceptions of Maulvi Muhammad Ali's 1917 Aḥmadiyya translation, whose English Yusuf Ali finds "decidedly weak," and Pickthall, whose minimal notes and "literal" rendition of the Qur'ān Yusuf Ali finds lacking, which lack he proceeds to fill with copious notes and a lyrical commentary on the text of the Qur'ān.

Muhammad Abdel Haleem's important English translation of the Qur'ān bears witness to the continued hegemony of the defensive position. Consider the frequency with which the word "respect" and its antonym, offense, return over the two pages in which he reviews the history of English translations of the Qur'ān (those categories are applied mainly to non-Muslim translators of the Qur'ān; Muslim translators are faulted for being outdated and archaic):

> In 1861 the Revd J.M. Rodwell undertook a translation of the Qur'an. His perspective on the Qur'an was a strongly biblical one. [note: In his notes he is over-eager to claim biblical sources for Qur'anic material, and quick to claim that there are contradictions between verses where none exists.] One oddity is his disregard for the traditional Muslim arrangement of the suras, rearranging them into what he thought to be the chronological order; moreover some of his footnotes include material that is incorrect and offensive to Muslims …
>
> The next translator of the Qur'an into English, E.H. Palmer (1840–82), is claimed to be the first who had direct and long-lasting contact with the Arabs and sight, in style, to retain some of the "rude, fierce eloquence" of the Qur'an but without becoming "too rude or familiar." His translation appeared in 1880. He was the first to reflect, in his footnotes, some real respect for the text and the Prophet of Islam …
>
> Arthur J. Arberry's translation, *The Koran Interpreted*, appeared in 1955 and is undoubtedly one of the most respected translations of the Qur'an in English. Arberry shows great respect towards the language of the Qur'an, particularly its musical effects …
>
> In the following year (1956), N.J. Dawood produced his translation for Penguin Books … However, from the beginning his translation was seen to take too many liberties with the text of the Qur'an and

to contain many inaccuracies, as was immediately pointed out by reviewers; moreover many Muslims were deeply offended by the way he translated key terms and by some of the notes to the translation.

In 1980 an English translation by Muhammad Asad was published ... His language and choice of words too are original, but he inserts many bracketed explanatory words which, though useful, make his sentences cumbersome. Also his "rationalistic" approach leads him to translations that some Muslim theologians disagree with: for example, his translation of 50:17 as "the two demands of his nature ..." rather than "recording [angels]", or *hammim* in 56:93 as "burning despair" rather than "scalding water".[11]

The opposition that Abdel Haleem sets up between disrespect and outright offence on the non-Muslim side, and stylistic differences on the Muslim side, are telling. Questionable though Rodwell's translation might be, his re-arrangement of the sūras was based in part on research into the chronology of the Qur'ān by Gustav Weil and, more significantly, Theodor Nöldeke's epoch-making *Geschichte des Qorāns* (though some of the latter's comments about the style of the Qur'ān do seem offensive, especially coming from a man well versed in Arabic language and literature). In addition to parallels between Qur'ānic and biblical material, Rodwell was especially sensitive to the form and oral character of the Qur'ān. Whether or not there was an intention to offend behind Rodwell's translation, Abdel Haleem's comments convey the deep suspicion toward Orientalist scholarship that exists in the wake of the imperialist age. The default working hypothesis seems to be that Western translators and students of the Qur'ān are automatically suspect; those who do show "real respect" toward Islam and its scripture are the exception rather than the rule.

A similar concern with respect is shown in several recent French translations of the Qur'ān, though there is a markedly different attitude toward Orientalist scholarship due, perhaps, to the fact that some of the most influential translators (Blachère, Berque, Masson) trained as Orientalists. Like Boubakeur, most of these translators are aware of the reception of their work in a France with a large and growing Muslim population. Denise Masson's groundbreaking translation was published in 1967 with a short preface by Jean Grosjean, who would himself publish a translation of the Qur'ān five years later. By far the largest intellectual shadow cast over this project is that of Louis Massignon, whose ideas about the three monotheisms and the approach to the other are very much in evidence. Grosjean points out that Massignon was looking forward to the Masson translation when he died, and Masson's lengthy introduction makes clear that she situates her reading of Islam on the side of intercultural contact rather than conflict.[12] Similarly Massignon's ideas about Arabic being a synthetic Semitic language shape the project. The result is not without resemblance to the Anglophone discourse of respect. Like any good student of Massignon, Grosjean situates himself in the position of the believer to argue for the quality of the translation faced with the inimitability of the Qur'ān: "Le texte coranique fut un miracle. Est-ce qu'un traducteur peut refaire un miracle? Il peut du moins, à force de respect pour ce texte, en livrer le reflet."[13] ["The Coranic text was a miracle. Can a translator perform a miracle a second time? He can, at least, transmit the reflection thereof, out of respect for the text."] Furthermore, the onus will be on the French reader to effect a linguistic shift of perspective in order to receive the Qur'ān properly; for Semitic languages lend themselves to revelations in ways that Indo-European ones do not:

Le lecteur français doit toutefois se rappeler que, voilées par nos langues indo-européennes, les notions sur lesquelles se fonde tout monothéisme sont évidentes dans les langues sémitiques. Par exemple, le verbe y exprime plus le mode que le temps. Ses formes indiquent avec naturel si l'acte non seulement est subi ou se réfléchit mais encore son intensité, son intention, son effet ou sa cause, sa réciprocité, etc. Au contraire, nos précisions de temps sont secondaires et ne s'obtiennent que par de moyens accessoires. Les deux seuls temps réels ne font que distinguer ce qui est achevé, certain, et ce qui ne l'est pas, sans préjuger l'époque, au point qu'une action future peut être déjà faite. C'est donc à travers nos conjugaisons d'occasion que la version laissera sentir l'omniprésence de Dieu et les nuances de ses initiatives. (Les impasses de nos théologies sur les rapports entre la prédestination et la liberté, viennent de l'infirmité de nos grammaires plus aptes à la mécanique qu'à la métaphysique.) Sera déroutée aussi une autre de nos habitudes mentales, la distinction du profane et du sacré ou du politique et du mystique, car les religions vivantes y voient moins une différence de nature que de degré.

[The French reader must nevertheless remember that, veiled as they are by our Indo-European languages, the notions on which all monotheism is founded are obvious in the Semitic languages. For example, the verb in those languages expresses moods rather than tenses. Its forms naturally indicate whether or not the action is passive or reflexive as well as its intensity, its intention, its cause or its effect, its reciprocity, etc. Our precisions of time, on the contrary, are secondary and are only obtained by accessory means. The only two real tenses are there to distinguish between that which is accomplished and certain and that which is not, without indicating the time frame, so much so that a future action could have been already performed. It is therefore through our occasional conjugations that the translation will convey the omnipresence of God and the nuances of His initiatives. (The impasses of our theologies on the relationship between predestination and freedom come from the infirmity of our grammars, which are better suited to mechanics than to metaphysics.) Another one of our mental habits will also be disconcerted; namely the distinction between the sacred and the profane or the political and the mystical; for living religions see in them a difference less of nature than of degree.][14]

The opposition between East and West is contained in the structure of their languages: synthetic and paratactic Semitic languages as opposed to analytic and hypotactic Indo-European ones. Although one might cavil about the description of Arabic as a synthetic language, the net result is that the linguistic and cultural space that Grosjean associates with it is one that better accommodates communication with the divine. It is difficult to make another culture more respectable than that.

Grosjean's translation of 1972 was prefaced by Jacques Berque (who would himself publish a translation of the Qur'ān in 1990, and who would have frequent occasion to return to the subject). The tone of this preface differs radically from that of most others by its concern with the historical and political framework surrounding the reading and interpretation of the Qur'ān in the Arab world during the twentieth century. Berque was nothing if not sensitive to the hopes, dreams, and nightmares that affected the Arab and Muslim worlds over the course of the twentieth century, from imperialism to independence, and from reform to fundamentalism. Berque's text moves gracefully between the dawn of Islam and its contemporary uses, between the desert and the city, to weave an introduction to the Qur'ān that moves away from the opposition respect/offense and toward a fuller, more rounded consideration of the Qur'ān as a sacred text and a thing of beauty in the world. Berque's attention to the Qur'ān's worldliness recalls Edward Said's remarks on the subject:

> My position is that texts are worldly, to some degree they are events, and, even when they appear to deny it, they are nevertheless a part of the social world, human life, and of course the historical moments in which they are located and interpreted ...
>   A text in its actually *being* a text is also a being in the world; it therefore addresses anyone who reads ... The point is that texts have ways of existing that even in their most rarefied form are always enmeshed in circumstance, time, place and society – in short they are in the world, and hence worldly.[15]

Accordingly, Berque spends far more time mapping the circulation of the Qur'ān in the linguistic and cultural space of Muslim belief rather than dividing the reception of the Qur'ān into positive and negative poles. In his treatment, names like Vico, Nöldeke, and Meschonnic share the page comfortably with Labīd b. Rabī'a, and Imru'l Qays to give a preface that succeeds in explaining the importance of the Qur'ān in contemporary cultural life. His reading reminds the reader of the reasons behind the hypnotic "insuperability" (his translation of *I'jāz*) of the Qur'ān; its sound and rhythm, its linguistic and textual music that makes all of Arabic and Muslim culture resonate around it.

Berque pursues his analysis in a lengthy afterword to his 1990 translation of the Qur'ān (the modestly sub-titled *Essai de traduction*) and a series of lectures at the Institut du Monde Arabe (*Relire le Coran*). On both occasions Berque deepens his analysis of the form of the text to give an intriguing account of the standard arrangement of the sūras and their impact – semantic and aesthetic – on both the reader and listener of the Qur'ān. In a radical departure from received Western opinion, Berque links the literary quality of the Qur'ān to its (claims about its) clarity. Commenting on the term *bayān*, which he defines as "l'exposition claire, la faculté de s'exprimer de façon intelligible, l'expressivité la supême qualité d'un langage et, partant, d'une literature" ["clear exposition, the ability to express oneself intelligibly, expressivity as the supreme quality of a language and thus of its literature"], Berque relates the Qur'ān's intelligibility to its self-representation, as a text that reflects on itself, forged from the articulation (*tafṣīl*) of syntagms that work together to form the clear fabric of meaning.[16] In another attempt at bringing modern

(Saussurean) linguistics to bear on the Qur'ān, he claims that the language of the Qur'ān is the *koinê* of the Quraysh transposed: "C'est bien la *parole* de Quraysh, mais transcrite dans une autre *langue*." ["It is certainly the *parole* of the Quraysh, but transcribed into another *langue*."][17] The textual power of the Qur'ān derives from this transcription – or, to stretch the phrase, this translation – of a *parole* into a new idiom, with all of the social historic implications that the term *langue* implies, an idiom that can contain the transcendent within the finite: Berque speaks of a linguistic unveiling that signifies unspeakable depths ("une sorte de nudité de la parole, malgré la profondeur et la complexité du sens, jointe à une très grande économie de moyens"[18] ["a sort of nudity of language, despite the depth and complexity of meaning, joined to a great economy of means"]). Of course, the aspects of the Qur'ān that Berque identifies here, and which he uses to explain the *I'jāz*, are not entirely new: multiple medieval commentators have gone to great length to explain the stylistic operation of the Qur'ānic text.[19] But what Berque brings out with the word "transcription" is precisely the displacement of the ordinary tools of seventh-century Arabic into something rich and strange. This translation within a language has a name: literary production. The origin of the Qur'ān is found at the intersection between *koiné* and poetry, between speech and *saj'*, between *kalām* and *qirā'a*.

Berque compared the text of the Qur'ān to a carpet with motifs that emerge following certain patterns that are symmetric but not necessarily sequential:

> Le tissu du Coran me rappelle ces tapis maghrébins où la même couleur reparaît un peu partout sur la surface, où la même palmette ou rosace illustre le centre et les angles et les plages intermédiaires. Supposez qu'au lieu que ce soit une surface, un étalement dans l'espace, ce soit un flux verbal dans le temps. Il en est ainsi du Coran où les mêmes thèmes reviennent et s'entrecroisent.

> [The texture of the Coran reminds me of these Maghrebi carpets where the same color reappears all over the surface, where the same palmette or rosace patterns illustrate the center, the angles and the intermediary spaces. Suppose that, instead of being a surface, a spreading-out in space, it were a verbal flux in time. This is how it is with the Coran, where the same themes return and crisscross each other.][20]

Berque refers to this structure as an interlacing structure ("structure d'entrelacs") as a way of foregrounding the woven character of the discourse of the Qur'ān, illustrating his case with close readings of Q12:50–52 and Q3:124–128, and, still more powerfully, through a nineteenth-century Qur'ānic manuscript where the disposition of certain words on facing pages is perfectly symmetrical.[21] Berque, in other words, brings the character of Qur'ānic discourse back to the etymology of the word *text* (from *textus*: woven), demonstrating that the Qur'ān is the text par excellence, and whose textual excellence is demonstrated by what most readers find to be its most difficult characteristic: its non-linearity.

As of this writing, Berque's skill and sophistication remain unmatched. He has moved away from what I have been calling the defensive posture of the translator without in any way yielding to the cause of Western political hegemony over the Muslim world. Like all of the other translations that we have examined, his work is deeply enmeshed in the surrounding historical moment. However, what the world's numerous translations and translation projects have not yet managed to produce is a critical translation of the Qur'ān, taking full account of the genesis of the text, variants, origins, and their relationship to the history of Islam; in short, a more complete archaeology that would inform the process of translation, performing for it the same service as what the higher criticism has for the Bible. To a certain extent aspects of this method are evident in the translations of Richard Bell (1937), who went so far as to re-arrange the wording of certain verses in his translation, as well as Regis Blachère's translation (1947; second edition 1957), where there are consistent references to variant readings, and Rudi Paret (1962), who set out to render the text of the Qur'ān "as it was first heard from the Prophet's mouth."[22] Tarif Khalidi's recent landmark translation into English (2008) is unsurpassed in communicating the literary urgency and vividness of the Qur'ān to a contemporary Anglophone audience, but does so, alas, without the detailed notes that might have given the reader an idea of the many linguistic and historical layers beneath the text. Still, a proper implementation of a critical translation project would require a team of translators rather than, as has been the case hitherto, one translator working in splendid isolation over several years.[23] All hope is not lost, however: as calls for such work are repeated, they are bound to be heeded sooner or later; perhaps once there has been a collective de-escalation of anxieties surrounding the idea of bringing textual criticism to a sacred text, and a realization that the course of research into the text and history of the Bible over the past two centuries has destroyed neither Judaism nor Christianity. Translation, that most political art, always finds a way of responding to the demands of the *polis*.

ENDNOTES

PREFACE

1 Gunny, *Images of Islam*, pp. 9–36; MacLean, *The Rise of Oriental Travel*, pp. 33–47, 126–176; and MacLean, "Learn of a Turk."

2 See Dimmock, *New Turkes*.

CHAPTER 1

1 My account of Peter the Venerable's project relies on Kritzeck's *Peter the Venerable and Islam*. Excellent coverage of the translations of Robert of Ketton and Mark of Toledo, as well as numerous others, is found in Burman, *Reading the Qur'ān*. On the life of Robert, see Charles Burnett, "Ketton, Robert of." My account of the Western translations of the Qur'ān is not exhaustive: for many of the details not mentioned here the reader is referred to Bobzin, "Translations of the Qur'ān."

2 Pseudo al-Kindī's *Letter* was probably the most influential single source of Christian polemic in the medieval West. On its reception and impact, see Daniel, *Islam and the West*, pp. 22, 113–129, 256–257. On its assumed author, see Troupeau, "al-Kindī, 'Abd al-Masīḥ b. Isḥāḳ." On 'Abd Allāh b. Salām's *Masā'il*, see Horovitz, "'Abd Allāh b. Salām," and Daiber, "Masā'il Wa-adjwiba."

3 Burman, *Reading the Qur'ān*, pp. 29–35.

4 *KZR*, p. 229.

5 Thomas Burman makes a strong case in defense of Robert of Ketton's version, while acknowledging its tendency toward freewheeling paraphrase, by comparing it to Mark of Toledo's translation and accounting for the incorporation of exegetical material into the language of the translation. See his "Tafsir and Translation."

6 Much of the following account of Bibliander's edition of the Qur'ān is based on *KZR*, pp. 159–275, and Burman, *Reading the Qur'ān*, pp. 110–121. Good, if

partial, summaries are found in Bobzin, "Pre-1800 Preoccupations of Qur'ānic Studies," and "'A Treasury of Heresies.'" Although I emphasize the anti-Muslim position prevalent in many of these texts, there is a certain tendency to compromise both with the authorities and with the Muslim viewpoint that becomes more evident with successive generations of translators. One place where this can be seen is in the occasional, if inconsistent, use of illustrations in the translations of the Qur'ān. See Hamilton, *Forbidden Fruit*.

7 *KZR*, pp. 153–156.

8 Ibid., pp. 92, 95–152. Luther did not translate the Qur'ān, but was sufficiently persuaded of the ideological threat of Islam to produce a German translation and abridgement of Ricoldo da Monte Croce's *Contra legem Saracenorum* under the title *Widerlegung des Alkorans* in 1542. Even this exercise left him with the ardent desire to see the Qur'ān translated in order that everyone might find out what an awful book it was. Bobzin demonstrates that Luther's interest in the Qur'ān stemmed from his desire to unmask similarities and sympathies between the members of the church and the Turks. Ibid., pp. 15–20. A detailed account of Luther's interaction with Islam and the Qur'ān is found in Francisco, *Martin Luther and Islam*, especially pp. 91–94, 104–108, 180–217.

9 On the *Cribratio* and its place in the Reformation along with Riccoldo's *Contra legem saracenorum*, especially their influence on Luther's thinking about Islam, see *KZR*, pp. 29–34, and Bisaha, *Creating East and West*, pp. 144–147. On Riccoldo more generally, see Daniel, *Islam and the West*, pp. 77–97, 149–150, 196–197, 207–209.

10 On the significance of Pius II's letter to Mehmed II and the questions of sincerity that it raises as a conversion piece, see Bisaha, *Creating East and West*, pp. 147–152, 167–170. Bisaha concludes that the letter "belongs more to the realm of humanist history and pro-Western rhetoric than it does to any other genre." Ibid., p. 152. Paolo Giovio's treatise on Turkish matters composed for Emperor Charles V in 1530–1531, the *Commentario de le cose de' Turchi*, was included in Latin translation in Bibliander's edition. Although he urged a rapid, decisive military campaign against the Turks, Giovio's objectivity and broad-mindedness nevertheless brought him accusations of being a Turkish sympathizer. See Zimmermann, *Paolo Giovio*, pp. 121–123.

11 *KZR*, p. 267 n.

12 On Postel, see ibid., pp. 365–497, and, more generally, Kuntz, *Guillaume Postel*, and Balagna Costou, *Arabe et humanisme*. A witty summary is found in Irwin's *For Lust of Knowing*, pp. 66–73, where Postel is called "the crazy father of Orientalism."

13 Burman gives a rich account of the manuscript summaries and Widmanstetter's reliance on them in *Reading the Qur'ān*, pp. 103–110. For a more detailed account of Widmanstetter, see *KZR*, pp. 277–363.

14 See De Frede, *La prima traduzione italiana del Corano*, pp. 31–48.

15 Khairallah, "Arabic Studies in England," pp. 38–39; Toomer, *Eastern Wisedome and Learning*, pp. 108–110. Matthew Dimmock has compiled a very useful database of printed copies of the Qur'ān in circulation before 1700. The database, which is unfortunately still unpublished, lists some forty copies of Bibliander's edition of the Qur'ān in ecclesiastical and university libraries in Britain.

16 Matar, *Islam in Britain*, pp. 21–72. John Gregory explains the difficulty of obtaining the Qur'an in seventeenth-century England by the fact that the text

should only be touched by those who are pure, "And the Law is yet in force among the Turks for some special Alcorans of note, one of which sort inscribed in the same manner may be seen in the Archives of our publick Library." Ibid., p. 75.

17 Toomer, *Eastern Wisedome and Learning*, pp. 111–115.

18 Hamilton and Richard, *André Du Ryer*, pp. 101–103.

19 Ibid., pp. 96–101.

20 Ibid., pp. 46–57, 93–96.

21 Ibid., pp. 110–116.

22 Du Ryer, *L'Alcoran de Mahomet*, n.p.

23 Hamilton and Richard, *André Du Ryer*, pp. 110–114; Matar, "Alexander Ross." Matar points out that copies printed in England were available in the American colonies by the end of the seventeenth century, as witness Cotton Mather's reliance on the text in his *Pastoral Letter to the English Captives in Africa from New England* (1698).

24 Harrison, *"Religion,"* pp. 39–45, 130–172, 191–192.

25 Nallino, "Le fonti arabe manoscrite;" Levi della Vida, *Ricerche sulla formazione*; Hamilton, "Eastern Churches and Western Scholarship"; Wakefield, "Arabic Manuscripts in the Bodleian Library"; Feingold, "Oriental Studies."

26 Toomer, "Pococke, Edward."

27 Russell, "The Seventeenth Century"; Holt, "The Study of Arabic Historians"; Khairallah, "Arabic Studies in England," pp. 44–90; Hamilton, "The English Interest in the Arabic-Speaking Christians."

28 Toomer, *Eastern Wisedome and Learning*, pp. 116–126, 159–167, 212–226.

29 Hamilton, *William Bedwell the Arabist*, pp. 55–96, and, more briefly, "Bedwell, William."

30 On the importance of the form of the compendium in early Orientalism, see Fück, *Die Arabischen Studien in Europa*, pp. 59–101; Holt, "The Study of Arabic Historians," pp. 451–452; Laurens, *Aux sources de l'orientalisme*, pp. 59–60.

31 A very thorough account of Marracci's life and work is found in Pedani-Fabris, "Ludovico Marracci." On Marracci the Orientalist in particular, see Ross, "Ludovico Marracci," and Levi della Vida, "Ludovico Marracci." On Marracci's translation of the Qur'an, see Nallino, "Le fonti arabe manoscrite"; Shellabear, "Is Sale's Koran Reliable?"; Pedani-Fabris, "Intorno alla questione della traduzione del Corano"; Rizzardi, "Il modello controversistico di Ludovico Marracci"; Borrmans, "Ludovico Marracci." I am deeply grateful to Maria Pia Pedani, Emanuele Colombo, and Geneviève Gobillot for bringing some of this material to my attention under severe temporal constraints.

32 *RE*, pp. 47–50.

33 Grafton, "The Vatican and its Library"; Hamilton, "Eastern Churches and Western Scholarship" and *Forbidden Fruit*; Hankins, "The Popes and Humanism"; Fumaroli, *L'Âge de l'éloquence*, pp. 116–152, 202–226; Rizzardi, "Il modello controversistico di Ludovico Marracci," pp. 82–89.

34 Hamilton, "A Lutheran Translator for the Quran."

35 Daniel, *Islam and the West*, p. 321.

36 Martino, *L'Orient dans la littérature française*, pp. 162–163.

37 The importance of this aspect of Marracci's text should not be underestimated. This is, as Sale would later point out, only the second available printed Qur'ān

in Arabic, after the edition published by Abraham Hinckelmann in 1694. There had been a previous attempt at publishing the Qur'ān in Arabic by Paganino and Alessandro Paganini in Venice in 1537–1538, but the project seems to have failed. Maurice Borrmans speculates that the sole surviving copy of this edition is probably the first page proof of a commercial project aimed at printing the Qur'ān and selling it to Muslims in the Middle East, whence the absence of any introductory material in a Western language (with which contrasts the Latin introduction to Hinckelmann's edition). Having listed many of the innumerable errors in this edition, Borrmans concludes that it was this, rather than a papal interdiction, that probably persuaded the Paganinis to abandon the enterprise. See Borrmans, "Présentation de la première édition." Until the mid-nineteenth century, the Hinckelmann and Marracci editions were the only available vocalized versions of the Arabic text of the Qur'ān.

38 "Hactenus Alcorano contra Alcoranum pugnavi et Mahometum gladio suo jugulare pro mea virili parte conatus sum." Marracci, *Prodromus ad Refutationem Alcorani*, vol. 4, p. 124. A similar phrase occurs in the subtitle to the second part of his *Alcorani textus universus*: *Refutatio alcorani, in qua ad Mahumetanicae superstitionis radicem securis apponitur; & Mahumetus ipse gladio suo jugulatur*. On Marracci's military language, see Levi della Vida, "Ludovico Marracci," p. 196. Nallino argues that Marracci found inspiration in the strident anti-Christian polemic of Ibn Taymiyya, so Marracci's claim of having fought Islam on its own terms may not be entirely unjustified. "Le fonti arabe manoscrite," p. 348. Hartmut Bobzin usefully places Marracci in the long history of other Latin translations of the Qur'an, while maintaining that his "crude" tactics put paid to any hope of worldly success for his *refutatio.* Indeed, it was only with the publication of Christian Reineccius's Latin epitome of Marracci (Leipzig, 1721), which contains the Latin text of Marracci's translation without the Arabic text, notes, and refutations, that the latter's ideas became widespread, especially among those members of the scholarly community who could not read Arabic. Bobzin, "Pre-1800 Preoccupations of Qur'ānic Studies."

39 Poggi, "Grandezza e limiti di Ludovico Marracci," p. 51.

40 Khairallah, "Arabic Studies in England," pp. 132–157; Daniel, *Islam and the West*, pp. 309–310, 323. It bears pointing out that despite his hostility to Muhammad and indifference to Arabic studies, Humphrey Prideaux was generous with his assistance to younger scholars such as Simon Ockley, whose views of Islam were far more positive than his own.

41 On Reland's intellectual genealogy, see Hamilton, "Arabists and Cartesians at Utrecht."

42 Bayle, *Dictionnaire historique*, vol. 10, pp. 66–67; English translation, Bayle, *A General Dictionary*, vol. 7, p. 328.

43 Labrousse, *Pierre Bayle*, pp. 520–543; Bost, *Pierre Bayle*, pp. 285–297; Minuti, *Orientalismo*, pp. 192–214.

44 This particular point was also a staple in medieval refutations of Islam as evidence of its many contradictions, not least those evinced by its own scripture. Daniel, *Islam and the West*, pp. 83–98.

45 Gunny, *Images of Islam*, pp. 73–76.

46 Said, *Orientalism*, pp. 63–66; Gunny, *Images of Islam*, pp. 45–54; Dew, "The Order of Oriental Knowledge," pp. 249–252. On Kātib Čelebi and the

Kashf, see Gökyay, "Kātib Čelebi," as well as Pearson, "Bibliography of Translations."

47 Ménage, "Kateb Celebiana," pp. 173–175.

48 Laurens, *Aux sources de l'orientalisme*, pp. 60–61.

49 Ibid., pp. 68–70.

50 Ibid., pp. 71–75.

51 Dew, "The Order of Oriental Knowledge," p. 246.

52 Brugman and Schröder, *Arabic Studies*, p. 22. See also Hamilton, "Arabists and Cartesians at Utrecht," pp. 104–105; Minuti, *Orientalismo*, pp. 180–186.

53 Champion, *Republican Learning*, p. 25.

54 References are to the English translation of Reland's *De religione Mohammedica, Of the Mahometan Religion*, pp. 8–9.

55 Ibid., pp. 9–12.

56 Ibid., p. 12.

57 Ibid., p. 19.

58 Ibid., pp. 86, 99.

59 Prideaux, *The True Nature of Imposture*, pp. xiii–xiv.

60 Ibid., pp. 137–138.

61 Prideaux, "Letter to the Deists," p. 130.

62 Berti, "*L'Esprit de Spinosa*," p. 5.

63 Much of the following account is taken from Champion, *The Pillars of Priestcraft Shaken*, pp. 106–132. In a related continental development, a text written by a former Benedictine monk who converted to Protestantism and fled France to become librarian to the King of Prussia, namely Mathurin Veyssière de la Croze, explored the affinities between Islam and Socinianism. This text, the *Réflexions historiques et critiques sur le mahométisme et sur le socinianisme*, would eventually be translated into English in 1712 as part of the *Four Treatises* that also included the English translation of Reland's *De religione Mohammedica*. Veyssière de la Croze argues that it was the relatively free atmosphere of Arabia that allowed Islam to flourish, along with a number of other sects (a point that would later be made by Boulainvilliers and George Sale, though the latter does not mention Veyssière de la Croze in his translation of the Qur'ān), and makes the case for the Qur'ān and the social teachings of Islam (mainly alms) as key vectors in its rapid transmission. The overall critique is much harsher toward Socinianism than Islam. See Gunny, *Images of Islam*, pp. 76–79; Minuti, *Orientalismo*, pp. 217–230; Mulsow, *Die drei Ringe*, pp. 68–75.

64 Bury, *The Naked Gospel*, n.p.

65 Arnoud Vrolijk, Sale's biographer for the *Oxford Dictionary of National Biography*, calls this attribution "improbable," despite the fact that the arguments in "Mahomet No Impostor" anticipate some of those put forward in the Sale translation of the Qur'ān. Vrolijk, "Sale, George." Vrolijk's reasons include the early publication date, the absence of any mention of Muslim sources in the text, and the author's apparent ignorance of Arabic (e-mail communication, October 30, 2007). Even if the text is not by George Sale, the attribution bears witness to the extent to which his name has become synonymous with the defense of Islam by 1720; something that comes through with equal clarity in the attacks on his translation of the Qur'ān.

66 Khairallah, "Arabic Studies in England," pp. 204–225.

67 Haydon, Colin, *Anti-Catholicism in Eighteenth-Century England*, p. 58. In an essay on the early years of the SPCK, Craig Rose denies that anti-Catholicism was a key policy of the SPCK, and that most of their enmity was reserved for Socinians, deists, and, above all, Quakers. Rose, "The Origins and Ideals of the SPCK," pp. 185–187. Haydon's evidence is, however, very convincing.

68 Khairallah, "Arabic Studies in England," p. 216.

69 This episode demonstrates the complicated operation of sectarian activity in the early Enlightenment: Negri was born in Damascus, sent by the Jesuits to the Sorbonne in the hope that he would convert to Catholicism (he didn't), where he met and worked with such Orientalists as Job Ludolf and Frederick Rostgaard, and taught at La Sapienza College in Rome, before returning to England as King's Interpreter of Oriental Languages in 1719. Dadichi's life followed a similarly tortuous itinerary that took him from Aleppo to France, Germany, Spain, Italy, and Belgium before he finally landed in London in 1723, becoming, in turn, King's Interpreter of Oriental Languages. In other words, neither Negri nor Dadichi embodied the rigid orthodoxy emblematized by the SPCK, and yet the society was only happy to employ their services to advance its cause. Jean Gagnier, on the other hand, who was born in France, raised a Catholic, became a canon regular at the Church of Ste Geneviève-du-Mont, moved to England in 1702, converted to Anglicanism, and enjoyed powerful anti-Catholic patronage in the person of William Lloyd, Bishop of Worcester, going so far as to publish an anti-Catholic tract, *L'Eglise Romaine convaincue de depravation, d'idolatrie, et d'antichristianisme, en forme de lettre* in 1706, merely acted as a consultant on the project and offered the SPCK the use of Oxford University's Arabic type. Khairallah, "Arabic Studies in England," pp. 173–180, 209–220; Fück, *Die Arabischen Studien in Europa*, pp. 95–97; Franklin, "Gagnier, John."

70 Osborn, "Thomas Birch"; Khairallah, "Arabic Studies in England," pp. 229–230; Ricuperati, "*Universal History*," pp. 20–23.

71 Abbattista, "The Literary Mill"; Ricuperati, "*Universal History*," pp. 29–30.

72 Ricuperati, "*Universal History*," pp. 62–68.

73 Anthony Grafton considers Bayle to be the "inventor" of the modern footnote, with its critical and referential functions. *The Footnote*, pp. 190–212. The critical evaluation of sources can be related to Jean Le Clerc's plea for the proper use of evidence in historical writing instead of the indiscriminate reliance on rhetoric and classical sources. Champion, *The Pillars of Priestcraft Shaken*, pp. 30–31; Grafton, *What Was History?*, pp. 1–33, 46–49. A similar encyclopedic approach to sacred texts becomes apparent in a different but related register with the publication of Haug's encyclopedic Berleburger Bible (1726–1740), which combined critical scholarly inquiry with enthusiastic theology and universalism. Sheehan, *The Enlightenment Bible*, pp. 73–85. Sheehan underlines the similarities between the Berleburger Bible and Bayle's *Dictionary*, adding that they were not lost on Haug's contemporaries.

74 Allison, *The Crescent Obscured*, pp. 37–43.

75 Laurens, "Histoire, anthropologie et politique," p. 19.

76 Champion, "Legislators, Impostors and the Politic Origins of Religion," pp. 340–341.

77 Champion, *The Pillars of Priestcraft Shaken*, pp. 99–132.

78 Stubbe, Henry, *An Account of the Rise and Progress of Mahometanism*, p. 146.
79 Ibid., p. 151.
80 Ibid., p. 103.
81 Ibid., p. 166.
82 Ibid., p. 169.
83 Holt, *A Seventeenth-Century Defender of Islam*, pp. 19–24; Champion, "Legislators, Impostors and the Politic Origins of Religion," p. 348.
84 Geertz, "Thick Description," p. 10.
85 The classic, and still the best, account of this topic is Zuber's *Les "Belles infidèles,"* but see also Ballard, *De Cicéron à Benjamin*, pp. 147–197, where the topic is approached from a more technical perspective.
86 Racine, *Oeuvres complètes*, vol. 1, p. 699.
87 Voltaire, *La Philosophie de l'histoire*, p. 111.
88 Laurens, "L'Egypte dans le mythe-histoire de la raison," p. 33.
89 Steiner, *After Babel*, pp. 437–460.
90 But see also Rizzardi's analysis of the (mainly ecclesiastical and institutional) reasons that drove Marracci to his refutation: "Il modello controversistico di Ludovico Marracci," pp. 88–89.
91 *RE*, pp. 23–58.
92 Gunny, *Images of Islam*, pp. 65–83.
93 Harrison, "*Religion*," p. 146.
94 The indispensable references on this trend are Hazard, *La Crise de la conscience européenne*; *RE*; and Israel, *Enlightenment Contested*.
95 *RE*, pp. 338–341. Despite Bayle's importance as a vector of Spinoza's ideas, his ambivalence seems to have attenuated their impact – indeed, none of Sale's seven references to Bayle's *Dictionary* in his translation are to the article "Spinoza." Good histories of the *Traité* and its transmission are found in Berti, "*L'Esprit de Spinosa*"; Benítez, "Une Histoire interminable"; Wade, *The Clandestine Organization*, pp. 124–140; *RE*, pp. 694–703; Mulsow, *Moderne aus dem Untergrund*, pp. 115–159. Gunny gives a detailed analysis of the text with respect to Islam, taking into account significant variations in the extant manuscripts. Gunny, *Images of Islam*, pp. 84–88. Massignon locates the earliest version of the theory of the three impostors, and a forerunner of the medieval treatise *De tribus impostoribus*, in a set of tenth-century Qarmatian documents, some 150 years before the appearance of these theories in the West. "La légende 'de tribus impostoribus.'" The possibility of pan-religious equivalence also appears in titles from across the spectrum of ideology and religious belief, as witness Alexander Ross's *Pansebeia, or View of all Religions in the World ... Together with a Discovery of all known Heresies* (1653), which is less a plea for a Spinozist perspective than a catalogue of world religions, and John Toland's more radical *Pantheisticon*. The argument for the equivalence of the three monotheisms also comes to the fore in the revival and diffusion of the legend of the three rings in the clandestine literature of the period and, eventually, in Lessing's *Nathan der Weise*. For a genetic and intellectual history of this text, see Mulsow, *Die drei Ringe*, and on its place in Enlightenment Orientalism, Hamilton, "Western Attitudes," pp. 77–78.
96 Curiously, the impact of Simon's biblical criticism on Sale's translation seems to have been minimal: Sale only mentions him twice, and only in passing.

Still, few things better illustrate the rapid spread of heterodox thinking on scripture than Jurieu's paranoid fantasms of seeing Socinians everywhere, and Simon's remark that the Socinians were continuing the Calvinist project by other means. Gunny, *Images of Islam*, pp. 72–73, 78–79; Hazard, *La Crise de la conscience européenne*, pp. 92–96; *RE*, pp. 449–454.

97 There is an important precedent to this translatability, albeit in an extremely different key, in Postel's work on the concordance of all the world's religions.

98 Israel, *Enlightenment Contested*, pp. 135–163.

99 Assmann, *Moses the Egyptian*, p. 3.

100 Sale, p. 178.

101 Spinoza, *Opera*, vol. 4, p. 322. In the original the words "quem tantopere laudas" follow the opening phrase "Ordinem Romanae ecclesiae."

102 *RE*, pp. 224–229.

103 It does bear pointing out, however, that Sale, like Marracci and Pococke, makes a point of defining Islam along sectarian lines, thereby repeating the error of mapping the political and scholastic quarrels on to doctrinal and theological ones. This habit of seeing Islam through the lens of Christianity, whereby Sunni and Shī'a differences are understood through the difference between Catholic and Protestant, can be traced to a series of misunderstandings of (and in) Al-Shahrestani's *Kitāb al-milal wa-l-niḥal*, whereby the term *shu'ba* is re-transmitted as *milla* or *firqa*. Goldziher, "Le Dénombrement des sectes mahométanes." Sale cites Shahrestani via Pococke's *Specimen*:

> For *Mohammedans* seem ambitious that their religion should exceed others even in this respect; saying that the *Magians* are divided into seventy sects, the *Jews* into seventy one, the *Christians* into seventy-two, and the *Moslems* into seventy-three, as *Mohammed* had foretold; of which sects they reckon one to be always orthodox, and entitled to salvation. [Sale, p. 158.]

The *ḥadīth* in question is cited in Pococke, *Specimen*, pp. 209–210. Ironically, the absence of profound doctrinal differences in Islam to match those between Catholic and Protestant show Spinoza to be closer to the mark, perhaps, in his assessment of the unity of Islam.

104 *RE*, pp. 565–574.

105 Venturino, *Le Ragioni della tradizione*, pp. 1–38.

106 Boulainvilliers, *La Vie de Mahomed*, p. 33; Venturino, *Le Ragioni della tradizione*, pp. 169–178.

107 Boulainvilliers, *La Vie de Mahomed*, p. 144; Venturino, *Le Ragioni della tradizione*, pp. 186–191.

108 Boulainvilliers, *La Vie de Mahomed*, p. 268.

109 Venturino, *Le Ragioni della tradizione*, pp. 160–162, 178–186.

110 Hazard, *La Crise de la conscience européenne*, pp. 144–145.

111 Daniel, *John Toland*, p. 6.

112 *RE*, pp. 599–614, and Israel, *Enlightenment Contested*, pp. 94–114; Porter, *Enlightenment*, pp. 116–118.

113 Sale, pp. 33–36.

114 Bobzin, "Translations of the Qur'ān."

115 Khairallah, "Arabic Studies in England," p. 241; Porter, *Observations*, p. 55.

CHAPTER 2

1 Marracci, vol. 1, p. 1.
2 Ibid., vol. 1, p. 2.
3 Reland, *La Religion des Mahométans*, cxxv–clxi.
4 Marracci, vol. 1, p. 4.
5 "Ego enim semper in ea opinione fui (experientia id mihi, & ratione suadente) quòd si Alcoranus, & Euangelium Gentibus illis proponantur, semper Alcoranum potius & Mahumetican superstitionem, quàm Euangelium & Christianam religionem amplexurae sint, nisi anteà & de Euangelii veritate, & de Alcoranii mendaciis ac fraudibus probè instruantur. Prima quippe facie ea, quae hic habet, naturae, praesertim corruptae, dictamini magis conformia apparent, quàm quae illud proponit: nempè unum esse Deum, omnipotentem, omniscientem, rerum ominium conditorem ac moderatorem, cui nihil commune sit cum rebus creatis: pias ac frequentes ad illum preces fundendas: eleemosynas in pauperes erogandas: peregrinationes sacras obeundas, jejuniis corpus afflictandum: justitiam servandam: modestiam, beneficentiam, pietatem, aliasque virtutes excolendas: nemini injuriam faciendam: a furtis, adulteriis, caedibus, aliisque criminibus abstinendum: res mundanas, utpote fluxas, spernendas: bonis operibus incumbendum. Praetereà reddendam esse rationem Deo ab omnibus operum suorum: Bonis paratam esse in caelo aeternam felicitatem in iis rebus, quas humana natura vehementiùs solet appetere: Malis perpetuum in gehenna suplicium; & alia hujusmodi, quae revera passim in Alcorano leguntur. Si verò audiat ethnicus proponi sibi à Ministro Euangelico, Deum unum, & trinum: Deum hominem factum: Deum pauperem, crucifixum, mortuum, ac sepultum: mysterium Eucharistiae, necessitatem sacramenti poenitentiae: Monogamiam; conjugii nexum indissolubilem: vitam perpetuae cruci conjunctàm; beneficentiam erga inimicos: felicitatem summam sitam in bonis, quae nec oculus vidit, nec auris audivit, nec in cor hominis ascenderunt; & alia hujusmodi, vel humani intellectus captum excedentia; vel naturali conditioni & imbecillitati difficillima, si non impossibilia; & haec cum Alcoranica doctrina comparaverit: statim ab his refugiet, & ad illa obviis ulnis accurret … nisi anteà instruatur, etiam testimonio ipsius Alcorani, nihil Religionem Christianam continere vel absurdum, vel falsum, quantumvis captu arduum, factuque difficile; sed omnia in ea vera, certa, & divino testimonio in Pentateucho & Euangelio (quos Mahumetus ipse libros à Deo traditos, & certissimae veritatis esse affirmat) comprobata … Mahumetum porrò nihil aliud fecisse, quàm veram & propè universalem in Orbe religionem corrupisse; novamque ac perversam superstitionem armis, fraudibus, aliisque malis artibus invexisse: à qua, si ea à Christiana desumpsit, auferantur, *moveat cornicula risum furtivis nudata coloribus*." [i.e. Horace, *Ep.* 1.3.19.] [Ibid., vol. 2, p. 9.]
6 Sale, "Dedication," n.p.
7 Ibid.
8 Ibid.
9 Porter, *Enlightenment*, pp. 51–70. Porter quotes George Thomson's injunction that the focus of knowledge should be on "Things, not Thinking … Operation, not merely Speculation" (p. 53). Sale's phrase should also be read against the history of the perceived usefulness of Arabic studies in England. See Khairallah, "Arabic Studies in England," pp. 44–90, 203–263.

10 Sale, p. iii.
11 Ibid., pp. iii–iv.
12 Haydon, *Anti-Catholicism in Eighteenth-Century England*, pp. 4–5.
13 Ibid.
14 Dumont, *Homo aequalis, II*, pp. 15–31; Descombes, *Philosophie par gros temps*, pp. 51–53, and "Louis Dumont," pp. 227–232.
15 Descombes, *Philosophie par gros temps*, 136.
16 Hegel, *Die Vernunft in der Geschichte*, pp. 74–78, but see also the interpretation of Hegel's statement that world history is the progress of the consciousness of freedom and the intercultural dialogue that this necessarily entails in Houlgate, "World History as the Progress of Consciousness."
17 Hourani, *Islam in European Thought*, pp. 7–60.
18 Laurens, *Aux sources de l'orientalisme*, pp. 60–61.
19 Hourani sums up the perplexed Christian reaction toward Muhammad and Islam as one of puzzlement before a prophet who is no prophet in the usual sense – the prophecy of the Old Testament having been fulfilled in the New and thereby dispensing with the need for new prophets – and bafflement before the communication between God and humanity: the God of Islam is "a God who seems to be the God of Abraham, who speaks to mankind and makes His will known, and holds out the prospect of a Final day of Judgement, but who speaks through a Book which Muslims do, and Christians do not, accept as literally the word of God." *Islam in European Thought*, p. 48.
20 Massignon, "Réflexions sur la structure primitive," p. 615. See also the connotations and etymologies listed by Lecerf for the term "Djiwār" in his eponymous article: stranger, enemy (cf. Latin *hostis*) as well as guest, client. Lecerf adduces several examples of Semitic texts that carry connotations of seeking protection in a sacred place or temple.
21 Massignon's sentence is found in an article linking the deep structure of Semitic languages to some of the insights made available by early structural anthropology:

> J'ai rêvé parfois d'écrire … une introduction "du dedans" à l'étude de l'arabe … – Pour que les lecteurs "expatrient" leur désir de comprendre hors de leurs normes; en le décentrant, comme Copernic son univers ptoléméen, en passant, comme le géomètre transforme son système de coordonnées cartésiennes en système de coordonnées polaires réaxé sur le centre axial de l'autre. – Pour comprendre l'autre, il ne faut pas se l'annexer, mais devenir son hôte. Le caractère "exogamique" du langage n'est réalisable qu'en usant du Droit d'Asile: "dakhīlak." [Massignon, "Réflexions sur la structure primitive," p. 615.]

> [I have sometimes dreamed of writing … an introduction "from within" to Arabic … – So that readers might expatriate their desire for understanding beyond their norms; by decentring it, as Copernicus did to his Ptolemean universe, in passing, as the geometer transforms his system of Cartesian co-ordinates into a system of polar co-ordinates re-centred on the geometric origin of the other. – To understand the other, we must not annex him, but become his host/guest. The "exogamic" character of language cannot be realized unless we use the right of asylum: "dakhīlak."]

Elsewhere, Massignon relates this particular moral injunction to his study of Al-Ḥallāj, using identical language (decentring the self, substitution of the self for the other, transformation of Cartesian into Polar co-ordinates) and linking it to the mystical station of *qurb* (proximity). Massignon, *Essai sur les origines*, p. 43, and "L'Involution sémantique," p. 631.

22 Steiner, *After Babel*, pp. 312–318.

23 Ibid., pp. 248–282.

24 Ibid., p. 413. It bears pointing out that Steiner's model predicts a greater tension between languages of the same family than between more distant ones: "Out of the tension of resistance and affinity, a tension directly proportional to the proximity of the two languages and historical communities, grows the elucidative strangeness of the great translation. The strangeness is elucidative because we come to recognize it, to 'know it again', as our own" (ibid.). Steiner's conclusion is based on his fine analyses of the English translations of Flaubert and German translations of Shakespeare, in contradistinction to Ezra Pound, who "can make *Cathay* spare and translucent because he, and his Western readers, know next to nothing of the original" (ibid., p. 412). I am not sure that this is entirely accurate when it comes to the translations of the Qur'ān under scrutiny here: whereas the "elucidative strangeness" to which Steiner refers is there on nearly every page of Sale's text, it is difficult to relate this quality to any proximity between the Arabic and English languages.

25 "The radical generosity of the translator ('I grant beforehand that there must be something there'), his trust in the 'other' as yet untried, unmapped alterity of statement, concentrates to a philosophically dramatic degree the human bias toward seeing the world as symbolic, as constituted of relations in which 'this' can stand for 'that', and must in fact be able to do so if there are to be meanings and structures." Ibid., p. 312.

26 The historical classification that underlies Steiner's model has come under attack from a number of quarters, notably Michel Ballard and Antoine Berman, who use the critique as a point of departure for their histories of translation (Berman, unfortunately, seems to ignore the second half of *After Babel*). Nevertheless, Steiner's model does have the advantage of explaining the success of (mostly literary) translations that would otherwise seem too close to one or the other extreme of the three-part traditional model, one case in point being Ezra Pound's *Cathay* poems. Steiner, *After Babel*, pp. 375–380; Ballard, *De Cicéron à Benjamin*, pp. 13–20; Berman, *L'Epreuve de l'étranger*, pp. 12–17.

27 "The English text has not been translated into the German language, says Gundolf, it *has become that language*." Friedrich Gundolf, *Shakespeare und der Deutsche Geist* (1927), quoted in Steiner, *After Babel*, p. 402.

28 My phrasing is borrowed from Mark Strand, who offers the following suggestion in an imaginary dialogue with Borges in a series of prose poems on translation: "Wouldn't it be best to think of translation as a transaction between individual idioms, between, say, the Italian of D'Annunzio and the English of Auden? If we did, we could end irrelevant discussions of who has and who hasn't done a correct translation." Strand, *The Continuous Life*, "Translation 5," p. 53.

29 For George Steiner, Borges' parable is "the most acute, most concentrated

commentary anyone has offered on the business of translation." *After Babel*, p. 73.

30 An excellent account of the history of the arguments surrounding this verse is found in McAuliffe, "Text and Textuality," pp. 58–65. Detailed treatments of the *muḥkam/mutashābih* opposition as a basis for *tafsīr* are found in Abū Zayd, *Ittijāh*, pp. 164–190, and more briefly in Heath, "Metaphor," as well as Gilliot and Larcher, "Language and Style." With specific reference to Al-Zamakhsharī in the context of Mu'tazili exegesis, see Goldziher, *Die Richtungen*, pp. 101–178, esp. pp. 127–129 on Q3:7. John Wansbrough uses the history of the commentaries surrounding Q3:7 to develop his concept of *Deutungsbedürftigkeit* – the need for interpretation – as a key principle of exegesis (see below). *Quranic Studies*, pp. 148–172.

31 Sale, p. 35.

32 Ibid.

33 Ibid., "Preliminary Discourse," p. 69.

34 For a useful catalogue of the failure of other translators, including Robert of Ketton, André Du Ryer, and Marracci, to capture and appreciate the full significance of this distinction, see Hamilton and Richard, *André Du Ryer*, p. 101 n. There is an important precedent for Sale's position in Reland, *Of the Mahometan Religion*, pp. 93–95. Bobzin points out that Postel displays an accurate understanding of the distinction between *muḥkam* and *mutashābih* but does not translate Q3:7 in *De orbis terrae Concordia*. Bobzin, *KZR*, pp. 472–473.

35 Marracci, vol. 1, pp. 34–35, 39–40.

36 Cf. Zamakhsharī *ad loc.* and Helmut Gätje, *The Qur'an and its Exegesis*, pp. 55–57.

37 On the related question – just what qualifies someone to be declared "grounded in knowledge" – see Izutsu, *God and Man in the Qur'an*, pp. 55–60. According to Izutsu, the term *'ilm* means knowledge derived from an absolutely reliable source, namely divine revelation. Thus those who are "rooted in knowledge" are the true believers. We see here an important proposition regarding faith and knowledge that announces the divergence between Marracci and Sale (see below): for the former, knowledge of scripture is necessarily mediated by an institution, while the latter is comfortable with a direct relationship between God and the believer. Daniel Madigan has recently pushed the semantic analysis of the term *kitāb* further to adduce a key relationship between it and *'ilm*, namely that the term *kitāb* operates as a unifying symbol for all the positive connotations of knowledge (*'ilm*) and authority (*ḥukm*). *The Qur'ān's Self-Image*, pp. 144–165.

38 This reading can be traced as far back as the commentary by Mujāhid b. Jabr (d. 100 AH), though it is doubtful that either Sale or Marracci had copies of his *tafsīr*. McAuliffe, "Text and Textuality," p. 61.

39 Marracci, vol. 2, p. 105.

40 Cf. Cicero's references to feigned virtue in *Pro Caelio* 14 as "virtus adsimulata."

41 Marracci, vol. 2, p. 108.

42 Ibid.

43 "Neque objiciant Moslemi, in Pentateucho & Evangelio multa esse assimilata, seu metaphorica, aut allegorica. Quamvis enim hoc verissimum sit: ea tamen

non sunt hujusmodi, ut à solo Deo intelligi possint, sed ex antecedentibus & consequentibus, & ex ipso modo loquendi, ab hominibus saltem sapientoribus, seu doctioribus verae fidei lumine illustrates, non multo saepè cum labore intelliguntur, & ab iis, quae sunt propriè dicta, facile distinguuntur." Ibid.

44 See McAuliffe's account of this and other arguments regarding the *mutashābihāt* as a justification of faith. "Text and Textuality," pp. 64–65.

45 Wansbrough, *Quranic Studies*, p. 149.

46 Ibid., p. 100. Auerbach attributes all of the terms quoted to biblical narrative. *Mimesis*, pp. 26–27.

47 Wansbrough, *Quranic Studies*, pp. 142–178.

48 Massignon, who took an essentialist view of Semitic languages and their relationship to Revelation, also holds fast to the distinction between Greek and Hebrew:

> Il y a une espèce de transcendence dans le langage déjà, que j'ai sentie à travers l'arabe. Je ne dis pas que chez d'autres langages on ne puisse la trouver, mais je crois que, toutes choses égales d'ailleurs, les langues sémitiques sont celles qui sont predestinées pour un certain maintien du problème du langage. C'est le principe de la Révélation et des rapports du langage et de la Révélation. Sous quelle forme Dieu a-t-il révélé sa Loi à Moïse? C'est le problème de l'inspiration qu'on minimise chez un certain nombre d'exégètes, en comparant le Livre de Job à Eschyle ou de Saint Jean à des Dialogues de Platon. Il y a dans les langues sémitiques un certain *témoignage* de ce que le langage, en quelque manière, doit exprimer … [Massignon, "L'Involution sémantique," p. 629.]

> [There is a sort of transcendence in language that I have felt through Arabic. I do not claim that it cannot be found in other languages, but I believe that, all other things being equal, the Semitic languages are those destined for a certain maintenance of the problem of language. It is the principle of Revelation and of the relationship of language to Revelation. In what form did God reveal his Law to Moses? It is the problem of inspiration that is minimized by a number of exegetes, as they compare the Book of Job to Aeschylus or St. John to the Dialogues of Plato. There is in the Semitic languages a certain *witnessing* to what language, somehow, must express …]

Henri Meschonnic has a thorough examination of Massignon's theological linguistics and an incisive critique of what he calls the idealism underlying Western translations of the sacred, especially with reference to the Bible. *Pour la poétique II*, pp. 229–237, 412–413; *Poétique du traduire*, pp. 427–444.

49 Whence, too, perhaps, the appalling quality of some of his translations. This becomes especially apparent when complex figurative language occurs in the Qur'ān, e.g. Q3:7, Q17:42 (where he omits the phrase جَنَاحَ الذُّلِّ مِنَ الرَّحْمَةِ), Q55:17–20 (where he fails to translate بَرْزَخ), and so on. See Hamilton and Richard, *André Du Ryer*, pp. 101–103.

50 Auerbach, *Mimesis*, p. 15.

51 Ibid., p. 16.

52 Qtd. Khairallah, "Arabic Studies in England," pp. 241–242.

53 قَدْ خَسِرَ الَّذِينَ كَذَّبُوا بِلِقَاءِ اللَّهِ حَتَّى إِذَا جَاءَتْهُمُ السَّاعَةُ بَغْتَةً قَالُوا يَا حَسْرَتَنَا عَلَى مَا فَرَّطْنَا فِيهَا وَهُمْ يَحْمِلُونَ أَوْزَارَهُمْ عَلَى ظُهُورِهِمْ أَلَا سَاءَ مَا يَزِرُونَ.

In Sale's translation:

> They are lost who reject as a falsehood the meeting of GOD *in the next life*, until the hour cometh suddenly upon them. *Then will* they say, Alas! for that we have behaved ourselves negligently in *our lifetime;* and they shall carry their burdens on their backs; will it not be evil which they shall be loaden with? [Sale, p. 101.]

54 Ibid., p. 102.

55 Champion, *Republican Learning*, pp. 98–105; Griffin, *Regaining Paradise*, pp. 11–42.

56 Toland, "The Life of John Milton," p. 43.

57 Milton, *A Complete Collection*, vol. 1, p. 274.

58 On the place of the individual reader in *Paradise Lost* see Fish, *Surprised by Sin*, pp. 1–56, 286–356. On Milton's radicalism and his argument for the spiritual power of the "kingdom within" the self, see Loewenstein, *Representing Revolution*, pp. 202–268. On the extent to which Milton's name had become synonymous with the cause of toleration in debates related to the Ottoman Empire and his recent reception in the Middle East, see MacLean, "Milton, Islam and the Ottomans."

59 Sale, "Preliminary Discourse," p. 61.

60 In an excellent paper that remains, unfortunately, unpublished, Jan Loop gives a thorough account of the Western reception of the style of the Qur'ān and the doctrine of its *I'jāz* during the seventeenth and eighteenth centuries, carefully situating Sale within contemporary arguments about the incomprehensibility of the Qur'ān and the suspicion shown by many thinkers toward religious "enthusiasm," claiming that Sale was indeed the first to treat *I'jāz* positively. "Heiliger Poesie," pp. 23–26.

61 Sale, "Preliminary Discourse," p. 61 n.

62 Porter, *Enlightenment*, pp. 160–161.

63 Shaftesbury, *Characteristics*, vol. 3, p. 235.

64 Champion, *The Pillars of Priestcraft Shaken*, pp. 212–218; Klein, *Shaftesbury and the Culture of Politeness*, pp. 154–212; *RE*, p. 67.

65 Marracci, vol. 1, pp. 33–34.

66 "Pindarem quisquis studet aemulari/Jule ceratis ope Daedale/Nititur pennis, vitreo daturus/Noumina Ponto." ["Whoever tries to rival Pindar, Julus, is just flying with Daedalean feathers, destined to [fall and] give his name to the glassy sea below."] Qtd. Marracci, *Prodromus ad Refutationem Alcorani*, vol. 1, p. 70.

67 Ibid., vol. 1, pp. 69–74.

68 See Williams, *Tradition and Originality in Roman Poetry*, pp. 429–431, 764–765. On the poet's deliberate self-positioning with respect to the size of his project, the risks he is taking and his political situation in imperial Rome, see Lowrie, *Horace's Narrative Odes*, pp. 212–213, 317–352.

69 For a detailed discussion of the Hellenistic nuances and background to *Ars. P.* 139 and Horace's views of the nature of Homeric subject matter (*Ars. P.* 140–152), see Brink, *Horace on Poetry II*, pp. 208–224, 488–490. The impact of Homer on the Alexander histories is examined in Elizabeth Carney, "Artifice and Alexander History."

70 Marracci, vol. 2, p. 108.

CHAPTER 3

1 Robinson, "Jesus." McAuliffe gives the following portrait of Qur'ānic Christians:

> Created in the interplay of text and interpretation, Qur'ānic Christians are those whose fundamental submission to God, whose Islam was undertaken within the context of following the prophet Jesus. To him had God vouchsafed a revelation that, given its divine origins, obviously could not be inconsistent with God's culminating revelation in the Qur'ān. Qur'ānic Christians guarded this revelation in its pristine purity, keeping themselves free from the eventual dogmatic aberrations of their co-religionists. Scripturally anticipating the advent of God's final prophet, they stood ready to acknowledge him as the fulfillment of that same divine graciousness that had sent their earlier prophet, Jesus. For Qur'ānic Christians there was not, nor could there be, any incongruity between the two prophets, Jesus and Muhammad. Those who had faithfully followed the former would necessarily be eager to welcome the latter. Qur'ānic Christians, then, are Christians who either accepted the prophethood of Muhammad and the revelation entrusted to him or would have done so had their historical circumstances permitted. [McAuliffe, *Qur'ānic Christians*, p. 287.]

2 Rubin, *Between the Bible and the Qur'ān*, p. 4.
3 Toland, *Nazarenus*, p. 117.
4 Sale, "Preliminary Discourse," p. 70.
5 A more detailed account is found in Champion's "Introduction" to Toland, *Nazarenus*, pp. 39–53.
6 Ibid., p. 117.
7 Ibid.
8 Ibid., p. 116.
9 Ibid., p. 118.
10 Ibid., pp. 140–141.
11 Ibid., p. 142. On the history of the identification of Muḥammad (or Aḥmad) with Περίκλυτος, see Shacht, "Aḥmad"; Anawati, "'Īsā"; Watt, "His Name is Ahmad." Anawati implies that the equivalence between Περίκλυτος and Aḥmad is original to Sale, "relying on a suggestion of Marracci," but the date of Toland's text proves that it was he rather than Sale who forged the connection.
12 Sale, p. 449.

13 Ibid.

14 In his epistle to the reader, Sale calls the Gospel of Barnabas a "barefaced forgery" but attributes it to "some renegade Christian."

15 Sale, "Preliminary Discourse," pp. 74–75.

16 Champion (ed.), "Introduction" to Toland, *Nazarenus*, p. 77–78.

17 Marracci, vol. 1, pp. 42–43.

18 Abu Al-Qāsim Hibat Allāh b. Salāma b. Naṣr b. 'Ali Al-Baghdādī's (Sale's 'Abu'lKasem Hebat Allah' d. 1019) *Kitāb Al-Nāsikh wa-l-mansūkh min kitāb Allāh*. For more on Hibat Allāh b. Salāma, see *GAL*, vol. 1, p. 205 (192); *GAS*, vol. 1, pp. 47–48; as well as Nöldeke, *Geschichte des Qorāns*, vol. 1, pp. 52–54. On abrogation more generally and its relationship to the textual historicity of the Qur'ān, see Burton, "Naskh," "Abrogation," *The Collection of the Qur'an*, pp. 46–137, and *The Sources of Islamic Law*, pp. 165–213; Powers, "The Exegetical Genre *nāsikh al-Qur'ān wa mansūkhuhu*."

19 Ibn Salāma, *Al-Nāsikh wa-l-mansūkh*, pp. 20–22.

20 Marracci, vol. 1, p. 43.

21 Schöller, "Post-Enlightenment Academic Study of the Qur'ān"; Neuwirth, "Form and Structure"; Burton, *The Collection of the Qur'ān*. Burton notes correctly that the word "Qur'ān" refers not to a physical object but to an idea; a notion that receives full treatment in Abū Zayd, *Mafhūm al-Naṣṣ*.

22 Sale, "Preliminary Discourse," p. 66.

23 Sale, p. 8.

24 McAuliffe, *Qur'ānic Christians*, pp. 91–128.

25 Sale, pp. 8–9 n.

26 Marracci, vol. 2, p. 33.

27 The anti-Muslim polemic on this point can be traced as far back as Nicetas of Byzantium, who notes the oddity of Mary being greeted as the sister of Aaron (Q19:28). Robinson, *Christ in Islam and Christianity*, p. 9. Marracci also makes much of the putative identification of 'Isā with Esau. See Anawati, "'Īsā." A full account of the Muslim Mary's genealogy is found in Arnaldez, *Jésus fils de Marie*, pp. 33–34.

28 Marracci, vol. 2, p. 107.

29 Marracci, vol. 2, p. 115.

30 Marracci, vol. 2, p. 434.

31 Marracci's translation of Q19:28 is straightforward: "O soror Aaron; non fuit pater tuus vir malus & non fuit mater tua scortatrix." His refutation of this failure of identification rehearses the arguments he presents *ad* Q3:

> Quemamodùm supra Mahomet vocavit Mariam Deiparam filiam Amram: ita vocat hic sororem Aaron. Confoundit scilicet hand um Maria illa, quae verè fuit filia Amran & sororem Aaron. Hunc tamen errorem tàm crassum Mahumetani agnoscentes, excusare conantur, ut vidimus in notis: sed frustra & rationibus prorsùs frivolis, ac ridiculis. Neque enim Maria erit ex stirpe Aaron, sed Jude, neque potuit habere fratrem illum tàm sanctum, nomine Aaron; cùm orta sit primogenita & unigenita ex parentibus sterilibus. Quòd si etiam poneremus, post illam natum hunc Aaron fictitium; fuisset certè, eo tempore valdè puer: erat enim Maria, juxta Mahumetanos, trecim annos nata. Ineptè vero vocassent eam sororem Aaron propter similitudinem cum Aaron fratre Moysi

in pudicitia (cf. Zamakhshari); cùm nullam in hoc praerogativum Aaron habuerit. Rationabiliùs vocassent eam sororem alicujus foeminae castitate insignis, veluti Juditae, vel ipsius Mariae sororis Aaron: vel saltem alicujus viri ejusdem virtutus laude conspicui, veluti Joseph filii Jacob, vel Eliae. Omitto alias circa hoc ineptias. Unum addo: si ita licet nomina, ac personas fingere, vel pervertire, nihil tam absurdum erit, quod defendere non possimus. Vide supre in Sura 3 & in Prodorumus p. 4 cap. Ult. Pag. 76. [Marracci, vol. 2, pp. 431, 435–436.]

32 Marracci, *Prodromus ad Refutationem Alcorani*, Part 4, Chapter 27, vol. 1, p. 105.

33 Sale, p. 38 n.

34 This possibility is found as early as a tradition from *Ṣaḥīḥ Muslim* mentioned by Ibn Kathīr *ad* Q19:28. Qtd. Robinson, *Christ in Islam and Christianity*, p. 63. Reland devotes a chapter to the question of Mary's relationship to Moses, seeing in it an instance of mistaken Christian belief about the Qur'ān: "A great many are so proud of this enormous Mistake, as they think, that neglecting the rest, they believe, that this alone, like *Medusa*'s Head, should be made use of against the *Mahometans*." Reland, *Of the Mahometan Religion*, p. 80.

35 According to Neal Robinson, another possible source for the identity of the two Marys is the Syriac Christian literature current in the age of Muḥammad: "The description of Mary as the 'Sister of Aaron' (19:28), which seemed such a blunder to the polemicists, would surely not have seemed in the least odd to Christians who thought of Mary as having been present on Mount Horeb as the burning bush which was not consumed," citing E. Gräf on a hymn by Rabbulah, the Orthodox bishop of Edessa (fifth century) ("Zu den christlichen Einflüssen im Koran," J. Henninger Festschrift *al-bahit* [Bonn, St. Augustin, 1976]). Robinson, *Christ in Islam and Christianity*, pp. 18, 196.

36 Sale, pp. 250–251.

37 Ibid., n.

38 The relevant sections are the Homeric *Hymn to Apollo*, 18, 117, 123–132 and Callimachus' *Hymn to Delos*, 210. In his translation of Callimachus, Mair lists the following additional references to the palm motif: Callimachus, *Hymn* 2.4 (reference to the Delian palm in Callimachus' *Hymn to Apollo*), Homer, *Od.* 6.162, Hesiod, *Theognis* 5, and Euripides, *Hecuba* 458. Walter Burkert stresses the importance of trees as markers of sanctuary and the link of this particular aspect of Greek religion with Near Eastern tradition. *Greek Religion*, pp. 85–86. Another common element, albeit one that Sale does not emphasize, is nourishment from a divine, as opposed to a human, source: Homer says that Apollo was not fed by his mother, but rather was served nectar and ambrosia by Themis (*Hom. Hymn Apollo*, 123–124), which parallels the *nourritures terrestres* topos running through the Qur'ānic Jesus and Mary story and the concomitant leitmotif of the benefits of the palm tree in both the Qur'ān and hadīth. See Viré, "Nakhl"; Waines, "Date Palm."

39 Needless to say, this is the position of Marracci. It bears pointing out that many, if not all, of the points on which Islam and Christianity diverge with respect to the Jesus story are found in Tatian's attempt at harmonizing the four gospels in his *Diatessaron* (c. 175 CE) and apocryphal infancy gospels, most of

which would not have been deemed legitimate by Marracci. Robinson, *Christ in Islam and Christianity*, pp. 17–22. Once again, the extent to which the early modern representation of Islam relied on intra-Christian religious controversy is made clear.

40 Sale's approach bears comparison with Georges Dumézil's, whereby the very large corpus of Indo-European epics is shown consistently to yield a tripartite structure. Dumézil's trifunctional model is treated extensively in *Mythe et épopée I*. On the applicability of the adjective "structural" to this method and the intellectual context of his research, see Dumézil's preface and François Dosse's brief but useful discussion of Dumézil's relationship to the structuralist movement. Dumézil, ibid., pp. 9–27; Dosse, *Histoire du structuralisme*, vol. 1, pp. 53–57.

41 Sale, pp. 42–43.

42 Ibid., p. 43 n.

43 McAuliffe, *Qur'ānic Christians*, pp. 144–146; Arnaldez, *Jésus fils de Marie*, pp. 187–204.

44 Sale, p. 43 n.

45 *Al-Kashshāf ad loc.*, qtd. and trans. McAuliffe, *Qur'ānic Christians*, p. 149.

46 Sale, p. 79.

47 Robinson, *Christ in Islam and Christianity*, pp. 127–141.

CHAPTER 4

1 See Pomeau, *La Religion de Voltaire*; Badir, *Voltaire et l'Islam*; Hadidi, *Voltaire et l'Islam*; Gunny, *Images of Islam*, pp. 134–62.

2 Pomeau et al., *Voltaire en son temps*, vol. 2, pp. 151–159. *Mahomet* receives exhaustive treatment in Badir, *Voltaire et l'Islam*, pp. 73–146.

3 Grimm, *Correspondance littéraire*, vol. 2, p. 310.

4 Voltaire, "Mahométans," pp. 20–21. Like many of Voltaire's articles dealing with religion, this one was originally written as part of the *Questions sur l'Encyclopédie* and added to the *Dictionnaire philosophique* in the Kehl edition of Voltaire's complete works.

5 Pomeau, *La Religion de Voltaire*, p. 145.

6 See Ahmad Gunny's introduction and notes to his critical edition of the text in *The Complete Works of Voltaire*, vol. 20B, pp. 329–345.

7 *Notes marginales*, vol. 4, pp. 654–664.

8 There are bookmarks between pages 136–137 and 176–177 of the 1734 edition of the Sale Qur'ān, which cover Q7:175–190 and Q11:6–29 respectively. The choice of verses singled out above is mine alone, based on the presumed interest of Voltaire in the lack of attribution of any divine quality to Muhammad and in Voltaire's presumed interest in the thesis that Muhammad composed the Qur'ān.

9 *EM*, vol. 1, p. 273.

10 Ibid., vol. 1, pp. 269–270.

11 Ibid., vol. 1, p. 274.

12 Voltaire, "Alcoran," pp. 100–101.

13 Sale, pp. 65–66.

14 Voltaire, "Alcoran," pp. 100–101.

15 An inquiry into the vast questions of the codification and legality of women's rights and the laws of marriage in the Qur'an is beyond the scope of this study, but good points of departure are provided by Margot Badran, "Feminism and the Qur'ān"; Kohn, *Die Eheschliessung im Koran*; Nada Tomiche, "Mar'a" and "La Femme en Islam"; Motzki, "Marriage and Divorce" and "Geschlechtsreife une Legitimation zur Zeugung im frühen Islam"; Ahmed, *Women and Gender in Islam*, pp. 41–123.

16 Roland Mousnier calls the society of absolutist France a "society of lineages," although he does argue for a gradual departure from considerations of lineage in favor of the home and hearth ("la maison et le ménage"). Similarly, the power exercised by the market in ranks and titles had great impact on family life during this period. *Institutions*, pp. 47–82, 618–632. A good account of the quotidian complications of French married life is found in Hardwick, *The Practice of Patriarchy*, pp. 77–158.

17 Voltaire, "Alcoran," p. 100.

18 Ibid., p. 98.

19 Here Voltaire anticipates later arguments to this effect by Porter and Anquetil-Duperron. Laurens, *Origines intellectuelles*, pp. 53–62.

20 Lazarus-Yafeh, "The Religious Dialectics of the Hadjdj," p. 20. An extensive account of this transition is found in Wellhausen, *Reste arabischen Heidentums*, pp. 68–129. Mohammed Arkoun reads the ḥajj as the locus of the replacement of a pagan semantic system by a Muslim one in his "Le Hajj dans la pensée islamique."

21 Sale, "Preliminary Discourse," pp. 121–122.

22 *EM*, vol. 1, p. 273.

23 Sale, "Preliminary Discourse," p. 142.

24 *EM*, vol. 1, p. 256.

25 Ibid., vol. 1, p. 258.

26 Ibid., vol. 1, p. 260.

27 Ibid., vol. 1, p. 265.

28 Ibid., vol. 1, p. 267.

29 Ibid., vol. 1, p. 275.

30 It bears pointing out that fanaticism has not been completely eliminated from Voltaire's perspective. To his comment on the caliphate as the "puissance qui a menacé toute la terre," he adds: "Leurs ordres étaient autant d'oracles, et leurs soldats autant de fanatiques." Ibid., vol. 1, p. 267.

31 Ibid., vol. 1, p. 234.

32 Ibid., vol. 1, p. 223.

33 Ibid., vol. 1, p. 279.

34 Ibid., vol. 2, pp. 917–918.

35 A thorough account of Voltaire's relationship to previous historians, including Bayle, is found in Brumfitt, *Voltaire Historian*, pp. 26–45, esp. pp. 104–106 on the question of causation.

36 Ibid., pp. 136–138.

37 Ibid., p. 141.

38 Banier, *La Mythologie*, vol. 1, pp. 19–20, qtd. Brumfitt, "Introduction" to *La Philosophie de l'histoire*, p. 47.

39 Voltaire, *Oeuvres complètes*, Besterman ed., vol. 33, p. 164.

40 Becker, *The Heavenly City*, pp. 17–19. Needless to say, the idea of the accomplishment of the transcendent in human history does not disappear immediately, as the example of Hegel makes abundantly clear.

41 *EM*, vol. 1, p. 196.

42 Ibid., vol. 1, p. 255.

43 Ibid., vol. 1, p. 256.

44 Ibid., vol. 1, p. 263.

45 Ibid.

46 Ibid., vol. 2, p. 915.

47 Sale, p. iii.

48 *EM*, vol. 1, p. 260.

49 Ibid., vol. 1, p. 115.

50 Pomeau et al., *Voltaire en son temps*, vol. 4, pp. 66–79.

51 Voltaire, *Dieu et les hommes*, p. 415.

52 *EM*, vol. 1, p. 259 n.

53 Ibid., vol. 1, p. 256. If, following the editorial note of René Pomeau in *Voltaire en son temps*, we assume a very rough exchange rate of 100 1990 French Francs to the *livre* of the mid-eighteenth century, this translates into a figure of 90,000 1990 French Francs or 13,700 Euros today – a tidy sum, perhaps, but hardly enough to change the world. On Voltaire's financial skills more generally, see Donvez, *De quoi vivait Voltaire?*

54 Voltaire, "De l'Alcoran et de Mahomet," p. 340, emphasis added.

55 *EM*, vol. 1, p. 257.

56 Voltaire, "De l'Alcoran et de Mahomet," p. 341. Ahmad Gunny identifies this as a mistake – Muhammad was wounded at the battle of Uhud, not Badr (his first battle with the Meccans). Voltaire's mistake underlines the importance of Badr for his understanding of Muhammad (see below).

57 *EM*, vol. 1, pp. 257–258.

58 Ibid., vol. 1, pp. 258–259.

59 Voltaire, *La Philosophie de l'histoire*, p. 142.

60 *EM*, vol. 1, p. 260.

61 Ibid., vol. 1, pp. 260–261.

62 Ibid., vol. 1, pp. 266–267.

63 Ibid., vol. 1, p. 264.

64 Ibid., vol. 1, pp. 264–265.

65 Later on in the *Essai*, as he tries to make a case for the similarities between Islam and other religions, Voltaire argues that, "Le dogme de la predestination absolue, et de la fatalité, qui semble au jour'dui caractériser le mahométisme, était l'opinion de toute l'antiquité: elle n'est pas moins claire dans l'*Iliade* que dans l'*Alcoran*." ["The dogma of absolute predestination and fatalism, which seems to characterize Mahometism today, was believed in by all antiquity: it is no less clear in the *Iliad* than in the *Alcoran*."] Ibid., vol. 1, p. 273.

66 Ibid., vol. 1, p. 269. It bears pointing out that, like Rousseau, Voltaire is impressed by the longevity of the Arabic language and Muslim civilization:

> La langue arabe avait l'avantage d'être perfectionnée depuis longtemps; elle était fixée avant Mahomet, et ne s'est point altérée depuis. Aucun des jargons qu'on parlait alors en Europe n'a pas seulement laissé la moindre trace. De quelque côté que nous nous tournions, il faut avouer

que nous n'existons que d'hier. Nous allons plus loin que les autres peuples en plus d'un genre; et c'est peut-être parce que nous sommes venus les derniers.

[The Arabic language had the advantage of being perfected long ago; it had been fixed before Mahmet and has never been altered since. None of the jargons that were spoken in Europe at the time has left the slightest trace. No matter which side we turn to, we must admit that we were born yesterday. We go farther than other peoples in several respects, and it is perhaps because we are the last to arrive.]

67 D'Herbelot, *Bibliothèque orientale*, p. 190.
68 *EM*, vol. 1, pp. 256–257.
69 Sale, p. 44.
70 To take one example near the verse cited above, consider Sale's translation of and commentary on Q3:23 اللَّهِ لِيَحْكُمَ بَيْنَهُمْ ثُمَّ يَتَوَلَّى فَرِيقٌ مِنْهُمْ وَهُمْ مُعْرِضُونَ [: أَلَمْ تَرَ إِلَى الَّذِينَ أُوتُوا نَصِيبًا مِنَ الْكِتَابِ يُدْعَوْنَ إِلَى كِتَابِ "Hast thou not observed those unto whom part of the scripture was given [that is, the Jews]? They were called unto the book of GOD, that it might judge between them; then some of them turned their backs, and retired afar off." Sale's footnote reads:

This passage was revealed on occasion of a dispute Mohammed had with some Jews, which is differently related by the commentators.

Al Beidâwi says that Mohammed going one day into a Jewish synagogue, Naïm Ebn Amru and al Hareth Ebn Zeid asked him what religion he was of? To which he answering, "Of the religion of Abraham"; they replied, "Abraham was a Jew." But on Mohammed's proposing that the Pentateuch might decide the question, they would by no means agree to it.

But Jallalo'ddin tells us that two persons of the Jewish religion having committed adultery, their punishment was referred to Mohammed, who gave sentence that they should be stoned, according to the law of Moses. This the Jews refused to submit to, alleging there was no such command in the Pentateuch; but on Mohammed's appealing to the book, the said law was found therein. Whereupon the criminals were stoned, to the great mortification of the Jews.

It is very remarkable that this law of Moses concerning the stoning of adulterers is mentioned in the New Testament [John 7:5] (though I know some dispute the authenticity of that whole passage), but is not now to be found, either in the Hebrew or Samaritan Pentateuch, or in the Septuagint; it being only said that such *shall be put to death* [Leviticus 20:10]. This omission is insisted on by the Mohammedans as one instance of the corruption of the law of Moses by the Jews. [Sale, p. 37.]

For the Abrahamic center of gravity of Q3, Voltaire was probably also thinking of the verse that followed Q3:67: "Verily the men who are the nearest *of kin* unto Abraham are they who follow him; and this prophet, and they who believed *on him:* GOD is the patron of the faithful." Sale, p. 44. For an extended analysis of this topic, see Robinson, "Sūrat Al 'Imrān."

71 *EM*, vol. 1, p. 259.

72 ذَلِكَ الْكِتَابُ لَا رَيْبَ فِيهِ هُدًى لِلْمُتَّقِينَ (2) الَّذِينَ يُؤْمِنُونَ بِالْغَيْبِ وَيُقِيمُونَ الصَّلَاةَ وَمِمَّا رَزَقْنَاهُمْ يُنْفِقُونَ

Sale's translation reads: "There is no doubt in this book; it is a direction to the pious, who believe in the mysteries of faith, who observe the appointed times of prayer, and distribute alms out of what we have bestowed on them." Sale explains the word "mysteries" thus: "The Arabic word is *gheib*, which properly signifies a thing that is *absent, at a great distance, or invisible*, such as the resurrection, paradise, and hell. And this is agreeable to the language of scripture, which defines faith to be the *evidence of things not seen* [Heb. 11:1; see also Rom. 24:25; 2 Cor. 4:18 and 5:7]." Sale, p. 2.

73 The falsity of this conversion story, as well as the myth of the *mu'allaqāt*, has been demonstrated by Nöldeke, *Beiträge zur Kenntniss der Poesie der alten Araber*, pp. xvii–xxiii. As Navid Kermani points out, however, narratives like these constitute an important part of the cultural memory of Islam and the way in which it is understood by both believers and opponents. Kermani, *Gott ist schön*, pp. 14–24.

74 *EM*, vol. 1, p. 259.

75 Ibid., vol. 1, p. 269.

76 Ibid., vol. 1, p. 271. Q7:199, خُذِ الْعَفْوَ وَأْمُرْ بِالْعُرْفِ وَأَعْرِضْ عَنِ الْجَاهِلِينَ is translated by Sale as follows: "Use indulgence, and command that which is just, and withdraw far from the ignorant." Sale, p. 38. Sale adds the following commentary at the phrase "Use indulgence" (his translation of خذ العفو): "Or, as the words may also be translated, *Take the superabundant overplus* – meaning that Mohammed should accept such voluntary alms from the people as they could spare. But the passage, if taken in this sense, was abrogated by the precept of legal alms, which was given at Medina." Voltaire's version is very far indeed from the original, since he is quoting a commentary rather than a verse. It does, however, confirm his preoccupation with another constant in his analysis of religion: alms. The detailed definition of alms-giving made enough of an impression on him that he returned to it repeatedly, both in the *Questions sur l'Encyclopédie* (passage quoted above) and in the *Essai sur les moeurs*, where we read: "Il n'y a point de religion dans laquelle on n'ait recommandé l'aumône. La mahométane est la seule qui en ait fait un précepte légal, positif, indispensable. *L'Alcoran* ordonne de donner deux et demi pour cent de son revenu, soit en argent, soit en denrées." ["There is no religion in which alms are not recommended. The Mahometan is the only one that has made it into an indispensable, positive, legal precept. The *Alcoran* commands giving two and a half per cent of one's income, either in money or in kind."] *EM*, vol. 1, p. 273. One (anecdotal) indication of the fact that this was one of Voltaire's obsessions might be gleaned from a marginal note on the following sentence from d'Holbach's *Le Bon sens* (1774): "La Religion chrétienne, prêchée dans son origine par des mendiants et des hommes très misérables, sous le nom de charité, recommande très fortement l'aumône: la Religion de Mahomet en fait également un devoir indispensable." Voltaire's note reads: "Vous vous trompez. Jesus conseille l'aumône. Mahomet l'ordonne" (*Notes marginales*, vol. 4, p. 419). Clearly the fact that Islam had overtaken Christianity's central virtue – charity – was an historical irony that left its mark on the sage of Ferney.

77 In fact "les Interprétes" seems to refer to one: Ja'far Al-Ṣādiq, who is reported
    as saying that this verse contains the best summary in the entire Qur'ān of the
    noblest virtues: ليس في القرآن آية أجمع لمكارم الأخلاق منها . (Zamakhsharī *ad loc.*)

78 This seems to be a mis-translation of the phrase attributed to Gabriel,
    أن تصل من قطعك, which might be better rendered by "keep a good relationship
    even with those who cut off contact with you." Cf. Zamakhsharī *ad loc.*

79 *Notes marginales*, vol. 4, p. 379.

80 Peterson, "Forgiveness"; Rahbar, *God of Justice*, pp. 141–175.

81 *EM*, vol. 1, p. 271.

82 *Notes marginales*, vol. 4, p. 664.

83 Ibid., vol. 4, p. 661; Sale, p. 81.

84 *EM*, vol. 1, p. 275. There is a similar passage in "De l'Alcoran et de Mahomet,"
    pp. 335–336: "Il était bien difficile qu'une religion si simple et si sage
    enseignée par un homme toujours victorieux ne subjuguât pas une partie de
    la terre. En effet les musulmans ont fait autant de prosélytes par la parole que
    par l'épée. Ils ont converti à leur religion les Indiens et jusqu'aux Nègres. Les
    Turcs même leurs vainqueurs se sont soumis à l'islamisme." ["It would have
    been difficult for such a simple and wise religion taught by a man who was
    always victorious not to take over part of the globe. In fact the Muslims made
    as many converts by the word as by the sword. They even converted Indians
    and Negroes. Even the Turks, who beat them, were converted to Islam."]

85 *EM*, vol. 1, p. 272.

86 Ibid., p. 275. Cf. Sale's comment on the Christian and Jewish laws of war:

> The Jews, indeed, had a divine commission, extensive and explicit
> enough, to attack, subdue, and destroy the enemies of their religion;
> and Mohammed pretended to have received one in favour of himself
> and his Moslems, in terms equally plain and full; and therefore it is no
> wonder that they should act consistently with their avowed principles:
> but that Christians should teach and practise a doctrine so opposite to
> the temper and whole tenour of the Gospel, seems very strange; and
> yet the latter have carried matters farther, and shown a more violent
> spirit of intolerance than either of the former. [Sale, "Preliminary
> Discourse," p. 143.]

87 Heck, "Politics and the Qur'ān"; Schoeck, "Moses."

88 Assmann, *Moses the Egyptian*, pp. 91–143.

89 Hadot, *Le Voile d'Isis*, pp. 265–284. The combination of these two qualities
    in Moses – the legislator and the interpreter of nature – eventually makes its
    way into the languages of revolution and empire, as witness the following
    passage from Volney's *Ruines*: "Soyez le législateur de tout le genre humain,
    ainsi que vous serez l'interprète de la même nature; montrez-nous la ligne qui
    sépare le monde des chimères de celui des réalités, et enseignez-nous, après
    tant de religions et d'erreurs, la religion de l'évidence et de la vérité." ["Be the
    legislator of the entire human race as well as the interpreter of nature; show us
    the line that separates the world of dreams from that of reality, and teach us,
    after so many false and erroneous religions, the religion of clarity and truth."]
    (Pp. 241–243, qtd. Laurens, *Origines intellectuelles*, p. 192: the words are
    addressed to Napoleon.)

90 Voltaire's anti-Egyptian rhetoric probably has much to do with his attempt at discrediting biblical history and the story of Exodus. In the *Philosophie de l'histoire*, Voltaire attacks the Egyptians up to the point where he turns his attention to the crusaders: "Jamais les Egyptiens, dans les temps connus, ne furent redoutables, jamais l'ennemi n'entra chez eux qu'il ne les subjuguât … Il n'y a jamais eu que nos seuls croisés qui se soient fait battre par ces Égyptiens, le plus lâche de tous les peoples, comme on l'a remarqué ailleurs; mais c'est qu'alors ils étaient gouvernés par la milice des Mammeluks de Colchos." ["The Egyptians have never been known to be frightening, and no one has ever invaded them without subjugating them … Only our crusaders were beaten by the Egyptians, the most cowardly of all people, as we have noted elsewhere, but that is because at the time they were ruled by the Mammeluks of Colchos."] *La Philosophie de l'histoire*, p. 161.

91 According to Moubarac, Moses is mentioned in 502 verses, while Abraham is mentioned in 245. Third and fourth place in Moubarac's ranking belong to Noah (131 verses) and Jesus (93 verses). *Abraham dans le Coran*, p. 28.

92 One significant difference between the Mosaic and Abrahamic narratives in the Qur'ān concerns the *Straflegende*: Abraham follows a split development as both Patriarch and champion of monotheism, with the narration separating the two, while the majority of the Mosaic pericopes present him as a prophet sent to warn Pharaoh of God's impending doom. Moubarac, *Abraham dans la Coran*, pp. 25–26, 36.

93 These developments are dealt with at length in Rubin, *Between the Bible and the Qur'ān*, though the emphasis there is mainly on the ḥadīth and historiography. A good survey of the treatment of Jews in the Qur'an is found in Rubin, "Jews and Judaism," where this bi-partite structure is also in evidence. On the urge to differentiate Muslims from Jews and Christians alike, Vajda links the consistent imperative to "break their laws" (*khālifūhum*) to the Talmudic command to disobey the laws of the unbelievers (*ḥuqqôt-ha-gôy*): "Ahl Al-Kitāb." The relationship between distinctions (between belief and unbelief) and the idea of "God's boundaries" (حدود الله) in the Qur'an is explored in Richard Kimber's suggestive article, "Boundaries and Precepts." John Wansbrough, on the other hand, argues that the technical legal term *ḥadd* is only symbolically related to scriptural *ḥudūd*, which have a much closer relationship to the hermeneutic concept *muḥkam*. *Quranic Studies*, p. 177.

94 Assmann, *Moses the Egyptian*, pp. 57–77.

95 Wade, *The Clandestine Organization*, pp. 138–140. Wade cites a manuscript that contains a striking anticipation of Voltaire's language in his description of the battle of Badr:

> The *Parallèle entre Mahomet et Moïse* [par Zélim Musulman dans une lettre qu'il écrit à Nathan Rabbin, Rouen, 1580] is presented in the form of a letter purported to have been written to a Rabbi. After confirming the principle that one should accept no opinion without previously having submitted it to the "coupole de la raison," the Musulman [sic] proceeds to give a short history of Muhammad. He related how the prophet, happily married to a rich widow, and suddenly afflicted with epilepsy, was forced to feign divine inspiration to retain the esteem of his wife. Having gotten together some converts,

he proceeded to organize an army, first attacked a rich caravan, and finally besieged and took the town of Mecca. "Car pour lors Dieu combattait pour Mahomet comme il avait anciennement combattu pour Moïse." Turning from Muhammad, whom the Jew had willingly called an impostor, to Moses, Zélim gives two accounts of his life, one according to Tacitus, the other according to Doxios. The first contains nothing miraculous about the leader of the Jews, the second is an "admirable tragic-comédie." God is presented in the account of Doxios as cruel, unjust and even ignorant. His treatment of Pharaoh in hardening his heart and then punishing him for it was certainly not entirely fair. The impression is given that Moses, as well as Muhammad is an impostor. The treatise concludes with a brief comparison of the two legislators: both gained their reputation through their genius and their ambition, both introduced their religion in the same way; both had recourse to arms. But while Muhammad established his Kingdom like Alexander the Great, Moses used the methods of the Spanish in America. Muhammad spared the innocent while Moses sacrificed without mercy a whole nation. Muhammad was good to his people while Moses was a "tyran avaricieux et cruel." [Wade, *The Clandestine Organization*, p. 139.]

96 Madigan, "Criterion"; Mir, "Names of the Qur'ān"; Schoeck, "Moses"; Paret, "Furḳān"; Bell and Watt, *Bell's Introduction to the Qur'ān*, pp. 145–147.

97 Causse, "Théologie de rupture et théologie de la communauté."

98 Badir, *Voltaire et l'Islam*, pp. 159–182.

99 Voltaire, *Œuvres complètes*, Moland ed., vol. 30, p. 121 n.

100 *EM*, vol. 1, p. 139.

101 Ibid., vol. 2, p. 918.

102 Ibid. Although important, the details of Voltaire's sinophilia are beyond the scope of this study. Good accounts are found in Etiemble, *L'Europe chinoise*, vol. 2, pp. 207–306; Song, *Voltaire et la Chine*, pp. 153–179.

103 Bell, *The Origin of Islam*, pp. 120–125; Watt, *Muhammad at Medina*, p. 16, and "Badr"; Marshall, *God, Muhammad and the Unbelievers*, pp. 136–137; Nawas, "Badr."

104 Assmann, *Moses the Egyptian*, pp. 3–4.

105 Bell and Watt, *Bell's Introduction to the Qur'an*, pp. 145–147. The occurrences listed are Q2:53, Q2:185, Q3:4, Q8:29, Q8:41, Q21:48, Q25:1.

106 Sale, p. 139.

107 Ibid., p. 85.

108 Ibid.

109 For an account of the patterns that dominate the *Straflegende* in the Qur'ān, see Welch, "Formulaic Features of the Punishment Stories."

110 In a remarkably sensitive and detailed reading of Q25, Anthony H. Johns shows the extent to which the use of the word *furqān* in Q25:1 points beyond itself to connote the entirety of the Qur'ānic message. The content of this chapter "announces" decisive cleavages in the life of Muhammad – Badr and the emigration to Medina – and ways of overcoming the division between belief and unbelief – conversion and repentance. Most significantly, Johns emphasizes the reciprocity in the relationship between God and his creatures:

He will not turn to them unless they turn to Him first. Johns, "Reflections on the Dynamics and Sprituality of *Sūrat al-Furqān*."

111 Sale, p. 268.

112 Ibid., p. 141.

113 Gagnier, whose *Vie de Mahomet* is another one of Voltaire's sources, narrates the following incident which shows that the parallel Egyptians/Jews/Unbelievers/ Muslims held even for early chroniclers of Islam. When 'Abdullah b. Mas'ūd decapitates Muhammad's arch-enemy Abu Jahl and brings his head back to the prophet, the latter cries out: *Cet homme était le Pharaon de notre Nation.* Nor could Voltaire have overlooked the declaration attributed to Abu'l Feda: "Ce fut dans cette guerre, dit Abu'l Feda, que Dieu manifesta la Religion par une victoire signalée." ["Abu'l Feda says that it was in this war that God made manifest the true Religion by a victory foretold."] Gagnier, *Vie de Mahomet*, vol. 2, p. 23.

114 Rothschild, *Economic Sentiments*, pp. 116–156.

CHAPTER 5

1 Jean Starobinski relies on the French translation for his annotations to Rousseau's *Essai sur l'origine des langues* in Rousseau, *OC*, vol. 5, pp. 371– 429. The only reference to George Sale in the Rousseau corpus comes indirectly on October 28, 1763, when Rousseau writes to Rey requesting all volumes of the *Universal History* that have been translated into French: *CC*, vol. 18, pp. 244–245. For a discussion of Rousseau's other sources of information about Islam, see Neaimi, *L'Islam au siècle des Lumières*, pp. 24–25.

2 The deconstruction of the distinction between legislator and impostor and the following reading rely on Bennington, *Dudding*, pp. 69–80.

3 *OC*, vol. 4, p. 977.

4 Ibid., vol. 3, p. 381. A good summary of the legislator's importance is found in Gagnebin, "Le Rôle du législateur." Rousseau seems to substitute the legislator, who makes the social universe run like clockwork, for the *dieu-horloger* of the early eighteenth century. Ehrard, *L'Idée de nature en France*, pp. 48–71; Lefebvre, "Jean-Jacques Rousseau." On the Malebranchian genealogy of the link between the clockmaker and the legislator, both of whom establish general laws that regulate machines and men respectively, see Riley, *The General Will before Rousseau*, pp. 24–100.

5 Wisner, *The Cult of the Legislator in France*, pp. 25–49.

6 Burgelin, *La Philosophie de l'existence*, pp. 297–304, 556–565.

7 Burgelin, *Jean-Jacques Rousseau*, pp. 55–57.

8 Shklar, *Men and Citizens*, pp. 160–164. Burgelin mentions the following line from a letter to Mirabeau (1767): "Je voudrais que le despote pût être Dieu." Burgelin, *Philosophie de l'existence*, p. 561.

9 *OC*, vol. 3, p. 500.

10 Ibid., vol. 3, pp. 383–384.

11 Grotius, *Traité de la vérité*, p. 358. The persistence of this particular myth chez Rousseau is very odd, especially in view of Pococke's criticism of Grotius, Grotius's own admission that it was not based on any Muslim sources, Bayle's detailed refutation in his *Dictionary* (a text that Rousseau

would presumably have read attentively), and Voltaire's numerous attempts at its refutation once and for all. See Khairallah, "Arabic Studies in England," pp. 48–51; Holt, "The Study of Arabic Historians," p. 554; Bayle, "Mahomet" (rem. N), vol. 10, pp. 60–61; *Notes marginales*, vol. 4, pp. 201, 685.

12 *OC*, vol. 3, pp. 462–463.

13 *CC*, vol. 17, pp. 205, 215, L 2906, vol. 8, pp. 208–209, L 1337.

14 Ibid., vol. 16, p. 313, L 2760.

15 Ibid., vol. 41, p. 16, L 7187.

16 Ibid., vol. 49, pp. 198–199, L 8358.

17 Ibid., vol. 49, p. 202 n.

18 Wansbrough, *Quranic Studies*, pp. 4, 7–8. On the sectarian character of Rousseau's disciples see Masson, *La Religion de Jean-Jacques Rousseau*, vol. 2, pp. 93–96.

19 *Voyage à Erménonville*, pp. 17–19.

20 The auditory and oratorical primacy of this (monotheistic) mode of prophecy, where word triumphs over vision, is discussed in Meschonnic, *Pour la poétique II*, pp. 267–269.

21 Izutsu, *God and Man in the Qur'an*, pp. 178–199.

22 See Gilliot and Larcher, "Language and Style"; Neuwirth, "Form and Structure." Toufic Fahd provides a very useful history, with examples, of the Arabic literature and practice of divination and oracular utterance in *La Divination arabe*, pp. 77–90, 150–169. Fahd defines *saj'* as "l'expression formelle de l'oracle" (p. 151) and cites Ibn Khaldūn's argument that the *kāhin* is closest to the status of prophecy (*nubuwwa*) when he speaks in *saj'* (p. 81 n.). Alan Jones has published a series of articles in which he explores the linguistic registers of the Qur'ān (which he groups under four rubrics – *kāhin*, *khaṭīb*, *qāṣṣ*, and the [Medinan] documentary style) and tries to map them on to the historical situation of Islamic Arabia. See "The Language of the Qur'an" and "The Oral and the Written."

23 O' Dea, *Jean-Jacques Rousseau*, pp. 55–72.

24 *OC*, vol. 5, p. 428.

25 Kelly, "'To Persuade without Convincing,'" pp. 329–331.

26 Ibid., p. 329.

27 *OC*, vol. 5, pp. 56–57.

28 Ibid., vol. 5, p. 383.

29 Ibid., vol. 5, p. 383.

30 See Starobinski's notes, *OC*, vol. 5, pp. 1546–1553. On the extent of Lamy's influence on Rousseau, see Masson, *La Religion de Jean-Jacques Rousseau*, vol. 1, pp. 81–90.

31 Lamy, *La Rhétorique*, Preface, pp. 103–104.

32 In his *Glossarium universale hebraicum* (1697) Louis Thomassin – *the* point of reference with respect to which Lamy positions himself – identifies Hebrew as the Adamic *Ur-sprache*, and consequently the mother of all languages. On the relationship between Thomassin and Lamy, see Noille-Clauzade, "Introduction," in Lamy, *La Rhétorique*, pp. 92–93. Needless to say, this characterization of Hebrew is not original to Thomassin, and is part of a long history of attempts to identify the first language of humanity. Eco, *La Ricerca della lingua perfetta*, pp. 84–127. In his description of this language

in the *Essai*, Rousseau distances himself from the monogenetic hypothesis according to which all languages are derived from one mother tongue. Ibid., pp. 117–118.

33 Lamy, *La Rhétorique*, vol. 4.6, pp. 343–344.

34 Ibid., vol. 1.10, pp. 146–147.

35 Sale, "Preliminary Discourse," p. 26.

36 Ibid., p. 62.

37 *OC*, vol. 5, p. 409.

38 Ibid., vol. 5, p. 1822.

39 The numerous conversion stories centered on listeners being so moved by the beauty and eloquence of the Qur'ān that they decide to convert immediately is analyzed in Kermani, *Gott ist schön*, pp. 31–43. One constant element in these narratives is the listener's reaction, which centers on the beauty of the text rather than any exhortation to violence. Indeed, there are quite a few stories of people being sent to kill Muhammad (as is the case with one variant of the 'Umar b. al-Khaṭṭāb conversion story) and softening their stance after hearing the Qur'ān, rather than begging Muhammad to lead them to war, but Gagnier's version makes this sound like a distinct possibility.

40 *OC*, vol. 5, pp. 409–410.

41 See Starobinski's note, ibid., vol. 5, p. 1548. Leone Caetani presents the narrative as transmitted by the various historians in *Annali dell'Islam*, vol. 1, pp. 284–286.

42 Gagnier, *La Vie de Mahomet*, vol. 1, pp. 163–164.

43 Sale, p. 466.

44 Gagnier, *La Vie de Mahomet*, vol. 1, pp. 165–166.

45 In some respects Turpin thus anticipates Geiger's *Was hat Mahomet aus dem Judenthume aufgenommen* (1832), though of course Turpin, by his own admission, had no Oriental languages. Although *L'Histoire de l'Alcoran* is a marked improvement over previous books about Islam, Turpin's text is nevertheless marred by inaccuracies, including such things as a reference to a certain "116th" chapter of the Qur'ān. *Histoire de l'Alcoran*, vol. 1, p. 332.

46 Ibid., vol. 1, p. xii.

47 Ibid., vol. 2, p. 83.

48 Gunny, *Images of Islam*, pp. 183–187.

49 Pastoret, *Zoroastre, Confucius et Mahomet*, p. 234.

50 Ibid., pp. 206, 234, 320; Savary, *Le Koran*, p. 107.

51 Pastoret, *Zoroastre, Confucius et Mahomet*, pp. 237–252.

52 Ibid., p. 300.

53 Ibid., p. 400.

54 Ibid., pp. 412–413.

CHAPTER 6

1 Said, *Orientalism*, pp. 80–84.

2 Laurens, *L'Expédition d'Egypte*, p. 31.

3 Ibid., pp. 31–32; Laurens, *Origines intellectuelles*, pp. 30–34.

4 *Pièces diverses*, pp. 152–153.

5 A military rank sometimes applied to civilian notables. See Uzunçarşili, "Čorbadjī."

6 My translation. Arabic text and English translation in Abd al-Raḥmān Al-Jabartī, "Tārīkh Muddat al-Faransīs bi-Miṣr," in Moreh ed. and trans., *Al-Jabartī's Chronicle*, pp. 40–42, Arabic text 7–10, 2b–3b. Subsequent references to this edition of Al-Jabartī's chronicle will be to the English text, Arabic text and manuscript page respectively.

7 Laurens, *Origines intellectuelles*, pp. 61–82. Laurens covers the many parallels between the invasion of Egypt and the 2003 American-led invasion of Iraq in "Volonté de réformes et changements, le modèle de Bonaparte à Bush."

8 Laurens, *Origines intellectuelles*, pp. 26–31.

9 Savary, *Le Koran*, p. 2.

10 Ibid., p. 14.

11 Ibid., p. 42.

12 Ibid., p. 110.

13 Ibid., p. 108.

14 Du Ryer, *L'Alcoran de Mahomet*, vol. 2, p. 458.

15 Marracci, vol. 2, p. 787.

16 Ibid.

17 Savary, *Le Koran*, p. 560.

18 Admittedly "lectulos sponsales" is an accurate, literal translation of الأرائك , which follows the definition found in the standard commentaries of الأسرة في الحجال (beds in the marital chamber). See Jalālayn, Bayḍāwī *ad loc.*

19 On the identification with Muhammad, see Healey, *The Literary Culture of Napoleon*, pp. 99–103. On Napoleon's relationship with writers and artists more generally, see Charpentier, *Napoléon et les hommes de lettres de son temps*.

20 On Napoleon, the *philosophes*, and religion, see Healey, *The Literary Culture of Napoleon*, pp. 62–78.

21 Qtd. ibid., p. 100.

22 Rémusat, *Mémoires*, vol. 1, p. 274.

23 Healey, *The Literary Culture of Napoleon*, pp. 79–117.

24 Laissus, *L'Egypte, une aventure savante*, pp. 32–35, 60–66.

25 Healey, *The Literary Culture of Napoleon*, pp. 103–104.

26 Cf. "Al-Muḳannaʿ" and Laoust, *Les Schismes dans l'islam*, pp. 74–75. Martin identifies Napoleon's source as Marigny's *Histoire des arabes sous les califes* in "The Mask of the Prophet," p. 319. In the Postface to his translation of Borges's *Historia universal de la infamia*, Roger Caillois assumes that Napoleon would have come across the story of Al-Muqannaʿ in the *Bibliothèque orientale*. Borges, *Histoire universelle*, pp. 243–244. Cf. D'Herbelot, *Bibliothèque orientale*, "Hakem ben Haschem," pp. 412–413, and "Mahadi," p. 530, as well as Marigny, *Histoire des Arabes*, vol. 3, pp. 49–54.

27 Las Cases, *Mémorial de Sainte-Hélène*, vol. 1, p. 529, qtd. Healey, *The Literary Culture of Napoleon*, p. 100.

28 Qtd. ibid., p. 102.

29 Savary, *Le Koran*, pp. 30–31.
30 Ibid., pp. 32, 156. Emphasis mine. Savary's translations of the Qur'anic verses dealing with Badr are found in both his introduction and under the relevant chapters; page numbers are to the passage in the introduction and the passage in the body of the Qur'ān translation respectively. Savary numbers this verse Q3:119. Both in this verse and Q3:125, the connotation of speed and the incorrect verse numbering are original to Savary – they do not appear in any of the other major translations.
31 Sale, p. 51.
32 Savary, *Le Koran*, pp. 31, 156–157. Emphasis mine. Savary numbers these verses 120–121.
33 Sale, p. 51.
34 Savary, *Le Koran*, pp. 32, 232.
35 Sale, p. 141.
36 Savary, *Lettres sur l'Egypte*, vol. 2, pp. 189–273. On the impact of this revolt on the European view of the Middle East, see Laurens, *Origines intellectuelles*, pp. 159–169. For a less romantic account of Ali Bey's revolt and the "reaction" of Abu Dahab, which was seen as a short Golden Age by many of the *'ulamā'* of Egypt, see Laurens, *L'Expédition d'Egypte*, pp. 78–106.
37 Savary, *Lettres sur l'Egypte*, vol. 2, p. 295.
38 Ibid., vol. 2, p. 251.
39 Ibid., vol. 2, pp. 246–247.
40 Laurens, *Origines intellectuelles*, pp. 166–169.
41 *Pièces diverses*, p. 158.
42 Takim, "Saul"; Marlow, "Kings and Rulers"; Ayalon, "Malik."
43 Plessner, "Mulk"; Marlow, "Kings and Rulers."
44 Sale, p. 29; Du Ryer, *L'Alcoran de Mahomet*, vol. 1, p. 414; Marracci, vol. 2, p. 91; Savary, *Le Koran*, p. 140.
45 *Pièces diverses*, pp. 158–159.
46 Sale, p. 22; Du Ryer, *L'Alcoran de Mahomet*, vol. 1, p. 404; Marracci, vol. 2, p. 75; Savary, *Le Koran*, p. 133.
47 *Pièces diverses*, pp. 161–162.
48 *Al-Jabartī's Chronicle*, pp. 120–121, Ar. 96–97, 26a.
49 Ibid., p. 119, Ar. 95, 25b. Al-Jabartī's view of the French is unstable, varying from episode to episode and chronicle to chronicle. Cf. Delanoue, *Moralistes et politiques*, vol. 1, pp. 67–83; Moreh, "Al-Jabarti as Writer," pp. 23–25.
50 *Pièces diverses*, pp. 111–112.
51 Napoleon's account seems to confuse a number of traditions, especially ones identifying the Mahdī with Jesus (who is supposed to return at the end of time) and with profligate spending. Madelung, "Al-Mahdī." See also the text and notes in Goldziher, *Introduction to Islamic Theology and Law*, pp. 196–200, 264–266.
52 One of Napoleon's Oriental fantasies would be indirectly realized in the mid-twentieth century when a French journalist with the pseudonym Jean Barois (taken from the eponymous novel by Roger Martin du Gard [1913]) wrote a biography of Muhammad entitled *Mahomet, le Napoléon du Ciel* (Paris, Colbert, 1943) as a way of dealing with his imprisonment during WWII. See Salazar ed., *Mahomet*, pp. 291–310.

CHAPTER 7

1 Mommsen, *Goethe und die arabische Welt*, pp. 157–165.

2 Goethe, *Briefe*, vol. 1, p. 132. Goethe is alluding to the verse قَالَ رَبِّ اشْرَحْ لِي صَدْرِي , which Sale translates as, "Moses answered, LORD, enlarge my breast" and Megerlin, "Er sprach: O mein Herr! Mache mir Raum in meiner engen Brust." Sale, p. 257; Megerlin, *Die türkische Bibel*, p. 422.

3 Mommsen, *Goethe und die arabische Welt*, pp. 172–176.

4 "Wie dank ich ihm er hat meine Brust geöffnet, die harte Hülle meines Herzens weggenommen, daß ich sein Nahen empfinden kann." *SWS*, vol. 1.1, p. 517.

5 Andrea Polaschegg sees in Goethe's turn to the East a flight from contingency and arbitrariness, re-enacting the processes of linguistic and cultural understanding and production that would prove essential to his self-definition. *Der andere Orientalismus*, pp. 311–397, esp. pp. 373–395.

6 *SWS*, vol. 1.2, pp. 443–446.

7 Qtd. Mommsen, *Goethe und die arabische Welt*, p. 176.

8 On Goethe's struggle with and use of Arabic script, which oscillates between the icon and signifier in his writings, see Polaschegg, *Der andere Orientalismus*, pp. 316–343.

9 Not much will be said in what follows about Goethe's translation of Voltaire's *Mahomet*, a task he found unpleasant because it went against his convictions about Muhammad and which seems to have been conjured up by Duke Carl August to inaugurate an age of improved German taste through translations from French classical drama. Goethe softened the tone of Voltaire's text, which cast Muhammad too negatively for his taste. See Mommsen, *Goethe und die arabische Welt*, pp. 218–238; Kilchenmann, "Goethes Übersetzung der voltairedramen *Mahomet* und *Tancred*."

10 Mommsen, *Goethe und die arabische Welt*, p. 215.

11 Goethe's preoccupation with the spoken word stays with him until the *Divan*, where we read in the opening poem that "Wie das Wort so wichtig dort war,/ Weil es ein gesprochen Wort war" ["How important the word was there/ Because it was a spoken word"]. "Hegire," *SWS*, vol. 11.1.2, p. 12.

12 Ibid., vol. 11.1.2, p. 132.

13 Sheehan, *The Enlightenment Bible*, pp. 148–151; Kugel, "Poets and Prophets," pp. 21–25.

14 Sheehan, *The Enlightenment Bible*, p. 157.

15 Ibid., p. 172.

16 A full examination of the tense relationship between poetry and the Qur'ān is beyond the scope of this study, but see Zwettler, "A Mantic Manifesto"; Jones, "Poetry and Poets"; and Kermani, *Gott ist schön*, pp. 315–364.

17 *SWS*, vol. 11.1.2, pp. 147–148. Goethe's next paragraph cites Arnold's retranslation of Sale, Q2:2–7.

Goethe:

> Der ganze Inhalt des Korans, um mit wenigem viel zu sagen, findet sich zu Anfang der zweiten Sura und lautet folgendermaßen. "Es ist kein Zweifel in diesem Buch. Es ist eine Unterrichtung der Frommen, welche die Geheimnisse des *Glaubens* vor wahr halten, die bestimmten Zeiten des *Gebets* beobachten und von demjenigen, was wir ihnen verliehen

haben, *Almosen* austeilen und welche der Offenbarung glauben, die den *Propheten* vor dir herabgesandt worden, und gewisse Versicherung des zukünftigen Lebens haben: diese werden von ihrem Herrn geleitet und sollen glücklich und selig sein. Die Ungläubigen betreffend, wird es ihnen gleichviel sein, ob du sie vermahnest oder nicht vermahnest; die werden doch nicht glauben. Gott hat ihre Herzen und Ohren versiegelt. Eine Dunkelheit bedeckt ihr Gesicht und sie werden eine schwere Strafe leiden."

Sale:

There is no doubt in this book; *it is* a direction to the pious, who believe in the mysteries *of faith,* who observe the appointed times of prayer, and distribute *alms* out of what we have bestowed on them, and who believe in that *revelation*, which hath been sent down unto thee and that which hath been sent down *unto the prophets* before thee and have firm assurance of the life to come:, these are directed by their LORD, and they shall prosper. As for the unbelievers, it will be equal to them whether thou admonish them, or do not admonish them; they will not believe. GOD hath sealed up their hearts and their hearing; a dimness covereth their sight, and they shall suffer a grievous punishment. [Sale, p. 2.]

18 *SWS*, vol. 11.1.2, p. 149: "Der Stil des Korans ist, seinem Inhalt und Zweck gemäß, streng, groß, furchtbar, stellenweis wahrhaft erhaben; so treibt ein Keil den andern, und darf sich über die große Wirksamkeit des Buches niemand verwundern. Weshalb es denn auch von den echten Verehrern für unerschaffen und mit Gott gleich ewig erklärt wurde."

19 Mommsen, *Goethe und die arabische Welt*, p. 167.

20 *SWS*, vol. 16, pp. 641–654, 670–673; Boyle, *Goethe*, vol. 1, pp. 141–142, 149–151.

21 "Ich konnte weder dem einen noch dem andern völlig zustimmen: denn mein Christus hatte auch seine eigne Gestalt nach meinem Sinne angenommen." *SWS*, vol. 16, p. 653.

22 "Bei meiner überfreien Gesinnung, bei meinem völlig zweck- und planlosen Leben und Handeln konnte mir nicht verborgen bleiben, daß Lavater und Basedow geisige, ja geistliche Mittel zu irdischen Zwecken gebrauchten ... Weil ich nun aber alle Betrachtungen dieser Art bis aufs Äußerste verfolgte und über meine enge Erfahrung hinaus nach ähnlichen Fällen in der Geschichte mich umsah, so entwickelte sich bei mir der Vorsatz, an den Leben Mahomets, den ich nie als einen Betrüger hatte ansehen können, jene von mir in der Wirklichkeit so lebhaft angeschauten Wege, die, anstatt zum Heil, vielmehr zum Verderben führen, dramatisch darzustellen." Ibid., vol. 16, pp. 670–671.

23 This is Goethe's direct observation of both Lavater and Basedow: "Indem ich nun beide [Lavater and Basedow] beobachtete, ja ihnen freiheraus meine Meinung gestand und die ihrige dagegen vernahm, so wurde der Gedanke rege, daß freilich der vorzügliche Mensch das Göttliche was in ihm ist, auch außer sich verbreiten möchte. Dann aber trifft er auch auf die rohe Welt, und um auf sie zu wirken, muß er sich ihr gleichstellen; hierdurch aber vergibt er jenen hohen

Vorzügen gar sehr, und am Ende begibt er sich ihrer gänzlich." Ibid., vol. 16, p. 671.

24 Ibid., vol. 16, p. 613.

25 Mommsen, *Goethe und die arabische Welt*, pp. 205–209.

26 *SWS*, vol. 16, p. 614.

27 The concept of "worldly gospel" should be read against the shift in reading habits that occurred at the turn of the nineteenth century. As the German book trade and reading population grew alongside increasing secularization, attention shifted from devotional to "high" literature, although this was somewhat limited. Those who did read high literature read it again and again like devotional literature, as witness Novalis's use of *Wilhelm Meisters Lehrjahre* (thereby fulfilling at least one of Goethe's poetic-prophetic ambitions). More generally, Saul points out that "Metaphors signaling a text's intention to be the new Gospel are among the most common in the literature of the age." "Aesthetic Humanism," p. 205. Lessing called for a new and rational Bible, for which Schiller suggested art (or rather beauty) and Novalis history. Ibid., pp. 205–210; Saul, *History and Poetry in Novalis*, pp. 101–125.

28 Kermani, "Revelation," p. 219.

29 A fuller account of Goethe's relationship to the *Sturm und Drang*'s ideas on genius is found in Schmidt, *Geschichte des Genie-Gedankens*, vol. 1, pp. 69–78, 129–140, 150–192, and on Goethe in particular, pp. 193–353.

30 *SWS*, vol. 16, pp. 604–605.

31 Ibid., vol. 16, p. 672.

32 Ibid., vol. 16, p. 672.

33 "Alles was das Genie durch Charakter und Geist über die Menschen vermag, sollte dargestellt werden, und wie es dabei gewinnt und verliert." Ibid., vol. 16, p. 673.

34 Grappin, "Notice," p. 1562.

35 Goethe also transcribes related passages where we see cosmology being adduced as evidence of God's creative power, such as Q2:115 and Q2:164. Megerlin's verse numbering is frequently unorthodox – e.g. he counts Q2:1 and Q2:2 as one verse, with the result that the numbering of Goethe's excerpts is usually off by several verses. Goethe's wording also varies somewhat from Megerlin's. Megerlin's translation of Q2:115 reads: "Uebrigens gehöret Gott sowohl der Aufgang, als der Niedergang der Sonnen (d.i. alle Gegenden sind sein), daher wo ihr euch auch (im Gebet) hinwendet: so ist Gottes Angesicht da." Megerlin, *Die türkische Bibel*, p. 57. Goethe's transcription: "Gott gehöret der Aufgang und Niedergang der Sonnen, und wohin ihr euch wendet, ist Gottes Angesicht da." *SWS*, vol. 1.2, p. 443.

36 *SWS*, vol. 1.2, p. 445. Marracci's text reads:

> 75. Et *memento*, cùm dixit Abraham patri suo Azar: An accipis simulacri in deos? Certè ego video te, & gentem tuam in errore manifesto. 76. Et ita ostendimus Abrahae regnum Coelorum, & terrae: & ut esset ex firmiter credentibus. 77. Cumque obtenebrata fuisset super eum nox, vidit stellam (*scilicet Venerem*). Dixit: Hic est Dominus meus. Cùm autem *illa* occidisset, dixit: Non amo *dominos* occumbentes. 78. Cùm verò vidisset lunam orientem, dixit: Hic est Dominus meus. Sed cùm *illa* occubuisset, dixit: Profectò, nisi direxerit me Dominus

meus, ero certè ex gentibus errantibus. 79. Cùm posteà vidisset Solem exorientem, dixit: Hic est Dominus meus: Hic est major *stella & luna*. Sed cùm occidisset, dixit: O popule meus, certè ego immunis sum ab eo, quod associatis (*id est ab idolatria vestra*.) 80. Certè ego converti faciem meam ad eum, qui condidit Caelos, terram; Orthodoxus *sum*, & non sum ego ex Associantibus. [Marracci, vol. 2, p. 254.]

Sale translates this passage as follows:

> *Call to mind* when Abraham said unto his father Azer, Dost thou take images for gods? Verily I perceive that thou and thy people *are* in a manifest error. And thus did we show unto Abraham the kingdom of heaven and earth, that he might become *one* of those who firmly believe. And when the night overshadowed him, he saw a star, *and* he said, This is my LORD; but when it set, he said, I like not *gods* which set. And when he saw the moon rising, he said, This is my LORD; but when he saw it set, he said, Verily if my LORD direct me not, I shall become *one* of the people who go astray. And when he saw the sun rising, he said, This is my LORD, this is the greatest; but when it set, he said, O my people, verily I am clear of that which ye associate *with God:* I direct my face unto him who hath created the heavens and the earth; *I am* orthodox, and am not *one* of the idolaters. [Sale, p. 106.]

37 *SWS*, vol. 1.1, p. 517, original not divided into individual verses.

38 Jølle, "The River and its Metaphors," pp. 434–436.

39 "Wenn er [Pindar] die Pfeile ein übern andern nach dem Wolkenziel schiest steh ich freilich noch da und gaffe; doch fühl ich indeß, was Horaz aussprechen konnte, was Quintilian rühmt, und was tätiges an mir ist lebt auf da ich Adel fühle und Zweck kenne. Ειδος φυα, ψεφηνος ανηρ, μυριαν αρεταν αστελει νοω γευεται, ουποι αστπεχει κατεβα ποδι, μαθοντες pp." Goethe, *Briefe*, vol. 1, p. 131.

The allusions to Horace and Quintilian have been identified as allusions to *Carm.* 4.2 (which, as has been mentioned, praises Pindar and compares him to a mighty river) and *Inst. Orat.* 10.1.61 (where Quintilian calls Pindar the greatest lyric poet, refers to his "river of eloquence," and again alludes to Horace *Carm.* 4.2). Goethe, *Briefe*, vol. 1, pp. 586–587. Goethe's "citation" from Pindar joins two separate verses. Ειδος φυα come from *Ol.* 2.86, while the rest are from *Nem.* 3.41. The conjunction implies that, to Goethe's mind in 1772, poetry and heroism were bound inextricably with one another. It is precisely in the *Ol.* 2 that Pindar compares his words to arrows.

40 Jølle, "The River and its Metaphors," p. 435; Boyle, *Goethe*, vol. 1, pp. 158–160; Schmidt, *Die Geschichte des Genie-Gedankens*, vol. 1, pp. 199–254.

41 Jølle, "The River and its Metaphors," pp. 440–441.

42 Strich, *Goethe und die Weltliteratur*, pp. 48–49, 154–157.

43 Sheehan, *The Enlightenment Bible*, pp. 148–181.

44 *SWS*, vol. 1.2, p. 217. Cf. Polaschegg, *Der andere Orientalismus*, pp. 312–316.

45 *SWS*, vol. 1.2, p. 216.

46 *The Warehouse of Eastern Treasures/and the Mine of Foreign Symbols/by/A Group of Authors/An Enterprise under the Care of the Finest of the Nobles/ Wenzeslaus Count Rzewusky/Say unto God belongeth the east and the west: He directeth whom He pleaseth into the right way./Printed in the City of Vienna the Seat of the Imperial Austrian Sultanate/In the Year 1809 after the Birth of Christ, by which I mean/The Year 1223 after the Hijra of Muhammad.*

47 This changes in the second and subsequent volumes, where Rzewusky's name appears in both the Arabic and Western title pages.

48 Hammer-Purgstall, *Fundgruben*, vol. 1, pp. III–IV; Sale, p. 17. Very freely translated from the original, with Q2:142 in the Sale translation.

49 Indeed, whole sections of the *Fundgruben* make their way into Goethe's notes and commentary on the *Divan*. The section on the language of flowers, for one, is mostly an adaptation of Hammer's French article, "Sur le langage des fleurs." *SWS*, vol. 11.1.2, pp. 196–198; *Fundgruben*, vol. 1, pp. 32–42.

50 The Qur'anic background to this verse should serve to mitigate Edward Said's reading of "Talismane," which he considers an example of the empty, unbounded Orient on to which Western desires, fantasies and violence are eventually projected. *Orientalism*, pp. 167–168.

51 *SWS*, vol. 11.1.2, p. 11. Q6:97 reads:

قَدْ فَصَّلْنَا الْآيَاتِ لِقَوْمٍ يَعْلَمُونَ وَهُوَ الَّذِي جَعَلَ لَكُمُ النُّجُومَ لِتَهْتَدُوا بِهَا فِي ظُلُمَاتِ الْبَرِّ وَالْبَحْرِ

Sale's translation: "It is He who hath ordained the stars for you, that ye may be directed thereby in the darkness of the land and of the sea. We have clearly shown forth *our* signs, unto people who understand." Sale, p. 106.

52 "Über die Sternbilder der Araber, und ihre eigenen Namen für einzelne Sterne." *Fundgruben*, vol. 1, pp. 1–15. Oddly enough, Hammer's article incorrectly identifies this verse as Q98:21. In the second volume of the *Fundgruben*, the verse appears translated and numbered as Q6:98 as follows: "Er ists, der die Gestirne euch gesetzt zur Leitung in der Finsterniß zu Land und See; und diese Zeichen haben wir verliehn den Völkern, so sie die Wahrheit anerkennen." *Fundgruben*, vol. 2, p. 348.

53 *Fundgruben*, vol. 2, p. 25.

54 There is an important precedent to Hammer in the Qur'ān translation of Friedrich Boysen (Halle, 1773), though it is not clear that his translation had much of an impact on Goethe. Boysen's translation was followed by Johann Wilhelm Glein's *Halladat oder das Rote Buch* (1774), where we see a more radical attempt at setting the Qur'ān to verse. Loop, "Heiliger Poesie," pp. 34–39. One of the most important consquences of Hammer's publications and teaching was Friedrich Rückert's project of a fully poetic, rhyming translation of the Qur'ān in verse. See Bobzin, "Friedrich Rückert und der Koran."

55 Hammer makes some strange mistakes for someone so seriously committed to transmitting the acoustic effects of the Qur'an: Q 36 (*Yā sīn*) is entitled *Jas* and the first verse is translated as *Jas*. Hammer does not even use the term *Geheimnisvolle Buchstabe*, the formula that he uses for the other mysterious letters in the Qur'an. *Fundgruben*, vol. 4, p. 68.

56 Carlyle often spurs Goethe to reflect on world literature. Goethe returns to the subject in his introduction to the German translation of Carlyle's *Life of Schiller*. Goethe, *Goethes Werke: Hamburger Ausgabe*, vol. 12, p. 364.

57 *SWS*, vol. 18.2, p. 86.

58 The terms that Goethe uses to describe the literary marketplace in his review are the same as those used by Carlyle in the preface to *German Romance*, where the ultimate question seems to be how to decide the worth of a given work of literature both in its own culture and to the target audience. Carlyle writes:

> No Leipzig Fair is unattended by its mob of gentlemen that write with ease; each duly offering his new novel, among the other fancy-goods and fustians of that great emporium ... The inspirations of the Artist are rare and transient, but the hunger of the Manufacturer is universal and incessant. The novel, too, is among the simplest forms of composition; a free arena for all sorts and degrees of talent; and may be worked in equally by a Henry Fielding and a Doctor Polydore. In Germany, accordingly, as in other countries, the Novelists are a mixed, innumerable, and most productive race. Interspersed with a few Poets, we behold whole legions and hosts of Poetasters, in all stages of worthlessness ...
>
> On the whole, as the light of a very small taper may be useful in total darkness, I have sometimes hoped that this little enterprise might assist, in its degree, to forward an acquaintance with the Germans and their literature; a literature and a people both well worthy of our study. Translations, in this view, can be of little avail, except in so far as they excite us to a much more general study of the language.' [*German Romance*, vol. 1, pp. vi–vii, xi–xii.]

59 Q13:8 reads: وَيَقُولُ الَّذِينَ كَفَرُوا لَوْلا أُنزِلَ عَلَيْهِ آيَةٌ مِنْ رَبِّهِ إِنَّمَا أَنتَ مُنذِرٌ وَلِكُلِّ قَوْمٍ هَادٍ
Sale's translation: "The infidels say, Unless a sign be sent down unto him from his LORD, *we will not believe*. Thou art *commissioned to be* a preacher only, *and not a worker of miracles:* and unto every people *hath* a director *been appointed*."
Q14:4 reads:

وَمَا أَرْسَلْنَا مِنْ رَسُولٍ إِلا بِلِسَانِ قَوْمِهِ لِيُبَيِّنَ لَهُمْ فَيُضِلُّ اللَّهُ مَنْ يَشَاءُ وَيَهْدِي مَنْ يَشَاءُ وَهُوَ الْعَزِيزُ الْحَكِيمُ

Sale's translation: "We have sent no apostle but with the language of his people, that he might declare *their* duty plainly unto them; for GOD causeth to err whom he pleaseth; and he is the mighty, the wise." Sale, pp. 201, 205. Hammer translates Q13:8 (which he numbers 13:9, having counted the mysterious letters [*Geheimnisvolle Buchstaben*] with which the chapter opens as a separate verse) as "Es sagen die Ungläubigen: Ward nicht ein Zeichen des Herrn über ihn gesendet? Ist er denn nicht ein Prediger? Ein jedes Volk hat seinen Leiter" and Q14:4 (which, again, he numbers as 14:5, having counted the mysterious letters with which the chapter opens as a separate verse) as "Wir sandten keinen Propheten als in der Sprache seines Volks, die Wahrheit aufzuklären. Gott führt irre, und leitet wen er will, Er ist der Allerhöchste Allerweiseste." *Fundgruben*, vol. 3, pp. 231, 235. Megerlin translates Q13:8 as "Weiter sagen einige Ungläubige von dir: Ist dann nicht ein Wunderzeichen von seinem

Herrn on ihm herabgeschickt worden?" Doch du bist nur ein Prediger (kein Wundertäter) und ist einem jeden Volk sein Lehrer zur Unterweisung gegeben worden" (the text in Goethe's *Koran-Auszüge* matches this closely) and Q14:4 as "Wir haben auch einen Gesandten nur gesandt, in einer einem jeden Volk bekannten Sprache: daß er die deutlich unterweise. Darum läßt Gott niemand irren, als wen er will, und führt auch auf den rechten Weg, wen er will. Dann er ist mächtig und weise." *Die türkische Bibel*, pp. 339, 347. Marracci translates Q13:8 (which he numbers 13:9): "Et dicunt, qui sunt increduli, *irrisoriè*: Nonne demissum fuit super eum (*idest Mahumetum*) signum à Domino suo? Tu certè est praedicator (*idest missus ad praedicandum, non ad miracula facienda*) & unicuique genti *datus fuit* director" and Q14:4 (which he numbers 14:5) by "Et non misimus ullum legatum, nisi cum lingua gentis suae, ut declareret eis *veritatem*. Porrò errare faciet Deus, quem vult, & diriget quem vult, & ipse est Praepotens, Sapiens." Marracci, vol. 2, pp. 367–368, 375. Overall, Goethe's stands as the most fluid expression of God's providence in sending to every people a prophet who speaks their language. Cf. Pierre Larcher, "Concept of Language."

60 A good summary of the uses to which the notion of world literature has been put in the past two centuries is found in Pizer, "Goethe's 'World Literature' Paradigm."

61 Rippin, "The Commerce of Eschatology," and "Trade and Commerce." One such Qur'anic *locus* is Q101 and Q102, which Goethe would have known at the very least from his perusal of the *Fundgruben*, vol. 2, p. 44.

62 *SWS*, vol. 18.2, pp. 178–179; Berman, *L'Epreuve de l'étranger*, pp. 91–92.

63 Berman, *L'Epreuve de l'étranger*, p. 90.

64 Ibid., p. 93.

65 Strich, *Goethe und die Weltliteratur*, pp. 19–20; Berman, *L'Epreuve de l'étranger*, pp. 95–97.

66 *SWS*, vol. 11.1.2, pp. 261–265. On p. 264 Goethe defines the translations of the third phase as ones "wo man die Übersetzung dem Original identisch machen möchte, so daß eins nicht anstatt des andern, sonder an der Stelle des andern gelten solle" ["where one would want to make the translation identical to the original, so that the one does not substitute for the other but rather is valid in the place of the other"].

67 Strich, *Goethe und die Weltliteratur*, pp. 165–170. Despite their tremendous value, Strich's insights are dulled by his insistence on a unitary, monolithic Oriental mind. Goethe's insistence on specular relationships reappears in his writing on metempsychosis: "Die schönste Metempsychose ist die, wenn wir uns im andern wieder auftreten sehn." ["The most beautiful metempsychosis is the one in which we see ourselves reappear in others."] Qtd. ibid., p. 33.

68 See Polaschegg, *Der andere Orientalismus*, pp. 96–101, 367–373.

69 Ibid., p. 18.

70 Ibid., pp. 25–26.

71 Watt, "Carlyle on Muhammad."

72 Ashton, *The German Idea*, pp. 19–22, 67–104.

73 Norton ed., *Correspondence between Goethe and Carlyle*, pp. 33–35.

74 Ibid., p. 333.

75 In light of the foregoing it is difficult to agree with Said's account of Carlyle's account of Muhammad as being one written mainly to allay Western anxieties

about the Orient, though the argument certainly holds when applied to Macaulay's "Minute on Indian Education." *Orientalism*, p. 152.
76 Strich, *Goethe und die Weltliteratur*, p. 21.

AFTERWORD

1 Lockman, *Contending Visions*; Said, *Orientalism*; Johansen, "Politics and Scholarship"; Irwin, *For Lust of Knowing*; Schöller, "Post-Enlightenment Academic Study of the Qur'ān."
2 Johansen, "Politics and Scholarship," pp. 79–83.
3 Bobzin, "Translations of the Qur'ān."
4 *Les Livres sacrés de l'orient*, pp. xxiv–xxv. Pauthier cites verse numbers keyed to the Kazimirski translation in a footnote; verse numbers cited here are to the verse numbers in the standard edition.
5 Boubakeur, *Le Coran*, p. 12.
6 Gilliot, "Review of *Le Coran*," Boubakeur trans., pp. 209–210.
7 Boubakeur, *Le Coran*, pp. 49–50.
8 *The Meaning of the Glorious Quran*, Pickthall trans., p. vii.
9 A concise account of this debate is found in Welch, "Al-Ḳur'ān," and a more detailed one of both the debate and its legacy in Jansen, *The Interpretation of the Koran in Modern Egypt*.
10 Yusuf Ali, *The Holy Qur'an*, n.p.
11 Abdel Haleem, *Understanding The Qur'an*, pp. xxviii–xxix.
12 Massignon repeatedly invokes the laws of *djiwār* and asylum to oppose Europe's intransigence in dealing with the colonial populations. Massignon's vocabulary is striking by its prescience:

> Je ne partage pas la conception cartésienne de "clash" des cultures opposant une culture moderne technique à une culture périmée non technique … Il y a quelque chose de plus: j'ai un homme devant moi, un homme qui se prétend lésé, qui me réclame *sa* "justice" et la réclame dans *mon* système de justice, au nom d'un principe de participation prélogique essentiel, qu'on appelle le caractère *sacré* du *droit d'asile*. Le premier contact entre deux usuf civilisations, primitives et hostiles, c'est le principe de l'hospitalité. L'hospitalité, c'est de supposer que l'étranger, l'ennemi, a quelque chose de bon, tout de même, à nous donner. ["L'Occident devant l'orient," pp. 209, 213.]

In his "Avertissement" to his edition of Massignon's *Opera minora*, Youakim Moubarac describes him as "un savant français … qui a dit 'qu'il n'était pas un arabisant, mais un 'arabisé', au sens classique, un 'dakhīl', un hôte." "Avertissement," n.p.
13 Masson, *Le Coran,* p. ix.
14 Ibid., pp. ix–x.
15 Said, *The World, the Text and the Critic*, pp. 4, 33, 35.
16 Berque, *Relire le Coran*, p. 109.
17 Ibid., p. 128.

18 Ibid., p. 125.
19 Grunebaum, "Bayān"; Kadi and Mir, "Literature and the Qur'ān."
20 Berque, *Relire le Coran*, p. 34.
21 Ibid., pp. 34–36, 42–43.
22 Bobzin, "Translations of the Qur'ān"; Bellamy, "Textual Criticism of the Qur'ān"; Blachère, *Le Coran (al-Qor'ân)*; Bell, *A Commentary on the Qur'ān*; Paret, *Der Koran*.
23 Gilliot, "Le Coran: trois traductions récentes," p. 177. Among many possible reasons for the current state of Qur'ān translations one might adduce Walid Saleh's assessment and diagnosis of recent scholarship on the Qur'ān in his "In Search of a Comprehensible Qur'ān," though he does not deal with translation per se.

BIBLIOGRAPHY

ABBREVIATIONS

CC	*Correspondance complète* (various authors)
EI	*Encyclopaedia of Islam*, ed. P. Bearman et al. Brill, 2008. Brill Online. <http://www.brillonline.nl>
EM	Voltaire, *Essai sur les moeurs*
EQ	*Encyclopaedia of the Qur'ān*, ed. J. D. McAuliffe. Brill, 2008. Brill Online. <http://www.brillonline.nl>
GAL	C. Brockelmann, *Geschichte der arabischen Literatur*
GAS	F. Sezgin, *Geschichte der arabischen Schrifttums*
KZR	H. Bobzin, *Der Koran im Zeitalter der Reformation*
Marracci	*Alcorani textus universus ...*
Notes marginales	*Corpus des notes marginales de Voltaire*, ed. T. P. Voronova
OC	*Œuvres complètes* (various authors)
ODNB	*Oxford Dictionary of National Biography*. Oxford University Press, Sept 2004; online edn. Jan 2008 <http://www.oxforddnb.com>
RE	J. Israel, *Radical Enlightenment*
Sale	*The Koran*, trans. G. Sale
SWS	Goethe, *Sämtliche Werke, nach Epochen seines Schaffens*

All online resources accessed various dates, September 2006–April 2008.

Abbreviations of classical sources follow eds. A. Spawforth and S. Hornblower, *Oxford Classical Dictionary* (3rd edn.).

TRANSLITERATIONS

'	ء
a, ā	ا
b	ب
t	ت
th	ث
j	ج
ḥ	ح
kh	خ
d	د
dh	ذ
r	ر
z	ز
s	س
sh	ش
ṣ	ص
ḍ	ض
ṭ	ط
ẓ	ظ
'	ع
gh	غ
f	ف
q	ق
k	ك
l	ل
m	م
n	ن
h	ه
w, ū	و
y, ī	ي

SOURCES

Abbattista, G. "'The Literary Mill:' per una storia editoriale della *Universal History* (1736–1765)," *Studi Settecenteschi*, 1:2, 1981, pp. 91–133.

Abdel Haleem, M. A. S. trans. *The Qur'an: A New Translation*. Oxford: Oxford University Press, 2005.

—— *Understanding the Qur'ān: Themes and Styles*. London and New York: I. B. Tauris, 2001.

Abu Zayd, N. H. *Al-Ittijāh al-'aqlī fī-l-tafsīr: Dirāsah fī qaḍiyyat al-majāz fī-l-Qur'ān 'ind Al-mu'tazalah*. Beirut and Casablanca: Al-Markaz Al-Thaqāfī Al-'Arabī, 2003 (5ᵗʰ edn.).

—— *Mafhūm al-naṣṣ: Dirāsah fī 'ulūm al-Qur'ān*. Beirut and Casablanca: Al-Hay'ah al-'Āmmah li-l-Kitāb, 1994 (2ⁿᵈ edn.).

Adang, C. "Belief and Unbelief," *EQ*.

Ahmed, L. *Women and Gender in Islam: Historical Roots of a Modern Debate*. New Haven, CT, and London: Yale University Press, 1992.

Al-Jabartī, A. "Tārīkh Muddat al-Faransīs bi-Misr," in ed. and trans. S. Moreh, *Al-Jabartī's Chronicle of the First Seven Months of the French Occupation of Egypt, Muḥarram-Rajab 1213 / 15 June–December 1798*. Leiden: Brill, 1975.

Al-Qadi, W. "Authority," *EQ*.

Allison, R. C. *The Crescent Obscured: The United States and the Muslim World, 1776–1815*. New York: Oxford University Press, 1995.

Anawati, G. C. "'Īsa," *EI*.

Anon. "Al-Muḳanna'," *EI*.

Arkoun, M. "Le Hajj dans la pensée islamique," in M. Arkoun, *Lectures du Coran*. Paris: Maisonneuve et Larose, 1982, pp. 157–175.

Arnaldez, R. *Jésus fils de Marie, prophète de l'Islam*. Paris: Desclée, 1980.

—— "Khalḳ," *EI*.

Ashton, R. *The German Idea: Four English Writers and the Reception of German Thought 1800–1860*. Cambridge: Cambridge University Press, 1980.

Assmann, J. *Moses the Egyptian: The Memory of Egypt in Western Monotheism*. Cambridge, MA: Harvard University Press, 1997.

Auerbach, E. *Mimesis: Dargestellte Wirklichkeit in der abendländischen Literatur*. Tübingen and Basel: A. Francke, 1994 (9ᵗʰ edn.).

—— *Mimesis: The Representation of Reality in Western Literature*, trans. W. R. Trask. Princeton: Princeton University Press, 2003 (50ᵗʰ anniversary edn.).

Ayalon, A. "Malik," *EI*.

'Azab, M. "Problématique de la traduction du Coran," *Islam de France*, 4, 1999, pp. 33–83.

Baczko, B. "Moïse, législateur ..." in eds. S. Harvey et al., *Reappraisals of*

Rousseau: Studies in Honour of R. A. Leigh. Manchester: Manchester University Press, 1980, pp. 111–130.

Badir, M. G. *Voltaire et l'Islam*. Oxford: Voltaire Foundation, 1974.

Badran, M. "Feminism and the Qur'ān," *EQ*.

Balagna Costou, J. *Arabe et humanisme dans la France des derniers Valois*. Paris: Maisonneuve et Larose, 1989.

Ballard, M. *De Cicéron à Benjamin: traducteurs, traductions, réflexions*. Lille: Presses Universitaires de Lille, 1992.

Banier, A. *La Mythologie et les fables expliquées par l'histoire*. Paris: Briasson, 1738–1740, 3 vols.

Al-Bayḍāwī, A. *Anwār al-tanzīl wa asrār al-ta'wīl*. Cairo: Dār Al-Kitāb al-'Arabī, n.d.

Bayle, P. *Dictionnaire historique et critique*, ed. Beuchot. Paris: Hachette, 1820–1824 (11th edn.); Geneva, Slatkine, 1969, 16 vols.

—— *A General Dictionary, Historical and Critical: in which a new and accurate translation of that of the celebrated Mr. Bayle, with the corrections and observations printed in the late edition at Paris, is included, and interspersed with several thousand lives never before published*, ed. J. P. Bernard et al. London: Bettenham, 1734–1741, 10 vols. Volumes 1–4 contain the phrase 'And articles relating to Oriental History by George Sale, gent.'

Becker, C. L. *The Heavenly City of the Eighteenth-Century Philosophers*. New Haven, CT, and London: Yale University Press, 2003 (2nd edn.).

Bell, R. *A Commentary on the Qur'an*, eds. C. E. Bosworth and M. E. J. Richardson. Manchester: University of Manchester Press, 1991, 2 vols.

—— *The Origin of Islam in Its Christian Environment: The Gunning Lectures, Edinburgh University 1925*. London: Cass, 1968 (reprint).

—— trans. *The Qur'an: Translated with a Critical Re-arrangement of the Surahs*. Edinburgh: University of Edinburgh Press, 1937–1939.

—— and Montgomery Watt, W. *Bell's Introduction to the Qur'an, Enlarged and Completely Revised by W. Montgomery Watt*. Edinburgh: Edinburgh University Press, 1970.

Bellamy, J. A. "Textual Criticism of the Qur'ān," *EQ*.

Benítez, M. "Une Histoire interminable: origines et développement du *Traité des trois imposteurs*," in eds. S. Berti et al., *Heterodoxy, Spinozism, and Free Thought in Early Eighteenth-Century Europe: Studies on the Traité des Trois Imposteurs*. Dordrecht, Boston, and London: Kluwer, 1996, pp. 53–74.

Bennington, G. *Dudding: Des noms de Rousseau*. Paris: Galilée, 1991.

Bergier, M. *Le Déisme réfuté par lui-même, ou Examen, en forme de lettres, des principes d'incrédulité répandus dans les divers ouvrages de M. Rousseau* (1765). Paris: Vrin, 1981 (reprint).

Berman, A. *L'Epreuve de l'étranger*. Paris: Gallimard, 1984.

Berque, J. *Relire le Coran*. Paris: Albin Michel, 1993.

Berti, S. "*L'Esprit de Spinosa:* ses origines et sa première édition dans leur contexte spinozien,'" in eds. S. Berti et al., *Heterodoxy, Spinozism, and Free Thought in Early Eighteenth-Century Europe: Studies on the Traité des Trois Imposteurs*. Dordrecht, Boston, and London: Kluwer, 1996, pp. 3–51.

—— Charles-Daubert, F. and Popkin, R. H. eds. *Heterodoxy, Spinozism, and Free Thought in Early Eighteenth-Century Europe: Studies on the Traité des Trois Imposteurs*. Dordrecht, Boston, and London: Kluwer, 1996.

Besterman, T. *Voltaire*. Oxford: Blackwell, 1976 (3rd edn.).

Bisaha, N. *Creating East and West: Renaissance Humanists and the Ottoman Turks*. Philadelphia, PA: University of Pennsylvania Press, 2004.

Blachère, R. trans. *Le Coran (al-Qor'ân)* (1956). Paris: Maisonneuve et Larose, 2005.

—— *Introduction au Coran* (1959). Paris: Maisonneuve et Larose, 2002 (reprint).

Bobzin, H. "Friedrich Rückert und der Koran,'" in eds. H. Bobzin and W. Fischer, *Der Koran in der Übersetzung von Friedrich Rückert*. Würzburg: Ergon, 1995, pp. vii–xxxiii.

—— *Der Koran im Zeitalter der Reformation: Studien zur Frühgeschichte der Arabistik und Islamkunde in Europa*. Beirut and Stuttgart: Steiner, 1995.

—— "Latin Translations of the Koran: A Short Overview,'" *Der Islam*, 70:2, 1993, pp. 193–206. Reprinted in Turner, C. ed. *The Koran: Critical Concepts in Islamic Studies*. London and New York: RoutledgeCurzon, vol. 4, pp. 116–127.

—— "Pre-1800 Preoccupations of Qur'ānic Studies,'" *EQ*.

—— "Translations of the Qur'ān,'" *EQ*.

—— "'A Treasury of Heresies:' Christian Polemics against the Koran,'" in ed. S. Wild, *The Qur'ān as Text*. Leiden, New York, and Cologne: Brill, 1996, pp. 157–175.

Borges, J. L. *Histoire universelle de l'infamie/Histoire de l'éternité*, trans. R. Caillois and L. Guille. Paris: UGE, 1994.

Borrmans, M. "Ludovico Marracci et sa traduction latine du Coran,'" *Islamochristiana*, 28, 2002, pp. 73–85.

—— "Observations à propos de la première édition imprimée du Coran à Venise,'" *Quaderni di Studi Arabi*, 8, 1990, pp. 3–12.

—— "Présentation de la première édition imprimée du Coran à Venise,'" *Quaderni di Studi Arabi*, 9, 1991, pp. 93–126.

Bost, H. *Pierre Bayle*. Paris: Fayard, 2006.

Boubakeur, Si H. *Le Coran: Traduction francaise et commentaire d'après la tradition, les différentes écoles de lecture, d'exégèse, de jurisprudence et de théologie, les interprétations mystiques, les tendances schismatiques et les doctrines hérétiques de l'Islâm, et à la lumière des théories scientifiques, philosophiques et politiques modernes.* Paris: Maisonneuve et Larose, 1995.

Boulainvilliers, H. *La Vie de Mahomed; avec des réflexions sur la religion mahometane, & les coutumes des musulmans.* Amsterdam: P. Humbert, 1731.

Boullata, I. "Literary Structures of the Qur'ān," *EQ.*

—— ed. *Literary Structures of Religious Meaning in the Qur'ān.* Richmond: Curzon, 2000.

Boyle, N. *Goethe: The Poet and the Age.* Oxford and New York: Oxford University Press, 1991–2000, 2 vols.

Brink, C. O. *Horace on Poetry II: The "Ars Poetica."* Cambridge: Cambridge University Press, 1971.

Brockelmann, C. *Geschichte der arabischen Literatur.* Leiden: Brill, 1942–1947, 3 vols.

Brugman, J. and Schröder, F. *Arabic Studies in the Netherlands.* Publications of the Netherlands Institute of Archaeology and Arabic Studies in Cairo, vol. 3. Leiden: Brill, 1979.

Brumfitt, J. H. "Introduction" to *La Philosophie de l'histoire.* Geneva and Toronto: Institut et Musée Voltaire and University of Toronto Press, 1969 (2nd edn.), pp. 13–89.

—— *Voltaire Historian.* London and New York: Oxford University Press, 1958.

Burgelin, P. *Jean-Jacques Rousseau et la religion de Genève.* Geneva: Labor et Fides, 1962.

—— *La Philosophie de l'existence de Jean-Jacques Rousseau.* Paris: Presses Universitaires de France, 1952.

Burkert, W. *Greek Religion,* trans. J. Raffan. Cambridge, MA: Harvard University Press, 1985.

Burman, T. E. *Reading the Qur'ān in Latin Christendom, 1140–1560.* Philadelphia, PA: University of Pennsylvania Press, 2007.

—— "Tafsir and Translation: Traditional Arabic Qur'ān Exegesis and the Latin Qur'āns of Robert of Ketton and Mark of Toledo," *Speculum,* 73:3, July 1998, pp. 703–732.

Burnett, C. "Ketton, Robert of (*fl.* 1141–1157)," *ODNB.*

Burton, J. "Abrogation," *EQ.*

—— *The Collection of the Qur'ān.* Cambridge: Cambridge University Press, 1977.

—— "Naskh," *EI.*

—— *The Sources of Islamic Law: Islamic Theories of Abrogation.* Edinburgh: Edinburgh University Press, 1990.

Bury, A. *The Naked Gospel.* London, 1690.

Caetani, L. *Annali dell'Islam*. Milan: Ulrico Hoepli, 1905–1926, 10 vols.

Callimachus. *Callimachus: Hymns and Epigrams. Lycophron: Alexandra. Aratus: Phaenomena*, trans. A. W. and G. R. Mair. Cambridge, MA: Harvard University Press, 1989.

Carlyle, T. *German Romance: Specimens of Its Chief Authors*. Boston: James Munroe, 1841, 2 vols.

Carney, E. "Artifice and Alexander History," in eds. A. B. Bosworth and E. Baynham, *Alexander the Great in Fact and Fiction*. Oxford and New York: Oxford University Press, 1999, pp. 263–285.

Causse, M. "Théologie de rupture et théologie de la communauté. Etude sur la vocation prophétique de Moïse d'après le Coran," *Revue d'histoire et de philosophie religieuses*, 44:1, 1964, pp. 60–82.

Champion, J. "Introduction" to J. Toland, *Nazarenus*, ed. J. Champion. Oxford: Voltaire Foundation, 1999, pp. 1–112.

—— "Legislators, Impostors and the Politic Origins of Religion: English Theories of 'Imposture' from Stubbe to Toland," in eds. S. Berti et al., *Heterodoxy, Spinozism, and Free Thought in Early Eighteenth-Century Europe: Studies on the Traité des Trois Imposteurs*. Dordrecht, Boston, and London: Kluwer, 1996, pp. 333–356.

—— *The Pillars of Priestcraft Shaken: The Church of England and Its Enemies, 1660–1720*. Cambridge: Cambridge University Press, 1992.

—— *Republican Learning: John Toland and the Crisis of Christian Culture, 1696–1722*. Manchester and New York: Manchester University Press, 2003.

Charpentier, J. *Napoléon et les hommes de lettres de son temps*. Paris: Mercure de France, 1936.

Daiber, H. "Masā'il wa-Adjwiba," *EI*.

Daniel, N. *Islam and the West: The Making of an Image*. Edinburgh: Edinburgh University Press, 1960; Oxford: Oneworld, 1993.

Daniel, S. H. *John Toland: His Methods, Manners and Minds*. Kingston and Montreal: McGill–Queen's University Press, 1984.

De Frede, C. *La prima traduzione italiana del Corano sullo sfondo dei rapporti tra Cristianità e Islam nel Cinquecento*. Naples: Istituto Universitario Orientale, 1967.

Delanoue, G. *Moralistes et politiques musulmans dans l'Egypte du dix-neuvième siècle (1798–1882)*. Cairo: Institut Français d'Archéologie Orientale du Caire, 1982, 2 vols.

Denny, F. M. "Community and Society," *EQ*.

—— "Face," *EQ*.

Derathé, R. *Jean-Jacques Rousseau et la science politique de son temps*. Paris: J. Vrin, 1974 (2nd edn.).

Descombes, V. "Louis Dumont ou les outils de la tolérance," *Esprit* 253,

240 *The Enlightenment Qur'ān*

June 1999. Reprinted in V. Descombes, *Le Raisonnement de l'ours et autres essais de philosophie pratique*. Paris: Seuil, 2007, pp. 227–253.

—— *Philosophie par gros temps*. Paris: Minuit, 1989.

Dew, N. "The Order of Oriental Knowledge: The Making of D'Herbelot's *Bibliothèque orientale*," in ed. C. Prendergast, *Debating World Literature*. London: Verso, 2004, pp. 233–252.

Dimmock, M. *New Turkes: Dramatizing Islam and the Ottomans in Early Modern England*. Aldershot and Burlington, VT: Ashgate, 2005.

Donvez, J. *De quoi vivait Voltaire?* Paris: Deux Rives, 1949.

Dosse, F. *Histoire du structuralisme*. Paris: La Découverte, 1991, 2 vols.

Dousse, M. *Marie la musulmane*. Paris: Albin Michel, 2005.

Du Ryer, A. *L'Alcoran de Mahomet. Translaté d'arabe en françois, par le sieur Du Ryer, sieur de la Garde Malezair.* Paris: Antoine de Somaville, 1647.

—— *The Alcoran of Mahomet, translated out of Arabique into French; by the sieur Du Ryer, Lord of Malezair, and resident for the King of France, at Alexandria. And newly Englished, for the satisfaction of all that desire to look into the Turkish vanities.* London, 1649.

—— *L'Alcoran de Mahomet. Traduit de l'arabe, par André Du Ryer, sieur de la Garde Malezair, avec la traduction des Observations historiques et critiques sur le Mahométisme, mises à la tête de la version anglaise de M. George Sale.* Nouvelle edition, qu'on a augmentée d'un Discours Preliminaire, extrait du nouvel Ouvrage Anglois de *Mr. Porter*, Ministre Plenipotentiaire de S. M. Britannique en Turquie. Amsterdam and Leipzig: Arkstée & Merkus, 1775, 2 vols.

Dumézil, G. *Mythe et épopée I. L'idéologie des trois fonctions dans les épopées des peuples indo-européens*. Paris: Gallimard, 1986 (5th edn.).

Dumont, L. *Homo aequalis, II. L'Idéologie allemande: France-Allemagne et retour*. Paris: Gallimard, 1991.

Eco, U. *La Ricerca della lingua perfetta nelle cultura europea*, ed. J. Le Goff. Rome and Bari: Laterza, 1993.

Ehlert, T. "Muḥammad," *EI*.

Ehrard, J. *L'Idée de nature en France à l'aube des Lumières*. Paris: Flammarion, 1970.

Etiemble. *L'Europe chinoise*. Paris: Gallimard, 1989, 2 vols.

Fahd, T. *La Divination arabe. Etudes religieuses, sociologiques et folkloriques sur le milieu natif de l'islam*. Paris: Sindbad, 1987.

Feingold, M. "Oriental Studies," in ed. N. Tyacke, *Seventeenth-Century Oxford*, vol. 4 of *The History of the University of Oxford*. Oxford: Clarendon Press, 1997, pp. 449–504.

Fish, S. *Surprised by Sin: The Reader in Paradise Lost*. Cambridge, MA: Harvard University Press, 1997 (2nd edn.).

Franklin, M. J. "Gagnier, John (*c*.1670–1740)," *ODNB*.

Fumaroli, M. *L'Âge de l'éloquence. Rhétorique et 'res litteraria' de la Renaissance au seuil de l'époque classique*. Paris: Albin Michel, 1994.

Fussner, R. E. *The Historical Revolution*. Westport, CT: Greenwood Press, 1976.

Fück, J. *Die Arabischen Studien in Europa bis in den Anfang des 20. Jahrhunderts*. Leipzig: Harrassowitz, 1955.

Gagnebin, B. "Le Rôle du législateur dans les conceptions politiques de Rousseau," in *Etudes sur le* Contrat social *de Jean-Jacques Rousseau. Actes des journées d'étude organisées a Dijon pour la commémoration du 200e anniversaire du* Contrat social. Paris: Les Belles Lettres, 1962, pp. 272–290.

Gagnier, J. ed. and trans. *Ismael Abu'l-Feda, de vita, et rebus gestis Mohammedis, Moslemici religionis auctoris, et imperii Saracenici fundatoris ... textum arabicum primus edidit, latine vertit, prefatione, & notis illustravit Joannes Gagnier, A. M*. Oxford: E Theatro Sheldoniano, 1723.

—— *La Vie de Mahomet, traduite et compilée de l'Alcoran, des traditions authentiques de la Sonna et de meilleurs auteurs arabes*. Amsterdam: Weinsteins and Smith, 1748, 3 vols.

Gätje, H. *The Qur'an and its Exegesis: Selected Texts with Classical and Modern Muslim Interpretations* (1971), ed. and trans. A. T. Welch. Oxford: Oneworld, 2004.

Geertz, C. "Thick Description: Towards an Interpretive Theory of Culture," in C. Geertz, *The Interpretation of Cultures: Selected Essays*. New York: Basic, 1973, pp. 3–30.

Gilliot, C. "Review of *Le Coran*, translated by Cheikh Si Hamza Boubakeur," *Studia Islamica*, 84, 1996, pp. 207–212.

—— "Le Coran: trois traductions récentes [Jacques Berque, André Chouraqui, René Khawam]," *Studia Islamica*, 85, 1992, pp. 159–177.

—— and P. Larcher. "Language and Style," *EQ*.

Goethe, J. W. von. *Briefe*, ed. K. R. Mandelkow. Munich: C. H. Beck, 1988, 6 vols.

—— *Goethes Werke: Hamburger Ausgabe*, ed. E. Trunz. Munich: C. H. Beck, 1981–1989, 14 vols.

—— *Sämtliche Werke, nach Epochen seines Schaffens. Münchner Ausgabe*, eds. K. Richter et al. Munich: Carl Hanser, 1987.

Gökyay, O. Ş. "Kātib Čelebi," *EI*.

Goldziher, I. "Le Dénombrement des sectes mahométanes" (1892), reprinted in I. Goldziher, *Sur L'Islam. Origines de la théologie musulmane*. Paris: Desclée de Brouwer, 2003, pp. 269–277.

—— *Introduction to Islamic Theology and Law*, trans. A. and R. Hamori. Princeton, NJ: Princeton University Press, 1981.

—— *Die Richtungen der islamischen Koranauslegung.* Leiden: Brill, 1920.

Grafton, A. *The Footnote: A Curious History.* Cambridge, MA: Harvard University Press, 1997.

—— ed., *Rome Reborn: The Vatican Library and Renaissance Culture.* Exhibition Catalogue, Library of Congress, Washington, DC; New Haven, CT: Library of Congress and Yale University Press in association with the Biblioteca Apostolica Vaticana, 1993.

—— "The Vatican and Its Library," in ed. A. Grafton, *Rome Reborn: The Vatican Library and Renaissance Culture.* Exhibition Catalogue, Library of Congress, Washington, DC; New Haven, CT: Library of Congress and Yale University Press in association with the Biblioteca Apostolica Vaticana, 1993, pp. 3–45.

—— *What Was History? The Art of History in Early Modern Europe.* Cambridge: Cambridge University Press, 2007.

Graham, W. A. "Scripture and the Qur'ān," *EQ.*

Grappin, P. "Notice" to *Mahomet*, in eds. P. Grappin and E. Henkel, *Goethe, Théâtre complet.* Paris: Gallimard, 1988, pp. 1559–1562.

Griffin, D. *Regaining Paradise: Milton and the Eighteenth Century.* Cambridge: Cambridge University Press, 1986.

Gril, D. "Miracles," *EQ.*

Grimm, F. M. *Correspondance littéraire, philosophique et critique*, ed. M. Tourneux. Paris: Garnier Frères, 1877; Nendeln, Liechtenstein: Kraus, 1968, 16 vols (reprint).

Grosjean, J. trans. *Le Coran.* Précédé d'une étude de Jacques Berque, traduit de l'arabe par Jean Grosjean, illustré de sérigraphies originales par Zenderoudi, accompagné d'un manuscrit d'Ibn al-Bawwab commenté par D. S. Rice. Paris: Le Club du Livre, 1972.

Grotius, H. *Traité de la vérité de la religion chrétienne*, trans. P. Le Jeune. Amsterdam: E-J Ledet, 1728.

Grunebaum, G. E. von. "Bayān," *EI.*

Guer, J-A. *Moeurs et usages des Turcs, leur religion, leur gouvernement civil, militaire et politique, avec un abrégé de l'histoire ottomane.* Paris: Coustelier, 1746–1747, 2 vols.

Gunny, A. *Images of Islam in Eighteenth-Century Writings.* London: Grey Seal, 1996.

Hadidi, D. *Voltaire et l'Islam.* Paris: Publications Orientalistes de France, 1979.

Hadot, P. *Le Voile d'Isis. Essai sur l'histoire de l'idée de Nature.* Paris: Gallimard, 2004.

Hallaq, W. "Law and the Qur'ān," *EQ.*

Hamilton, A. "Arabists and Cartesians at Utrecht," in eds. P. Hoftijzer and T. Verbeek, *Leven na Descartes. Zeven opstellen over ideeëngeschiednis in Nederland in de tweede helft van de zeventiende eeuw*. Hilversum: Uitgeverij Verloren, 2005, pp. 97–105.

—— "Bedwell, William (*bap.* 1563, *d.* 1632)," *ODNB*.

—— "Eastern Churches and Western Scholarship," in ed. A Grafton, *Rome Reborn: The Vatican Library and Renaissance Culture*. Exhibition Catalogue, Library of Congress, Washington, DC; New Haven, CT: Library of Congress and Yale University Press in association with the Biblioteca Apostolica Vaticana, 1993, pp. 225–249.

—— "The English Interest in the Arabic-Speaking Christians," in ed. G. A. Russell, *The "Arabick" Interest of the Natural Philosophers in Seventeenth-Century England*. Leiden, New York, and Cologne: Brill, pp. 30–53.

—— *The Forbidden Fruit: The Koran in Early Modern Europe*. The Hadassah and Daniel Khalili Memorial Lecture in Islamic Art and Culture. London: London Middle East Institute, 2008.

—— "A Lutheran Translator for the Quran: A Late Seventeenth-Century Quest," in eds. A. Hamilton, M. van den Boogert, and B. Westerwell, *The Republic of Letters and the Levant*, special issue of *Intersections: Yearbook for Early Modern Studies*, 5, 2005, pp. 197–221.

—— "The Study of Islam in Early Modern Europe," *Archiv für Religionsgeschichte*, 3, 2001, pp. 169–182.

—— *William Bedwell the Arabist, 1563–1632*. Leiden: Brill and Leiden University Press, 1985.

—— "Western Attitudes to Islam in the Enlightenment," *Middle Eastern Lectures*, 3, 1999, pp. 69–85.

—— and Richard, F. *André Du Ryer and Oriental Studies in Seventeenth-Century France*. London and Oxford: The Arcadian Library in association with Oxford University Press, 2004.

Hammer-Purgstall, J. von. *Fundgruben des Orients*. Vienna: Anton Schmid, 1809–1816, 6 vols.

Hankins, J. "The Popes and Humanism," in ed. A. Grafton, *Rome Reborn: The Vatican Library and Renaissance Culture*. Exhibition Catalogue, Library of Congress, Washington, DC; New Haven, CT: Library of Congress and Yale University Press in association with the Biblioteca Apostolica Vaticana, 1993, pp. 47–85.

Hardwick, J. *The Practice of Patriarchy: Gender and the Politics of Household Authority in Early Modern France*. University Park: Pennsylvania State University Press, 1998.

Harrison, P. *"Religion" and the Religions in the English Enlightenment*. Cambridge: Cambridge University Press, 1990.

Haydon, C. *Anti-Catholicism in Eighteenth-Century England, c. 1714–80: A Political and Social Study*. Manchester: Manchester University Press, 1993.

Hayes, K. J. "How Thomas Jefferson Read the Qur'an," *Early American Literature*, 39:2, 2004, pp. 247–261.

Hazard, P. *La Crise de la conscience européenne, 1680–1715* (1961). Paris: Livre de Poche, 2005.

Healey, F. G. *The Literary Culture of Napoleon*. Geneva: Droz, 1959.

Heath, P. "Metaphor," *EQ*.

Heck, P. L. "Politics and the Qur'ān," *EQ*.

Hegel, G. W. F. *Die Vernunft in der Geschichte*, vol. 1 of ed. J. Hoffmeister, *Vorlesungen über die Philosophie der Weltgeschichte*. Hamburg: Felix Meiner, 1970 (5th edn.).

D'Herbelot, B. *Bibliothèque orientale, ou Dictionnaire universel contenant généralement tout ce qui regarde la connaissance des peuples de l'Orient*. Paris: Compagnie des Libraires, 1697.

Holt, P. M. *A Seventeenth-Century Defender of Islam: Henry Stubbe (1632–76) and His Book*. London: Dr. William's Trust, 1972.

—— "The Study of Arabic Historians in Seventeenth-Century England: The Background and Work of Edward Pococke," *Bulletin of the School of Oriental and African Studies*, 19:3, 1957, pp. 444–555.

—— "The Treatment of Arab History by Prideaux, Ockley and Sale," in eds. P. M. Holt and B. Lewis, *Historians of the Middle East*. London: Oxford University Press, 1962, pp. 290–302.

Homer. *Homeric Hymns. Homeric Apocrypha. Lives of Homer*, ed. and trans. M. L. West. Cambridge, MA: Harvard University Press, 2003.

Horace. *Odes and Epodes*, ed. and trans. N. Rudd. Cambridge, MA: Harvard University Press, 2004.

Horovitz, J. "'Abd Allāh b. Salām," *EI*.

Houlgate, S. "World History as the Progress of Consciousness: An Interpretation of Hegel's Philosophy of History," *The Owl of Minerva*, 22, 1990, pp. 69–80; reprinted in ed. R. Stern, *G. W. F. Hegel: Critical Assessments*. London and New York: Routledge, 1993, pp. 402–416.

Hourani, A. *Europe and the Middle East*. Berkeley: University of California Press, 1980.

—— *Islam in European Thought*. Cambridge: Cambridge University Press, 1991.

Ibn Salāma, H. *Al-Nāsikh wa-l-mansūkh min Kitāb Allāh 'Azza wa Jall*, eds. Z. Al-Shawīsh and M. Kan'ān. Beirut and Damascus: Al-Maktab al-Islamī, 1986 (2nd edn.).

Irwin, R. *For Lust of Knowing: The Orientalists and their Enemies*. London: Allen Lane, 2006.

Israel, J. *Enlightenment Contested: Philosophy, Modernity and the Emancipation of Man, 1670–1752*. Oxford: Oxford University Press, 2006.

—— *Radical Enlightenment: Philosophy and the Making of Modernity, 1650–1750*. Oxford: Oxford University Press, 2001.

Izutsu, T. *God and Man in the Qur'an: Semantics and the Qur'anic Weltanschauung* (1964). Kuala Lumpur: Islamic Book Trust, 2002 (2nd edn.).

Jansen, J. J. G. *The Interpretation of the Koran in Modern Egypt*. Leiden: Brill, 1974.

Johansen, B. "Politics and Scholarship: The Development of Islamic Studies in the Federal Republic of Germany," in ed. T. Y. Ismael, *Middle East Studies: International Perspectives on the State of the Art*. New York, Westport, CT, and London: Praeger, 1990, pp. 71–130.

Johns, A. H. "Reflections on the Dynamics and Sprituality of *Sūrat al-Furqān*," in ed. I. Boullata, *Literary Structures of Religious Meaning in the Qur'an*. Richmond: Curzon, 2000, pp. 188–227.

Jones, A. "The Language of the Qur'an," *The Arabist: Budapest Studies in Arabic*, 6–7, 1993, pp. 29–48.

—— "Narrative Technique in the Qur'an and in Early Poetry," *The Arabist*, 8, 1994, pp. 45–54.

—— "The Oral and the Written: Some Thoughts about the Quranic Text," *The Arabist*, 10, 1996, pp. 57–66.

—— "Poetry and Poets," *EQ*.

Jølle, J. "The River and its Metaphors: Goethe's 'Mahomets Gesang,'" *Modern Language Notes*, 119:3, 2004, pp. 431–450.

Kadi, W. and Mir, M. "Literature and the Qur'ān," *EQ*.

Katsh, A. I. *Judaism in Islam: Biblical and Talmudic Backgrounds of the Koran and Its Commentaries*. New York: New York University Press, 1954.

Kelly, C. "'To Persuade without Convincing:' The Language of Rousseau's Legislator," *American Journal of Political Science*, 31:2, May 1987, pp. 321–335.

Kermani, N. "The Aesthetic Reception of the Qur'ān as Reflected in Early Muslim History," in ed. I. Boullata, *Literary Structures of Religious Meaning in the Qur'an*. Richmond: Curzon, 2000, pp. 255–276.

—— *Gott ist schön: Das ästhetische Erleben des Koran*. Munich: Beck, 2003.

—— "Revelation in its Aesthetic Dimension," in ed. S. Wild, *The Qur'ān as Text*. Leiden, New York, and Cologne: Brill, 1996, pp. 213–224.

Khairallah, S. "Arabic Studies in England in the Late Seventeenth and Early Eighteenth Centuries" (Ph.D. diss., Faculty of Arts, University of London, 1972).

Khalidi, T. trans. *The Qur'an*. London: Penguin, 2008.

Kilchenmann, R. J. "Goethes Übersetzung der voltairedramen *Mahomet* und *Tancred*," *Comparative Literature*, 14:4, Autumn 1962, pp. 332–340.

Kimber, R. "Boundaries and Precepts," *EQ*.

Klein, L. E. *Shaftesbury and the Culture of Politeness: Moral Discourse and Cultural Politics in Early Eighteenth-Century England*. Cambridge: Cambridge University Press, 1994.

Kohn, S. *Die Eheschliessung im Koran*. London: Austin, 1934.

Kritzeck, J. *Peter the Venerable and Islam*. Princeton: Princeton University Press, 1964.

Kugel, J. L. ed. *Poets and Prophets: The Beginnings of a Literary Tradition*. Ithaca: Cornell University Press, 1990.

—— "Poets and Prophets: An Overview," in ed. J. L. Kugel, *Poets and Prophets: The Beginnings of a Literary Tradition*. Ithaca: Cornell University Press, 1990, pp. 1–25.

Kuntz, M. L. *Guillaume Postel, Prophet of the Restitution of All Things: His Life and Thought*. The Hague and Boston, MA: Martinus Nijhoff, 1981.

Labrousse, E. *Pierre Bayle*. The Hague: Mouton, 1963–1964.

—— *Pierre Bayle. Hétérodoxie et rigorisme*. Originally published as the second volume of *Pierre Bayle* (1963–1964). Paris: Albin Michel, 1996 (2nd edn.).

Laissus, Y. *L'Egypte, une aventure savante. Avec Bonaparte, Kléber, Menou, 1798–1801*. Paris: Fayard, 1998.

Lamy, B. *La Rhétorique, ou l'art de parler*, ed. C. Noille-Clauzade. Paris: Champion, 1998.

Laoust, H. *Les Schismes dans l'islam. Introduction à une étude de la religion musulmane*. Paris: Payot, 1983.

Larcher, P. "Concept of Language," *EQ*.

Laurens, H. *Aux sources de l'orientalisme: La Bibliothèque Orientale de Barthélémi D'Herbelot*. Paris: Maisonneuve et Larose, 1978.

—— "Histoire, anthropologie et politique au siècle des Lumières, le cas de l'orientalisme islamisant," *L'Information historique*, 44, 1982, pp. 167–174, reprinted in *Orientales I. Autour de l'expédition d'Egypte*. Paris: CNRS, 2004, pp. 15–29.

—— "L'Egypte dans le mythe-histoire de la raison," *Le Miroir égyptien*, 1984, pp. 183–187, reprinted in *Orientales I. Autour de l'expédition d'Egypte*. Paris: CNRS, 2004, pp. 33–37.

—— *L'Expédition d'Egypte*. Paris: Seuil, 1997.

—— *Les Origines intellectuelles de l'expédition d'Egypte. L'Orientalisme islamisant en France (1698–1798)*. Istanbul and Paris: Editions Isis and Institut Français d'Etudes Anatoliennes d'Istanbul, 1987.

—— "Volonté de réformes et changements, le modèle de Bonaparte à Bush," in eds. A. Hammoudi et al., *La Démocratie est-elle soluble dans l'islam?* Paris: CNRS, 2007, pp. 59–76.

Lazarus-Yafeh, H. "The Religious Dialectics of the Hadjdj," in H. Lazarus-

Yafeh, *Some Religious Aspects of Islam: A Collection of Articles*. Leiden: Brill, 1981, pp. 17–37.

Le Coat, N. "Allegories Literary, Scientific and Imperial: Representations of the Other in Writings on Egypt by Volney and Savary," *The Eighteenth Century: Theory and Interpretation*, 38:1, Spring 1997, pp. 3–22.

Lecerf, J. "Djiwār," *EI*.

Lefebvre, F. "Jean-Jacques Rousseau, de la montre du Sérail au gouvernement du *Contrat social*," eds. P. Dumont and R. Hildebrand, *L'Horloger du Sérail. Aux sources du fantasme oriental chez Jean-Jacques Rousseau*. Paris: Maisonneuve et Larose, Institut Français d'Etudes Anatoliennes, 2005, pp. 137–154.

Levi della Vida, G. "Ludovico Marracci e la sua opera negli studi islamici," in *Aneddoti e suaghi, arabi e non arabi*. Milan and Naples: Riccardo Ricciardi, 1959, pp. 193–210.

—— *Ricerche sulla formazione del più antico fondo dei manoscritti orientali della Biblioteca Vaticana*. Vatican City: Biblioteca Apostolica Vaticana, 1939.

Lockman, Z. *Contending Visions of the Middle East: The History and Politics of Orientalism*. Cambridge: Cambridge University Press, 2004.

Loewenstein, D. *Representing Revolution in Milton and His Contemporaries: Religion, Politics and Polemics in Radical Puritanism*. Cambridge: Cambridge University Press, 2001.

Loop, J. "Heiliger Poesie – Die europäische Rezeption des Koran als poetischer Text im 17. und 18. Jahrhundert." Warburg Institute, 2007.

Lowrie, M. *Horace's Narrative Odes*. Oxford: Clarendon Press, 1997.

Lowry, J. "Lawful and Unlawful," *EQ*.

MacLean, G. "Learn of a Turk," *Prose Studies*, 29:1, April 2007, pp. 36–58.

—— "Milton, Islam and the Ottomans," in eds. S. Achinstein and E. Sauer, *Milton and Toleration*. Oxford: Oxford University Press, 2007, pp. 284–298.

—— *The Rise of Oriental Travel: English Visitors to the Ottoman Empire, 1580–1720*. New York: Palgrave Macmillan, 2006.

Madelung, W. "Al-Mahdī," *EI*.

Madigan, D. "Criterion," *EQ*.

—— *The Qur'ān's Self-Image: Writing and Authority in Islam's Scripture*. Princeton: Princeton University Press, 2001.

Al-Maḥallī, J. and Al-Suyūṭī, J. *Tafsīr al-Jalālayn*. Cairo: Dār Al-Kitāb Al-'Arabī, n.d.

Marigny, F., abbé de. *Histoire des Arabes sous le gouvernement des califes*. Paris: Estienne & fils, Desaint & Saillant, Jean-Thomas Herrissant, 1750, 4 vols.

Marlow, L. "Kings and Rulers," *EQ*.

Marracci, L. *Alcorani textus universus ex correctioribus Arabum exemplar-*

ibus summa fide atque pulcherrimis characteribus descriptus. Padua: 1698, 2 vols.

—— *Prodromus ad Refutationem Alcorani. In quo per quatuor præcipuas veræ religionis notas Mahumetanæ Sectæ falsitas ostenditur; Christianæ Religionis veritas comprobatur.* Rome: 1691, 4 vols.

Marshall, D. *God, Muhammad and the Unbelievers: A Qur'ānic Study.* Richmond: Curzon, 1999.

Martin, A. "The Mask of the Prophet: Napoleon, Borges, Verne," *Comparative Literature*, 40:4, Autumn 1988, pp. 318–334.

Martino, P. *L'Orient dans la littérature française au dix-septième et au dix-huitième siècle.* Paris: Hachette, 1906; Geneva: Slatkine, 1970.

Mason, H. *Pierre Bayle and Voltaire.* London: Oxford University Press, 1963.

Massignon, L. *Essai sur les origines du lexique technique de la mystique musulmane.* Paris: 1968; Paris: Editions du Cerf, 1999 (reprint).

—— "La légende 'de tribus impostoribus' et ses origines islamiques," *Opera Minora*, ed. Y. Moubarac. Paris: Presses Universitaires de France, 1969, vol. 1, pp. 82–85.

—— "L'Involution sémantique du symbole dans les cultures sémitiques," *Opera Minora*, ed. Y. Moubarac. Paris: Presses Universitaires de France, 1969, vol. 2, pp. 626–637.

—— "L'Occident devant l'orient: Primauté d'une solution culturelle," *Opera Minora*, ed. Y. Moubarac. Paris: Presses Universitaires de France, 1969, vol. 1, pp. 208–223.

—— "Réflexions sur la structure primitive de l'analyse grammaticale en arabe," *Opera Minora*, ed. Y. Moubarac. Paris: Presses Universitaires de France, 1969, vol. 2, pp. 613–625.

—— "La syntaxe intérieure des langues sémitiques et le mode de recueillement qu'elles inspirent," *Opera Minora*, ed. Y. Moubarac. Paris: Presses Universitaires de France, 1969, vol. 2, pp. 570–581.

—— "Les 'Sept Dormants,' apocalypse de l'Islam," *Opera Minora*, ed. Y. Moubarac. Paris: Presses Universitaires de France, 1969, vol. 3, pp. 104–118.

—— *Opera Minora*, ed. Y. Moubarac. Paris: Presses Universitaires de France, 1969, 3 vols.

Masson, D. trans. *Le Coran.* Préface par J. Grosjean. Introduction, traduction, et notes par D. Masson. Paris: Gallimard, 1967.

Masson, P-M. *La Religion de Jean-Jacques Rousseau.* Paris: Hachette, 1916; Geneva: Slatkine, 1970 (reprint).

Matar, N. "Alexander Ross and the First English Translation of the Qur'an," *Muslim World*, 88, January 1998, pp. 81–92.

—— *Islam in Britain, 1558–1685.* Cambridge: Cambridge University Press, 1998.

McAuliffe, J. D. *Qur'ānic Christians: An Analysis of Classical and Modern Exegesis*. Cambridge: Cambridge University Press, 1990.

—— "Text and Textuality: Q3:7 as a Point of Intersection," in ed. I. Boullata, *Literary Structures of Religious Meaning in the Qur'ān*. Richmond: Curzon, 2000, pp. 56–76.

—— Walfish, B. D. and Goering, J. W. eds. *With Reverence for the Word: Mediaeval Scriptural Exegesis in Judaism, Christianity and Islam*. Oxford: Oxford University Press, 2002.

Megerlin, D. F. *Die türkische Bibel, oder des Korans allererste Uebersetzung aus der Arabischen Urschrift selbst verfertiget* ... Frankfurt: Johann Gottlieb Garbe, 1772.

Meschonnic, H. *Poétique du traduire*. Paris: Verdier, 2002.

—— *Pour la poétique II: Épistemologie de l'écriture, poétique de la traduction*. Paris: Gallimard, 1973.

Ménage, V. L. "Kateb Celebiana," *Bulletin of the School of Oriental and African Studies*, 26:1, 1963, pp. 173–175.

Milton, J. *A Complete Collection of the Historical, Political and Miscellaneous Works of John Milton*, ed. J. Toland. Amsterdam: 1698, 3 vols.

Minuti, R. *Orientalismo e idee di tolleranza nella cultura francese del primo '700*. Florence: L. S. Olschki, 2006.

Mir, M. "Names of the Qur'ān," *EQ*.

Miscellanea Aurea: or the Golden Medley. London: A. Bettesworth & J. Pemberton, 1720.

Mommsen, K. *Goethe und die arabische Welt*. Frankfurt: Insel, 1988.

Moreh, S. "Al-Jabarti as Writer," in ed. and trans. S. Moreh, *Al-Jabarti's Chronicle of the First Seven Months of the French Occupation of Egypt, Muharram-Rajab 1213/15 June–December 1798*. Leiden: Brill, 1975, pp. 23–30.

—— ed. and trans. *Al-Jabarti's Chronicle of the First Seven Months of the French Occupation of Egypt, Muharram-Rajab 1213/15 June–December 1798*. Leiden: Brill, 1975.

Motzki, H. "Geschlechtsreife une Legitimation zur Zeugung im frühen Islam," in ed. E. W. Müller, *Geschlechtsreife une Legitimation zur Zeugung*. Freiburg and Munich: Karl Alber, 1985, pp. 479–550.

—— "Marriage and Divorce," *EQ*.

Moubarac, Y. *Abraham dans le Coran. L'Histoire d'Abraham dans le Coran et la naissance de l'Islam*. Paris: Vrin, 1957.

—— "Avertissement" in L. Massignon, *Opera Minora*, ed. Y. Moubarac. Paris: Presses Universitaires de France, 1969, 3 vols.

Mousnier, R. *Les Institutions de la France sous la monarchie absolue, 1598–1789* (1974). Paris: Presses Universitaires de France, 2005.

Mulsow, M. *Die drei Ringe. Toleranz und clandestine Gelehrsamkeit bei*

Mathurin Veyssière de la Croze (1661–1739). Tübingen: Max Niemeyer, 2001.

—— *Moderne aus dem Untergrund: Radikale Frühaufklärung in Deutschland, 1680–1720.* Hamburg: Felix Meiner, 2002.

Nallino, C. A. "Le fonti arabe manoscrite dell'opera di Ludovico Marracci sul Corano," *Rendiconti della Reale Accademia Nazionale dei Lincei – Classe di scienze, morali, storiche e filologiche.* Seria 6, vol. 7, Seduta del 15 novembre 1931, pp. 303–349.

Nawas, J. "Badr," *EQ.*

Neaimi, S. *L'Islam au siècle des Lumières. Image de la civilisation islamique chez les philosophes français du dix-huitième siècle.* Paris, Turin, and Budapest: L'Harmattan, 2003.

Neuwirth, A. "Cosmology," *EQ.*

—— "Form and Structure," *EQ.*

Noille-Clauzade, C. ed. "Introduction" to B. Lamy, *La Rhétorique.* Paris: Champion, 1998, pp. 9–97.

Nöldeke, T. *Beiträge zur Kenntniss der Poesie der alten Araber.* Hanover: C. Rumpler, 1864.

—— *Geschichte des Qorāns*, ed. F. Schwally. Leipzig: Dieter, 1909–1938; Hildesheim, New York: G. Olms, 1981.

—— *Remarques critques sur le style et la syntaxe du coran*, ed. and trans. G-H. Bosquet. Paris: Maisonneuve, n.d.

Norton, C. ed. *Correspondence between Goethe and Carlyle.* London and New York: Macmillan, 1887.

Osborn, J. M. "Thomas Birch and the 'General Dictionary' (1734–41)," *Modern Philology*, 36:1, August 1938, pp. 25–46.

O'Dea, M. *Jean-Jacques Rousseau: Music, Illusion and Desire.* New York: St. Martin's, 1995.

Paret, R. "Furḳān," *EI.*

—— *Der Koran: Kommentär und Konkordanz* (1971). Stuttgart: W. Kohlhammer, 1977 (2nd edn.).

Pastoret, C., marquis de. *Zoroastre, Confucius et Mahomet comparés comme sectaires, législateurs et moralistes: avec le tableau de leurs dogmes, de leurs lois et de leur morale.* Paris: Buisson, 1787.

Pauthier, G. ed. *Les Livres sacrés de l'orient, comprenant le Chou-king ou le livre par excellence; –les Sse-chou ou les quatre livres moraux de Confucius et de ses disciples; –les lois de Manou, premier législateur de l'Inde; –le Koran de Mahomet*, trans. G. Pauthier and M. Kasimirski. Paris: Firmin Didot, 1840.

Pearson, J. D. "Bibliography of Translations of the Qur'ān into European Languages," in ed. A. F. L. Beeston, *Arabic Literature to the End of the Umayyad Period.* Cambridge: Cambridge University Press, 1983, pp. 502–520.

—— "Bibliography," *EI*.

Pedani-Fabris, M. P. "Intorno alla questione della traduzione del Corano," in eds. L. Billanovich and P. Gios, *Gregorio Barbarigo, patrizio veneto, vescovo e cardinale nella tarda Controriforma (1625–1697). Atti del convegno di studi, Padova 7–10 novembre 1996*. Padua: Istituto per la storia ecclesiastica padovana, 1999, pp. 353–365.

—— "Ludovico Marracci: La vita e l'opera," in ed. G. Zatti, *Il Corano: Traduzioni, traduttore e lettori in Italia*. Milan: IPL, pp. 9–29.

Peterson, D. C. "Forgiveness," *EQ*.

Pickthall M. M. trans. *The Meaning of the Glorious Quran* (1930). Des Plaines, IL: Library of Islam, 1992.

Pièces diverses et correspondances relatives aux opérations de l'armée d'Orient en Egypte. Imprimées en exécution de l'arrêté du Tribunat en date du 7 Nivôse an 9 de la République française. Paris: Baudouin, Messidor an 9 (1801).

Pindar. *Nemean Odes. Isthmian Odes. Fragments*, ed. and trans. W. H. Race. Cambridge, MA: Harvard University Press, 1997.

—— *Olympian Odes. Pythian Odes*, ed. and trans. W. H. Race. Cambridge, MA: Harvard University Press, 1997.

Pizer, J. "Goethe's 'World Literature' Paradigm and Contemporary Cultural Globalization," *Comparative Literature*, 52:3, Summer 2000, pp. 213–227.

Plessner, M. "Mulk," *EI*.

Pococke, E. *Specimen historiae Arabum, sive, Gregorii Abul Farajii Malatiensis de origine & moribus Arabum succincta narratio, in linguam Latinam conversa, notisque è probatisimis apud ipsos authoribus, fufiùs illustrata*. Oxford: H. Hall, 1650.

Poggi, V. "Grandezza e limiti di Ludovico Marracci attraverso la 'Sura della Caverna'," in ed. G. Zatti, *Il Corano: Traduzioni, traduttore e lettori in Italia*. Milan: IPL, pp. 31–81.

Polaschegg, A. *Der andere Orientalismus. Regeln deutsch-morgenländischer Imagination im 19. Jahrhundert*. Berlin and New York: De Gruyter, 2005.

Pomeau, R. *La Religion de Voltaire*. Paris: Nizet, 1969 (2nd edn.).

—— et al., eds. *Voltaire en son temps*. Oxford: Voltaire Foundation, 1986–1994, 5 vols.

Porter, J. *Observations on the Religion, Law, Government, and Manners of the Turks*. London: J. Nourse, 1771.

Porter, R. *Enlightenment: Britain and the Creation of the Modern World*. London: Penguin, 2000.

Powers, D. S. "The Exegetical Genre *nāsikh al-Qur'ān wa mansūkhuhu*," in ed. A Rippin, *Approaches to the History of the Interpretation of the Qur'ān*. Oxford: Clarendon Press, 1987.

Prideaux, H. *The True Nature of Imposture Fully Display'd in the Life of*

Mahomet with a Discourse Annexed for the Vindicating of Christianity from this Charge ... London: William Rogers, 1697.

Racine, J. *Œuvres complètes*, ed. G. Forestier. Paris: Gallimard, 1999.

Rahbar, D. *God of Justice*. Leiden: Brill, 1960.

Reineccius, C. *Mohammedis Filii Abdaliae pseudo-prophetae Fides Islamitica, i.e. Al-Coranus ex idiomate arabico quo primum a Mohammede conscriptus est, Latine versus per Ludovicum Marracium* ... Leipzig: Sumtibus Lanckisianis, 1721.

Reland, A. *La Religion des Mahométans, tiré du latin de Mr. Reland (par David Durand) et augmenté d'une Confession de foi Mahométane qui n'avait point encore paru*. The Hague: Isaac Vaillant, 1721.

—— *Of the Mahometan Religion in Four Treatises Concerning the Doctrine, Discipline and Worship of the Mahometans*. Translation of *De religione Mohammedica libri duo* (1705) compiled with other texts. London: Darby, 1712.

de Rémusat, C. *Mémoires de Madame de Rémusat, 1802–1808*, ed. P. de Rémusat. Paris: Calmann-Lévy, 1880, 3 vols (12th edn.).

Ricuperati, G. "*Universal History*. Storia di un progetto europeo. Impostori, storici ed editori nella *Ancient Part*," *Studi Settecenteschi*, 1:2, 1981, pp. 7–91.

Riley, P. *The General Will Before Rousseau: The Transformation of the Divine into the Civic*. Princeton: Princeton University Press, 1986.

Rippin, A. ed. *Approaches to the History of the Interpretation of the Qur'ān*. Oxford: Clarendon Press, 1987.

—— "The Commerce of Eschatology," in ed. S. Wild, *The Qur'ān as Text*. Leiden, New York, and Cologne: Brill, 1996, pp. 125–135.

—— "Trade and Commerce," *EQ*.

Rizzardi, G. "Il modello controversistico di Ludovico Marracci,' in ed. G. Zatti, *Il Corano: Traduzioni, traduttore e lettori in Italia*. Milan: IPL, pp. 81–110.

Robinson, N. *Christ in Islam and Christianity: The Representation of Jesus in the Qur'an and the Classical Muslim Commentaries*. London: Macmillan, 1991.

—— "Jesus," *EQ*.

—— "Surat Āl 'Imrān and Those with the Greatest Claim to Abraham," *Journal of Qur'anic Studies*, 6:2, 2004, pp. 1–21.

Rose, C. "The Origins and Ideals of the SPCK, 1699–1716," in eds. J. Walsh, C. Haydon, and S. Taylor, *The Church of England, c. 1689–c. 1833: From Toleration to Tractarianism*. Cambridge: Cambridge University Press, 1993, pp. 172–190.

Ross, E. D. "Ludovico Marracci," *Bulletin of the School of Oriental Studies*, 2:1, 1921, pp. 117–123.

Rothschild, E. *Economic Sentiments: Adam Smith, Condorcet and the Enlightenment.* Cambridge, MA: Harvard University Press, 2001.

Rousseau, J-J. *Correspondance complète*, ed. R. A. Leigh. Geneva, Madison, WI and Banbury, Oxford: Institut et Musée Voltaire; University of Wisconsin Press and the Voltaire Foundation, 1968–1955, 52 vols.

—— *Du contrat social, édition originale annotée par Voltaire.* Facsimile of the original edition published by Jean-Michel Rey, Amsterdam, 1762. Paris: Le Serpent à Plumes, 1998.

—— *Œuvres complètes*, eds. B. Gagnebin and M. Raymond. Paris: Gallimard, 1959–1995, 5 vols.

Rubin, U. *Between the Bible and the Qur'an: The Children of Israel and the Islamic Self-Image.* Princeton: Darwin Press, 1999.

—— "Jews and Judaism," *EQ.*

—— "Muhammad," *EQ.*

Russell, G. A. ed. *The "Arabick" Interest of the Natural Philosophers in Seventeenth-Century England.* Leiden, New York, and Cologne: Brill, 1994.

—— "The Seventeenth Century: The Age of 'Arabick,'" in ed. G. A. Russell, *The "Arabick" Interest of the Natural Philosophers in Seventeenth-Century England.* Leiden, New York, and Cologne: Brill, 1994, pp. 1–19.

Rycaut, P. *The History of the Present State of the Ottoman Empire.* London, Broome, 1682 (5th edn.).

Said, E. *Orientalism* (1978). New York: Vintage, 1994.

—— *The World, the Text and the Critic.* Cambridge, MA: Harvard University Press, 1983.

Salazar, P-J. ed. *Mahomet. Récits français de la vie du Prophète.* Paris: Klincksieck, 2005.

Sale, G. *The Koran: commonly called the Alkoran of Mohammed, translated into English from the original Arabic, with explanatory notes taken from the most approved commentators, to which is prefixed a preliminary discourse by George Sale.* London: J. Wilcox, 1734.

—— *Observations historiques et critiques sur le mahométisme, ou Traduction du discours préliminaire mis à la tête de la version anglaise de l'Alcoran, publiée par George Sale.* Geneva: Barrillot et fils, 1751.

Saleh, W. "In Search of a Comprehensible Qur'ān: A Survey of Some Recent Scholarly Works," *Bulletin of Royal Institute for Inter-Faith Studies*, 5:2, Autumn/Winter 2003, pp. 143–162.

Saul, N. "Aesthetic Humanism (1790–1830)," in ed. H. Watanabe-O'Kelly, *The Cambridge History of German Literature.* Cambridge: Cambridge University Press, 1997, pp. 202–271.

—— *History and Poetry in Novalis and in the Tradition of the German Enlightenment.* London: Institute of Germanic Studies, 1984.

Savary, C. *Le Koran; traduit de l'arabe, accompagné de notes précédé d'un abrégé de la vie de Mahomet, tiré des écrivains orientaux les estimés par M. Savary.* Paris: Garnier, 1960.

—— *Lettres sur l'Egypte.* Paris: Onfroi, 1786, 3 vols.

Schacht, J. "Ahmad," *EQ.*

Schmidt, J. *Die Geschichte des Genie-Gedankens in der deutschen Literatur, Philosophie und Politik, 1750–1945.* Heidelberg: Carl Winter, 2004, 2 vols (3rd edn.).

Schoeck, C. "Moses," *EQ.*

Schöller, M. "Post-Enlightenment Academic Study of the Qur'ān," *EQ.*

Sells, M. "Ascension," *EQ.*

Sezgin, F. *Geschichte des arabischen Schrifttums.* Leiden: Brill, 1967–, 13 vols.

Shaftesbury, A., Third Earl. *Characteristics of Men, Manners, Opinions, Times* (1711, 3 vols.). Hildesheim and New York: Georg Olms, 1978.

Sheehan, J. *The Enlightenment Bible: Translation, Scholarship, Culture.* Princeton: Princeton University Press, 2005.

Shellabear, W. G. "Is Sale's Koran Reliable?" *Moslem World,* 21:2, April 1931, pp. 126–142.

Shklar, J. *Men and Citizens: A Study of Rousseau's Social Theory.* Cambridge: Cambridge University Press, 1969.

Song, S-C. *Voltaire et la Chine.* Aix-en-Provence: Université de Provence, 1989.

Spellberg, D. A. "'Aisha bint Abī Bakr," *EQ.*

Spinoza, B. *Opera,* ed. C. Gebhardt. Heidelberg: Carl Winter, 1925, 4 vols.

Steiner, G. *After Babel: Aspects of Language and Translation.* Oxford and London: Oxford University Press, 1998 (3rd edn.).

Stowasser, B. F. "Mary," *EQ.*

Strand, M. *The Continuous Life: Poems.* New York: Knopf, 1999.

Strich, F. *Goethe und die Weltliteratur.* Berne: Francke, 1957 (2nd edn.).

Stubbe, H. *An Account of the Rise and Progress of Mahometanism with the life of Mahomet, and a vindication of him and his religion from the calumnies of the Christians,* from a manuscript copied by Charles Hornby of Pipe Office in 1705 with some variations and additions, ed. H. M. K. Shairani. London: Luzac, 1911.

Takim, L. "Saul," *EQ.*

Tibawi, A. L. "Is the Qur'an Translatable?" *Muslim World,* 52:1, January 1962, pp. 4–16.

Toland, J. "The Life of John Milton," in ed. J. Toland, *A Complete Collection of the Historical, Political and Miscellaneous Works of John Milton.* Amsterdam: 1698, pp. 6–47.

—— *Nazarenus,* ed. J. Champion. Oxford: Voltaire Foundation, 1999.

—— *Nazarenus, or Jewish, Gentile and Mahometan Christianity*. London: J. Brotherton, J. Roberts and A. Dodd, 1718.

Tomiche, N. "La Femme en Islam," in ed. P. Grimal, *Histoire mondiale de la femme*. Paris: Nouvelle Librairie de France, 1965–1966, vol. 3, pp. 97–156.

—— "Mar'a," *EI*.

Toomer, G. J. *Eastern Wisedome and Learning*. Oxford: Clarendon Press, 1996.

—— "Pococke, Edward (1604–1691)," *ODNB*.

Troupeau, G. "al-Kindī, ʿAbd al-Masīḥ b. Isḥāk," *EI*.

Turner, C. ed. *The Koran: Critical Concepts in Islamic Studies*. London and New York: RoutledgeCurzon, 4 vols.

Turpin, F-H. *Histoire de l'Alcoran, où l'on découvre le Système Politique & Religieux du Faux-Prophête, & les Sources où il a puisé sa Législation*. London and Paris: De Hansy, 1775, 2 vols.

Uzunçarşili, İ.H . "Čorbadjī," *EI*.

Vajda, G. "Ahl Al-Kitāb," *EI*.

Venturino, D. *Le Ragioni della tradizione: nobiltà e mondo moderno in Boulainvilliers, 1658–1722*. Florence: Le Lettere, 1993.

Viré, F. "Nakhl," *EI*.

Voltaire. "Alcoran, ou plutôt Le Koran" (1770), in *Dictionnaire Philosophique*, vol. 17 of *Œuvres complètes*, ed. L. Moland. Nouvelle édition. Paris: Garnier, 1877–1885, pp. 98–107.

—— *Correspondance*, eds. T. Besterman and F. Deloffre. Paris: Gallimard, 1977–.

—— "De l'Alcoran et de Mahomet," in *Mahomet*, vol. 20B of *The Complete Works of Voltaire*, ed. A. Gunny. Oxford: Voltaire Foundation, 2002, pp. 329–345.

—— *Dieu et les hommes*, vol. 69 of *Œuvres complètes*, ed. R. Mortier. Oxford: Voltaire Foundation, 1994.

—— *Essai sur les moeurs et l'esprit des nations et sur les principaux faits de l'histoire depuis Charlemagne jusqu'à Louis XIII*, ed. R. Pomeau. Paris: Garnier, 1963, 2 vols.

—— "Mahométans," (1770), in *Dictionnaire Philosophique*, vol. 20 of *Œuvres complètes*, ed. L. Moland. Nouvelle édition. Paris: Garnier, 1877–1885, pp. 20–21.

—— *Mélanges*, ed. J. van den Heuvel. Paris: Gallimard, 1961.

—— *Œuvres complètes*, ed. L. Moland. Paris: Garnier, 1877–1885, 46 vols.

—— *Œuvres complètes*, ed. T. Besterman. Geneva: Institut et Musée Voltaire, 1968–.

—— *Œuvres historiques*, ed. R. Pomeau. Paris: Gallimard, 1978, vol. 128.

—— *La Philosophie de l'histoire*, vol. 59 of *The Complete Works of Voltaire*, ed. J. H. Brumfitt. Geneva and Toronto: Institut et Musée Voltaire and University of Toronto Press, 1969 (2ⁿᵈ edn.).

—— *Voltaire's Correspondence*, ed. T. Besterman. Publications de l'Institut et Musée Voltaire, Geneva: Institut et Musée Voltaire, 1953–1968, 107 vols.

Voronova, T. P. ed. *Corpus des notes marginales de Voltaire*. Berlin: Akademie, 1988–.

Voyage à Erménonville, ou Lettre sur la Translation de Jean-Jacques Rousseau au Panthéon. Paris: Meurant, 1794.

Vrolijk, A. "Sale, George (*b*. in or after 1696, *d*. 1736)," *ODNB*.

Wade, I. O. *The Clandestine Organization and Diffusion of Philosophic Ideas in France from 1700 to 1750*. Princeton: Princeton University Press, 1938; New York: Octagon, 1967 (reprint).

Waines, D. "Date Palm," *EQ*.

Wakefield, C. "Arabic Manuscripts in the Bodleian Library: The Seventeenth-Century Collections," in ed. G. A. Russell, *The "Arabick" Interest of the Natural Philosophers in Seventeenth-Century England*. Leiden, New York, and Cologne: Brill, 1994, pp. 128–146.

Wansbrough, J. *Quranic Studies: Sources and Methods of Scriptural Interpretation* (Foreword, Translations and Expanded Notes by A. Rippin). Amherst, NY: Prometheus, 2004.

Watt, W. Montgomery. "Badr," *EI*.

—— "Carlyle on Muhammad," *Hibbert Journal*, 53, 1954–1955, pp. 247–254.

—— *The Formative Period of Islamic Thought*. Edinburgh: Edinburgh University Press, 1973.

—— "His Name is Ahmad," *Muslim World*, 43:2, 1953, pp. 110–117.

—— *Muhammad at Medina*. Oxford: Oxford University Press, 1956; Karachi: Oxford University Press, 2004.

Welch, A. T. "Formulaic Features of the Punishment Stories," in ed. I. Boullata, *Literary Structures of Religious Meaning in the Qur'ān*. Richmond: Curzon, 2000, pp. 77–116.

—— "Al-Ḳur'ān," *EI*.

Wellhausen, J. *Reste arabischen Heidentums*. Berlin: G. Reimer, 1897 (2ⁿᵈ edn.).

Wheeler, B. M. *Moses in the Quran and Islamic Exegesis*. London: RoutledgeCurzon, 2002.

Wild, S. ed. *The Qur'ān as Text*. Leiden, New York, and Cologne: Brill, 1996.

—— "The Self-Referentiality of the Qur'ān: Sura 3:7 as an Exegetical Challenge," in eds. J. D. McAuliffe, B. D. Walfish, and J. W. Goering, *With Reverence for the Word: Mediaeval Scriptural Exegesis in*

Judaism, Christianity and Islam. Oxford: Oxford University Press, 2002, pp. 422–436.

—— "'We Have Sent Down to Thee the Book with the Truth': Spatial and Temporal Implications of the Qur'ānic Concepts of Nuzūl, Tanzīl and Inzāl," in ed. S. Wild, *The Qur'ān as Text.* Leiden, New York, and Cologne: Brill, 1996, pp. 137–153.

Williams, G. *Tradition and Originality in Roman Poetry.* Oxford: Clarendon Press, 1968.

Wisner, D. A. *The Cult of the Legislator in France 1750–1830: A Study in the Political Theology of the French Enlightenment.* Oxford: Voltaire Foundation, 1997.

Woolf, S. "The Construction of a European World-View in the Revolutionary-Napoleonic Years," *Past and Present,* 137, November 1992, pp. 72–101.

Yusuf Ali, A. trans. *The Holy Qur'an: Text, Translation and Commentary* (1934). Beirut: Dār Al-'Arabiyya, 1968.

Al-Zamakhsharī, M. b. 'Umar. *Al-Kashshāf 'an ḥaqā'iq ghawāmiḍ al-tanzīl wa 'uyūn al-aqāwīl fī wujūh al-ta'wīl,* ed. M. H. Ahmad. Cairo: Dār Al-Kitāb Al-'Arabī, n.d., 4 vols.

Zatti, G. ed. *Il Corano: Traduzioni, traduttore e lettori in Italia.* Milan: IPL, 2000.

Zimmermann, T. C. P. *Paolo Giovio: The Historian and the Crisis of Sixteenth-Century Italy.* Princeton: Princeton University Press, 1995.

Zuber, R. *Les "Belles infidèles" et la formation du goût classique.* Paris: Albin Michel, 1995.

Zwettler, M. "A Mantic Manifesto: The Sura of 'The Poets' and the Qur'anic Foundations of Poetic Authority," in ed. J. L. Kugel, *Poets and Prophets: The Beginnings of a Literary Tradition.* Ithaca: Cornell University Press, 1990, pp. 75–119.

INDEX

INDEX OF QUR'ĀNIC VERSES